A

DATE
BOOK

The Philip E. Lilienthal imprint
honors special books
in commemoration of a man whose work
at University of California Press from 1954 to 1979
was marked by dedication to young authors
and to high standards in the field of Asian Studies.
Friends, family, authors, and foundations have together
endowed the Lilienthal Fund, which enables the Press
to publish under this imprint selected books
in a way that reflects the taste and judgment
of a great and beloved editor.

The publisher gratefully acknowledges the generous contribution to this book provided by the Philip E. Lilienthal Asian Studies Endowment Fund of the University of California Press Foundation, which is supported by a major gift from Sally Lilienthal.

Publié avec le concours du Ministère français chargé de la culture, Centre national du livre. Published with the assistance of the French Ministry of Culture's National Center for the Book.

Authenticating Tibet

Authenticating Tibet

Answers to China's 100 Questions

Edited by

ANNE-MARIE BLONDEAU

and

KATIA BUFFETRILLE

With a foreword by
Donald Lopez

University of California Press

BERKELEY   LOS ANGELES   LONDON

Adapted and updated translation of *Le Tibet est-il chinois ? Réponses à cent questions chinoises,* edited by Anne-Marie Blondeau and Katia Buffetrille, *Sciences des religions* (Paris: Albin Michel, 2002)

University of California Press, one of the most distinguished university presses in the United States, enriches lives around the world by advancing scholarship in the humanities, social sciences, and natural sciences. Its activities are supported by the UC Press Foundation and by philanthropic contributions from individuals and institutions. For more information, visit www.ucpress.edu.

University of California Press
Berkeley and Los Angeles, California

University of California Press, Ltd.
London, England

Library of Congress Cataloging-in-Publication Data

Authenticating Tibet : answers to China's *100 questions* / edited by Anne-Marie Blondeau and Katia Buffetrille ; with a foreword by Donald Lopez.
    "Adapted and updated translation of Le Tibet est-il chinois ? : réponses à cent questions chinoises."
        p.   cm.
    Includes bibliographical references.
    ISBN: 978-0-520-24464-1 (cloth : alk. paper)
    ISBN: 978-0-520-24928-8 (pbk. : alk. paper)   1. Tibet (China)—Politics and government—1951–.   2. Tibet (China)—History.   3. Human rights—China—Tibet.   I. Blondeau, Anne-Marie.   II. Buffetrille, Katia.   III. Jing, Wei. Xizang bai ti wen da. IV. Tibet est-il chinois? : réponses à cent questions chinoises. V. Title: Answers to China's *100 questions*.
DS786.T4963413   2008
951'.505—dc22   2007012135

Manufactured in the United States of America

15   14   13   12   11   10   09   08
10   9   8   7   6   5   4   3   2   1

This book is printed on Natures Book, which contains 50% postconsumer waste and meets the minimum requirements of ANSI/NISO Z39.48-1992 (R 1997) (*Permanence of Paper*).

CONTENTS

True or false: Tibet has always been a part of China. True or false: Prior to 1959, the majority of the Tibetan population were serfs living under feudal lords. True or false: Between 1959 and 1979, more than one million Tibetans were killed by the Chinese. True or false: China's primary motivation for invading Tibet was to gain access to Tibet's mineral resources. These statements—each of which is false—are commonly repeated in the war of words that has been waged for almost half a century between the People's Republic of China and supporters of the Dalai Lama. Despite occasional, and never corresponding, conciliatory gestures from one side toward the other, charges and countercharges have continued to be exchanged, largely unabated over the decades.

The "Tibet question" has captivated the interests, and the passions, of people around the world since troops of the People's Liberation Army entered Tibet in 1950, and especially since the young Dalai Lama's escape into exile in 1959. For most Chinese, Tibet has always been a part of China, and the events of the 1950s represented a peaceful liberation and a return of Tibet to the Chinese motherland after a brief period of foreign interference by colonial powers (particularly the British) in the first half of the twentieth century. From the Chinese perspective, Tibet was a backward and uncivilized land, where the people suffered under the cruel rule of lamas and aristocrats. Since their overthrow of the latter, Tibetans have been welcome to share in the hard-won benefits of China's modern miracle. This view of Tibet is not limited strictly to members of the Chinese Communist Party or to the citizens of the PRC; it is widely held by Chinese in Taiwan and around the world as well.

The opposing view, widely held outside China, is that the entry of Chinese troops into Tibetan territory in 1950 was the invasion of a sovereign nation, a nation that was different from China in language, history, culture, and religion; that in 1951 a Tibetan delegation in Beijing was coerced into signing an agreement that ceded Tibet to the People's Republic of China; that a popular uprising against the Chinese occupiers was brutally repressed; that since then Tibet has become a Chinese colony, with indigenous Tibetan culture, and especially Tibetan religion systematically destroyed; that hundreds of thousands of Tibetans have perished in this process. In the more extreme forms of this account, traditional Tibet has been portrayed as a peaceful land overseen by benevolent Buddhist masters, its people devoted to ethereal pursuits, a land bypassed by the horrors of modernity until it was overwhelmed by fanatical Communists, who have obliterated all that was ancient and spiritual, replacing it with the modern and material.

These renditions of the events of the past fifty years in Tibet are mutually contradictory. Both cannot be true. Yet each has persisted, each with its own rhetoric, one view held in China and broadcast abroad with the full force of the central government of the world's most populous nation, the other propagated less systematically and without the apparatus of state; the case against China and in support of the cause of Tibetan independence (or at least autonomy) has been made by the Dalai Lama, his government in exile in India, and his supporters around the world.

Despite this apparent mismatch, and their unquestioned military and political control of what was once called Tibet, the Chinese have not desisted from their claims. Tibet continues to be the most persistent of China's public relations problems. Long after the horrors of the Cultural Revolution could be ascribed to the excesses of dead leaders, the Tibet problem remains.

One element in the Chinese arsenal designed to combat the claims of the Dalai Lama and his supporters was a small book entitled *100 Questions about Tibet*, published in English in 1989. It has been translated into a number of languages and reprinted in slightly different editions since then and is available now online. The book, which appeared just as Tibet was beginning to attract a large number of European and American tourists, was published to present the facts about Tibet to a European and North American audience and to counter what the Chinese regard as the misinformation dispensed by the Dalai Lama and his followers. Despite its wide dissemination, the book has had little effect on the Tibetan independence movement and has been largely dismissed by proponents of a free Tibet as yet another rendition of familiar Chinese lies.

Two French scholars decided to take the book somewhat more seriously. Anne-Marie Blondeau and Katia Buffetrille, two of the leading scholars of the renowned Tibetan Studies faculty at the École pratique des Hautes Études in Paris, assembled an international group of distinguished experts from France, Switzerland, Germany, Norway, England, Canada, and the United States, specialists in Tibetan history, language, religion, economics, politics, and society. They assigned a number of the Chinese questions to each of these experts according to his or her area of expertise, and asked each to write clear, concise, and historically accurate answers. The project resulted in a book entitled *Le Tibet est-il chinois?* (Is Tibet Chinese?), which appeared under the imprint of the leading French publisher Albin Michel in Paris in 2002. The present volume is not simply a translation of this important French work. The editors went back to the original contributors and asked them to revise and update their answers in light of most recent events in Tibet and among the Tibetan community in exile.

The format of the book is simple. The Chinese question is given, followed by a summary of the Chinese answer. That answer is followed by a detailed response by one of fifteen scholars. The book seeks to avoid the polemics that so commonly surround the Tibet question. The new answers are in almost every case rather different from those provided by the Chinese. At the same time, the book is by no means a simple confirmation of the claims of the "pro-Tibet" movement. The rich history of Tibet's past and the highly charged circumstances of Tibet's present are described in balanced and accurate detail, set forth in clear, straightforward prose. The two editors, in addition to providing responses to a number of the questions themselves, have supplied maps, a glossary, and a historical timeline.

It would, however, be disingenuous to claim that this book is entirely neutral, at least in its motivation. If the answers to the questions in the original Chinese book were historically accurate, there would be no need for the present volume. The scholars who provide new answers to the Chinese questions here do so, however, without deference to the positions of the Dalai Lama's government-in-exile. Indeed, they often take exception to those positions.

100 Questions about Tibet is a work of propaganda, filled with Chinese rhetoric extolling the "multi-national Motherland" and condemning supporters of Tibetan independence as "splittists," that is, those who seek to split Tibet from China. As a work of propaganda, it seeks to promote a particular point of view. The questions that are asked are formulated to present the Chinese case, and the answers to those questions provide information selectively in order to portray the Chinese case in the best possible light. Although the one hundred questions and their Chinese answers range widely, they return again and again to three themes: (1) that Tibet is, and has long been, a part of China, (2) that the life of the Tibetan people has improved greatly since the "peaceful liberation" of Tibet, and (3) that the people of Tibet enjoy freedom of religion. A further motif is that whatever suffering and deprivation may have occurred in Tibet since its "liberation" were the result of the excesses of the Cultural Revolution, which affected all regions of the PRC, including Tibet.

The present volume, in contrast, is a work of scholarship. As such, it seeks to gather information from all available sources and then provides an evaluation of that information, allowing the reader to draw his or her own conclusions.

One of the differences between propaganda and scholarship is that propaganda is confident and unambiguous in its assertions; its goal is to present a particular point of view in the most compelling way possible. Scholarship must acknowledge and engage ambiguity, often raising questions in the process of answering others. Propaganda simplifies what seems complicated. Scholarship complicates what seems simple. Scholarship, therefore, cannot always provide a monosyllabic answer to a "true or false question." For example, in the present volume, there is a detailed discussion of the relationship of Tibetan peasants to the land and to landowners in traditional Tibet in an effort to determine the accuracy of the Chinese claim that prior to 1950, the majority of the Tibetan people were "serfs." The answer is not a simple "yes" or "no." Proponents of Tibetan independence have made their own claims, and these are also examined. It is commonly stated, for example, that when the Chinese established the Tibet Autonomous Region (TAR) in 1965, they effectively reduced the area of the region of Tibet by two-thirds. The accuracy of this statement depends upon how one defines the word "Tibet." If, by Tibet, one means the region inhabited by peoples who spoke a dialect of the Tibetan language and practiced Tibetan Buddhism, a region that scholars refer to as "ethnic Tibet" or "cultural Tibet," then the statement is true. Large parts of this region, including the Tibetan areas known as Kham and Amdo, were incorporated into the Chinese provinces of Sichuan, Qinghai, Gansu, and Yunnan. However, if by Tibet, one means the region that was under the direct rule of the Dalai Lama's government in Lhasa, what scholars refer to as "political Tibet," then the borders of the TAR correspond roughly to this realm.

The analysis of propaganda entails the evaluation, not only of what is said, but also what is not said. This is an important focus of the chapters of this volume. Some things are not said by the Chinese authors of *100 Ques-*

tions about Tibet, simply because they are assumed. For example, readers unfamiliar with the terminology of the Chinese Communist Party might infer that because the central provinces of traditional Tibet are called the Tibet Autonomous Region, this region enjoys, or should enjoy, some degree of autonomy. However, we learn that for the Chinese, an "autonomous region" is defined as an area where an ethnic minority lives in "compact communities," such that the Chinese Communist Party must adapt its policies in accordance with local "characteristics."

Elsewhere in the volume, one learns information crucial to understanding premodern Tibet, information that is not typically mentioned by either the Chinese or their opponents. For example, the large-scale destruction of Buddhist monasteries is generally lamented for the damage done to the Buddhist dharma and those who practice it, as well as the loss of religious texts, paintings, statues, and works of architecture. What is not widely known is that the Buddhist monastery, of which there were hundreds in Tibet, played a crucial role in the traditional Tibetan economy. The monastery was the primary financial center for the local economy, providing credit to farmers, nomads, and traders. In 1959, it is estimated that Drepung Monastery, located outside Lhasa, the largest monastery in Tibet, had outstanding loans equivalent to U.S.$5 million (approximately U.S.$34 million in 2006 dollars) and 130,000 metric tons of grain. The Chinese policy of shutting down (and in many cases physically destroying) the monasteries and laicizing the monastic population thus had devastating effects on the Tibetan economy, contributing to severe hardship throughout Tibet over several decades. Indeed, as this volume makes clear, the improved standard of living that the Chinese claim to have brought to Tibet is a reality only for the small percentage of Tibetans living in the few urban areas. It is unclear whether the standard of living of the majority of Tibetans living in the countryside has in fact improved under Chinese rule.

These are examples of the kinds of issues explored in the pages of this book. There are detailed discussions of Tibetan culture, religion, education, medicine, and economy both prior to Chinese rule as well as over the course of the past half-century. Chinese policy has ebbed and flowed between periods of ideological stringency and relative liberalization over the decades, with attendant consequences for the Tibetans and their culture.

Today, almost sixty years after troops of the People's Liberation Army entered Tibetan territory, the fate of Tibet and the Tibetan people (both in Tibet and in exile) remains a highly charged issue, with profound political, cultural, and human consequences. The image of Tibet offered in this volume is not that of a picture painted in broad strokes, a picture that one might describe as "rosy" or "dark." It seeks instead the documentary accuracy of a photograph. Yet like all photographs, it is open to interpretation. Most would agree that the perspective it provides does not offer reason for optimism. Yet, without understanding the past and the present of Tibet in some depth, an understanding that can be gained from the pages of this volume, it is difficult to know how to move forward.

Donald Lopez

Following the "peaceful liberation" of Tibet by the new communist government of China that led to the Lhasa uprising and the escape of the Dalai Lama to India in 1959, the debate on Tibetan issues has been continuing. Advocates of the Tibetan and Chinese sides have raised diametrically opposing views and presented endless arguments to prove their assertions, without being able to convince the other side.

In 1989, a booklet entitled *100 Questions about Tibet* was published in English by the Beijing Review Press and distributed around the world through Chinese embassies.[1] Printed on cheap paper and illustrated with poor-quality pictures in black and white, the booklet was written by "numerous government officials and scholars of Tibetan history at the Nationalities Institute under the Chinese Academy of Social Sciences." Its stated aim was to be "of use to all those who are concerned to know and understand the truth about Tibet."

This propaganda booklet presented nine chapters, starting with "The Historical Facts"—the main issue in the debate between pro-Chinese and pro-Tibetans—and followed by "Human Rights," "Policies Towards the Dalai Lama," "Population," "Religious Belief," "The Right to Autonomy," "Culture and Education," "Economic Development," "Livelihood of the People," and "The Riots in Lhasa." It must be noted that topics such as the Great Leap Forward and the Cultural Revolution, which have greatly affected Tibet and the Tibetans, were barely mentioned.

In order to understand the ins and outs of the situation that Tibet faces under Chinese control, it appears essential to deal with the topics that the

---

1. Jing 1989. The French version (Jing 1988) appeared one year earlier.

Chinese authorities consider most important in the context of their relations with the Tibetans both inside and outside Tibet. What better opportunity could there be than to answer these Chinese questions with a book adopting a scholarly approach?

Consequently, at Anne-Marie Blondeau's initiative and with the help of Western Tibetologists specialized in each of the fields concerned, we published *Le Tibet est-il chinois ? Réponses à cent questions chinoises* in 2002. Aiming at a broad audience, the book addressed each of the questions raised in the Chinese booklet, faithfully summarized the Chinese arguments, and provided a critical and concise commentary based on a full range of sources and data.

On such a polemical topic, it is always the sources used that are the main bone of contention. Neither official Chinese sources nor Tibetan ones from the government in exile at Dharamsala in India can be entirely relied upon, because they are obviously not neutral. The same can be said of information from pro-Chinese or pro-Tibetan organizations. But they have to be used, compared, and complemented both with independent sources and with experience gathered in the course of field research. The contributors, being specialists in the region, travel to Tibet on a regular basis and have a concrete knowledge of the actual situation.

While the French book was in the process of being printed, a second version of the Chinese booklet, without any authors' names or an introduction, appeared in 2001, printed this time on a much better paper and illustrated with good-quality color pictures. Instead of the previous nine chapters, the booklet was divided into five sections, titled "Tibet Is an Inalienable Part of China's Territory," "Democratic Reform and Regional Ethnic Autonomy," "Economic Development, People's Livelihood and Environmental Protection," "Population, Health, Culture, Education and Tourism," and "Policies of the Central Government toward the Dalai Lama."

The tone and rhetoric remain the same, but the Chinese claim to Tibet is more clearly stated in this second version, as illustrated in the title of the first section. Much more emphasis is put on the economy, a sector that showed marked improvement between 1988 and 2001, and also on the environment, a domain of utmost importance worldwide. China's environmental policies are under close scrutiny by many foreign organizations. But not a single word is said in the 2001 publication about what are called "The Riots" in the previous, 1989 version, namely the Tibetan demonstrations against Chinese occupation of 1987 and 1988.

Although China has been through tremendous changes since the creation of the People's Republic of China in 1949, neither the position of the Chinese Government nor the vocabulary used in relation to the "ancien régime" in Tibet and the Dalai Lama have changed. This appears clearly in the 1989 and the 2001 versions of *100 Questions,* as well as in a recent interview with Zhang Qingli, the new hard-line head of the Communist Party in Tibet (see Zhang 2006) and articles in *China Daily,* the national English-language newspaper (e.g., May 18, 2007). Moreover, in spite of the endless efforts of the Chinese authorities to denigrate the actions of the Dalai Lama and undermine his influence, Tibetans are still extremely supportive of him.

Every year, numerous Tibetans illegally cross the border to Nepal without legitimate travel documents, knowing perfectly well the hardships and dangers they risk. If some of them are children sent by their parents to get a Tibetan schooling, the others can be qualified as pilgrims and expect to meet the Dalai Lama. The case of Kelsang Namtso, a 17-year-old nun who was shot in September 2006 by Chinese border guards close to the Nangpa Pass, which marks the border between Tibet and Nepal, has attracted international media attention. The shooting was witnessed by a large number of international climbers, and pictures and video footage have spread on the Net. This is the only documented case, but reports from refugees suggest that such incidents are not rare. This does not necessarily mean that Tibetans would like to return to the situation prior to 1950. Everyone agrees that Tibet had to be modernized. China did bring material progress to Tibet, but Tibetans have had to pay a very high price for this modernization. The Chinese market is booming and is attracting investors and businessmen from all over the world, whereas the situation of human rights in the People's Republic has not improved at all, as recent reports prove. In 2006, the Chinese authorities were even planning to open Tibet to tourism without special permit in order to take advantage of the economic benefits (a decision that has yet to happen), yet the press and Internet are still totally controlled. The coverage of the inauguration of the Beijing-Golmud-Lhasa railway provided by Chinese and "invited" foreign journalists demonstrates this fact clearly. The Chinese authorities drew lots to select the foreign correspondents in Beijing who might observe the festivities. Those who were not selected were not granted a permit to go to Lhasa, and those who tried to go were stopped and their passports confiscated. In addition, the practice of blacklisting journalists still continues; consequently, *Le Monde*'s retired correspondent Jean-Claude Buhrer has been banned from entering China because of his articles about Tibet (WTN, August 8, 2006).

Even though several new books on contemporary Tibet have appeared in the past few years (see, e.g., Powers 2004, Heath 2005, and Sautman and Teufel Dreyer 2006), a new, updated English version of *Le Tibet est-il chi-*

nois? should be a useful tool that will help everyone to form an opinion about the Sino-Tibetan situation. Certainly, updating our French book in English was a challenge, given the many developments that happen almost daily, not only in the Tibet Autonomous Region, but in the ethnic Tibetan regions of Gansu, Yunnan, Qinghai, and Sichuan. Each section of the book could indeed have been developed into a full book. However, our objective was simpler. The solid documentation is written in a clear, straightforward style for a nonspecialist audience and complemented with a comparative chronology of Tibetan and Chinese history from the seventh century C.E. on, a glossary, a list of references, and two maps. We retained the specific question-and-answer format of the 1989 English edition of *100 Questions*,[2] which should help make this book more useful as a reference work.

The year 2008 will be crucial for Beijing—the attention of the whole world will be on China as it hosts the Olympic Games. Thousands of tourists (Chinese as well as foreign) will take this opportunity to visit the country and certainly the different Tibetan areas in the People's Republic of China. One of the many objectives in providing answers to *100 Questions about Tibet* was the restoration of Tibetan toponyms (and personal names) to their original forms and hence returning a cultural identity to those places and people. The phonetic transcription adopted in China gives a sinicized pronunciation and conceals the meaning of the words in Tibetan. This sinicization of proper nouns denies not only the existence of Tibet as a political entity, established historically on a concrete geographical territory, but the identity of the Tibetans as an ethnic group distinct from the Han. As a result, it is often difficult, not to say impossible, to identify the Tibetan original behind its Chinese rendering. For instance, how could one recognize the regent Reting Rinpoche (Rwa sgreng) under "Rabchen Hutuktu" (Question 10), the famous Drepung ('Bras spungs) Monastery under "Zhaibung" (Question 55) or "Daipung" (Question 71), and Cagpori behind "Yaowangshan" (Question 74)?[3] In addition, instead of sinicizing Tibetan toponyms, a new Chinese name is sometimes created. This can be observed especially in areas with a strong Chinese immigrant population (see Chayet 1997: 35–51). But Tibetan toponyms can also be replaced by names that convey a myth totally foreign to the Tibetan world. Hence, following a competition to determine the Chinese area closest to the Western imaginary concept of Shangri-La (the name of the monastery of the Blue Moon Valley in

---

2. If not specified, quotations are taken from the 1989 English edition.

3. The 2001 version of *100 Questions* was slightly improved in this regard, using "Sherpas," for example, instead of the 1989 version's "Xiaerbas."

James Hilton's best-selling 1933 novel *Lost Horizon* and the 1937 Frank Capra film of the same title), the county (and not the monastery) of Gyeltang (rGyal thang) was selected in 2001 after a long "scientific" debate. From that year on, the name "Shangrila" has officially replaced the Tibetan Gyeltang.

The aim of this book is not to give a stark black-and-white picture of the situation in Tibet. Past and present history is far more complex. Even if we do defend the rights of the Tibetans, we are neither committed supporters of the Dalai Lama and the Tibetan government in exile nor systematic detractors of Chinese policy, and the book is free from the polemics that so commonly surround the Tibet question.

Our aim has been to give the reader the information necessary to achieve a balanced picture of the relations between Tibet and China, and, in doing so, to contribute to safeguarding the civilization of Tibet.

Katia Buffetrille

ACKNOWLEDGMENTS

We would like to express our gratitude to Martine van Workens for inviting us to publish the French original of this book in her collection at Albin Michel in 2002. We are also grateful to the contributors, who kindly agreed to update their original articles for this English version. Vincent Micoud kindly helped prepare the map. Reed Malcolm and Suzanne Knott of the University of California Press provided good counsel throughout the publication process. Finally, we are indebted to Peter Dreyer for his careful editing of the manuscript.

CCP	Chinese Communist Party
Chin.	Chinese language
CPPCC	Chinese People's Political Consultative Conference
CPSY	[PRC, National Bureau of Statistics] *China Population Statistical Yearbook*
CSY	[PRC, National Bureau of Statistics] *China Statistical Yearbook*
Dharamsala	The Government of Tibet in Exile (www.tibet.com)
FBIS	[U.S.] Foreign Broadcast Information Service
GDP	gross domestic product
ICT	International Campaign for Tibet
IIAS	International Institute for Asian Studies (www.iias.nl)
lit.	literally
NGO	nongovernmental organization
PLA	People's Liberation Army
PRC	People's Republic of China
QSY	[PRC, Qinghai Bureau of Statistics] *Qinghai Statistical Yearbook*
TAP	Tibetan Autonomous Prefecture
TAR	Tibet Autonomous Region
TCHRD	Tibetan Centre for Human Rights and Democracy (www.tchrd.org)
THF	Tibet Heritage Fund
Tib.	Tibetan language

TIN	Tibet Information Network, London
TSY	[PRC, Tibet Bureau of Statistics] *Tibet Statistical Yearbook*
UN	United Nations
UNDP	United Nations Development Program
UNESCO	United Nations Educational, Scientific and Cultural Organization
UNICEF	United Nations Children's Fund
UNPO	Unrepresented Nations and Peoples Organization (www.unpo.org)
WDS	Western Development Strategy (PRC)
WTN	World Tibet Network News (www.tibet.ca/en/wtnarchive)
[ ]	editors' comments

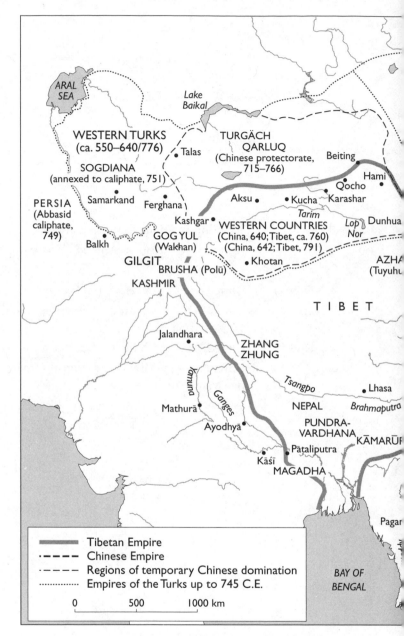

1. The Tibetan empire and Central Asia ca. 800. Based on Herbert Franke, Grosser historischer Weltatlas, pt. II, Mittelalter, ed. Josef Engel, 2d ed. (Munich: Bayer. Schulbuch-Verlag, 1979), map 54c.

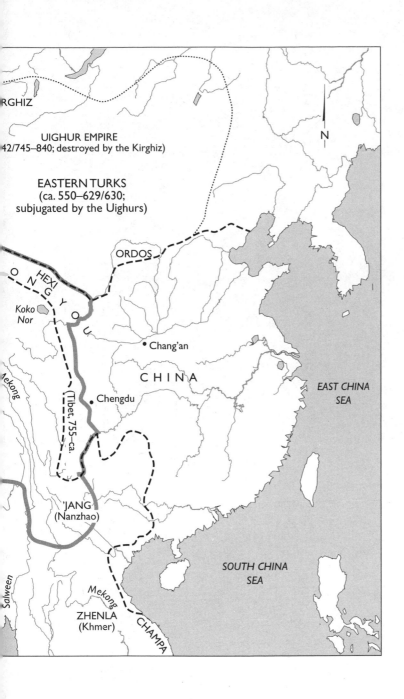

RGHIZ

UIGHUR EMPIRE
42/745–840; destroyed by the Kirghiz)

EASTERN TURKS
(ca. 550–629/630;
subjugated by the Uighurs)

ORDOS

ONGYOU

HEXI

Koko
Nor

Chang'an

C H I N A

Mekong

(Tibet, 755–ca.

Chengdu

EAST CHINA
SEA

'JANG
(Nanzhao)

Salween

SOUTH CHINA
SEA

Mekong

ZHENLA
(Khmer)

CHAMPA

N

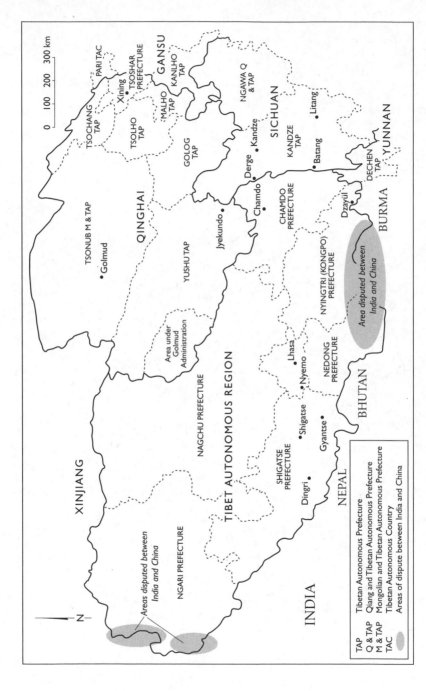

2. Modern Tibet. Map background by courtesy of TibetInfoNet.

PART ONE

Historical Facts

The Chinese authors quite logically begin with history, but they fail to provide a coherent account either of Tibet's history or of Sino-Tibetan relations. The aim of their questions and answers is merely to demonstrate that Tibet has been a part of China since the thirteenth century. The contributors to this section of the present volume locate the Chinese arguments in a broader historical context.

1

Some Tibetans in self-exile have repeatedly claimed
that Tibet and China are two different countries.
What does history have to say?

"This argument does not conform with recorded history. It is nothing but an excuse to conduct activities aimed at splitting Tibet from China and making it into an independent state."

"China is a multi-national country. The Tibetans . . . established the 'Tubo kingdom'" in the seventh century, which "friendly [sic] coexisted with the Tang Dynasty" for more than two hundred years; then it collapsed, and Tibet was in a "state of disintegration" for about three centuries.

[The end of the Chinese answer, which is much more detailed and deals with the rise of the Yuan dynasty in the thirteenth century, is quoted below, at the beginning of the second part of our reply. Inasmuch as the unchanging Chinese arguments invariably belittle the greatness of the Tibetan empire (or so-called Tubo kingdom), it seemed necessary to highlight this essential period of Tibetan civilization's formation.]

The Tibetan Empire (Seventh–Ninth Centuries)

HELGA UEBACH

Nonspecialist readers may be puzzled by the terms "Tubo dynasty," "Tubo kingdom," and "Tubo rule" in Chinese writings dealing with the early Tibetan empire. A few words of explanation are thus in order. The Tibetan name for Tibet is Bö. In Chinese texts of the period under consideration, the Tibetans are called Tu-fan. The Chinese claim that the pronunciation of the respective Chinese characters was Tu-po. However, this interpretation is not corroborated by any gloss to ancient Chinese texts, and it was long ago rejected by the famous French scholar Paul Pelliot (1878–1945). Its constant use in Chinese publications, even when translated into Western or other languages, may be explained by the wish to equate Tu po with Tu Bö. Given that the name Tibet is well established all over the world, adopting the questionable Chinese term for the country is both unnecessary and pointless.

3

Tibet's recorded history begins in the early seventh century C.E. with the reign of Trisong Tsen, more popularly known as Songtsen Gampo (r. 617–649/50). From this time on, the most important events of the empire were recorded in the *Tibetan Annals*. China, Tibet's great neighbor to the east, was at that time ruled by the Tang dynasty. In the *Annals of Tang Dynasty*, there are some chapters dealing with Tibetan affairs where the data and records of the *Tibetan Annals* can be counterchecked. These main sources of exact historical data are supplemented by inscriptions, documentary evidence from Central Asia, and information supplied by the histories of India to the south, the Arabs and Persians to the west, city-states with Indo-European populations in the oases along the Silk Road to the north, and various confederations of Turkic peoples still farther to the north, all of which were soon involved in Tibet's expansion.

An impression of how Tibetans see their early history—in a less strict sense of the term—is gained from fairly old chronicles. The Tibetan rulers are said to be of divine origin or, in the words of Old Tibetan inscriptions, their ancestor was a "god who descended from heaven to become ruler of men." There had been more than thirty generations of rulers prior to Songtsen Gampo whose names included the word *tsen*, "mighty." They resided in the fortress of "Tiger-Peak" in Chingwa, a side valley of the fertile Yarlung valley, watered by a right tributary of the river Tsangpo, or Brahmaputra, to the southeast of Lhasa. In the time of Namri Longtsen, the father of Songtsen Gampo, the chiefs of some great clans plotted against their overlords and allied themselves with Namri Longtsen. This conspiracy was the starting point of the coming into being of the Tibetan state. The surrounding principalities and petty kingdoms soon were subdued and bound by the ties of vassalage. The court moved to the strategically more favored northern bank of the Tsangpo River, while the valley of Chingwa farther on was significant as the site where the huge tombs of the rulers were built.

For the sake of simplicity, the name "Yarlung dynasty" has been introduced, but no Tibetan dynastic name has been transmitted. The epithet of the Tibetan rulers was transformed into their title, *tsenpo*, and it is by this title that they were generally known. Translating it as "the mighty one" does not quite seem to do it justice. In an early Old Tibetan–Chinese glossary, it is paraphrased by the Chinese characters for "Son of Heaven," and doubtless was taken as equivalent to the title otherwise exclusively used by and for the Chinese emperor. It is interesting to note that in the *Annals of the Tang Dynasty*, the title *tsenpo* is reproduced phonetically.

When Songtsen Gampo ascended to the throne, the various subjects of his father and those of his mother, including the people of Sumpa in present-day eastern Tibet, were hostile to him. They revolted but were soon put down. The *tsenpo* continued expanding the empire. He invaded the kingdom of Zhangzhung in the region around Mount Kailash, imposed tribute on it, and sent a Tibetan princess for matrimonial alliance. In the east, he step by step subdued the various Qiang tribes in the mountainous border regions and attacked the Azha kingdom (Chin. Tuyuhun) in the area of Koko Nor (Chin. Qinghai). By that time, the *tsenpo*'s forces had reached the confines of the Chinese empire. The *tsenpo* sent an embassy to the Chinese court at Chang'an (present-day Xi'an) in 634 C.E. and asked for a Chinese princess in matrimonial alliance. The Chinese emperor was reluctant and only consented under the threat of the Tibetan warriors. In 641, a Chinese princess was escorted to Lhasa, and for the first time the so-called "uncle–nephew" (i.e., father-in-law–son-in-law) alliance was established.

Matrimonial alliance was a political means frequently employed by the *tsenpo*. In addition to ladies of Tibetan noble clans, Songtsen Gampo is also said to have married a Nepalese princess. Both princesses, the Chinese and the Nepalese, were devout Buddhists, and each had a temple built in Lhasa. The Chinese princess founded the Ramoche temple, and the Nepalese princess built the Jokhang temple, a sanctuary still highly revered by Tibetans.

In about 647 C.E., a Tibetan army crossed the Himalayas—sometimes rashly considered an insuperable natural barrier—on a punitive expedition, because a Chinese embassy on a mission to India had been ill-treated, and China had called upon its Tibetan ally for help. Taking revenge, and doubtless also because it fitted in very well with the *tsenpo*'s policy of expansion, the Tibetan army penetrated deep into the North Indian plain.

The Tibetans had first become known to the Chinese as strong and powerful warriors. The *Tang Annals* note their fine weapons, their excellent armor, and their bravery with admiration. The empire they won by force might have been short-lived had it not been for Songtsen Gampo's far-sighted government and legislation. It was his grandson and successor Manglong Mangtsen (r. 650–676) who organized the Tibetan state and had the legal code written down in 655. Noble Tibetan youths were sent to the Chinese imperial academy at Chang'an for higher education and, although perhaps at a somewhat later date, also to India. An Indian alphabet had been adjusted to the peculiarities of the Tibetan language and henceforth served as script for Tibetan.

Diplomatic relations with China, once established, were maintained during the whole period of the Tibetan empire, and embassies were exchanged almost uninterruptedly. They were regularly sent to announce the death of the *tsenpo* or the Chinese emperor and to offer condolences. Apart from trade, which played an important role, the subjects discussed most frequently were problems connected with war and peace, such as negotiations over territorial claims, the exchange of prisoners of war, and peace treaties. At least eight bilateral peace treaties were concluded, and almost one hundred official missions are enumerated in the *Tang Annals*. The numerous missions reflect, not only the close contacts, but also the many conflicts between the Tibetan and Chinese empires provoked by their politics and geography.

In the early seventh century, in addition to the military governments of Longyou and Hexi (roughly present-day Qinghai and Gansu), the Chinese had established protectorates and the Four Garrisons in Central Asia, of which Kashgar was the farthest west, to prevent incursions on their western frontier, and doubtless also to control international trade. The Tibetans, who were continually trying to gain a foothold in the highly civilized city-states of Central Asia, which were important trading centers along the Silk Road, were thus in permanent conflict with Chinese interests. The Chinese military presence barred access to the two main routes linking central Tibet with Central Asia. One of these led to the northeast via Koko Nor. The other, to the north, ended at the crossroads near Lop Nor, from where two routes ran west to the southern and northern Tarim basin and another two ran northeast to Hexi and southeast to Koko Nor (see map 1).

Another route opening into Central Asia led over the high mountain passes in the Karakorum and Pamir ranges in the extreme west. During *Tsenpo* Manglong Mangtsen's reign, the Tibetans therefore concentrated on getting control of these strategically important mountain passes. Having subdued the small kingdoms of Brusha (Chin. Polü), the Gilgit area, and Gogyül (Wakhan), they allied themselves with the western Turks and launched an attack on the westernmost Chinese stronghold, Kashgar. From there, they proceeded to Khotan and, having taken it, reinforced by the Khotanese, they also conquered Aksu. The Chinese thus lost the southwestern and northern parts of the Tarim basin and withdrew their garrisons. At the same time, the Azha people in the northeast were subjugated. Their kingdom ceased to exist (663), and their territory came under Tibetan administration.

Tibet's Central Asian dominions were lost in 692 due to internal weakness resulting from *Tsenpo* Düsong's (676–704) struggle to put an end to the rule of the powerful Gar clan, whose members had hereditarily held the office of great councilor not only during the *tsenpo*'s infancy but since the time of Songtsen Gampo. Düsong set out at the head of his army. Having twice inflicted a defeat on the Chinese in Qinghai and Gansu, he proposed another marriage alliance with China. He then directed his army toward the southeast, subdued the kingdom of Jang (Chin. Nanzhao), and died on a campaign against the Mywa tribe in northern Yunnan.

One of the *tsenpo*'s elder sons managed to be enthroned but was soon deposed. During the infancy of the heir to the throne, Tride Tsugtsen (b. 704, enthroned 712), his grandmother Trimalö, of the noble clan of Dro, practically acted as regent. Negotiations for peace with China had been successful and the matrimonial alliance proposed by Düsong was concluded. In 710, a Chinese princess came to Tibet for the second time. The renewed alliance did not change things much, and obviously it was differently interpreted by Tibetans and Chinese. The *Tang Annals* report that the Tibetans insisted on being addressed in terms of equality in diplomatic correspondence. It is a characteristic feature of the Chinese to have taken this legitimate demand as hostile behavior.

Meanwhile, the Tibetans had entered into diplomatic relations with the Arabs and strengthened their position by an alliance not only with the Arabs but also with the Turgesh (a western Turkic tribe living in the Ili region, which at that time had formed a confederation). This was a matter of great concern among the small states in the west allied with or dependent on China. The Tibetans started to attack the Chinese garrisons in the Tarim basin and conquered Kucha (727). At the same time, they continued raiding China's northwestern border. A number of battles were fought against the Chinese army, with varying success. In 730, another peace treaty was concluded with China. According to the *Tang Annals* (Pelliot 1961), on this occasion the Chinese tried to trick the Tibetan councilor into accepting among other presents the fish insignia purse that was the mark of a tributary state. The Tibetan councilor politely refused, in Chinese, however, to accept the gift. (The fish insignia purse, a handsome bag meant to be worn on the belt, was presented by the Chinese to the representatives of foreign countries leading "tributary missions"; it contained one half of a bronze fish, the other half of which was kept in China so that it could be checked whether the two halves were a good match.) Peace between Tibet and China did not last. When war broke out again, the Chinese army managed to overrun the Tibetans far in the west and conquered part of Brusha. Moreover, although successful on the eastern border, the Tibetans lost battles in Central Asia and in the northeast. The series of Chinese victories came to an end in 751, however, when the Arabs and Qarluqs, a Turkic people in the region of Ili (Grousset 1941: 158), inflicted a great defeat on them in the battle of Talas. This marked the end of Chinese domination in Central Asia, and finally this whole region adopted the Muslim faith.

In 755, China was shaken by the rebellion of An Lushan (Gernet 1999:

227). In the same year, *Tsenpo* Tride Tsugtsen was murdered, and there was some turmoil in Tibet until his son, Trisong Detsen (742–797?), was enthroned with the help of loyal nobles. After having eliminated the disloyal nobles, Trisong soon took advantage of China's weakness. The Tibetan army advanced steadily in the northeast, occupying all of Longyou (Qinghai), east of Koko Nor. At the height of their military power, the Tibetans in 763 even occupied the Chinese capital, Chang'an (modern Xi'an), and installed a puppet emperor, thus endangering the very existence of the Tang dynasty. The victorious Tibetan general, Tara Lugong, was richly rewarded by the *tsenpo*. A huge inscribed stela commemorating his deeds and the rewards he received was erected at the foot of the hill on which the Potala Palace stands in Lhasa and still can be seen there today. After having enthroned their candidate for emperor of China, the Tibetans withdrew within a few weeks. Short-lived though it was, this episode is noteworthy because, conversely, no contemporary Chinese army—or any other army of the time—ever managed to penetrate deep into Tibetan territory, let alone central Tibet.

In the following years, the Tibetans conquered the important towns of Hexi (Gansu corridor) one after another, up to Hami, completely cutting off China from its Central Asian dominions. A peace treaty was again concluded in 783, confirming the Tibetan conquests in detail. In 791, the Tibetans also dominated Khotan and the southern part of the Tarim basin. During Trisong Detsen's reign, the Tibetan empire reached its greatest territorial extension. In order to protect the empire, which included peoples of different ethnic origin, like Indo-Europeans, Turks, and Chinese, speaking a variety of languages, military governments were established all along its frontier, stretching like a bow from the Karakorum range via the Tarim basin up to the Nanshan range and down to the Sichuan basin. Throughout the empire, Tibetan law and administration, in which local residents also took part, were applied.

Meanwhile, an important event had taken place in Tibet: Buddhism had been proclaimed the state religion. From the start of their expansion, the Tibetans had come into contact with adherents of all the great religions to be found at the confines of their empire: Buddhists, followers of the various other Indian religions, Christians, Muslims, Confucians, Taoists, and Manichaeans. It is known that the Tibetans asked for information on Islam, and it may be assumed that they showed similar interest in the other religions. Buddhism was widespread and flourishing in the surrounding regions, however, from Kashmir in the west to China itself, not to speak of the many monasteries in the states along the Silk Road. Many of these states were temporarily or permanently dominated by the Tibetans, who, to say the least, obviously tolerated Buddhism and other religious beliefs. Buddhist monks from Khotan fleeing the fighting in that kingdom in 739 sought refuge in Tibet. Thus, since the first contacts in the time of Songtsen Gampo, the ground for adopting the Buddhist way of life in Tibet had been continuously prepared.

Having decided to officially adopt Buddhism as state religion, *Tsenpo* Trisong Detsen took a great personal interest in Buddhist doctrine. He invited Indian and Chinese Buddhist masters who respectively represented the opposing views on the "gradual way" and the "immediate way" of attaining Enlightenment for a debate and concluded in favor of adopting the "gradual way" advocated by the Indians. However, there were no serious ill effects for the representatives of the Chinese side or for their adherents. Their doctrine coexisted with the officially adopted one, especially in the border regions of the Tibetan empire. The *tsenpo* made sure that Buddhism was disseminated as effectively as he had managed military affairs. Samye, the first monastery was built, provisions for the clergy were regulated and granted by the government, commissioners for Buddhist affairs were appointed, a number of colleges for the teaching of the Buddhist doctrine were established in Tibet itself, as well as in the northern and eastern border regions, and Indian scholars were invited in order to start the great work of translating the Buddhist canon into Tibetan.

Though the *tsenpo* himself was fervently engaged in the study of Buddhist doctrine, he did not neglect external affairs. Hostility with China soon had flared up again. The Chinese side had not kept the terms of an agreement of mutual military assistance. The Tibetans therefore attacked and occupied a number of Chinese prefectures in the Ordos region and farther in the east. During the ensuing peace negotiations, the Tibetans took revenge by kidnapping the Chinese negotiators.

Toward the end of the eighth century, the Uighurs, allies of China, had become a threat on Tibet's northern border. The Tibetans, together with their allies the Qarluqs, had taken the important city of Beiting from the Uighurs in 790. However, the Uighurs retook it in 792. In the same year, they also captured Qocho from the Tibetans. It was a setback when the Jang kingdom, Tibet's vassal in the southeast since the times of Düsong, refused to supply soldiers and defected to the Chinese in 794. But nevertheless Tibet was able to maintain its position.

The exact date of the death of the great *tsenpo* Trisong Detsen and the ascension to the throne of his son Tride Songtsen (r. 800?–817) is one of the problems in Tibetan history still not solved satisfactorily. Despite Tibet's involvement in a war with its former allies, the Arabs, in western Central Asia and although almost permanently engaged in fighting the Uighurs to keep them off their territory in the north and northeast, as well as the usual clashes with the Chinese, the new *tsenpo* continued the pious work of his father. It was during his reign that a translating committee consisting of a great number of Indian and Tibetan masters compiled a dictionary ordered by his father establishing the Tibetan equivalents of Sanskrit terms.

Negotiations for a new peace treaty with China came to an end only in 821 during the reign of Tride Songtsen's son Tritsug Detsen (r. 817–838 or 841?). In 823, the carefully drafted text of the treaty came into effect, after having been signed and sworn by both parties, each according to their own custom and to the custom of the other side.

The text of the treaty was inscribed on three pillars, erected in the Chinese capital, on the frontier, and in Lhasa. Only the pillar in Lhasa in front of the Jokhang temple survives, where the bilingual inscription of the treaty and the names of the Tibetan and Chinese signatories still can be deciphered. The treaty replaced the one concluded in 783 confirming the new Tibetan conquests and the actual frontiers. The Tibetans and Chinese are treated as equals, and the treaty concludes by saying: "Tibetans shall be happy in Tibet and Chinese shall be happy in China." The treaty was kept by both sides for almost two decades.

Under the patronage of the *tsenpo*, Buddhism spread and flourished throughout the empire. Many temples and monasteries were founded, and the number of monks increased. A great number of Buddhist texts were translated from Sanskrit, Chinese, and other languages. Numerous Tibetan manuscripts dating from that period found in a walled-up cave of the famous monastery of the "Caves of the Thousand Buddhas" near the oasis town of Dunhuang at the eastern end of the Silk Road give evidence of the translation activities.

Buddhist thought had also gained influence in the Tibetan government: the highest-ranking Tibetan official was a Buddhist monk. This fact was like a thorn in the flesh of those heads of Tibet's great noble clans who for centuries had tried to wrest power from the *tsenpo*. The Great Monk and Great Councilor Pelyön who had so successfully negotiated the treaty of 821/823 was murdered. In 838 (or 841?), the *tsenpo* shared his fate. Since he left no heir, his elder brother Ü Dumtsen, better known as Langdarma, ascended to the throne. The most popular account of his death in 842 says that a Buddhist monk killed him in order to put an end to his persecution of Buddhism. This "persecution" (for which there is no historical testimony) may have been the immediate cause, but, doubtless, the reason must be sought in the lack of central authority. After the *tsenpo* was murdered, one of his wives gave birth to a son, and another likewise claimed the dead ruler to have been the father of her son. Each had his partisans, and their struggle for power led to the disintegration of the empire. By the 860s, the Tibetans no longer dominated Gansu, and toward the end of that century, Tibetan domination of the Tarim basin also came to an end. The empire was partitioned between the two lines of heirs in the succession of the *tsenpo*, and there was no longer any central government.

This era when Tibet was a great military power, independent in every respect, with an extensive empire in Asia, ruled over by its *tsenpo*, who maintained international relations with and received embassies from China, the Arabs, and various Turkic states, is not well known. The renown of those centuries has given way to the perhaps more praiseworthy idea—equally rooted in that period—of Tibet as the "roof of the world," a country where Buddhism has penetrated every aspect of life and survived irrespective of all political changes.

The Yuan Dynasty (1279–1368)

[*A brief note is needed to fill the gap left by the Chinese authors between the Tibetan empire and the Yuan era.*

With the death of the last tsenpo *(ca. 842), what the Tibetans call "the first diffusion of the doctrine" came to an end. Tibet broke up again into several principalities waging war against one another. The blossoming of Buddhism, at least in its monastic form, stopped in central Tibet, but continued in the west and in the northeast, leading to the "second diffusion of Buddhism" at the end of the tenth century (see Question 56).*

Various schools of Tibetan Buddhism appeared at that time, composed of both monks and lay tantric practitioners. The inclusion of laypeople in this religious revival led to the transformation of the formerly warlike Tibet into a pious Buddhist country. Thanks to donations, the monasteries acquired prestige and economic power that foreshadowed both their political power and conflicts over that power. Later, the hegemony of the Sakyapas in the thirteenth and fourteenth centuries was replaced by that of the Phagmodrupas, until the Gelugpas gained control in the seventeenth century, with the reign of the 5th Dalai Lama.]

[*Continuation of the Chinese answer:*] In 1206, "the Mongolians of northern China . . . founded the Mongol Khanates." After having destroyed several kingdoms in China, Genghis Khan and his descendants established the Yuan Dynasty in 1271.

As early as the 1240s, various political forces in Tibet had pledged allegiance to the Mongols; Tibet then became an administrative region under the Yuan. "In the following 700 years, Tibet remained under the jurisdiction of China's central governments."

ELLIOT SPERLING

The question of whether Tibet has been a country separate from China cuts right to the heart of the ideological difficulties that China has had to deal with in redefining itself, in moving from what was recognized by other members of the world community as an empire at the beginning of the twentieth century to a "people's republic" at mid-century. The Chinese authorities have made the ideological leap by setting forth a Maoist interpretation of history that dictates that China is and always has been a "multinational" state; and moreover that it is not and never has been an empire. This manner of contextualizing China's claims to Tibet postulates that neighboring states and peoples that China has conquered and assimilated have been actors in an inexorable historical process that destined them to be (a priori, in some cases) "integral parts of China," incapable of true nationhood on their own. This worldview is not very far removed from that of older imperial Chinese ideologies that held that the peoples beyond China's frontiers were essentially subnational—peoples not at a level of nation formation comparable to China's, who could not but gravitate submissively into the sphere of China's influence and domination. Thus, China's modern claims that neighboring peoples are nothing but China's own "national minorities" mesh very well with Chinese worldviews from earlier centuries. To a large extent, this is nothing but the assimilation of much of China's traditional international environment into the People's Republic of China (PRC) as its frontier lands. As such, it represents a significant political and ideological development for China; but this is not to say that the worldviews of the peoples thus incorporated into China have developed, or have foreseen developments, along remotely similar lines.

Tibet, as much as any other Inner Asian dominion of China, has had its history distorted by modern Chinese writers in order to conform to the ideological requirements of the modern Chinese state. Thus the statement in *100 Questions* that Tibet became a part of China during the Yuan period assumes that the reader agrees that the Mongols who conquered and ruled China considered themselves "Chinese" and established their empire as a

Chinese empire, both rather untenable propositions. Assuredly, Tibet was incorporated into the Mongol dominions, but this was in a manner distinct from the Mongol conquest of China. In the late 1240s, the Tibetan lama Sakya Pandita (Sapan), leader of the Sakyapa sect of Tibetan Buddhism traveled with his nephews to the court of the Mongol prince Godan and sent a letter back to other leading figures in Tibet urging that they submit to Mongol authority. The letter that he is held to have sent (in 1249) and the acquiescence that other Tibetans accorded to the imposition of Mongol domination, as described in it, are generally considered to have marked the beginning of Mongol rule over Tibet. The Mongol hold weakened considerably in the fourteenth century, and the Mongols were ultimately unable to maintain their rule in Tibet, other than nominally, after 1354, when their local Sakyapa representatives began to suffer serious substantive losses of their broad authority to the rising power of Changchub Gyeltsen, a sectarian leader of the Phagmodrupa subsect of Tibetan Buddhism. These events are quite separate from the collapse of Mongol rule in China.

The submission of the Tibetans to the Mongols meant submission to the Mongol world empire. There is no doubt about the fact that Tibet was ruled, for the most part, by that branch of the Mongol empire based in China. There were also clear lines of influence between scattered areas of Tibet and the Mongols in Iran as well. However, the most telling indication of Tibet's status is the fact that the Yuan dynasty's official history (the *Yuanshi*, compiled a year after the dynasty collapsed), in detailing the geography of the Yuan realms, excludes Tibet from the relevant chapters. Clearly, Tibet, although under the domination of the Mongol rulers of the Yuan dynasty, was not attached by them to China, much less made an "integral part" of China. Interestingly enough, Chinese authors are either unable or unwilling to point to an actual act or decree that specifically designated Tibet "an integral part of China." Thus Chinese publications exhibit an inability to agree on when Tibet became a part of China: the *Beijing Review* (February 1988) has dated it to 1264; an article in *Social Sciences in China* (1984) dated it to Sakya Pandita's trip to Godan's court; and the "White Paper" published by the Information Office of the State Council of the PRC in the *Beijing Review* (September–October 1992), vaguely dates it to after the establishment of the Yuan central government (the same document dates the establishment of centralized Yuan rule to 1279). Evidently, the event that modern Chinese writers make so central to their arguments about China's claim to Tibet never registered among Yuan annalists and historiographers. There is a good reason for this, of course: it never happened. Moreover, the assertion that Tibet has been an integral part of China since the Yuan period is clearly a modern creation; when China, Tibet, and Britain met at Simla in 1914 to discuss the Tibetan question (see Question 10), the official Chinese response to Tibetan claims about the status of Tibet stated that definite Chinese sovereignty over Tibet commenced only during the Qing dynasty, after the conclusion of the Gurkha war in 1792.

2

SOME TIBETANS HAVE ARGUED THAT THE YUAN EMPEROR, KUBLAI KHAN, AND PAGBA, A LEADING TIBETAN LAMA OF THE SAGYA SECT, ONLY ESTABLISHED THE RELIGIOUS RELATIONSHIP OF "THE BENEFACTOR AND THE LAMA"; POLITICAL SUBORDINATION WAS NOT INVOLVED. IS THIS RIGHT?

The authors deny this theory [implicitly sustained by Tibetan historiography]. They summarize Tibeto-Mongol relations from Genghis Khan's accession (1206) and his conquest of the Xixia (1227) and Jin (1234) kingdoms up to the relationships established between Kublai and Phagpa.

"After Kublai's accession to the throne in 1260" [actually to the position of Great Khan; he founded the Yuan dynasty after his conquest of China in 1276, taking the emperor name Shizu], he granted Phagpa the title of "State Tutor" and in 1264, he appointed him to head the Zongzhiyuan [renamed Xuanzhengyuan in 1288], "to handle Buddhist affairs across his empire, including the government and religious affairs of Tibet."

"At the Yuan court, Kublai Khan always regarded Pagba as his subject." Thus "the relationship between Kublai Khan and Pagba was primarily one of political subordination." There were also religious bonds between them, and only when preaching did Pagba occupy a higher seat than Kublai.

ELLIOT SPERLING

It is true, as *100 Questions* states, that Tibet's relationship to the Mongol rulers of the Yuan was not limited to "priest-patron" links, as sometimes maintained by Tibetans (see the end of Question 5 for a definition and discussion of those links). Tibet was also subject to Mongol rule both militarily and politically (see Petech 1990). However, the nature of that rule, as stated in the preceding question, was quite different from the way in which Chinese writers have portrayed it. Similarly, the portrayal of the "priest-patron" relationship in *100 Questions* is also not wholly correct. The reasons for the Mongol incursion into Tibet, ordered by Godan, can in large part be traced to Mongol interest in the esoteric power that had been at the core of the brief "priest-patron" relationship that had existed between Tibetan lamas and the earlier Tangut rulers, whose state was destroyed by the Mongols in 1227. The Tangut state had occupied the area that came to be dominated by Godan and, not surprisingly, Godan hoped to make use of the religious practices of Tibetan Buddhists to augment his own power. That power was ultimately limited, but when Kublai began his rise to the Mongol throne, he asked that Godan send him the Sakyapa clerics who had been brought to the latter's court at Liangzhou. However, as indicated in *100 Questions*, the elderly Sakya Pandita had died, so his nephew Phagpa was sent to Kublai. We need not doubt that Kublai did exercise political domination over Tibet, and that the power that Phagpa and the Sakyapa sect enjoyed in Tibet was linked to their role under Kublai and his successors. The Chinese authors are unexpectedly straightforward, however, when discussing Kublai's appointment of Phagpa to head the Commission for Buddhist and Tibetan Affairs (Xuanzhengyuan), for they correctly state that the bureau was intended to handle Buddhist affairs throughout Kublai's "empire," which was in fact the case: Kublai's realms did not constitute a "multinational state," but rather an empire.

3

How did the Yuan Dynasty exercise its sovereignty over Tibet?

The Yuan government administered Tibet through a series of six measures:

1. The emperor Shizu [Kublai] "made Tibet a fief for his seventh son. . . . From then on, it was passed on to his descendants."
2. Officials were dispatched to Tibet, where they conducted three

censuses; tributes and taxes were fixed according to the results of the censuses.

3. "The Yuan central government founded the Zongzhiyuan in 1264" [see Question 2], which nominated Tibetan officials and reported directly to the emperor.

4. Three pacification commissioner's offices were set up, in Ü, Tsang, and Ngari [central Tibet], whose marshals administered garrisons of Mongolian troops posted there.

[For obvious ideological reasons, the authors do not mention the important territorial and administrative reorganization undertaken by the Mongols, dividing Tibet in three "districts" (chölkha): Ü and Tsang; Ngari; and Kham and Amdo. These eastern parts of Tibet are never taken into account in the contemporary Chinese works on Tibet, that is, the Tibet Autonomous Region (TAR).]

5. Courier stations and staging posts were established across the whole of Tibet.

6. All high-ranking Tibetan officials were appointed, promoted or dismissed by the central government.

"In sum, the Yuan Dynasty adopted a series of special measures to govern Tibet, which was always regarded as one of its provinces."

ELLIOT SPERLING

The description provided in *100 Questions* of the structures that the Yuan rulers established in their exercise of dominion over Tibet is essentially correct. However the extent to which these structures were actually involved in the daily administration of Tibetan affairs inside Tibet is exaggerated, for it ignores the very real role that the Sakyapas played in the country. We know that the administrative arrangements in Tibet allowed for a considerable amount of decentralization in the country, including the posting of local officials from the Iranian part of the Mongol empire to those areas considered to be under the jurisdiction of the Mongol ruling house in Iran; although this in no way undermined or affected the actual Yuan position in Tibet, it is indicative that Mongol arrangements for Tibet were far more complex than *100 Questions* otherwise implies. We may also point out here that the authors contradict themselves when they revert to usual form and state that the Xuanzhengyuan was established to handle Buddhist affairs "across the whole of China," rather than in Kublai's empire, as stated in their preceding answer.

4

IT HAS BEEN ARGUED THAT THE MONGOLIANS INCORPORATED
TIBET INTO CHINA BY CONQUEST IN A MANNER NOT TOO DISSIMILAR
TO BRITAIN'S OCCUPATION OF INDIA AND BURMA. WHAT DO YOU
THINK OF THE CLAIM THAT JUST AS INDIA CANNOT NOW REGARD
BURMA AS PART OF ITS TERRITORY, SO CHINA CANNOT CLAIM
SOVEREIGNTY OVER TIBET?

"This argument is utterly groundless, and those who raise it either
are ignorant of China's history or have ulterior motives.

" . . . China has been a multi-national country since ancient times. . . .
It is a mistake to believe . . . that China means the Han Nationality,
or that the Han Nationality means China. To do so is to be led into
the mistaken belief that the regimes established by China's ethnic minorities are 'foreign countries.'"

Before the Mongol takeover, China was "torn apart by many separatist feudal regimes": the Song, the Liao, the Western Xia, and the
Jin, the last three founded by non-Han ethnic peoples.

"From ancient times the Mongolians had been one of China's nationalities." Consequently, it is wrong to argue that the imposition of
the Mongol rule and the foundation of the Yuan dynasty was due to
a foreign power. The same occurred with the Manchus: it was always
"a case of one Chinese nationality replacing another."

"It is not hard to see that there is nothing in common with the
British war of aggression against India and Burma . . . and the Mongolians' war to unify China."

ELLIOT SPERLING

Here, in asserting that those who maintain that Tibet and China were both
incorporated by force into a Mongol empire are either ignorant of Chinese
history or have ulterior motives, the authors resort to invective rather than
reasoning. Alas, that means that practically all historians of the period, outside China, must be so categorized, for they too accept that the Mongols
established an empire that included China, Tibet, Iran, Russia, and so on.
Moreover, this group of supposedly ignorant or devious people includes the
authors of the Yuan's official history (among others), for, as we have noted,
they not only didn't bother to describe Tibet as a part of China, they also

failed to include Mongolia as such. Here too the authors advance the familiar argument that "China has been a multi-national country since ancient times," and the notion that China could ever have been part of an empire, or that it could have behaved as an imperial power, is sidestepped. More arguments along the same lines follow. It is a mistake, say the authors, "to believe . . . that China means the Han Nationality, or that the Han Nationality means China." But that, in fact, is one of the basic meanings of the term "Han." A number of pre- and post-Communist Chinese dictionaries clearly note this meaning. On the title page of any Chinese-English dictionary "Han-Ying" is translated as "Chinese-English," clearly showing the basic meaning of Han as equivalent to Chinese.

At heart here is the desire of the Chinese authorities to legitimize their hold over areas such as Tibet by imposing on the people of these areas the designation "Chinese," a designation with clear ethno-linguistic implications, thus suggesting that Chinese rule over these peoples is somehow an organic and natural development, and that the peoples concerned are essentially ethno-linguistically an organic whole. Of course, this is quite at odds with the tack taken by the Russians, who in the Soviet Union presided over a similarly multinational state composed of elements derived from an earlier empire. The Russians designated the component peoples of the state that they dominated as "Soviet," a term meaning "council" and bearing no specific ethno-linguistic connotations. Of late, Chinese writers have even demanded that the term "Sino" in the larger term "Sino-Tibetan" can only be used to mean "Han." What then of the "Sino" in "Sino-American?" It clearly means Chinese there. Such are the problems encountered when one seeks to enforce state-ordered political language. The fact of the matter is that "Han" is a legitimate synonym for "Chinese," as the dictionaries note. In spite of Chinese protests to the contrary, the incorporation of Tibet into the Mongol empire (like its incorporation into the PRC) was accomplished by force of arms, rather than by the normal movement of some predictable and inevitable historical process.

5

DID THE MING AND QING DYNASTIES CONTINUE TO EXERCISE THE
SOVEREIGNTY OVER TIBET ESTABLISHED BY THE YUAN DYNASTY?

"Yes. The Ming Dynasty . . . basically inherited the arrangements of the Yuan Dynasty." Tibetan officials were summoned to come to China for reconfirmation of their titles and offices. "Many of them did so." Later, the emperor created six new titles and bestowed them upon the high-ranking lamas who governed Tibet: "Great Treasure Prince of Dharma," and so forth.

[Before the fall of the Yuan, the power of the Sakyapas had weakened, and rule over Tibet fell into the hands of Changchub Gyeltsen (1302–1364), a remarkable statesman of the Phagmodrupa School. He unified Tibet and abolished the territorial division instituted by the Mongols in favor of the ancient division into provinces, to which he assigned governors. He reorganized the tax system and the code of laws, improved communications, and built roads and bridges. His successors ruled Tibet, first effectively then nominally until the accession to power of the 5th Dalai Lama and the Gelugpa School.

The authors of 100 Questions *are much more prolix when they present the situation under the Qing Dynasty (1644–1911); but their historical summary is misleading when they jump without transition from the diplomatic relations between the 5th Dalai Lama and the first Qing emperor in the mid seventeenth century to the details of the political and administrative reorganization imposed by China upon the government of the Dalai Lamas in 1793.*

The nature of the links between Tibet and China changed under the Qing, as explained by Elliot Sperling and Anne Chayet, who respectively specialize in the Ming and Qing Dynasties. The end of the Chinese answer is found at the beginning of the Section that deals with the Qing Dynasty.]

The Ming Dynasty (1368–1644)

ELLIOT SPERLING

The administrative structures that the Ming dynasty established for Tibet existed for the most part solely on paper. The primary unit established by the Ming for Tibet was the Xi'an Branch Regional Guard based at Hezhou, a frontier town in Gansu, well away from the Tibetan heartland. At its establishment, a Chinese official named Wei Zheng was placed at its head. The "White Paper" on Tibet published in the *Beijing Review* in September-October 1992 gives strong emphasis to the establishment of this office (terming it the "Shaanxi Itinerant High Commandery") as proof of Ming China's sovereignty over Tibet. However, Wei Zheng, whom one would therefore have to assume was the highest official in the region is unknown in any Tibetan historical sources and barely mentioned by traditional Chinese sources. Obviously, this supposed administrative unit was intended only to exercise ceremonial authority anywhere beyond the frontier region.

Thus, the titles that we find in Ming sources being accorded to Tibetan figures at this time cannot be taken as carrying real political authority in Tibet. Moreover, the official history of the Ming dynasty (like that of the Yuan) places Tibet outside the geography of Ming China. A letter informing the Tibetans of the establishment of the Ming, sent to Tibet by the dynasty's first emperor, and similar to letters sent by him to other foreign lands, also attests to the fact that the Ming rulers did not consider Tibet to be "Chinese"; in it, the emperor refers to Tibet as a state quite separate from China. Surely one cannot assume that the first Ming emperor, Zhu Yuanzhang, was also ignorant of Chinese history and possessed of ulterior motives, as *100 Questions* states with regard to those who view Tibet and China as having been constituent parts of a Mongol empire? Certainly, Zhu and the emperors who succeeded him did not deal with Tibet as if it were a province of China. Relations with important Tibetan hierarchs were not handled by provincial-level bureaucrats.

One sees the significance of this when one examines the most prominent titles presented to Tibetans during the Ming: those designating the hierarchs of the Karmapa, Sakyapa, and Gelugpa sects as "Great Precious King of the Dharma" (1407), "Great Vehicle King of the Dharma" (1413), and "Great Compassionate King of the Dharma" (1434); and five important secular figures as "Prince Who Spreads Magical Transformations" (1406), "Prince Who Spreads the Doctrine" (1413), "Prince Who Supports the Doctrine" (1413), "Prince Who Relies on Virtue" (1407), and "Prince Who Protects the Doctrine" (1407). The presentation of these titles and communication with their recipients were clearly treated as diplomatic affairs by the Ming and were handled by the same diplomatic bureaucracy that dealt with Ming China's relations with the lands of the South Seas. One cannot (as Chinese authors have sometimes done) extrapolate from the simple presentation of these titles a basis for claiming Ming sovereignty over Tibet. An examination of the events surrounding the presentation of these titles shows clearly that the recipients held power and/or influence in Tibet prior to their being granted. As such, the titles did not bestow power, but rather acknowledged it, and their granting must be seen as something akin to the not uncommon presentation of honors, titles, or awards by one country to nationals of another. The assertion made in the 1992 "White Paper" on Tibet that succession to these titles on the death of a holder required approval of the emperor is true, insofar as these were Chinese titles. But the further statement that such imperial approval was a prerequisite for the holder to assume his role is disingenuous, to say the least. While the title of "Great Precious King of the Dharma," for example, was an honor bestowed by the Ming court on the chief Karmapa incarnations, the role of these hierarchs in Tibet was well established before the title was given and was in no way dependent on it.

The Qing Dynasty (1644–1911)

ANNE CHAYET

During the Qing dynasty, a significant change affected Sino-Tibetan relations. By the end of the eighteenth century, Tibet had gradually become part of the Chinese political system. This evolution was one of the keys to the present situation, so it is necessary to ask what led to it.

Traditionally, China considered itself the center of the world, surrounded by an outer circle of barbarian countries, and very early on, it had formed a vivid consciousness of its uniqueness, one of the main components of its culture, as well as of its power and grandeur. The consciousness China had of its cultural identity followed its territorial expansion and its political and economic growth, leaving a limited place and role for the non-Chinese populations that were progressively merged into the empire.

It has already been said here (see "The Yuan Dynasty," above) that it is nonsensical to describe ancient China as a pluri-ethnic country, and to use recent Western concepts or references to contemporary international law to explain the past history of China or any part of Asia. It should not be forgotten that Han (that is to say, ethnically and culturally Chinese) literati used to consider—and sometimes still consider—the Manchu emperors of the Qing dynasty as mere usurpers.

Manchu sovereigns had had ambitions regarding China for a long time. They founded a claim to the succession of the Tungusic Jin Dynasty upon their ethnic relationship with that dynasty, which had reigned over North China (1115–1234). Consequently, they created their own dynasty on the Chinese model and called it the Latter Jin Dynasty (1616). Some years later, the Manchu sovereign altered the name of his dynasty to that of Qing, or "Pure," in a kind of solemn refounding. The designation "Manchu" for his people appears in the dynastic *Records* as early as 1613 and has sometimes been explained as a form of the Sanskrit name Mañjushrî, the famous bodhisattva and symbol of knowledge of the Buddhist tradition, considered to be the protector of China.

By the end of the sixteenth century, the increasing power of the Manchus became a direct threat to the declining Ming empire. In 1634, the Manchu sovereign Hung Taiji defeated the last Mongol khan in lineal descent from Genghis Khan, and the imperial seal of the Yuan, generally considered to be Genghis Khan's own seal, came into his hands. This token of legitimacy reinforced his claim to have inherited the Mongol empire, as well as the empire of China. The Mongol princes who submitted to him after 1634 were devoted Buddhists. They followed the rule of the Tibetan reformed school of the Gelugpas. To comply with their tradition, the Manchu sovereign declared himself a protector of Buddhism, as did his successors, the Qing emperors of China, at least as long as it was useful to their political purposes and as long as they were able to maintain an independent policy.

In 1578, a famous meeting took place between Sönam Gyatso, abbot of the Gelugpa Drepung monastery near Lhasa, and Altan Khan of the Tumed Mongols, which led to them bestowing honorific titles on each other: Sönam Gyatso received the title of Dalai Lama from Altan Khan and in turn gave the latter the title of Chögyel (King Ruling According to the Doctrine), as a protector of Buddhism (see Question 6). The Dalai Lama's prestige and influence among the Mongols became so great that it aroused both concern at the Ming court and jealousy among the other religious dignitaries in Tibet. When Sönam Gyatso died (1588), his reincarnation was discovered in Altan Khan's family. This meant a direct foreign influence in Tibet, which had not happened since the fall of the Yuan. The resulting troubles came to a climax in 1610, when the prince of Tsang (one of the two central provinces of Tibet) invaded Ü (Lhasa province) where the Gelugpas had their most important monasteries and support. The Gelugpas soon called on the Mongol princes for help, which deepened the breach between the two parties. Finally, in 1641–42, Gushri Khan, head of the Qoshot Mongols, who had settled in the vicinity of Koko Nor and were the most effective support of the Gelugpas, defeated the prince of Tsang. In April 1642, Gushri Khan solemnly presented the provinces of Tibet to the young 5th Dalai Lama.

Two years later, in 1644, the Ming dynasty was driven out by the Manchus, and the Qing dynasty ascended the Beijing throne. However, the pacification and unification of the empire under the new rule proved a rather lengthy task. Wu Sangui's rebellion in western and southwestern China began in 1674 and ended only in late 1681, and until his death in 1697, Galdan, prince of the Dzungar Mongols, made several attempts to restore the empire of Genghis Khan, threatening the northern frontiers of the Qing empire and endangering its Mongol allies. During the first half of the eighteenth century, the Qing emperors did their best to compel all the Mongol tribes to submit, either by diplomacy or by armed force. Emperor Kangxi (r. 1662–1722) asked the Dalai Lama several times to calm down trouble-some Mongol princes or to act as a mediator between them (see also Petech 1972). But as the Mongol tribes submitted one after the other to the new dynasty, Tibet lost part of the importance it had had in the imperial eyes, becoming merely one of the empire's borderlands, a part of its protective glacis, destined to be included in it as a precaution and submitted to its rule. Consequently, from 1720 on, there was a permanent Chinese presence in Tibet, either administrative or military, although the form of government was never that of an average province of China, even after the 1793 reform, which notably strengthened the role and power of the emperor's represen-tatives in Lhasa, the *ambans*.

During the nineteenth century, with the Qing in decline, the Chinese po-sition in Tibet weakened, which did not exclude crises or abuses. Beijing's power still expressed itself, but in an unrealistic conservative and formalist way. Tibetan society was unable to face reform, in spite of the 13th Dalai Lama's attempts at modernization. Tibet was brutally confronted with the twentieth century, first with the British invasion of 1904 and the Chinese counteroffensive, which led to two successive exiles of the Dalai Lama, then with the collapse of the Qing dynasty (1911).

> [*Continuation of the Chinese answer:*] "Tibet's incorporation into the Qing Dynasty was as smooth and voluntary as its acceptance of Ming rule." In 1642, the 5th Dalai Lama "sent envoys to establish relations and pay homage to the Qing court." In later years, the Qing dynasty strengthened its administrative grip on Tibet and in 1793 the "29-article regulations" were formulated. The main points concerned the equality with the Dalai Lama and the Panchen Lama of the high com-missioners [*ambans*] sent by Beijing; Tibetan officials were forbidden to correspond with foreign countries; foreign traders were controlled by the high commissioner; the reincarnations of the Dalai Lama, Panchen Lama and high lamas "should be decided by drawing slips from a gold urn . . . and approved by the emperor."

ANNE CHAYET

Westerners, especially the British, who established contacts with Tibet as early as the eighteenth century, described its status in terms typical of West-ern political thinking and international relations. The concepts of sovereignty and suzerainty unnecessarily complicated an issue that was already much vexed. Sino-Tibetan relations and their evolution between the seventeenth and twentieth centuries are extremely ambiguous, and it is not easy to find one's way in the official reports and documents, Tibetan or Chinese, contemporary or not, and to trace back what the Tibetan and Chinese rulers really thought of their mutual relations, especially if one considers that a great many present-day Tibetans think that the links between China and Tibet were merely religious.

MANCHUS, MONGOLS, AND TIBETANS

Part of Tibet's usefulness to the Qing was that although outside (*wai*) China, the Dalai Lama, thanks to his religious authority, was able to keep the quarrelsome (but devoted Buddhist) Mongol princes under control. However, after the general submission of the Mongols, Tibet lost part of its specific importance and might even become a danger to China if it were to enter into alliance with one of the new powers that had appeared in Asia: Russia at the northern border of the empire, and later Britain, south of the Himalayas.

In 1637, the Manchu sovereign Huang Taiji, assuming the role of a protector of Buddhism, courteously invited the Dalai Lama to preach the Doctrine in Manchuria. The Dalai Lama's answer (dated 1640, it arrived in Mukden in 1642) implied neither submission nor dependence. As we can judge from contemporary Tibetan documents, this invitation was considered merely as establishing religious links with a new protector of the Doctrine. However, when sending his invitation to the Dalai Lama, Huang Taiji also wrote to the prince of Tsang, asking him to let the hierarch go to Mukden and even to prompt him to do so. One may think that his reading of the situation was not realistic, for the prince of Tsang was then fighting decisive battles with the Tibetan and Mongol supporters of the Dalai Lama, but it proves that he distinguished between temporal and spiritual power in Tibet, attributing the first to the prince of Tsang and the second to the Dalai Lama, something his Mongol allies did not do as neatly.

In 1642, the Dalai Lama received temporal power over Tibet from Gushri Khan. It is difficult to understand the extent of the Dalai Lama's authority in the governmental system that was then established. This system depended so fundamentally on the distinct characters of Gushri Khan and the 5th Dalai Lama that it proved to be unmanageable after the latter's death. The Dalai Lama was, first of all, a spiritual master, guardian of the Doctrine. He did not concern himself with the daily affairs of civil government, and still less with the possible command of an army. The temporal power he had received placed him, from a religious point of view, in a rather paradoxical situation.

As can be seen from the 5th Dalai Lama's autobiography, he entrusted Gushri Khan with the command of the armies and charged a regent with the administration of the state. Between 1642 and 1655, the whole of the country was pacified and reorganized, and the Gelugpas' power continued to grow, showing a strong trend toward centralism. Gradually, the Dalai Lama came to rule more directly, the regent acting upon his orders. After Gushri Khan's death (1655), his sons succeeded him, but they were less efficient, did not often come to Lhasa, and neglected military defense, which no longer seemed to have the crucial importance it had had twenty years before. The 5th Dalai Lama proved to be a clever diplomat and a good administrator, but he could not be a commander-in-chief. The army, or more precisely the lack of a powerful and well-organized army, was to be the weak aspect of the Dalai Lamas' rule.

VISIT OF THE 5TH DALAI LAMA TO BEIJING

In 1644, the Manchu rulers ascended the Beijing throne and, as Qing emperors of China, henceforward spoke to the Dalai Lama in language different from what they had used before. They followed the formal Chinese tradition, which submitted more or less implicitly to the Son of Heaven all the populations outside China, and considered them to be tributaries. In Mukden, long before 1644, they had had Chinese councilors, and they were well aware of this tradition. When in Beijing, they also adopted its underlying concept of centralized and absolute power and its lordly formalism. Many of the neighboring countries accepted or were compelled to accept being considered tributary countries. The 5th Dalai Lama obviously had a different idea of his relations with the emperor and with China. Besides, the first Qing emperors did not pretend to rule over Tibet.

In 1648, the young emperor Shunzhi (r. 1644–1662) invited the 5th Dalai Lama to come to Beijing. The latter alludes in his autobiography to the religious significance of the proposed meeting and cites a prophecy heralding the coming of a manifestation in central Tibet of the bodhisattva Mañjushrî, protector of China, who would work for the welfare of Buddhism in Tibet, China, and Mongolia, which he believed indicated his meeting with the emperor of China, also designated as a form of Mañjushrî. The main point here is that he speaks of Tibet, China, and Mongolia as separate entities and always continued to regard them as such. The Dalai Lama knew that he had to make clear his position before his visit to Beijing to avoid being treated as an ordinary tributary ruler. The Buddhist tradition offers many examples of relations between spiritual and temporal powers, between a spiritual master and a ruler (at various levels, from local rulers to emperors), donor and protector of the Doctrine, which are broadly defined by the Tibetan term *chöyön* ("priest-patron"). When a special teaching is given by the master to the protector, the link is closer to that of master and disciple. But if the Dalai Lama wished to be considered the spiritual master in his relationship with China, he could not elude the fact that he was also a temporal ruler, and that his lay protector was, like himself, the manifestation of a deity. And he had to take for granted that the Qing emperors' conception of the relationship was what it had been in the time of the Yuan dynasty, which proved to be wrong. Some emperors of the Tang dynasty (618–907), when Buddhism flourished at the imperial court, gave themselves the title of bodhisattva. Did this mean that the emperor was invested with religious authority as well as temporal authority, as was the Dalai Lama? This is what the 5th Dalai Lama seems to suggest in styling the emperor bodhisattva Mañjushrî, when he was himself the bodhisattva Avalokiteshvara, protector of Tibet. The Dalai Lama certainly knew that even if he agreed to be called bodhisattva, the emperor of China was first of all the Son of Heaven, without equal or superior, and living according to ritualistic rules that placed him above all powers and authorities. By styling the emperor bodhisattva, like himself, the Dalai Lama may have been attempting to incorporate him into his own world and to impose a kind of equality between their positions.

The Dalai Lama left for Beijing in 1652. He obviously considered himself an independent sovereign; moreover, the young emperor, either because he agreed with this opinion or to comply with the wish of his Mongol allies, planned to go in person outside the symbolical frontier of the Great Wall to welcome the hierarch. However, the imperial chancery, whose members were mostly Han and not Manchus, decided to keep to the ancient imperial tradition, and persuaded Shunzhi to delegate an official of high rank to meet the Dalai Lama instead.

In his autobiography, the 5th Dalai Lama records an impressive list of the various marks of esteem and respect that were paid to him. The *Historical Records* of the Qing are more laconic, although they show that the Tibetan hierarch was given a more important reception than that normally granted to a tributary prince, perhaps because the new dynasty did not yet comply entirely with Chinese tradition. Nevertheless, this meeting was a confrontation of two different worlds, whose positions were incompatible.

For the two sovereigns, this visit was probably the occasion for a kind of judging of their situation. Obviously, China was the bigger power, but the Qing emperor's authority was not yet firmly established, something both of them knew very well. The Dalai Lama had a great influence on the Mongol princes. He frequently settled their disputes, and he gave them titles and functions. He also acted as a mediator, when required by the emperor, between China and the Mongol princes who had not yet submitted. This attitude, far from reinforcing his temporal power, progressively deprived him of the military support of the Mongol princes. After their general submission, Tibet would have to face China alone.

Emperor Kangxi (r. 1662–1723) ascended the throne when he was eight, wielding power after 1669. He had a very strong personality, and was not disposed to tolerate a policy of inaction, lack of precision about the frontiers between China and Tibet, or the traditional lack of discipline of the Mongol princes. He was soon confronted with Wu Sangui's rebellion (1674–82) and asked for the Dalai Lama's help. The rebellion involved regions of Sichuan and Yunnan bordering Tibet. The Dalai Lama did his best, without much result, thus revealing that since Gushri Khan's death, he had virtually lost his control over the Qoshot princes, who maintained a zone of political and military instability between China and Tibet. Subsequently, when Galdan, prince of the Dzungar Mongols of the Ili region, threatened the northern frontier of the empire, the Dalai Lama was again called upon to intervene, but the conflict remained unresolved.

In fact, the 5th Dalai Lama had actually died in 1682. However, the young regent, Sangye Gyatso, concealed this for fourteen years, not only from the Tibetans and the Mongol princes, but from Emperor Kangxi, who never forgave him for this, or for the help he was suspected to have given Galdan (although the latter suffered a first defeat in 1690, then a decisive one in 1696).

As early as 1680, the Emperor had made numerous rectifications and annexations in the border areas between China and Tibet (especially in the Tibetan province of Kham). In 1693–94, he annexed the Xining region, in the vicinity of Koko Nor, considering that the Qoshot Mongols were no longer able to protect it. After the Dzungars' defeat, the regent had to officially inform the emperor of the 5th Dalai Lama's death and of the search for and discovery of his successor, the 6th Dalai Lama.

The young Dalai Lama, enthroned at the end of 1697, proved to be unwilling to assume his obligations and soon renounced his monastic vows (1702), although without giving up his temporal power. But in 1703, Lazang Khan, one of Gushri Khan's descendants, supported by Kangxi, took over his great-grandfather's civilian and military functions in Lhasa. He wanted to get rid of the 6th Dalai Lama and, in 1706, with Kangxi's support, he had the Dalai Lama transported to China. The official records tell us that the young man died on the way. Then, in spite of strong Tibetan opposition, Lazang Khan enthroned a Dalai Lama of his own choice, who was recognized by the emperor in 1710. However, the traditional search discovered the true reincarnation of the Dalai Lama in Kham. This child was recognized by the Mongol princes of Koko Nor, who asked Kangxi to recognize him. Who would have imagined begging the emperor of China for such recognition fifty years before?

THE CONQUEST

Galdan died in 1697, but there were still Dzungar chiefs and armies. In 1717, they attacked Lazang Khan's forces on the pretext of bringing the young Dalai Lama born in Kham from his residence in the Koko Nor region to Lhasa. Lhazang Khan had become estranged from the traditional powers in Tibet, both lay and religious. His armies were soon defeated by the Dzungars, who took possession of Lhasa in November 1717, and then of a large part of central Tibet, and engaged in three years of looting, destruction, and slaughter. Even the Potala—the palace of the Dalai Lamas and seat of their government in Lhasa—was plundered, and the Nyingmapas (the followers of the oldest school of Tibetan Buddhism) were cruelly persecuted.

The Dzungars, having defeated and killed Lhazang Khan, deposed his Dalai Lama and established a government in their pay. Meanwhile, some of the surviving officers of Lhazang Khan and a part of the Tibetan nobility organized resistance against the invaders. Emperor Kangxi, reconsidering his earlier and wrong choice, officially recognized the true Dalai Lama, and sent two rescue armies (one of them escorting the young hierarch from his residence), which reached Lhasa in the autumn of 1720.

A six months' temporary military administration was succeeded by a new government in the spring of 1721. It consisted of a council of three (later five) members, theoretically subordinate to the Dalai Lama, who was still underage (the regent functions had been suppressed), and watched over by the commander of the garrison, representative of the emperor.

The largest part of the two imperial armies had retired, but a garrison of 3,000 soldiers remained in Lhasa. There were also garrisons in eastern Tibet to supervise communications with China. The governor of Sichuan was given authority over the Tibetan territories between the border of China and that of Lhasa province. Although this order was partly cancelled in 1725, the emperor obviously wanted well-defined frontiers and was in a position to impose his will. To make this clear, he had a pillar erected in Lhasa, at the foot of the Potala, to commemorate his victory. The Italian Jesuit Ippolito Desideri, who was then in Tibet, wrote that Tibet had had an independent king (which was not exactly correct as far as Lhazang Khan was concerned) and had been subjugated in 1720 by the emperor of China, whose rule over the country would probably last for many centuries.

In the same year, 1721, the *Great Atlas of China* was published. In 1708, Emperor Kangxi had ordered the Jesuits to do a general mapping of China, but his order did not include Tibet. In 1709, he sent a representative to Lhazang Khan to undertake the mapping of Tibet, which was done and published with the main atlas in 1721. This detail shows how Kangxi's opinion and attitude concerning Tibet changed by the end of his reign. The Dzungars' final defeat in Tibet confirmed Galdan's defeat of 1696, putting an end to their threat on the northern frontier. Kangxi had limited the Russians' progress in Central and East Asia and their possible alliance with the Mongols by the Nerchinsk treaty (1689). In 1691, the eastern Mongols submitted to him. The imperial order now prevailed in Tibet: Kangxi had completed the protective northern and western glacis of the empire.

Concerning the countries bordering China, the terms "inner" and "outer" are not literary fictions. The young emperor Shunzhi was once advised against going to greet the Dalai Lama *outside* the Great Wall (although it has never been a real frontier). Emperor Kangxi registered among the territories of the empire towns and places that had until then been considered to be Tibetan and consequently *outside* the empire. In 1795, Emperor Qianlong still styled the Tibetans *waifan*, meaning barbarians and tributary people living in the bordering regions *outside* the empire. The year 1721 was an important date for Tibet. As noted by Father Desideri, its fate was sealed. It had been a country "outside China." The next step would be to declare it an integral part of China. This was not to be done in a day, but it can be said that from 1721 on, relations between Lhasa and Beijing depended upon the importance of the Chinese garrison in Lhasa and its ability to keep order and uphold the law in Tibet.

ORGANIZATION OF THE IMPERIAL POWER IN TIBET

Emperor Kangxi died in 1722 and was succeeded by his son Yongzheng. In 1723, the new emperor ordered the withdrawal of the Lhasa garrison, arguing that it was an excessive burden for the Tibetan economy, and most probably because he wished to reduce his expenses *outside* China. He kept a garrison of 1,000 soldiers in Chamdo and reorganized the Xining garrison with 6,000 soldiers. However, the situation was more difficult than he had thought, and an army had to be sent to put down a rebellion by the Mongol princes in the Koko Nor region (1723–24).

In 1725, Emperor Yongzheng returned to Tibet the administration of the territories situated between the border of Sichuan and the border of Lhasa province, with the exception of places of strategic importance such as Litang, Batang, and Derge, with which he charged local chiefs. Nevertheless, in 1726, inconsistent with this conciliatory attitude, he sent an edict to Lhasa ordering a veritable persecution of the Nyingmapa School. The pious fiction of the *chöyön* (see above) burst into pieces. The Tibetan council was indignant, especially because the Dalai Lama was still underage, but did not dare to protest.

The members of this council were divided on the question of relations with China. However, the opponents of the increasing presence and power of China in Tibet among them cannot be described as nationalists, as has sometimes been done, for this concept did not exist then. They were merely opposed to the new rule because it was against their interests and their traditions. The supporters of the Chinese intervention did not think it could be the beginning of a process of annexation. They considered it a measure of protection, a warrant of order and security, which left the spiritual power of the Dalai Lama untouched. They did not see, or preferred not to see, that the Manchu emperors interpreted the *chöyön* differently, and that it was contrary to Chinese tradition. During the eighteenth century, successive emperors respected several aspects of the relationship as the Tibetans thought it had been defined. But the disorder and the many disturbances that occurred in Tibet led them to press more heavily on the Tibetan government because, whatever may have been their respect for the Doctrine, they could not tolerate a weak point in the frontier of the empire.

In 1727, as a consequence of many court intrigues and conspiracies, as well as the inflexibility of his attitude, Khangchene, the head of the Tibetan council, was assassinated. Civil war broke out. One year later, in July 1728, Pholane, Khangchene's faithful assistant, suppressed the rebellion and took control of Lhasa. After consideration, Emperor Yongzheng had sent a relieving army of 15,000 soldiers, but it reached Lhasa only in September, without any fighting.

The awful punishment inflicted upon the murderers and their accomplices was, however, soon forgotten. Yongzheng attributed the disorder to the Dzungars' evil influence, which was wrong, and considered more realistically that the young Dalai Lama's circle, especially his father, had played an important part in raising the rebellion. Accordingly, the young hierarch and his father were exiled to the border area of Gartar (today Qianning, Sichuan), where they remained for seven years.

From 1728 on, the representatives periodically sent to Lhasa by the emperor became resident representatives, the *ambans*, who were supported by a garrison of 2,000 soldiers, a number sufficient to maintain order. Nevertheless, the emperor left many of the powers that had been taken from the Dalai Lama (at least temporarily) to Pholane, as head of the new council. Certainly, Yongzheng trusted the faithful Pholane, but there was a tradition of realism among the first Manchu emperors that led them to prefer local authorities to often more greedy imperial officials for the administration of border regions.

Emperor Yongzheng died in 1735, and the same year the Dalai Lama returned to Lhasa. The succeeding emperor, Qianlong (r. 1736–1795), thought, as his father had done in 1723, to withdraw the Lhasa garrison, which now numbered only 500 soldiers, but his councilors advised against it. In 1740, Qianlong gave Pholane the important title of *junwang* (second-rank prince) thus recognizing him as a kind of "viceroy" of Tibet. When Pholane died in 1747, his son Gyurme Namgyel succeeded to his charge, but soon fell out with all the Tibetan parties and brought upon himself the distrust of the *ambans*. The situation came to such a point of crisis that the *ambans*, without imperial instructions, preferred to have Gyurme Namgyel assassinated (1750). His few remaining supporters then stirred up a riot. A clean sweep was made of the garrison, and the two *ambans* were assassinated. Thanks to the Dalai Lama's intervention, the riot soon came to an end. The emperor sent 3,000 troops to Lhasa, and cruel punishments were inflicted to prevent any relapse.

Henceforth, a garrison of 1,500 soldiers was to be stationed in Lhasa. The government was entrusted to a council of four ministers under the restored authority of the Dalai Lama, one of the ministers being a monk, to balance the influence of the aristocracy, whom Qianlong no longer trusted. The council had to rule in accordance with the *ambans*. The Dalai Lama appointed the governors of the provinces from the officials recommended to him by the Council and the *ambans* and chose the religious authorities himself. The appointment of the two generals in charge of the army had to be confirmed by the emperor. Corvée and the postal service—a vital point for Beijing—were reorganized under the rule of imperial officials.

From the death of the 7th Dalai Lama (1757) until the birth of the 13th Dalai Lama (1876), Tibet never really emerged from the complicated and dangerous regime of regencies. The 8th Dalai Lama (1758–1804), an extremely pious man, never wielded power. His successors, the 9th, 10th, 11th, and 12th Dalai Lamas, all died before their majority, or very soon afterwards; there is no way of knowing whether they may have been murdered.

After the 1751 reform, there were still several unsettled points that more or less directly concerned Sino-Tibetan relations, but Tibet entered a period of comparative calm.

The unjustified suspicion that there was a secret link between the Tibetan authorities and the Dzungars, notwithstanding the events of 1717–20, had embittered Sino-Tibetan relations between 1680 and 1750, but in 1756–57, Emperor Qianlong resolved the issue by definitively pacifying the Dzungar territories of Ili. After their submission, the Mongol tribes were reorganized according to the Manchu administrative system and no longer begged the Dalai Lama to give them titles or nominate their khans, as had happened in the days of the 5th Dalai Lama.

The Nerchinsk (1689) and Kiakhta (1727) treaties had stopped the Russians' progress in Inner and East Asia. However, two new powers had appeared south of the Himalayas, the Gurkhas in Nepal and the British in Bengal. Emperor Qianlong now had another reason to watch over Tibet especially carefully. But his *amban*s underestimated the situation or failed to rouse imperial attention.

From 1768 on, tension grew in the border areas south of Tibet; the number of frontier incidents and encroachments was increasing. The Lhasa government and the *amban*s displayed equal incompetence in dealing with the Gurkha leaders. In 1791, the Gurkhas invaded Tibet as far as the famous, rich Tashilhünpo monastery, residence of the Panchen Lama, which was damaged and looted. Qianlong was then forced into a difficult and costly winter counteroffensive, and a powerful army was sent from China, which duly drove the Gurkhas back to the Kathmandu valley.

Qianlong then decided to reform Tibetan institutions more deeply. The Gurkha war was not the only cause of his discontent. He had declared himself scandalized by the fact that the main incarnations of the Tibetan Buddhist clergy were regularly discovered in the same aristocratic families. In fact, the emperor's protest seemed justified, on the Tibetan side as well as on the Mongolian. His famous *Lama shuo* (*Dissertation on Lamaism*, 1792) was engraved upon a stela in Yonghegong monastery in Beijing. Unfortunately, the Tibetan authorities do not seem to have read this dissertation carefully.

Shortly afterwards, at the beginning of 1793, the imperial ordinance that is now usually called the "Twenty-Nine-Article Ordinance" was published. Its first article repeated the imperial decision concerning the main incarnations in Tibet and Mongolia as stated by the *Lama shuo*. From now on, the Dalai Lama and Panchen Lama, as well as all the other main incarnations, would be selected by drawing from among the candidates' names placed in a golden vase. Obviously, Qianlong had a rather different idea of his role as protector of the Doctrine from what had been suggested by the Tibetan interpretation of the *chöyön*. One may think, of course, that he proclaimed this new rule to put an end to the abuses of the Buddhist aristocracy in Tibet and Mongolia. But one has to notice that there were two golden vases, one in Lhasa, the other in Beijing, which created a separation between the high incarnates of Tibet and those of Mongolia, which some of the latter might have wished for. Thus, imperial realism, as it has been sometimes styled, was, from a religious point of view, a blow to the Dalai Lama's prestige and spiritual authority.

The regulations promulgated by the Twenty-Nine-Article Ordinance can be divided into four groups: the imperial intervention in the selection of the Dalai Lama and Panchen Lama has already been mentioned, but it also concerned the appointment of lesser religious authorities, and the supervision of their properties and of the clergy was initiated; the *ambans'* power was strengthened and they were proclaimed equal in rank to the Dalai Lama and obligatory intermediaries between him and the emperor; Tibetan officials were forbidden to maintain correspondence with a foreign country without the *ambans'* involvement, and the *ambans* supervised all inner and outer circulation of people and goods; the administration, army, and taxation were reorganized. These measures established what is often described as Chinese *sovereignty* over Tibet. Actually, they were far from being entirely successful. Qianlong died six years later, and the dynasty decayed rapidly and was unable to enforce its rule in the border regions. It is usually said that the names of most of the Dalai Lamas, Panchen Lamas, and other high incarnates selected during the nineteenth century came out of the golden vases, but that they were always those that had been chosen previously by the competent religious authorities. This shows yet again that the Tibetans and the Chinese did not speak the same language.

As far as the *chöyön* concept is considered to have been the basis of relations between Tibet and China since the time of the Yuan dynasty, it is necessary to specify that it could be carried out in very different ways, and that, from the moment the emperor intervened in the religious affairs of Tibet, *chöyön* was respected by only one of the parties. The comparative liberalism of the first Qing emperors did not last long; later, they progressively imposed their power over Tibet, and the supremacy of the temporal power over the spiritual power.

6

CAN YOU OUTLINE THE ORIGINS OF THE DALAI LAMA AND THE
BAINQEN ERDINI [PANCHEN LAMA]? DID THE ESTABLISHMENT
OF THESE POSITIONS HAVE ANYTHING TO DO WITH THE
CHINESE CENTRAL GOVERNMENT?

They are the most prominent hierarchs among the "Yellow sect" founded by Tsongkhapa and "represent two different branches of this sect" [from the French version]. In 1578, Altan Khan of the Tumed Mongol tribe invited Sönam Gyatso to preach. They exchanged honorific titles: Altan Khan named Sönam Gyatso "Dalai Lama." "[T]his was a private matter without any political or legal implications."

In 1653, the 5th Dalai Lama, invited to Beijing, was formally titled "Dalai Lama" by the Qing emperor. "Thus the political and legal title 'Dalai Lama' was born." Then, in 1751, "the Qing dynasty's central government ordered the seventh Dalai Lama to take charge of the region's [Tibet] administration. It is evident, therefore, that both the title and the political and religious powers of Dalai Lama were granted by China's central government."

"The word 'Bainqen' [Panchen] first appeared in 1645, when Gushri Khan bestowed it upon the fourth Bainqen." In 1713, the Qing emperor Kangxi changed it to "Bainqen Erdini." "Erdini" means "brightness" in Mongolian. Both titles have been handed down through the reincarnation system and since the 5th Dalai Lama and Bainqen, "every new holder of these titles had had to be ratified by the central government." In 1792, Qianlong imposed a new system of "drawing lots from a golden urn" and almost all Dalai and Panchen Lamas were chosen through this system, under the supervision of the commissioners of the Qing court.

"This procedure makes it clear that the conferment of the titles of Dalai and Bainquen have always been subject to the political approvement [*sic*] of China's central government."

ANNE CHAYET

100 Questions tries to prove that the Dalai Lama and the Panchen Lama received their power and authority from China. The authors also try to justify the Manchu policy of divide and rule: that is to say, the rivalry that the imperial government did its best to create between the Dalai Lama and the Panchen Lama from the eighteenth century on.

The Gelugpa School was founded by the reformer Tsongkhapa. The habit of styling it "Yellow Sect" and then "Yellow Hats" appeared in China and spread during the Qing period. This name is supposed to distinguish them by the color of their hats from the unreformed schools, which are styled "Red Sect" without further distinction. The Qing dynasty dealt with the Gelugpas only and did not care for other branches of Tibetan Buddhism.

The Gelugpas had many monasteries throughout the whole of Tibetan territory, in Mongolia and even in China, where various kinds of teachings were given, but there were no subdivisions of the school, as suggested by *100 Questions*, which makes a distinction between the Dalai Lama and Panchen Lama branches. However, the two successive lines of the Dalai Lamas and the Panchen Lamas have to be distinguished. Considering the hierarchical order, the Dalai Lama comes first, because he is invested with the spiritual and the temporal supreme authority. The Panchen Lama, who has no temporal power, takes second place, but his spiritual role is highly considered and his prestige is very great.

The title of Dalai Lama appeared at the time when the Ming Dynasty (1369–1644) ruled over China, but it was not given by a Ming emperor. Since its foundation, the Gelugpa School had developed steadily, mainly because of its reputation of high moral virtue. By the end of the sixteenth century, the Gelugpas had acquired much power and influence. The eastern Mongols were then spreading toward the Koko Nor region, where they came into contact with Tibetan populations. The interest in Buddhism, which had lessened somewhat if not disappeared among the Mongol princes since the end of the Yuan dynasty, then regained strength, and the newcomers turned to the Gelugpas, widely settled in this region. In 1578, Sönam Gyatso, abbot of the Drepung monastery, met Altan Khan (1502–1582), ruler of the Tumed Mongols, who had repeatedly invited the abbot to meet with him. The purpose of the meeting was to solemnly celebrate the conversion to Buddhism of the eastern Mongol princes. Sönam Gyatso might have had an ulterior motive, for the political circumstances were then extremely difficult for the Gelugpas in central Tibet.

Sönam Gyatso was the second reincarnation of Gedün Drub (1391–1475), one of the main disciples of the founder, Tsongkhapa, and himself founder of the Tashilhünpo monastery. As explained above, he received from Altan Khan the title Dalai Lama (Dalai, from the Mongol *Tale,* meaning "ocean," equivalent to the Tibetan *gyatso;* and *lama,* Tibetan *bla ma,* meaning "the highest," and designating the Indian *guru*). The title of Dalai Lama was given retroactively to the two predecessors of Sönam Gyatso, who consequently became the 3rd Dalai Lama. The relationship thus established between the Dalai Lama and Altan Khan was of the *chöyön* type (see above, Question 5), a subtle balance between spiritual and temporal authority in the complicated Tibetan context, combining Indian and Buddhist principles with Inner Asian and native traditions. The objective of this type of reciprocal and personal relationship was an engagement to study, teach, protect, and spread the Doctrine. This principle was applied in different ways, depending upon the period and the status of the persons involved. In the case of Sönam Gyatso and Altan Khan, there was no ambiguity. The Chinese authors consider the titles exchanged in 1578 to have had no value, either legal or political. From their point of view, the title of Dalai Lama existed only after it was confirmed by an imperial edict, particularly when the 5th Dalai Lama went to Beijing in 1653 and this title was *granted* to the Dalai Lama. Of course, they do not mention the notion of *chöyön*.

The title of Panchen Lama was conferred upon Lozang Chöki Gyeltsen (1570–1662), who officially recognized and ordained the 5th Dalai Lama. He was the third reincarnation of one of the foremost disciples of Tsongkhapa and was elected as the abbot of Tashilhünpo monastery. He was a great scholar as well as a clever diplomat. The abbots of Tashilhünpo were famous for their scholarship, and consequently most of them received the title of *Pan chen* (*pan* from the Sanskrit *pandita* and *chen* meaning "great" in Tibetan, *Panchen* is thus the translation of the Sanskrit *Mahâ-pandita*). The 5th Dalai Lama gave him the Tashilhünpo monastery and many estates, which can be interpreted as an aspect of the relationship between master and disciple (different from the *chöyön* relationship already mentioned), as well as a more political act, that is to say, to settle the Gelugpas firmly in Tsang. There were no further elections to the throne of Tashilhünpo. Lozang Chöki Gyeltsen's successors by reincarnation were recognized as both Panchen Lama and abbot of the monastery. And, as he was the fourth incarnation in his lineage, the habit was soon adopted of calling him the 4th Panchen Lama, as well as the 1st, which he actually was. Lozang Chöki Gyeltsen is systematically called the 4th Panchen Lama in China, perhaps to emphasize a parallel between the Dalai Lama and the Panchen Lama that does not really exist, for the two titles are of different origin and nature (see also Question 13). If the title of Panchen Lama does not seem to have been *officially* given to Lozang Chöki Gyeltsen by the Dalai Lama, Emperor Kangxi, in his own way, confirmed it to his successor in 1713, by granting him the title of Panchen Erdeni. Emperor Yongzheng went much further in 1728 in giving him temporal power over the territories west of the province of Tsang. The civil war was then the main concern of the Tibetans and their hierarchs. The imperial scheme seemed to be of no consequence, but it was a precedent and a point of contention to embitter the traditional opposition between the provinces of Ü and Tsang, and the conflicts between the circles of the two hierarchs. It may have been one of the causes of the financial dispute that led to the Panchen Lama's exile in 1923, and consequently to his death in China in 1937 (see Question 13).

The research for and discovery of the reincarnations and successors of the 5th Dalai Lama and the 2nd Panchen Lama did not occur under the supervision of the imperial government. The 6th Dalai Lama was discovered and recognized before the official disclosure of his predecessor's death. Kangxi never recognized him, but later recognized Lhazang Khan's candidate, then the real 7th Dalai Lama, who is usually numbered 6th in Chinese publications. The 2nd Panchen Lama's successor was born in 1738, during the rule of Pholane, and imperial supervision was not likely in these years of good relations between Beijing and Lhasa, although this situation would not exclude eventual observers, exchange of courtesies, gifts, and the usual diplomas. The *Lama shuo* was published only in 1792 (see Question 5 above).

7

ARE THERE ANY HISTORICAL DOCUMENTS WHICH PROVIDE
EVIDENCE THAT TIBET IS PART OF CHINA?

There are many, in both Chinese and Tibetan, among them, in Tibetan: *A Feast for Wise Men* (Khepe gatön, 1564), *Records of Tibetan Kings (Bökyi gyelrab)* written by the 5th Dalai Lama, *Lineage of the Sakyapas (Sakya dungrab,* 1629), *Records of Han and Tibetan History (Gyapö yigtsang,* 1434), *The Blue Annals (Debter ngönpo),* and so on.

In Chinese, the Ming Annals show that Mongols and Tibetans received their titles from the Ming court; the 29-article regulations (1792) and other official documents give much evidence of how the Qing Dynasty ruled Tibet.

"After the foundation of the Republic of China (1912–49), Tibet remained one of China's provinces. . . . The current 14th Dalai Lama was ratified by the Kuomintang government" and a film shows his enthronement presided over by the central government's representative.

ANNE CHAYET

The Tibetan sources mentioned by *100 Questions* are actually some of the classical sources that are usually quoted when dealing with Tibetan historiography. *The Blue Annals (Debter ngönpo,* 1476–78) and the *Feast for Wise Men (Khepe gatön,* 1545–64) belong to the genre of works called

"Origin of Buddhism" (chöjung), an account of the origins and history of the Buddha, the history of Buddhism and its schools in India and then its spread to Tibet. Consequently, the issue of Sino-Tibetan relations is not much dealt with in these works, even if some of them contain a chapter on the history of Buddhism in China and Mongolia. The later (1748) history of Buddhism in India, Tibet, China, and Mongolia by the Oirat Mongol scholar Sumpakhenpo Yeshe Peljor belongs to this genre. 100 Questions also mentions the Chronicle written by the 5th Dalai Lama, which belongs to the Royal Chronicles or Genealogies genre (gyelrab, dungrab) and is an account of the successive rulers of Tibet from its first kings to the Gelugpa hierarchs. It is a pity that the authors of 100 Questions did not consult the 5th Dalai Lama's autobiography, which would have provided them with an interesting Tibetan point of view on Sino-Tibetan relations. The authors also mention the New Red Annals (Debter marpo sarma, 1538) and the Sakya Genealogies (Sakya dungrab, 1629), of the gyelrab genre, where much information can be found concerning relations between Tibet and the Yuan dynasty, but the final interpretation they give of the second of these works is questionable. This is also the case with the Anthology of Histories concerning China and Tibet (Gyabö yigtsang chenmo, 1434).

This very short selection could have been more accurate. Moreover, the information concerning Sino-Tibetan relations found in these works being mostly of a religious nature, they are generally formulated with the intent of glorifying the holy doctrine and need a careful critical reading, which does not appear in the conclusions reached by the authors of 100 Questions.

Obviously, the authors of 100 Questions have more closely followed the conclusions of the Chinese sources they mention, the Dynastic Records of the Ming (Ming shilu) and the Twenty-Nine-Article Ordinance (see Question 5 above). The Dynastic Records of the Yuan (Yuan shi) and Dynastic Records of the Qing (Qing shilu) and many other important documents are not mentioned, but this seems to be a mere omission, for one cannot believe that sincere historians, trained in the great Chinese tradition of scholarship would neglect or misread the sources to this extent.

Concerning the period of the Chinese Republic, the authors mention no precise source, Chinese or Tibetan, probably because the "documents" vaguely referred to do not confirm the authors' phantasmagoric and univocal description of the situation in Tibet. Concerning the enthronement of the 14th Dalai Lama in 1940, the representative of the Chinese government was received with great honor, but he never had a leading part in it, in spite of his much exaggerated reports.

8

WHY WAS THE ISSUE OF "TIBETAN INDEPENDENCE" RAISED EARLY IN THIS CENTURY?

The difference of understanding the word "Tibet": the Qinghai-Tibet Plateau according to Westerners, and for the Chinese, "Tibet proper" [i.e., the TAR], is noteworthy. The answer comes back, then, to the events during the last period of the Qing dynasty. Weakened and corrupted, the dynasty was neither able to resist foreign attacks (the opium wars of 1840 and 1860) nor to protect Tibet from the British invasion (1904). Defeated, the 13th Dalai Lama fled "to the interior [China] and was temporarily relieved of his official title," which was given back to him two years later.

Returning to Lhasa, the Dalai Lama came into conflict with the Chinese commissioner; fearful of the Chinese troops, he fled to India in 1910 and "was punished . . . with the removal of his official title." "Foreign writers have often mistakenly believed this event was caused by the arrival of Zhao Erfeng's troops," but Zhao, the commissioner for Sichuan and Yunnan "only reached Qamdo [Chamdo]." Actually, it was the arrival of Zhong Yin, a member of the imperial family, with a "poorly disciplined" force of 1,000 troops that frightened the Dalai Lama and his followers.

When news of the Chinese revolution arrived in Tibet in October 1911, a fierce struggle began among the military and civil Chinese stationed there. The Dalai Lama took this opportunity and gave orders for expelling the commissioners and the Chinese troops to China via India. The troubled situation in China, with "the careerist politician" Yuan Shikai at the head of the new Republic of China, didn't make possible "normalizing the political relationship between Tibet and the interior."

The expulsion of the Qing officials from Tibet aimed at overthrowing the Qing dynasty; it has been referred to as "exclusion of the Hans" or a "declaration of Tibetan independence," but it was not. At this time, "many provinces declared 'independence'. In this context, 'independence' involved ending Qing dynasty rule rather than the establishment of a new nation." Besides, the 13th Dalai Lama never asked China for independence for Tibet; he even denied having signed a treaty with Mongolia (1913), in which the two countries declared themselves independent nations.

"Up to this time, the question of Tibet's status had remained a purely internal matter of China." The problem arose in 1912 when the British refused to recognize the Republic of China and to let Chinese officials travel via India, forcing Yuan Shikai to appoint officials to participate in the Simla Conference (1913–14). "Although the talks broke down, one of its results was to hinder the resumption of normal political relations between Tibet and the interior."

In 1919, however, the Dalai Lama in receiving a delegation of the "national patriotic and anti-imperialist May 4th Movement" declared that "he had never established good terms with Britain and . . . had never had any intention of separating Tibet from China."

"On May 23, 1951, the Central Government of the People's Republic of China and Tibet's local government signed an agreement on Tibet's peaceful liberation" [see Question 14], which was endorsed by the 14th Dalai Lama.

"Even now, there are still some people who . . . try to convince others that there had existed a so-called problem of 'Tibetan Independence.' It has to be asked, what government across the world has ever recognized Tibet as an independent state?" [See Question 11].

Tsering Shakya and Anne-Marie Blondeau

100 Questions gives an unusually lengthy answer to this question. It is true that the final decades of the long nineteenth century were a very complex period in Asia, characterized not only by the profound upheavals provoked by Occidental and Russian imperialism, but, in the case of China, by the 1911 revolution that transformed the country from an empire that was several millennia old into a republic. Complexity comes from both numerous intrigues and maneuvers between the different actors and the ambiguous nature of the documents we have access to; the biases and coloration of embassy papers, official histories, and letters differ according to the nationality of the authors. Consequently, the historical facts reported in *100 Questions* are generally accurate, but their interpretation is often tendentious. Moreover, the Chinese answer essentially takes as its starting point the famous expedition of Colonel Francis Younghusband to Lhasa in 1904, without explaining its reasons. The British role really determined the fate of Tibet—we shall see this better in the following questions—but understanding it requires some knowledge of earlier history. The end of the Chinese answer will not be treated here, since the 17-Point Agreement of 1951 and the Dalai Lama's position regarding this agreement are the subject of comments in Questions 14 and 15. Likewise, we shall not speak here of the 1904 Anglo-Tibetan Treaty or the 1914 Simla Conference, which are detailed in connection with the Chinese answer to Question 10.

As has been noted, the traditional relationship between China and Tibet was characterized by the politico-religious term *chöyön* ("priest-patron"). China was seen as the political ally of an essentially noncoercive regime that existed in Tibet. This regime, particularly after the Gelugpa ascendancy, was preoccupied with resisting external aggression and suppressing any possibility of a concerted internal uprising. It thus sought to neutralize any possible threat and disarm potential aggressors by allying with the dominant regional power, namely, China.

However, by the late nineteenth century the traditional politico-religious ties came under severe strain for a number of reasons. The expansion of British colonial rule in the foothills of the Himalayas changed the traditional polity in the region. The advent of British interest in Tibet and Central Asia began to alter the existing trade and political systems that characterized China's relations with the neighboring states.

The British sought to expand their trade across the Himalayas into Central Asia and China; they wanted to regularize trade rights and relationship with Tibet with treaties and trade agreements. However, the Tibetan government was reluctant to allow entry for British merchants. The early period was particularly frustrating for the British, because the Tibetans ignored repeated British attempts to engage in diplomacy. In 1876, the British signed an agreement with China known as the Chefoo Convention. Although the agreement itself was not directly concerned with Tibet, a separate article conceded that China would grant the right of entrance for British merchants to Tibet, giving them passports (Deshayes 1997: 219). For the first time, China's authority in Tibet was thus recognized by a Western power.

Using the agreement reached with China, the British demanded the right to trade in Tibet. However, the government in Lhasa continued to resist British attempts to enter the country. Because of their isolation, the Tibetans could not understand the stake that their country represented, and they considered themselves masters of it; consequently, they judged the Chefoo Agreement not valid, since it had been signed without them. By 1890, they showed a greater determination to counter any British attempt to gain entry into Tibet by fortifying and improving defenses along the Tibet-Sikkim border. In 1890, an Anglo-Chinese Treaty was signed in Calcutta that sought to establish the border between Tibet and Sikkim. And three years later, the same protagonists signed the Tibet Trade Regulation, which allowed the British to establish a commercial agent in Yatung (in the Chumbi Valley in southern Tibet) and British India to export tea to Tibet, while certain goods were exempt from taxes.

Although these treaties were primarily concerned with trade, the legal consequence was, however, that the agreements recognized China's authority over Tibet and China's right to conduct Tibet's external relations. The difficulty was that the Chinese authorities in Beijing and the *amban*s in Lhasa were powerless to enforce these agreements. The border demarcation between Tibet and Sikkim remained ineffective, and the Tibetans rejected the trade regulations as invalid—as they did any agreement reached between China and Britain concerning Tibet—and refused to allow the British to trade in Tibet.

Becoming aware of China's lack of authority in Tibet, the British changed their policy in 1899 under the Indian viceroy Lord Curzon and tried to establish a direct relationship with the Tibetan government in Lhasa. The latter ignored British approaches and remained isolated.

By the early twentieth century, things had worsened, and in 1904, fearing Russian penetration of Tibet and increasing Russian influence on the frontiers of their empire, the British invaded Tibet. The Dalai Lama fled to Mongolia and then to China, which placed the Tibetans under Chinese control. In September 1904, an Anglo-Tibetan Convention was signed in Lhasa, whose terms, imposed by the leader of invading British force, Younghusband, allowed the British to establish a resident in Lhasa and imposed payment of an indemnity on Tibet.

Another important change was the shift in China's perception of its position in Tibet, which the Chinese began to regard as a "sovereign" one, in line with Western legal and political usage. However, the Chinese government was concerned about its lack of authority in Tibet and inability to enforce its wishes there. It appointed the warlord Zhao Erfeng, governor of Xining (nominated governor-general of Sichuan in January 1911, shortly before his assassination), as its resident in Lhasa, instructing him to bring Tibet firmly within the administrative structure of China. In 1908, Zhao Erfeng led a military invasion of Tibet (see Jagou 2000: 11–12). In 1909, the 13th Dalai Lama returned to Lhasa, and tried to dissuade the Chinese authorities from sending a military force to central Tibet. The Chinese ignored the Tibetans' appeal, and a Chinese force—which *100 Questions* regards as the *amban*s' military escort—occupied Lhasa in 1910. It is true that Zhao Erfeng himself did not reach Lhasa, but the rumor spread that he was approaching, and reports of his bloody exactions in eastern Tibet filled the population with terror. Moreover, the troops troubling Lhasa were, in fact, a detachment of the Sichuan army, according to the Chinese proclamation of the Dalai Lama's deposal, posted in Lhasa after he fled again, this time to India, where he stayed for three years (Goldstein 1989: 52–53).

After the 1911 revolution, Chinese authority in Tibet collapsed, and the Dalai Lama came back to Lhasa, after having the about 3,000 Chinese troops expelled. From his exile, he had sent a very strong memorandum to the chief of the Mongol and Tibetan Affairs Department in Beijing to be transmitted to the emperor. It coincided with the Chinese revolution, and it was Yuan Shikai, the temporary president of the new republic, who answered it with a telegram, published on October 28, 1912, in the Chinese *Government Gazette,* as if the memorandum had been addressed to him. In his response, he restored the Dalai Lama's title and function. Contrary to assertions in *100 Questions,* the Dalai Lama reacted immediately answering that "he was not asking the Chinese government for any rank, as he intended to exercise both temporal and spiritual rule" (Smith 1996: 182, quoting Charles Bell). Upon his return to Lhasa in 1913, he wrote a long proclamation, posted in all districts of Tibet, which gave the historical account of the "priest-patron" links that had ruled the Sino-Tibetan relations since the Yuan dynasty and his protests to the Manchu emperor who wanted to replace them with subordination. He had then regained power, and Tibetan troops were driving the remains of the Chinese army out of eastern Tibet. He added: "Now, the Chinese intention of colonizing Tibet under the Patron-Priest relationship has faded like a rainbow in the sky." And further: "We are a small, religious and independent nation. To keep up with the rest of the world, we must defend our country. . . . To safeguard and maintain the independence of our country, one and all should voluntarily work hard" (Goldstein 1989: 60–61).

For the Tibetans, it was clear that the Dalai Lama had severed all links with China and proclaimed Tibet's independence. Unfortunately, as a result of their ignorance of the international politico-diplomatic rules, the Tibetans—unlike the Mongolians—failed to win immediate recognition of this independence by communicating with the great powers and establishing diplomatic relations with them.

After 1911, the Tibetans wanted to conform the status of Tibet to a modern political system and establish direct foreign relations (see also Question 10). The question of the Tibeto-Mongol Treaty that the 13th Dalai Lama is also said to have signed in 1913 is more obscure. This treaty of mutual assistance, essentially containing a reciprocal recognition of the independence of both countries, had, in fact, been officially signed, but without the explicit endorsement by the Dalai Lama, who seems, effectively, to have in part disavowed it, probably to calm British fears of possible Russian interference in Tibet (Smith 1996: 185–86).

The above events show the background to the Tibetan declaration of independence. The main point is that advent of British rule in India and increasing British interest in Tibet changed the traditional religious-political balance that governed China's relationship with Tibet. Then, between 1913 and 1950, Tibet enjoyed independence, with total power over its internal and external affairs. This is what the International Commission of Jurists (a body with a consultative status with the United Nations) recognized in 1950 and 1959, saying: "Tibet was at the very least a de facto independent state when the Agreement of Peaceful Measures in Tibet was signed in 1951, and the repudiation of this agreement by the Tibetan Government in 1959 was found to be fully justified. . . . Tibet demonstrated from 1913 to 1950 the conditions of statehood as generally accepted under international law" (ICJ 1960: 346).

It might naïvely have been thought that this expert opinion would suffice for it to be recognized that Communist China had attacked, invaded, and occupied an independent state. This does not, however, take into account the economic and political interests of the great powers, which to this day have refused to recognize the independence of Tibet.

9

IT HAS BEEN CLAIMED THAT CHINA ONLY HAS
SUZERAINTY OVER TIBET. IS THIS RIGHT?

The British began using this term in their internal documents (Lord Curzon, 1904) for defining the ties uniting Tibet to China. The Petersburg Convention signed by Britain and Russia in 1907 is the first international document using it. The convention, whose aim was to delimitate the areas of influence of the two countries in Central Asia, comprised three sections, concerning Persia, Afghanistan, and Tibet. At the beginning of the Tibet section it was written that Great Britain and Russia recognized "China's right of suzerainty over Tibet." The second article stated that, according to this right of suzerainty, the two countries "engage not to enter into negotiations with Tibet except through the intermediary of the Chinese government." Nevertheless, the Chinese government neither validated this convention nor signed any treaty mentioning the word "suzerainty."

Moreover, the definition of this suzerainty has varied according to circumstances: when the 13th Dalai Lama fled to India, the *amban* revoked his title (although it was later restored by the Republican government) and the British refused to intervene, on grounds of Chinese suzerainty. Later, the notion was linked to the actual exercise of sovereignty over a local government, then to regional autonomy. "One point is clear, the use of the word concerning Tibet was aimed at denying China's sovereignty." This sovereignty being a fact, regional autonomy is a merely internal affair of a sovereign state.

Tsering Shakya

It is true that the British used the term "suzerainty" to describe China's authority or power over Tibet. It is also true that the Anglo-Russian convention of 1907 was the first international agreement where China's status in Tibet was defined as "suzerain." This resulted from the growing realization among the British that the Chinese power in the country was "nominal."

The term "suzerain" was first evolved in Europe in the Middle Ages to describe the relationship between a feudal lord and his vassal. The term implied that the vassal had to perform certain symbolic submission to the suzerain, pay tribute, and provide men in time of war. The suzerain provided military protection and funds to the vassal.

If we examine the traditional relationship between Tibet and China, it is clear that the term "suzerain" was not applicable to China's position in Tibet. The priest-patron relationship *(chöyön)* did not entail Tibet providing men in time of war to the Chinese emperor. Nor did Tibet pay any form of taxes to the Chinese government. The only area of overlapping is that Tibet traditionally sent missions to China, regarded as tributary according to the Chinese imperial system.

Neither the Chinese nor the Tibetans ever accepted the British term "suzerain." The Tibetans continued to use indigenous term *chöyön* to describe their relationship with China.

10
How did Britain and the United States interfere with China's domestic affairs with regard to Tibet in the past?

It was Great Britain, first, that, starting around the end of the eighteenth century, sought to interfere in China's internal affairs. The British East

India Company twice sent emissaries to Xigaze [Shigatse] to try to establish relations with the Panchen Lama. Then Britain took advantage of the Qing government's weakness to impose two treaties (1890 and 1893) on it, enabling Britain to open trade posts in Tibet. After the 1904 Younghusband invasion of Tibet, the Qing were forced to sign the so-called Treaty of Lhasa, which opened two more entrepôts (Gyantse and Gartok) to the British and imposed a "huge amount of military reparations" on China.

In 1907, Britain and Russia signed a treaty [see Question 9] that recognized Britain's "special rights" in Tibet. Later (1913–14), Britain forced the new Republic of China to take part in the Simla Conference, in which a secret agreement between the British and Tibetan representatives, "drew an arbitrary border along what has been so-called the 'McMahon Line,' thus occupying large tracts of Chinese territory." This was firmly rejected by the Chinese government.

Then, Britain backed the 'independence of Tibet' by "fostering pro-British groups among Tibet's upper classes. They sowed discord between the Dalai Lama and the 9th Bainqen [Panchen Lama]" and gave a large amount of weapons and ammunitions to Tibetan troops in order to establish a "great Tibet" under British protection. In 1940, they encouraged separatist elements to oppose the "patriotic regent Rabchen Hutukotu" [Reting Rinpoche].

The Americans interfered in Tibetan affairs during World War II, beginning with the Ilia Tolstoy mission in 1942. Then they hosted the "Shageba [Shakabpa] Mission" (1948), and finally they supported the separatists to oppose the PLA's entrance into Tibet. They attempted to persuade the Dalai Lama to denounce the 17-Point Agreement and to leave Tibet. After 1951, the CIA actively supported the Tibetan guerillas, and after 1955, "a large number of Tibetans" were "secretly sent to Taiwan and Okinawa for training in guerrilla warfare." It was also under the CIA's instigation that the 1959 rebellion in Lhasa took place. After the Dalai Lama's self-exile, the Americans continued to airdrop weapons and materials to the separatists who remained in Tibet.

In the 1960s, under President John F. Kennedy, the Americans began to restrain their interference in Tibet; but it was not before President Richard Nixon's visit to China in 1972 that they stopped their direct support of the Tibetan separatists. However some political forces in the United States still maintain close contacts with the "Dalai clique" and support his cause.

All these facts demonstrate not only the interference of Great Britain and the United States but also their failure to separate Tibet from China.

TSERING SHAKYA AND ANNE-MARIE BLONDEAU

We have seen above how the interests of the great powers, especially Britain and Russia, weighed on the fate of Tibet. The Chinese argue that the growing Tibetan assertion of independence was influenced and directed by the Western powers, the British in the early part of the twentieth century and the Americans in the latter half. After 1913, there was a growing awareness among Tibetans of the need to establish direct foreign relations without any reference to China (Question 8), and Tibet accordingly entered into direct relations with British India and other Western powers, notably by signing the conventions referred to in *100 Questions*.

The first convention was signed under constraint, because the Tibetans had just been defeated by the Younghusband expedition. Contrary to what *100 Questions* says, this Lhasa Treaty was not signed with the "Qing government" but with that of the Dalai Lama. The Chinese *amban*, a Bhutanese mediator, and the Nepalese representative attended the signing as simple witnesses and did not put their signatures to it. It was only in 1906 that—unbeknown to the Tibetans—Great Britain and China signed a convention ratifying the Lhasa Treaty, which opened two locations in Tibet to British commerce and imposed a £500,000 indemnity, later reduced to £166,000, on the Tibetans, which the Qing government hastily paid without even notifying the Lhasa government (Shakabpa 1967: 217–20, 253–54).

On the other hand, it was of their own accord that the Tibetans organized the Simla Conference (1913–14) with the British, in which the Chinese took part unwillingly. Although China's plenipotentiary initialed the resulting agreement, the Chinese government later refused to sign it. Only Britain and Tibet signed. The latter had to accept the reference in the text to the "suzerainty" of China. In exchange, China pledged not to intervene in Tibetan affairs. Under the agreement, Tibet's borders were fixed clearly, along a line named for the British plenipotentiary, Sir Henry McMahon (Shakabpa 1967: 251–57; see Goldstein 1989: 68–77, 832–41 for the text of the treaty and its annexes). But the Chinese, who have always denounced this convention, have never accepted the border thus drawn, hence the origin of the border conflict with India that degenerated into an open war in 1962 and is still not settled.

The Chinese authors of *100 Questions* also see the hand of the British in the discord between the 13th Dalai Lama and the 9th Panchen Lama, and later during the minority of the 14th Dalai Lama, in the resignation of his regent, Reting Rinpoche. Both the British and Chinese tried to use the Panchen Lama to checkmate the Dalai Lama, and certainly mistrust and hostility developed between their respective entourages. During the 13th Dalai Lama's exile in India, the *amban* sought to replace him with the Panchen Lama, whom he had brought to Lhasa and installed in the summer residence of the Dalai Lamas, the Norbulingka. He also paraded about the streets of Lhasa in the company of the Panchen Lama during the Great Prayer Festival *(Mönlam chenmo)*, as the Dalai Lama traditionally did on this occasion. But the break between the Panchen Lama and the Dalai Lama was clinched by the latter's reforms, especially his tax reform. The new tax scale, based on the size of properties and estates, imposed a heavy contribution on the vast lands of the Tashilhünpo Monastery, the seat of the Panchen Lama. Intimidated by stronger and stronger pressures from Lhasa, the Panchen Lama fled to Mongolia in 1923, and then to China. He died in 1937 on his way back to Tashilhünpo.

The 13th Dalai Lama died in 1933. Reting Rinpoche was nominated regent, but he resigned in 1941, not because of "pro-English separatists" but because his dissolute life did not allow him to confer novitiate vows on the young Dalai Lama as prescribed. Later, however, he became involved in a conspiracy to regain power and sought Chiang Kai-shek's help, which explains the reference to him as the "patriotic regent" in *100 Questions*. Upon the discovery of the conspiracy, he was arrested and died in prison in 1947, having probably been poisoned (Goldstein 1989: 464–510).

In 1947–48, the Tibetan government sent a commercial mission to the United States and England, officially in support of Tibetan exports and to buy gold to guarantee Tibet's currency, but unofficially for political motives (Shakabpa 1967: 294–95). Minister Shakabpa, the mission's leader, said at a press conference that the purpose of the mission was to show the world that "Tibet is an independent country and that its ties with China are of a religious nature." Perhaps by mistake, the U.S. and British consular officers in Hong Kong had visaed the passports issued by the Tibetan government to the mission members, which was tantamount to recognizing an independent status for Tibet, but their governments later disapproved the visas (Smith 1996: 257–60). According to Melvyn Goldstein (1997: 39), the British government disavowed the action of its consulate in Hong Kong only after China's protests, but prolonged the visas' validity by crossing out the "three months" term on the documents and adding by hand "nine months."

The United States got involved in the middle of the twentieth century. During World War II, Washington contemplated sending reinforcements through Tibet to its new ally Chiang Kai-shek, but the British disapproved of the idea and the Tibetans vetoed it. Nevertheless, in May 1942, President Franklin Roosevelt approved the plan and decided on a "reconnaissance mission from India to Tibet" with the aim of crossing Tibet up to Chongking, seat of the government of the Republic of China, to observe and investigate the attitudes of the Tibetans. This mission was entrusted to Captain Ilya Tolstoi, grandson of the Russian novelist, officially to bring a message and gifts from President Roosevelt to the young Dalai Lama. (Naïvely believing this to be the opening of diplomatic relations with the United States, the Dalai Lama's government wrote to Roosevelt to thank him and to reaffirm that Tibet had been independent "since immemorial times" [Shakabpa 1967: 287–89; Smith 1996: 245].) If the mission was a success on a personal level—Tolstoi stayed a month in Lhasa before proceeding on the planned route under the protection of a Tibetan escort—it does not seem to have achieved great results either for the Tibetans or for the Americans (Knaus 1999: 5–18). In reality, it was only in the 1950s, following the Communist victory in China, that the United States began to take a true interest in Tibet. This was largely due to the Cold War, when international relations overall were distorted by the conflict between the Communist and Western powers. Inevitably, the conflict in Tibet was influenced by Cold War strategies. The anti-Communist policy of the United States, rather than any particular desire to support Tibetan independence, largely determined the American involvement. The CIA's intervention in parachuting weapons to the Khampa guerrillas at the end of the 1950s and training some four hundred Tibetans in Guam, Okinawa, and at a Colorado camp (but not in Taiwan)[1] has long been known from Tibetan sources and CIA agents' reports (see Knaus 1999). Drawing on published memoirs and the recollections of Khampa guerrillas, Jamyang Norbu (1994) shows how the revolt, which started locally in Kham and Amdo as

---

1. Some Khampa fighters were, in fact, trained in Taiwan, but by the Kuomintang Nationalist government, which, prior to U.S. involvement, was already trying to make allies of the Tibetans in its struggle with the Communist regime in Beijing. The Kuomintang was pursuing its own interests in doing so and was not in collusion with the Americans.

early as 1950, won both of these provinces in 1956, and then central Tibet, without any external help at all. But coming back to the real U.S. intervention, as soon as Sino-American relations showed signs of improving, the United States stopped all support to the Tibetans. (John Kenneth Knaus [1999: 296] contends that Washington terminated its support for the Khampa guerrillas who had withdrawn to Mustang and Nepal in 1972 for operational rather than geopolitical reasons.)

The involvement of the United States and other Western powers cannot be suspected in the 1959 Lhasa revolt, which was a genuinely popular uprising (see Question 17). It was only after this that the Americans decided to strongly support the guerrillas (Smith 1996: 507–8). However, the Chinese can be excused for believing the contrary, since books on the CIA's activities by former agents published since 1973 "grossly exaggerate the CIA role in the revolt" and the escape of the Dalai Lama (Shakya 1999: 490n35; see also 201–2).

We can agree with *100 Questions* that "the United States and Great Britain have meddled into the Tibetan affairs." But all documents and written testimonies prove that, far from influencing the Tibetans and standing up for them, the foreign powers—notably the British and the Americans—continued to act in China's favor and refused to recognize the independent status of Tibet, which was asserting itself more and more. For all practical purposes, the British treated Tibet as an independent state and established direct relations with it, but they never accorded it de jure recognition (see the following Question).

11

WHAT ARE THE VIEWS OF FOREIGN COUNTRIES ON THE
"INDEPENDENCE OF TIBET"?

All the countries in the world have recognized and still recognize China's sovereignty over Tibet. The British led the way: in 1903, Lord Hamilton, secretary of state for India, declared that Tibet must be regarded "as a province of China." The British foreign secretary reiterated this in 1904.

"Since independence, India has repeatedly stated its respect for China's sovereignty over Tibet." On May 15, 1954, Nehru declared: "I am not aware that . . . Chinese sovereignty, or if you like suzerainty, was challenged by any outside country."

After the 1959 uprising, both the spokesmen of the U.S. State Department and the British Foreign Office reasserted China's sovereignty; in the American spokesman's words: "The United States never regarded Tibet as an independent state."

ANNE-MARIE BLONDEAU

In spite of the efforts of the governments of the 13th and then the 14th Dalai Lama to have the independence of Tibet prior to 1950 recognized, it is true that to this day, no government in the world has officially recognized this independence. But contrary to what the Chinese answer implies, it is not because everybody has found the Chinese territorial claim legally justified. It has been shown in Questions 8–10 that the foreign powers that have played a role on the Tibetan scene have merely pursued their own interests. Western cynicism emerges clearly in internal government documents and diplomatic exchanges between Great Britain and the United States. The most notorious example is the report of Lord Curzon, viceroy of India, delivered on January 8, 1903, to the secretary of state in charge of Indian affairs in London. In this document depicting the difficult relations with Tibet and recommending a military expedition to Lhasa, Lord Curzon writes: "We regard the so-called suzerainty of China over Tibet as a constitutional fiction, a political affectation which has been maintained because of its convenience to both parties" (quoted in Arpi 1999: 129). Similarly, the head of the British Foreign Office's Far Eastern Department wrote to the U.S. Embassy counselor in London on August 7, 1942: "In point of fact, the Tibetans not only claim to be but actually are an independent people" (quoted in Anand 1969: 423). And a U.S. State Department memorandum dated April 12, 1949, opines: "If Tibet possesses the stamina to withstand Communist infiltration . . . it would be to our interest to treat Tibet as independent rather than to continue to regard it as a part of China which has gone Communist" (quoted in Arpi 1999: 250–51).

The official position on Tibet of India, independent since 1947, was not based on political opportunism but on Nehru's personal views. Prior to the instauration of the PRC in 1949, Nehru implicitly recognized Tibet's independence, treating with it from government to government, and he even recommended to the British government that it raise the Tibetan question at the United Nations. However, his admiration for Mao's China led him to change his opinion and cultivate a Sino-Indian friendship that would lead to India and China becoming two superpowers sharing influence in Asia, he thought. This is why, while giving Tibet indications of sympathy, India asserted the rights of China and even prevented the appeal of the Tibetan government from being included in the UN agenda in 1951. The attack at the Tibetan-Indian border by Chinese troops in 1962 opened the eyes of the Indian government, but it was too late for Tibet. (However in Nehru's defense, the welcome and the asylum he granted in 1959 to the Dalai Lama, his entourage, and his government, and, later on, to 100,000 Tibetan refugees, must be taken into account.)

Politically and legally, foreign governments had good reasons not to move in 1950–59, when the People's Liberation Army (PLA) invaded and occupied Tibet. Politically, India still adhered to British Asian policy. India had its own problems and, as noted above, Nehru clung to the fantasy of Sino-Indian friendship. The Western countries had not yet embarked on decolonization and had their own troubles with separatists and "ethnic minorities." They did not wish to create a precedent in supporting the independence claim of a country they considered more or less a Chinese colony, which probably is one of the reasons why the report to the United Nations of the International Commission of Jurists (quoted in Question 8) went unanswered.

Legally, although this report and other specialists (see, e.g., Van Walt van Praag 1987) have directly recognized the de facto independence of Tibet between 1913 and 1950, that is not the universal opinion among jurists, who continue to split hairs over the principles of international law. For instance, even if one admits this independence before 1950, the fact that the Tibetan government agreed under duress to sign the 17-Point Agreement dictated by China in 1951,[2] and to collaborate with the Chinese up to 1959, weakens its position and enables the Chinese to appeal to the "stability of the international legal order" (Smith 1996: 661–67). What clearer proof that force trumps law! Governments are unwilling to clash with the PRC, whose markets are the target of fierce international competition, and to avoid taking sides, they are only too quick to cite Tibet's "insufficiently clear status." Although they regularly admonish China for its violations of human rights, both in China and Tibet, they thus refrain from championing Tibetan self-determination.

2. For the text of the 17-Point Agreement, see www.friends-of-tibet.org.nz/17-point-agreement.html (accessed February 23, 2007). See also Goldstein 1989: 763–70.

12

AN AMERICAN NEWSPAPER SAID THAT TIBET DID NOT BECOME PART
OF CHINA UNTIL 1950, AND ONLY IN THE LATE 1970S DID THE CARTER
ADMINISTRATION OFFICIALLY RECOGNIZE CHINA'S SOVEREIGNTY
OVER TIBET. DOES THIS ACCORD WITH HISTORY?

Historical facts prove that Tibet has been an "integral part" of China
since the Yuan dynasty, and that during the following 700 years, "the
Tibetan political and religious systems were established through the regulations of China's central government." The Qing dynasty strengthened its power over Tibet and reorganized the "local government's"
administration. "It sent two high commissioners [*ambans*] to reside
in Tibet and govern with the Dalai Lama and the Bainqen Lama." This
administration remained the same even when the Qing dynasty was
weakened after the 1840s, and it is with China that the British have
negotiated the conventions concerning Tibet.

The 17-Point Agreement negotiated in 1951 between the central
government and the "local government" of Tibet cannot be regarded
as the beginning of China's sovereignty: it is mere ignorance of
China's history. Before, the central government had also signed similar agreements with the local governments of Beijing, Hunan and Xinjiang for their peaceful liberation.

As for the U.S. government's position, diplomatic documents
indicate that Secretary of State John Hay instructed the U.S. ambassador to Britain, Joseph Choate, on June 3, 1904, to remind the British
that they had recognized Chinese sovereignty by negotiating with
China over Tibet on three occasions in the nineteenth century, and
that in 1943, when Britain "tried to dilute the status of Tibet as part
of China," the U.S. State Department informed the British ambassador in Washington: "The Chinese constitution lists Tibet among areas
constituting the territory of China. This Government has at no time
raised a question regarding the claim."

ANNE-MARIE BLONDEAU

Here *100 Questions* is seeking to hammer home an argument already
broadly set out and discussed in the preceding questions. This may be a good
propaganda technique, but it does not offer any new proof that Tibet was

part of China before 1950. Let us merely note an additional bit of fudging: although the Qing effectively reorganized the Tibetan government and put it under the tutelage of two *ambans*, they could not "govern with the Dalai Lama and the Bainqen Lama." This was for the excellent reason that the Panchen Lama, although head of a vast estate, had no role in Tibet's government. He played an important political role, starting in the nineteenth century, precisely because successive Chinese governments tried to use him against the Dalai Lama, as we shall see in connection with subsequent questions.

The question asked refers vaguely to "an American newspaper" and gives an imprecise date: "the late 1970s," when the Carter administration is said to have recognized that Tibet belonged to China. On the first point, many journalists in the world have written and continue to write that Tibet has been part of China only since the 1950 conquest. On the second point, one must recall that the United States was very late to recognize the PRC, which it did precisely in December 1978, when President Jimmy Carter announced the establishment of diplomatic relations between the two countries (up to then, the United States had recognized only the Nationalist Republic of China government, which had taken refuge in Taiwan). The first visible rapprochement was President Richard Nixon's visit to Beijing in 1972, one part of the price for which—according to Tsering Shakya (1999) and Warren W. Smith Jr. (1996: 554)—was the termination of American support to the Tibetan resistance. Many commentators emphasized that this recognition of the PRC simultaneously implied recognition of Chinese sovereignty over Tibet. Responding to a question on the subject in 1987, Deputy Assistant Secretary of State for East Asian and Pacific Affairs J. Stapleton Roy accepted that the United States had conceded that Tibet was a part of China in 1978 (Smith 1996: 555n46).

As far as the diplomatic documents quoted in the Chinese response are concerned, they probably derive from *Foreign Relations of the United States*, a series produced by the U.S. Department of State's Office of the Historian, which inter alia publishes various State Department documents as they are declassified.[3] The vacillation and hesitation of the Western powers on the status of Tibet have been described above; these diplomatic exchanges are only one example. In our view, their quotation by *100 Questions* goes against the thesis it seeks to demonstrate. If all the governments had recognized China's sovereignty without discussion, why would the diplomatic services

---

3. Presumably *Foreign Relations of the United States: Diplomatic Papers, 1943*, 6 vols. (Washington, D.C.: GPO, 1963–65). See also www.state.gov/www/about _state/history/frus.html (accessed February 23, 2007).

of various countries have needed reminders? In reality, Great Britain, India, and the United States sought in turn to support Tibet at different times, as their diplomatic correspondence shows (see, e.g., the documents from around 1950, when the Chinese attack was imminent, reproduced in Goldstein 1989: 749–57).

13
UNDER WHAT CIRCUMSTANCES DID THE PLA DECIDE TO MARCH INTO TIBET?

In 1949, when "[a]ll of China's inland territory except Tibet had been liberated," pro-imperialist elements in Tibet, collaborating with the American and British imperialists, "tried to block the PLA's advance." In July 1949, they expelled the Kuomintang representatives, publicized the "independence of Tibet," sent missions to the United States and Great Britain to seek aid and reinforced their troops along their eastern frontier, arousing "public indignation among people of all [Chinese] nationalities. Many requested that the Central People's Government send troops to liberate Tibet."

When he heard of the mission sent to Western countries by the Tibetan government, the Bainqen Lama's Bureau sent a cable to the central government (January 31, 1950), asserting: "Tibet is part of Chinese territory. . . . What the Lhasa authorities have done is a violation of national territorial integrity and against the will of Tibetan people. We, on behalf of the Tibetan people, request the prompt dispatch of the PLA to liberate Tibet."

Accordingly, the central government ordered the PLA to prepare to march into Tibet, while trying to persuade the Tibetan government to engage negotiations. It sent several peace missions to Lhasa to explain its position, hoping that "the local authorities could cut off [ties] with the imperialists and return to the multi-national family of the motherland." But the local government, headed by the regent Tagecha [Taktra], refused. It expelled Shirob Jaltso [Sherab Gyatso], commissioner of the central government, and exiled "the Living Buddha Datse" and three Han cadres. In addition "the Living Buddha Geda" was later killed by poison in Qamdo [Chamdo].

Consequently, the PLA entered into Tibet. On October 7, 1950, it defeated the Tibetan army at Chamdo and liberated the city. "In the spring of 1951, Regent Tagecha stepped down and the 14th Dalai Lama took over. The Tibetan authorities sent a delegation, headed by Ngapoi Ngawang Jigme, to Beijing and entered into negotiations. . . . After more than 20 days, the Agreement on Measures for the Peaceful Liberation of Tibet was signed on May 23, 1951."

SAMTEN KARMAY

When reading Chinese propaganda on Tibet, one must pay special attention to the terminology used. For instance, "local government" refers to that of an ethnic minority region such as Tibet, while "central government" refers to the government in Beijing. "China," which encompasses all the minorities (or "nationalities" as they are currently called), is treated as "inner," and bordering countries as "outer." All these terms and others, such as "liberate," "Han," "imperialist," "Western imperialist," "separatist," and so forth, alter the answer's meaning and are consequently prejudicial to an impartial understanding of the Tibetan issue.

Without reiterating what has been said above concerning the 13th Dalai Lama's declaration of independence, the Simla Conference, and so on, let us simply recall here a few things that illustrate Tibet's actual independence before 1949. First of all, after the 13th Dalai Lama expelled the Manchu *amban,* there were no Chinese representatives in Lhasa until 1934. Thereafter, the occasional presence of representatives of the Chinese Nationalist government was accepted—on the same basis as the presence of Indian and Nepalese representatives—in order to reestablish diplomatic relations.

In early 1946, the Tibetan government sent an official mission to India and China to congratulate the Allies on their victory in World War II. At the same time, the Tibetan government addressed a memorandum to the Chinese government indicating its intention to maintain Tibet's political status, in other words, Tibet's de jure and de facto independence, established since the signature of the Simla Convention (1913–14) with Great Britain (Goldstein 1989: 538–43).

In 1947, Tibet also participated in the pan-Asian conference organized by the Indian government in New Delhi. The Tibetan delegation sat alongside the delegations of thirty-two countries with its own newly created national flag and behind it a map of Asia with Tibet not included in China. Sampho, the head of the delegation, delivered his own personal speech. The flag was withdrawn owing to the protests of the Chinese delegation; according to Western authors, the map suffered a similar fate, although this is denied by Sampho's son (Arpi 1999: 175). We might also recall here the Tibetan trade mission, which, from 1947 to 1949, traveled with Tibetan passports not only to India but also to the United States and Great Britain.

Let us return, however, to the question that concerns us and to the events surrounding the invasion of Tibet in 1950 and the signing of the 17-Point Agreement. The Chinese authors would have us believe that the PLA intervened in Tibet as a result of the Chinese people's indignation, the Lhasa government's refusal to receive emissaries sent to negotiate, and the exile and murder of pro-Chinese Tibetans, as well as at the request of the Tibetan people. In reality, the integration of Tibet, Mongolia, and the Himalayan states (Nepal, Sikkim, Bhutan) was part of a plan long established by the Russian and Asian Communist parties to "liberate" Asian countries from the oppression of "reactionary" regimes. Moreover, for Communist China, Tibet was part of the heritage it had received from the Qing empire via Nationalist China (on the Nationalists' conquests in eastern Tibet and their armed conflicts with Tibet, see Jagou, 2000). The following radio broadcast by the New China Agency on January 1, 1950, left little doubt about the imminence of the invasion: "The tasks for the PLA for 1950 are to liberate Taiwan, Hainan and Tibet . . . Tibet is an integral part of China. Tibet has fallen under the influence of the imperialists" (Arpi 1999: 290).

The same radio station also stated that it was at the request of the Panchen Lama (discussed below) that the PLA was preparing to liberate Tibet. On January 2, 1950, Mao Zedong entrusted Deng Xiaoping, who was the political commissar for the Southwest Military Region at the time, with the task of preparing the invasion. Mao gave his support to Deng's plan according to which "the liberation of Tibet should be started simultaneously from all directions—from Sichuan in the east, from Yunnan in the south, from Qinghai in the north and from Xinjiang in the west" (Arpi 1999: 292).

In early October 1950, the Chinese army crossed the Yangtse, which had been the border between Tibet and China since the Chinese Nationalists' conquests, catching the Tibetans by surprise. Three armed divisions proceeded simultaneously: the Southwest Corps, consisting of 40,000 troops entered Kham, the eastern province of Tibet, from Yunnan; another division advanced from eastern Turkestan (Xinjiang) into Ngari, the western province of Tibet, after having crossed the Indian territory of Asai Chin; and the Northwest Division entered Amdo, the northeastern province of Tibet (Union Research Institute 1968: 2–3). On October 7, 1950, the Southwest Corps met with strong resistance by some 8,000 Tibetan soldiers and border guards. The fighting lasted for a week. After twenty engagements, half of the Tibetan forces had been put out of action. On October 17, Chamdo, the capital of Kham, fell to the Chinese. The province's governor, Ngapo

Ngawang Jigme, who was also a minister in the Dalai Lama's cabinet, was captured, together with Robert Ford, the British operator at Radio Chamdo. The latter was one of the two Westerners whom the Tibetan government had hired as radio operators (the other, Reginald Fox, had by then left Lhasa, which rendered communications between the Tibetan government and Kham difficult). Ford (1957) provides a firsthand account of the events.

To legitimate their annexation of Tibet by force, the Chinese Communists argued that they had done so to liberate the country from "Western imperialism" and to put an end to the feudal system, which oppressed the people. They also used one of the candidates for the reincarnation of the 9th Panchen Lama, who had died in 1937 at Jyekundo on his way back to central Tibet, after a long period spent in exile (see Question 10). After his death, his entourage, known collectively as the Nangang, turned back to Xining instead of returning to central Tibet. Later, the Nangang identified a young boy from the Koko Nor region as the reincarnation of the 9th Panchen Lama. It was in the name of this candidate that a "bureau of the Baiqen Lama's assembly" (i.e., the Nangang) allegedly sent a telegram dated January 31, 1950, to the Chinese government requesting them to send the PLA to Tibet. No trace of this telegram, which may have been written by the Chinese, has so far been found. Two other messages in the same vein, however, are known to us. Both were sent by the Panchen Erdeni (i.e., the Panchen Lama): one, dated October 1, 1949, was sent to Mao Zedong congratulating him on his victory in China and expressing the belief that Mao would soon liberate Tibet; the other, which was far more specific, was sent on the same date to the People's Revolutionary Military Committee with the following request: "We sincerely beseech that you will lead your righteous troops to liberate Tibet, eradicate the traitorous elements, and rescue the people of Tibet" (Goldstein 1989: 684n119).

A look back in time is necessary in order to understand the pro-Chinese attitude of the Panchen Lama and his entourage. As early as the nineteenth century, the Qing government had stirred up the potential rivalry between the Dalai Lama and the Panchen Lama in its attempt to make an ally of the latter. A conflict arose between the 13th Dalai Lama and the 9th Panchen Lama, to the extent that in 1923, the Panchen Lama, fearing for his life, fled to China. He established his residence in Xining, where he remained until 1937, when he was authorized to return to central Tibet, but, as noted, he died on the way.

As a result, the Nangang were inclined to co-operate with the Chinese. After the Panchen Lama's death, his entourage first went to Kandze in Kham, but came into conflict with the Chinese, who were already in control of part of the province (Jagou 2000). With the help of the Tibetan population, the Nangang nevertheless succeeded in sending the Panchen Lama's body and possessions to central Tibet. Despite this vicissitude in their relations with the Chinese government, the Nangang, under the aegis of the Kuomintang, left for Kumbum in Amdo to begin their search for the 9th Panchen Lama's reincarnation—without the authorization of the Tibetan government, which had begun its own search. The search was directed toward Amdo because of a prediction made by the state Oracle of Nechung (Ricca 1999), who was always consulted in important matters of this kind, that the reincarnation would be born in the northeastern part of the country. Fourteen boys from the Koko Nor region were identified as potential candidates, of whom two were selected. Both had been born in 1938, and they were from the same area in Amdo. One, named Gönpo Tseten, had been born into the family of a village chief, the other was named Sengdong. Lhasa, however, wanted to find other candidates in central Tibet and Kham: because the monastery of Tashilhünpo and, by extension, the Nangang had always been favorably inclined toward China, the Tibetan government was suspicious of their real intentions. While the search in central Tibet yielded no results, one boy in Kham was selected as a possible candidate. However, in 1944, the Nangang unilaterally decided to nominate one of their two candidates in Amdo, Gönpo Tseten. The ceremony took place at Kumbum Monastery, despite the disapproval of the Kuomintang authorities, who felt that the Panchen Lama could only be recognized in Lhasa. The Nangang's initiative made the Tibetan government realize the gravity of the situation; it was obvious that although, as a candidate, Gönpo Tseten now enjoyed considerable prestige, he nevertheless remained in the hands of the Chinese. In 1946, the Tibetan government ordered Tashilhünpo to dispatch a delegation to meet the Nangang and to return to Lhasa with the Amdo candidates for official tests. Another mission was sent to fetch the candidate from Kham to act as a counterweight to the Amdo candidates. However, when they met in Xining, a disagreement arose between the Tashilhünpo officials sent by Lhasa and the Nangang, who would support only the candidacy of Gönpo Tseten, also backed by the Chinese. The Nationalist Chinese officially recognized Gönpo Tseten as the 10th Panchen Lama on August 10, 1949—shortly before the Communists took power on October 1—very likely in response to the Tibetan government's expulsion, on July 8, of all Chinese nationals from Lhasa on the charges of espionage.

At every level, the members of the Nangang were the victims of Chinese intrigue and interference in Tibet's religious affairs, first under the Kuomintang and later under the Communists. Gönpo Tseten, together with the Nangang, fell into the hands of the Chinese Communists, who had just taken Xining. The other Amdo candidate died in 1949, and the candidate from Kham arrived in Lhasa.

The Dalai Lama was still a minor, and the government in Lhasa was deeply divided. The mission that was sent to India to set up negotiations with the Chinese was delayed for diplomatic reasons. The appeals sent on November 7, 1950, to the Indian and the British delegations at the United Nations went unanswered (although the Indian government did address a protest to PRC against its use of force in eastern Tibet). The Korean War had just broken out, and Mao Zedong had sent troops to back North Korea. The Soviet Union was sure to support the Chinese should the Tibetan question be raised. Moreover, for the Nationalist Chinese, who still represented China at the United Nations, the Tibetan issue was an internal affair.

Left to themselves, the Tibetans decided to enthrone the 14th Dalai Lama—who was then fifteen years old and had no political experience— earlier than planned. The ceremony took place on November 17, and on December 20, the news and eyewitness accounts from Kham prompted the cabinet and the National Assembly to prepare him for the possibility of exile in India, as well as to move the government's headquarters to Yatung near the Sikkim border, where the Dalai Lama remained until the signing of the 17-Point Agreement. In Delhi, the Tibetan emissaries finally met with the Chinese ambassador, who handed them a message containing Beijing's terms: (1) Tibet had to accept that it was a part of China; (2) Tibet's defense was to be handled by China; and (3) all political and trade matters concerning foreign countries were to be conducted through China (Goldstein 1989: 676).

If Tibet accepted these terms, the PLA would remain stationed on the border, if not, it would occupy Tibet. In the meantime, Ngapo, the former governor of Kham, who had been "reeducated" and had become a supporter of the Chinese, urged the Dalai Lama to undertake direct negotiations with the Chinese government. This was finally agreed to, and five negotiators, with Ngapo at their head, were sent to Beijing. On their way in Delhi, they met with Nehru, who made it clear that India would not intervene, and that when in Beijing, they should concede that Tibet was a part of China, since this fact had been internationally accepted (Shakya 1999: 64).

The Tibetan emissaries had received very precise instructions from their government: they were to stand firm concerning Tibet's independence. However, should the negotiations threaten to break down, they were to accept that Tibet was a part of China, but only on the following conditions: Tibet was to enjoy complete internal independence; no Chinese troops would be stationed inside Tibet; the Tibetan army would ensure the country's defense;

the entourage and military guard of the Chinese representative in Lhasa would not exceed one hundred men; and the Chinese representative would be a Buddhist (Shakya 1999: 64). After having discussed these terms among themselves, the delegates objected that the Chinese would never accept the condition refusing a Chinese military presence; the cabinet therefore suggested that the Tibetan army be incorporated into the Chinese army to ensure the country's defense. Ngapo assured his companions that since the Tibetan government had made two major concessions—concerning Tibet's political status and army—it would only be a waste of time to keep their government informed of the discussions' progress in minute detail.

In Beijing, Prime Minister and Minister of Foreign Affairs Zhou Enlai himself welcomed the Tibetan delegates. The negotiations, however, were conducted by the Communist Party's United Front Work Department and the National Minorities Commission, both primarily concerned with internal affairs; the inexperienced Tibetan delegates, who were unaware of this, thus believed they were dealing directly with the Chinese government. The Dalai Lama (1962: 80–82) explains how, in the end, his emissaries, deprived of direct contact with him and under Chinese pressure, exceeded the limits of their mission and signed the 17-Point Agreement on "the peaceful liberation of Tibet." Melvyn Goldstein (1989: 759–72) gives a day-to-day description of the negotiations, based on an account provided by one of the Tibetan delegates. It was evident that the Chinese were not prepared to accept any compromises and that the Tibetans were compelled, under the threat of immediate armed invasion, to sign the Chinese proposal.

Furthermore, at the beginning of the "negotiations" on April 29, 1951, the Chinese imposed as a preamble to any discussion that the Tibetan government accept the Panchen Lama. The Chinese authorities knew of course that the Tibetan government had not recognized the young boy from Amdo as the 10th Panchen Lama. The Chinese government's first demand was that the Tibetan delegation recognize this candidate as the real reincarnation of the 9th Panchen Lama. This demand astonished the Tibetan delegation, whose members did not understand why the Chinese insisted on this question, since the main purpose of the meeting was to discuss the "peaceful liberation of Tibet." The Tibetans refused to recognize the Chinese-backed candidate and explained that according to tradition, the candidate had to be chosen among at least three others following the outcome of divination and tests (recognition of objects that belonged to the late reincarnation placed among other objects, etc.), and finally by the Dalai Lama himself. During six or seven days, this was the only point discussed, until Li Weihan, the chairman of the National Minorities Commission, presented an ultimatum to the Tibetan delegation: "Because the Panchen Lama had recognized Mao as the new leader of China before the liberation of Qinghai and Mao had accepted the candidate as the true incarnation of the late Panchen Lama, the 'face' of Mao and China were at stake" (Goldstein 1989: 762; Goldstein, Sherap, and Siebenschuh 2004: 148). At this point, Ngabo was asked to wire Yatung, where the Dalai Lama and his government were established at the time. In his telegram, he explained that "negotiations" could not begin until the Tibetan government officially recognized the candidate chosen by the Chinese. The Chinese army was stationed on the threshold of Tibet, threatening to invade at any moment. In Yatung, the Dalai Lama and his government had no alternative other than to agree to this demand. After having conducted a lottery divination whose outcome favored the Chinese-backed candidate, they recognized the latter as the reincarnation of the 9th Panchen Lama (Goldstein 1989: 763).

This issue resolved, the seventeen articles prepared by the Chinese were briskly discussed and the agreement was signed on May 23, 1951, after Ngapo had thrice assured the Chinese that he had full power to do so, although this was not the case (as he himself admitted in 1989). In his autobiography (1962: 81), the Dalai Lama states that the Chinese made the Tibetan delegates use Chinese forgeries of the official Tibetan seals in the final signing. According to Goldstein (1989: 770n64), however, the new seals simply bore each delegate's name and were therefore not forgeries.

The content of the agreement and the Dalai Lama's reaction are discussed in relation to the following questions. Here, jumping ahead a little, we shall briefly describe the Panchen Lama's fate following the Dalai Lama's flight in 1959. The Communists had found in the person of Gönpo Tseten, who was recognized as the 10th Panchen Lama, a considerable asset. He was first presented as a rival of the Dalai Lama and then, after the latter's departure in 1959, as his replacement. However, as the Panchen Lama grew older, he became increasingly aware of the political manipulation of which he was the instrument. In 1962, after visiting central Tibet and other regions inhabited by Tibetans, he wrote a long report questioning Chinese policy in Tibet (see Barnett 1998a). As a result, he was dismissed from his post as acting chairman and vice-chairman of the Preparatory Committee for the Tibet Autonomous Region and deported to Beijing (Kunsang Paljor 1977: 25–31). Later, during the Cultural Revolution, he was asked to denounce the Dalai Lama as a "reactionary," which he categorically refused to do. Consequently, he suffered abuse and many years in prison (Lobsang 1989: 26). He was forced to marry a Chinese woman—who never appeared in public—and for this reason he could not wear monk's robes, even when he later sat on the Panchen Lama's throne in Tashilhünpo Monastery. He was not rehabilitated until the coming to power of Deng Xiaoping's government and was not permitted to return to Tibet until 1982, his first visit since 1964. He probably did not notice any improvement, since he repeated his criticisms of Chinese policy in Tibet in an energetic speech he made on March 28, 1987, before the National People's Congress Standing Committee in Beijing.

In 1989, he returned to Tibet to preside over the consecration of a new stupa at Tashilhünpo, built to house the relics of the 4th to 9th Panchen Lamas, whose tombs had been looted by the Red guards. Was the Panchen Lama unbearably distressed that his predecessors had been disturbed in their tombs for no reason? At any event, he fell ill in the middle of the ceremony. It is certain that by then he was profoundly disabused about his "collaboration"; a few days before his death, he said that "Tibet had lost more than it had gained in the past thirty years" (Shakya 1999: 429).

To clarify the Chinese Communist government's policy toward Tibet, mention should also be made of the "peace missions" that were supposedly sent to Lhasa before the arrival of the PLA in central Tibet. It is said that one such mission was led by a Shirob Jaltso. This name refers to Sherab Gyatso, a great scholar, or *geshe*. This renowned Drepung monk from Amdo had a great number of disciples and exercised considerable influence among the aristocracy and in monastic circles. He left Tibet in 1936 (following a disagreement concerning the revision of the Buddhist canon of which he was in charge) and became the president of the Association for the Promotion of Tibetan Culture in China. In reality, the Chinese Communists never sent him to Tibet as the head of a "peace mission." He was sent by Chiang Kai-shek in 1944 to improve relations between Tibet and China, which had deteriorated owing to border conflicts and Tibet's claims to independence during World War II. Sherab Gyatso arrived at Nagchuka in April 1944, accompanied by around fifty Chinese, most of whom were his disciples. The Tibetan government forbade his entourage to proceed farther, however, so he returned to China. From 1951 to 1968, he held various important posts under the Communist regime, but in 1968, during the Cultural Revolution, he was tortured and murdered in prison by the Chinese for having defended freedom of speech and beliefs and Tibetans' right to preserve their language (Stoddard 1988).

100 Questions also accuses "pro-imperialist elements" of having poisoned the "living Buddha Geda" of Peirei Monastery. Geta Trülku was a lama from Beri Monastery in the Kandze region of Kham. Geta's first contact with the Chinese Communists dated back to 1936, when they passed through Kandze during the Long March. At that time, Geta met the Chinese General Zhu De. The latter promised him future protection for having hidden and taken care of Communist soldiers. Later, when the Chinese Communists returned to Kandze during the PLA's invasion of Tibet, Geta is said to have gone out of his way to welcome the Chinese army. As a result, he was regarded by the Tibetan government as a traitor and a spy. Later, he was sent as an emissary to Chamdo, where he attempted, in vain, to obtain authorization to continue to Lhasa in order to persuade the Tibetan government to agree to the "peaceful liberation" of Tibet. He undoubtedly believed that by accepting the Chinese policy of "peaceful liberation," Tibet, as a part of the Republic of China, would be allowed to preserve its monasticism and theocratic system. Two weeks later, however, he died in mysterious circumstances while still in Chamdo. According to the minister Kashöba (1903–?), he was poisoned by Lhalu, the former governor of Kham. The Chinese accused Robert Ford, who denied any involvement during the five years he spent in prison in China. (The latter [1957], describes Geta's visit and death and how he immediately suspected that Geta had been poisoned, but refuses to say more and hopes that the murderer will never be discovered!)

The Panchen Lama, *Geshe* Sherab Gyatso, and Geta Trülku all three belonged to the Gelugpa School of Tibetan Buddhism, which since the Qing dynasty had always counted the staunchest supporters of collaboration with the Chinese among its members. Owing to the prestige and authority linked to their high religious status or scholarship, they were exploited and manipulated by the Chinese, who used them to serve their own political purposes in Tibet. On the other hand, all three voluntarily co-operated with the Chinese in the hope that one day China would understand the Buddhist monastic system and the Gelugpa School's political responsibility in Tibet. At the end of their lives, both the Panchen Lama and Sherab Gyatso were totally disillusioned with Communism and Chinese policy toward Tibet. They realized too late that they had been entrapped by the Chinese.

14
WHAT WAS THE CONTENT OF THE AGREEMENT ON MEASURES FOR THE PEACEFUL LIBERATION OF TIBET SIGNED BETWEEN CHINA'S CENTRAL GOVERNMENT AND THE LOCAL GOVERNMENT OF TIBET?

This agreement (the full text is appended) comprises 17 articles whose principal contents are: "The Tibetan people shall unite and drive out imperialist aggressive forces from Tibet; the local government of Tibet shall actively assist the PLA to enter Tibet and consolidate national defense; the Tibetan people have the right to national regional autonomy; the central authorities shall not alter the existing political system in Tibet; the central authorities also will not alter the established status, functions and powers of the Dalai Lama; the policy of freedom of religious belief shall be carried out, the religious beliefs, customs and habits shall be respected, and the monasteries shall be protected; Tibetan troops shall be reorganized by stages and made into a part of the national defense forces of the PRC; the spoken and written language and school education of the Tibetan nationality shall be developed step by step; Tibet's agriculture, animal husbandry, industry and commerce shall be developed step by step and the people's living standards shall be improved gradually in accordance with the actual conditions in Tibet; the PLA entering Tibet shall be fair in all buying and selling and shall not arbitrarily take a single needle or thread from the people; the Central People's Government shall be exclusively responsible for all external affairs in Tibet."

ANNE-MARIE BLONDEAU

We have just seen under what circumstances this agreement was signed. Let us now briefly examine some of its aspects.

The seventeen points of the agreement are preceded by a long preamble, not mentioned in the Chinese answer here, but of the essence, inasmuch as it starts with the assertion that Tibet is part of China. The Tibetan negotiators, who had arrived in Beijing with very firm instructions from their government (see the previous answer), were authorized to accept this Chinese claim as a last resort, but they had to remain inflexible about the stationing of Chinese troops in Tibet. According to the very interesting point-by-point comments by one of them, Sampho, to Goldstein: "There was no discussion regarding the Preamble. The Tibetan delegation was concerned only with the actual points of the Agreement" (Goldstein 1989: 765). The preamble begins (*100 Questions* version; emphasis has been added):

> *The Tibetan nationality is one of the nationalities* with a long history living *within the boundaries of China*. . . . But over the last 100 years or more, imperialist forces penetrated China and, in consequence, also penetrated *the Tibetan region*. . . . The *local government* of Tibet did not oppose these imperialist deceptions and provocations, and adopted an unpatriotic attitude toward our great motherland. Under such con-

ditions, the Tibetan nationality and people were plunged into the depths of enslavement and suffering.

The text goes on to speak of the victory in 1949 of the Communist forces, the establishment of the PRC, the fraternal union of all China's ethnic communities, the freedoms minorities are to have, and the duties of the central people's government.

To eliminate the imperialists "smoothly," unite the territory, and liberate the Tibetans so that they "return to the family of the PRC," the central people's government had ordered the PLA to enter Tibet. At the same time, it had "notified the local government of Tibet to send delegates to the central authorities to conduct talks for the conclusion of an agreement on measures for the peaceful liberation of Tibet. In the latter part of April 1951, the delegates *with the full powers* of the local government of Tibet arrived in Beijing. The Central People's Government appointed representatives with full power to conduct talks on a friendly basis."

The seventeen articles of the agreement follow. The commentary supplied by Goldstein reveals both the great naïveté of the Tibetan representatives, who were convinced that the continued existence of their government, customs, and religion were guaranteed, and the pitfalls they fell into on account of their insufficient knowledge of Chinese. For example, when they asked for the meaning of "local government," it was translated into Tibetan as "the government of an area" *(sane zhung)*, in which the term *zhung,* "government," reassured them, since it is how the Tibetan government is designated (Goldstein 1989: 765). These comments show too that the Chinese did not hesitate to use threats or blackmail. When the Tibetan delegates brought up the contradiction between article 15—which creates a military and administrative committee and a Chinese military headquarters in Tibet—and the articles guaranteeing the continuity of the Tibetan government, the Chinese became angry and threatened to dispatch the PLA immediately, which would not be peaceful. As Goldstein notes (1989: 769), it was a crucial article to them, for it allowed them to install their own administrative structure.

On top of this official agreement, three secret ones were signed (Goldstein 1989: 770). The first dealt with the incorporation of the Tibetan army into the PLA; the second, with what would happen if the Dalai Lama decided to take refuge in India: the agreement would remain in force, and the Dalai Lama could return when he wanted to; the third, not disclosed, probably related to the gradual suppression of the Tibetan currency.

After the signature, the delegates met with Mao Zedong for the first time.

15
What was the Dalai Lama's attitude towards this agreement?

He supported it. On October 24, 1951, he sent a telegram (full text appended) to Mao Zedong in which he declared that "the local government of Tibet and the Tibetan people, monks and laymen alike, would unanimously support the agreement." He added: "We will actively assist the PLA to enter Tibet and consolidate the national defense, drive out imperialist aggressive forces from Tibet, and safeguard the unified state territory and sovereignty under the leadership of Chairman Mao and the Central People's Government."

ANNE-MARIE BLONDEAU

The 17-Point Agreement was signed on May 23, 1951, but it was only on the 26th that the Dalai Lama and his government, still in Yatung, learned the news from Peking Radio, along with the rest of the world. As we have seen above, the Tibetan delegation did not have the right to inform its own government of the negotiations' progress before the official announcement by Beijing. The Dalai Lama's reaction in his memoirs suffices to offset the enthusiastic tone of the cited telegram of October 24 (which is remarkably late, five months after the signature of the agreement):

> Neither I nor my government were told that an agreement had been signed. We first came to know of it from a broadcast, which Ngapo made on Peking radio. It was a terrible shock when we heard the terms of it. We were appalled at the mixture of Communist clichés, vainglorious assertions which were completely false, and bold statements which were only partly true; and the terms were far worse and more oppressive than anything we had imagined. (1962: 81)

A little later, a telegram from Ngapo arrived, which indicated that secret agreements had also been signed. The Dalai Lama's cabinet answered it immediately, telling Ngapo that the conditions seemed extremely unfavorable and that he should have kept the government informed of the progress of the negotiations. It urged him to send the text of the agreement and of the secret clauses and to stay in Beijing with the whole delegation till further orders. But the members of the delegation refused, saying that if the Tibetan government wanted to resume the talks, it would be better to send new negotiators. Ngapo and another delegate went back to Lhasa with the documents, and the three others left for India and went from there to Yatung to report verbally to the Tibetan government.

Meanwhile, the departure for Lhasa of the Chinese representative—he was Zhang Jingwu, one of those who had negotiated the agreement—was announced. Zhang was to travel with the three Tibetan negotiators on their way back to India and would consequently pass through Yatung and meet with the Dalai Lama. Once more, the Tibetan government turned to the Americans—with whom they had secret exchanges during all this time— and asked for help. Minister Shakabpa assured the U.S. ambassador in Delhi that the Dalai Lama and his Tibetan government were rejecting the agreement, and they were waiting for the Tibetan negotiators to be out of China and for the Dalai Lama to take refuge in India before denouncing it publicly. Once again, too, the Indian government refused to interfere in what it considered a closed affair, and the British government advised the Americans to align themselves with the Indian position. However, the Americans were determined to help Tibet as long as the Tibetans clearly rejected the agreement and showed their resistance to the Chinese invasion. They consequently pushed the Dalai Lama to denounce it publicly before the arrival of the Chinese representative on Indian soil. But the Tibetan government wanted first to hear the report of its envoys to Beijing, and the Dalai Lama was also subjected to strong pressures, especially from the high clergy, to accept the agreement and return to Lhasa. Finally, it was a resort to divination that decided on this return, and the Dalai Lama set out for Lhasa on July 23, 1951.

Zhang Jingwu, who had preceded him there by a little, urged the Dalai Lama to confirm the agreement publicly. The cabinet did not know what to do and, finally, it was agreed to follow the advice of the National Assembly. This convened at the end of September and, after heated debates recommended the acceptance of the agreement, which after all, guaranteed the continuation of the traditional politico-religious system, with the Dalai Lama at its head. The latter then sent Mao Zedong the telegram quoted in the Chinese answer, whose style and jargon reveal the Chinese hand behind it. In fact, a draft had been written in Tibetan and translated by one of the Beijing negotiators. But Zhang Jingwu objected to the use of several terms (like "China and Tibet" since Tibet was not distinct from China, according to the Chinese), and one may suspect that he participated actively in the telegram's wording. The Chinese had won all the way.

The PLA had already entered Lhasa on September 9, and more Chinese troops were arriving every day.

The Chinese authors do not question the feelings of the Tibetans themselves here. In other answers (and in all the propaganda that went with the occupation of Tibet), it is asserted that the Tibetan people welcomed the Chinese soldiers as liberators. It is true that in the beginning, the Chinese army, having strict orders, behaved in a friendly manner, and the Chinese occupation appeared to many Tibetans to be a chance of improving their living conditions; this was particularly obvious in Kham. But feelings changed as soon as the Chinese imposed the collectivization of the land and cattle and began to persecute the clergy (see Sperling, next question). In central Tibet, it seems that the disenchantment was less rapid and initially arose from economic difficulties caused by having to support so large an army. In reality, the political awareness of the common people was nonexistent, and probably they did not understand the scope of the signed agreement, especially since, in the countryside, they were told about it by propaganda teams, which went systematically to villages showing movies, explaining the agreement, and promising that there would be no brutal change (Shakya 1999: 98). In Lhasa and Shigatse, the Chinese sought to seduce the Tibetan upper class with banquets, movies, performances of songs and dances, and the participation of high-ranking Tibetan civil servants on the different committees that were set up. The Chinese High Command even participated in the traditional distribution of alms to monks during the celebration of the Great Prayer *(Mönlam chenmo)* in 1951. Posters were already being put up in the streets of Lhasa, calling for the departure of the Chinese (Shakya 1999: 102). However, the politics of seduction was bearing fruit, not only with the upper class and big merchants, whose businesses were flourishing thanks to new regulations, but also with the people, who sincerely thought that the Chinese had come to modernize Tibet (most of them were seeing automobiles for the first time). The situation deteriorated starting in 1953–54, when China had to reduce its expenses on Tibet—for example, Tibetans were asked to voluntarily accept salary cuts—and wished to accelerate the starting of reforms with the creation of the Preparatory Committee for the Autonomous Region of Tibet. Moreover, refugees from Kham began to pour into Lhasa, bringing stories of exactions by the PLA in that region. Finally, on March 10, 1959, the growing popular dissatisfaction exploded in the Lhasa revolt (see Question 17).

As for the 17-Point Agreement, it was denounced as early as March 15, 1959, in Lhasa by a crowd assembled by the People's Assembly, a movement recently formed to protect the Dalai Lama, on the grounds that "the Chinese had betrayed the Agreement by undermining [his] authority" (Shakya 1999: 197–98). The Dalai Lama himself formally denounced the agreement when he arrived in exile in India, also accusing the Chinese of having already violated it.

On the Chinese side, a declaration signed by Zhou Enlai announced on

March 28 that the rebellion had in fact "torn up" the agreement; Tibet's government was dismissed and its responsibilities were handed to the Preparatory Committee for the Autonomous Region of Tibet. The Panchen Lama, in the absence of the Dalai Lama, was designated its president and Ngapo its vice president (Shakya 1999: 207). The 17-Point Agreement had had its day, and so had the traditional government of Tibet.

16
SINCE PEACEFUL LIBERATION, WHAT POLICIES HAS THE CHINESE GOVERNMENT PURSUED IN TIBET?

"Since the peaceful liberation of Tibet, the Chinese government has strictly upheld the policy of equality and unity of all nationalities, the policy of freedom for religious belief . . ." Until the "armed rebellion" in 1959, a policy of dialogue with the Tibetans was conducted, which took account of their actual economic and cultural situation. After the rebellion of March 1959, staged by "reactionary members of Tibet's upper classes," had been suppressed, the members of the upper classes were treated according to their participation in it, or not.

"After the democratic reform [following the Dalai Lama's flight in 1959], the central government adopted in 1961 the guiding principle of steady development in Tibet. . . . and the general standard of living in the region markedly improved."

During the Cultural Revolution [1966–1976], "China was plunged into the chaos," previous policies toward nationalities were abolished, "religious activities were banned and many monasteries were destroyed. The Tibetans suffered along with all the other peoples of China."

Since then, the central government has adopted "a series of special flexible policies suitable to Tibet's local conditions." For instance, "the exemption of tax and the cancellation of unified agricultural produce purchasing quotas for farmers and livestock breeders"; individual ownership of land, house, and livestock; and the development of the private economy along with the collective. "People who were wronged during the 'cultural revolution' have been rehabilitated and given compensation." Religious activities have resumed and the central government has given a large sum of funds to restore monasteries. Together with China's other provinces, it has "increased economic and technical aid to Tibet."

ELLIOT SPERLING

China's policies have varied since Tibet's "peaceful liberation" and the signing of the 17-Point Agreement decreeing the country's incorporation into the PRC. The general picture that emerges is not, as *100 Questions* would have it, one of stable policy developments, interrupted only by the chaos of the Cultural Revolution. Rather, it is a picture of wide variations and swings, which at times exacted a high toll in human suffering, of which the period of the Cultural Revolution represents only the most egregious example.

Following the incorporation of Tibet into the PRC in 1951, the policies adopted by China in the area that now constitutes the TAR differed considerably from those being followed in both Chinese areas of the PRC and Tibetan regions outside the borders of the modern TAR. As a result of the 17-Point Agreement, the social and economic structure of the state presided over by the Dalai Lama remained largely untouched, although the new Chinese military presence and its concomitant requisitions, as well as the political pressures exerted upon the Dalai Lama and his officials, did contribute to a sense of unease in the area. Elsewhere on the Tibetan Plateau, however, outside the area under the jurisdiction of the Dalai Lama's government, the stipulations of the 17-Point Agreement did not apply, and this produced a very different situation, with very serious consequences. Although China considers only the modern TAR to be "Tibet," events there cannot be understood in isolation from the other parts of the plateau. As the Chinese government implemented what it termed "democratic reforms" in Tibetan areas beyond the Dalai Lama's jurisdiction (Kham and Amdo, from now on incorporated into the Chinese provinces of Qinghai, Sichuan, Yunnan, and Gansu), it set off feelings of resentment and apprehension among the populations concerned; and these sentiments flowed back across the frontier of the modern TAR. One must bear in mind the close ties between the Tibetan populations throughout the plateau; the Dalai Lama and the late Panchen Lama were both born well outside the borders of the TAR, where most Tibetans still live.

In these areas, so-called democratic reforms were instituted, often as in China proper, in the attempt to change society and social relations throughout the PRC. These entailed the formation of cooperatives (later to lead to communes), land confiscations, and the denunciation of "class enemies," which was sometimes violent. At this time, the factors differentiating Tibetan and Chinese social and economic arrangements (for example, the fact that Tibetan areas had an overwhelming surplus of land and a dearth of population) counted for little in the ultimate scheme of reforming Tibetan society.

Thus, religious and political figures within the area of the modern TAR learned very early on in the 1950s that elsewhere on the Tibetan Plateau, the economic holdings and activities of Tibetan monasteries were being subjected to severe and often debilitating restrictions, while certain clergy and lay leaders were being denounced and attacked. The situation in these areas at that time runs very much counter to the statement by *100 Questions* that "[s]ince the peaceful liberation of Tibet, the Chinese government has strictly upheld the policy of equality and unity of all nationalities, the policy of freedom for religious belief, and the policy of uniting with personages in the upper classes to develop the patriotic united front." Already in 1956, when violent resistance had broken out in response to forced Chinese measures in the eastern parts of the Tibetan Plateau, *Geshe* Sherab Gyatso (see Question 13), was forced to concede that "disquiet" among Tibetans had been caused by the speed with which reforms (including the confiscation of land and animals for "cooperatives") had been implemented.

As is now well known, the armed resistance by Tibetans that developed in the eastern areas of the Tibetan Plateau spread into those areas under the Dalai Lama's jurisdiction, culminating in the uprising in Lhasa in March 1959. For more than a year, fighting continued as the Chinese army subdued Tibetan guerrillas in southern Tibet and began imposing, in the area previously under the Dalai Lama's government, many of the reforms that had been implemented elsewhere. All this is glossed in *100 Questions* as a rebellion by reactionary upper-class Tibetans.

The entire Tibetan Plateau soon became subject to many of the same sorts of policy changes and extremes that other parts of the PRC had been experiencing, in spite of the respite from the formation of cooperatives mentioned in *100 Questions*. Although the Chinese answer implies that Chinese policy toward Tibet has followed a consistent course (except for the period of the Cultural Revolution), the wide shifts in China's approach to Tibet were already visible in the 1950s, although their direct effects were felt largely outside the area ruled by the Dalai Lama. Leftist extremes produced periods in which strong Maoist and Stalinist principles dictated that the eventual withering away of nationality characteristics ought to be taking place with greater speed under China's socialist system; if this was not happening, it was said to be the result of class enemies using the nationality issue to cloak their reactionary class interests. Policy changes reflected the tensions between this position and the more moderate one, which, although still maintaining that nationality characteristics were destined to disappear, insisted that this process should be allowed to proceed normally and naturally, without coercive force. Examples of such swings can be seen, beginning in the late 1950s, in the liberal "Hundred Flowers Movement," which was followed by the leftist "anti-rightist" campaign (itself followed in turn by the leftist "Great Leap Forward" and another restoration of relative moderation). Such swings in policy culminated, of course, in the Cultural Revolution in 1966.

The leftist movements generally made no secret of their hostility to what was termed "local nationalism," a phenomenon to be wiped out among the PRC's national minorities. In extreme cases, such as the period of the Cultural Revolution, this entailed efforts to diminish the use of a minority nationality's own language, as well as other attacks on "nationality characteristics," which could be harsh and brutal. (In moderate periods such policies and the attitudes that generated them were disparaged as "Han chauvinism.")

In 1965, the TAR was created, in areas previously under the Dalai Lama's jurisdiction, although those areas had already been made subject to the whims of Chinese policy after the violent suppression of Tibetan resistance in 1959 and 1960. When the Cultural Revolution broke out in 1966, Tibet was soon swept up in it.

The ravages of the Cultural Revolution are sufficiently well known and there is no need to describe them in detail. Since the rise of Deng Xiaoping in the late 1970s, the Cultural Revolution has been denounced in official Chinese circles; the brief description in *100 Questions* is typical of these denunciations. In many cases, the specific sufferings of Tibetans and other peoples whose cultures and languages alone defined them as "non-progressive elements" in the thinking of that era are generally glossed over with words to the effect that, yes, Tibetans and other minorities suffered during the Cultural Revolution, but so did all of China's people. Thus in *100 Questions* the authors simply state: "Tibetans suffered along with all the other peoples of China."

Still, the fact is that minorities such as the Tibetans do seem to have suffered disproportionately. Recent documentary evidence from Inner Mongolia, for instance, indicates that Mongols were the main victims of the Cultural Revolution in the region, even though they were already only a small minority of the population.

Since the ascent of Deng Xiaoping, China has followed a policy of greater international openness, largely directed toward the development of its economy within the present world market system. This liberal swing away from the harsh policies of the Cultural Revolution has brought about certain liberal policies in pastoral and agricultural production (as noted in *100 Questions*) as well as liberalization in other aspects of Tibetan life and culture. It must be admitted that since the early 1980s, there has been a tremendous expansion in the limits allotted to cultural expression in Tibet.

But still, faced with expressions of Tibetan national aspirations, the Chinese authorities have used an increasingly heavy hand in certain areas of Tibetan policy.

17
WHAT CAUSED THE 1959 REBELLION IN TIBET?

After 1951, due to the conscientious implementation of the 17-Point Agreement by the PLA, "Tibet's economy and culture had made great progress." At the same time, "the million Tibetan serfs became increasingly conscious of their rights" and "strongly demanded the abolition of feudal serfdom." The Tibetan ruling classes were hostile to this demand; they persecuted the Tibetans who collaborated with the Chinese and "obstructed the implementation of the agreement."

The central government reacted cautiously and "decided not to conduct reforms in Tibet during the Second Five-Year Plan (1958–62)," waiting until the "Tibetan people and their leaders deemed it feasible." But "the reactionary clique of the Tibetan upper classes tried to perpetuate feudal serfdom. At the instigation of outside forces, they started an armed rebellion in a vain attempt to drive the PLA out. . . . This was the basic cause of the 1959 rebellion in Tibet."

As for the pretext that the Han planned to kidnap the Dalai Lama, the truth has been established in an article written by a former minister of the Tibetan local government, Ngapoi Ngawang Jigme [on whom, see Questions 13 and 14], vice-chairman of the National Popular Committee, which brands the rumor as entirely groundless and says that the Dalai Lama had himself fixed the date of his visit to PLA headquarters, and that the cabinet, including Ngapoi himself, had also been invited. [The full text of the article, published in *China Tibetan Studies*, no. 2 (1988), is given in an appendix.]

[This version is totally contradicted by the accounts given by the Dalai Lama (1962: 149–76) and Tsepon Shakabpa (1967: 316–20), a minister in the Tibetan government at that time. It is clear that neither the

Tibetan government, nor foreign powers were the instigators of this popular uprising, even if young officials took an active part in it. Here, we give the floor to one of the witnesses to these events, who explains the reasons for the uprising as he saw them.]

JAMPA PANGLUNG

On March 10, 1959, the Tibetan people rebelled against the Chinese occupying forces. The Chinese falsely branded this uprising a "putsch, precipitated by the reactionary clique of the Tibetan upper class in order to maintain serfdom."

This revolt of the Tibetans, however, had its roots in the occupation of Tibet by the PLA, which aimed at incorporating Tibet into China and thus forcing Communist ideology on the Tibetans. The Tibetan army, which consisted of a few thousand ill-equipped soldiers, armed with outdated weapons, put up a hopeless resistance, and the Communists pursued their aims relentlessly. Because of China's overwhelming military superiority, the Tibetan government, which nominally remained in office up to 1959, could do no more than drag its feet in negotiations.

Tibetans quickly grasped the intentions of the occupying Communist forces and felt the resulting hardships. For example, the questions asked of families in connection with the census begun in 1953 were taken as an encroachment on private life. Furthermore, the PLA had to buy food from the Tibetans, and since, despite its size and low population density, the country produced only enough for its inhabitants, the additional burden of provisioning an occupying army of more than 10,000 men inevitably led to food shortages. The lack of infrastructure led the Chinese to reinstitute the obligatory corvée system, or *ulag* (see Question 85), which they had formerly denounced as feudal, and this weighed heavily on the local people (Shakya 1999: 134ff.). Since Chinese currency was not valid in Tibet up to 1959, the Communists imported large quantities of "silver dollars" *(dayen)*, not only to pay for their food and lodging, but to cover the very high wages they paid Tibetans for road works, constructing barracks, and so on. Moreover, they tried to win over government officials by paying them an additional monthly salary in silver dollars. This led to inflation, which from 1950 to 1959 reached about 3,000 percent. For example, in 1950, a measure of barley, the principal food of the Tibetans, cost about twelve sang (Tib. *srang,* the currency introduced by the 13th Dalai Lama; in 1950, five sang equaled one Indian rupee), but by 1959, the price had risen to 350 sang. The extent of the inflation not only affected food but all other goods as well. Tibetans were thus soon on the brink of starvation.

In addition to the economic problems, the Tibetans suffered from a still more severe threat with regard to their cultural and national identity. For all Tibetans, the practice of Buddhist law has been the most essential part of everyday life. The Communists, however, while officially propagating freedom of religious practice, at the same time started trying to set people against monks and monasteries and also started to intimidate the monks. Slogans like "Religion is the opium of the people" and "Religion is superstition" were propagated in order to discredit Buddhist doctrine. The Communists insulted the monks by calling them "yellow robbers" or "red thieves," alluding to the color of their robes. The threat was continual and was made all the more evident by military bases being located within view of monasteries.

In the years 1953 to 1954, the Communists started to enforce the "Great Reform," the putting into practice of their ideology in Tibet. It is well known that Tibet is one of the few countries in the world whose culture has been deeply penetrated by Buddhism and whose particular social structures have in great part remained unchanged over centuries. There is no doubt about the need for reforms in some fields. However, it makes a big difference whether reforms are initiated by the Tibetans themselves or whether reforms aiming at eliminating their traditions, culture, and national identity are forced on the Tibetan people by a foreign occupying military power.

The Chinese started to ask government officials and renowned Buddhist dignitaries to take part in reeducation programs in regions east of the Yangtse River with Tibetan populations that had been under Chinese administration for some time. Arrests were made and oppression was intensified. As a result, local revolts in the eastern frontier areas of Amdo and Kham broke out. In contrast to the Tibetans of central Tibet, the local Tibetans of this region knew only too well how the Chinese people had suffered from Communist ideology. The PLA at times could not cope with the resistance movement in this area, so the Chinese air force resorted to bombing great monasteries like those of Litang and Chateng. Since a great number of Tibetans had taken refuge in these monasteries, the loss of life caused by these raids was great.

In April 1956, in order to take over political power in Tibet, the Chinese Communists had founded the "Preparatory Committee for the Autonomous Region of Tibet." In Lhasa, an opposition formed among the Tibetans distributed an ever-increasing number of anti-Communist and anti-Chinese leaflets. These activities brought about a difficult situation for the Tibetan government, which could not take the risk of any confrontation with the Chinese. Thus the Dalai Lama because of Chinese pressure had to dismiss a member of his cabinet and to officially criticize the resistance movement. Moreover, the Tibetan government had to arrest and imprison three leaders of an association called the "People's Assembly," founded in 1954, who had dared to present a petition demanding relief from the strict Chinese measures. At the same time, in the eastern part of the country, the Tibetans continued their guerrilla war. A great many of the area's inhabitants—Chinese from the frontier regions among them—left to take refuge in Lhasa and central Tibet.

In 1958, Khampas from eastern Tibet began to organize in resistance units in Lhasa and established their headquarters in southern Tibet. The PLA was highly alarmed. The Chinese reinforced their guards, erected bunkers in strategic places, and piled up sandbags on the roofs of their houses. Even Chinese civilian officials were issued weapons. Chinese pressure on the Tibetan government was intensified. It was demanded that it disarm the Khampa resistance fighters, who had the full support of the Tibetan people. The tension mounted.

The immediate cause for the revolt of the Tibetan people was a strange invitation made to the Dalai Lama by the Chinese. In February 1959, during the Great Prayer *(Mönlam chenmo)* following the New Year celebrations, he was expected to attend a dramatic performance in the Chinese military headquarters. On the occasion of the Great Prayer, about 40,000 monks from the surrounding monasteries and a great number of pilgrims had gathered in Lhasa. On the eve of the performance, a rumor spread that the Dalai Lama was to arrive at the PLA headquarters unescorted. The whole population was greatly alarmed at this, fearing that the Dalai Lama might be kidnapped.

It is noteworthy that the revolt broke out when the threat presented by the occupying Chinese Communists concerned the person of the Dalai Lama, the symbol of Buddhist doctrine, as well as of Tibet's cultural and national identity. On March 10, 1959, thousands of Tibetans hurried to Norbulingka, the summer palace of the Dalai Lama. Heedless of their lives, they formed a human barricade in order to prevent the Dalai Lama from going to the Chinese military headquarters. Their shouts of "Chinese go home!" and "Tibet for the Tibetans!" left no doubt as to their determination. In Lhasa, demonstrations spontaneously took place demanding that the Chinese occupiers leave Tibet. For the first time in Tibetan history, women also assembled, in great numbers, demanding that the Chinese return to their own country.

Since things were getting dangerously out of hand, the Tibetan resistance fighters organized the flight of the Tibetan government. Unaware of its escape, the PLA violently suppressed the desperate, spontaneous revolt of the Tibetan people during the night of March 20, and a great number of

Tibetans were killed. About 80,000, protected by the Khampa resistance fighters, were able to get away to India.

18
How did the Chinese government deal with those who participated in the March 1959 rebellion?

It was in order to preserve feudal serfdom and to "sabotage" the 17-Point Agreement that the "reactionary clique" launched this rebellion. "The broad masses of the Tibetan people and the patriotic members of the upper classes firmly . . . supported the PLA's suppression of the rebellion" ordered by the central government "in order to safeguard the unification of the motherland and the fundamental interests of the Tibetan people."

"Those captured in the rebellion were tried and sentenced according to law." The less guilty have been liberated in the 1960s; in 1979, all the remaining prisoners were set free.

Elliot Sperling

The comments in *100 Questions* to the effect that the fighting in Lhasa in 1959 was an attempt by Tibet's "reactionary clique" to preserve feudal serfdom distorts the complex factors that led to this confrontation, which have been briefly described in relation to Questions 16 and 17. The statement that the broad masses of the Tibetan people supported the suppression is not tenable. By now it is obvious to almost all observers that it is the Dalai Lama who commands (and who then commanded) the loyalty of most Tibetans.

It is true, as *100 Questions* states, that some Tibetans arrested in the wake of the rebellion were released in the 1960s and others were released in 1979 (twenty years after the 1959 fighting). However the authors do not give any figures for the number of Tibetans captured, nor do they describe the conditions of their incarceration. Moreover, they omit the slaughter that the Chinese army inflicted on Tibetans in its campaign against the rebellion (see Questions 21 to 25). Prisoners who survived and who have told of their experiences give similar accounts of forced labor, inadequate rations, and numerous deaths under brutal conditions. All that *100 Questions* says on this score is that they were "tried and sentenced according to law."

PART TWO

Human Rights

China maintains "that the realization of full human rights is a common pursuit of all countries," a formulation that suggests that each country should aspire to give its citizens access to human rights but in practice can implement this ideal only gradually. China ratified the Convention against Torture in 1988 and the International Covenant on Economic, Social and Cultural Rights in 2001, and in 2004, Beijing said that it was "actively considering approving" the International Covenant on Civil and Political Rights. It rejects the right of any other nation to criticize its human rights record, and most Western governments have replaced public criticism of China with closed "human rights dialogues," which generally discuss theoretical or institutional issues and not individual cases. China has increasingly emphasized economic and social rights over individual rights, and the 2001 edition of *100 Questions* removed all references to individual rights that had been included in the earlier edition, except for a discussion of religious rights. This chapter retrieves the questions and answers on human rights found in the 1989 edition. These covered issues of imprisonment, executions, travel, discrimination, and unemployment, which are absent from the later edition, as well as issues of local autonomy, social rights, education, health, and birth control, which are found in both versions.

19

WHAT WERE THE CONDITIONS REGARDING HUMAN RIGHTS IN TIBET BEFORE DEMOCRATIC REFORM? [QUESTIONS 12, 13, AND 92, 2001]

Before 1959, all except 5 percent of the Tibetan population were slaves or serfs in a feudal system in which they were regarded as saleable private property, had no land or freedom, and were subject to punishment by mutilation or amputation [from both the 1989 and 2001 editions]. The serfs were liable to be tortured or killed [from the 1989 edition]. Economy and culture were stagnant for centuries, life expectancy was 35.5 years, illiteracy was over 90 percent, 12 percent of Lhasa's population were beggars, and the Dalai Lama was responsible for all of this [from the 2001 edition].

ROBERT BARNETT

Official Chinese texts about Tibet treat the issue of human rights as comparative. So they argue that conditions in Tibet are better than they were before China took over direct administration of the region in 1959. All Chinese sources describe the previous conditions as "feudal serfdom," and the word "serf" occurs some thirty-five times in the 2001 edition. This approach skirts the question of whether current conditions meet international standards and implies increasingly that individual rights have to be sacrificed for economic or social rights to exist. Since 1990, Chinese leaders have justified this in terms of the need to ensure "stability."

Melvyn Goldstein, an American anthropologist who carried out research within Tibet into pre-1959 social relations, concluded that most Tibetans before 1959 were bound by written documents to the land on which they were based and to the lord who owned that land, and so he argued that they could be described as "serfs" (Goldstein 1986, 1988). Most Western scholars accept that this was broadly the case, but query the extensiveness of the practice and the politics behind the terms used to describe it. Franz Michael and Beatrice Miller argued that the less loaded words "commoner" or "subject" are more accurate than the word "serf," partly because of ample evidence that a large number of Tibetans were able to moderate their obligations to their lords by paying off some of their dues, and so could move from place to place. Tibet also had a functioning legal system to which they could appeal in some cases (Miller 1987, 1988; Michael 1986, 1987). Dieter Schuh (1988) showed that those who might technically be called "serfs" were in fact relatively prosperous—the majority were often poorer, but in many cases they were not "bound to the land" and so were not technically "serfs." Girija Saklani (1978) argued that the feudal-type institutions in Tibetan society were counterbalanced by factors that reflected "the principle of cohesion and collectivity" rather than of a rigid hierarchy. W. M. Coleman (1998) has pointed out that in practice the Tibetans had more autonomy than appears in the written documents, and that Tibetans could equally well be described simply as peasants with particular kinds of debts and taxation responsibilities, rather than using a politically and morally loaded term such as "serf." Other scholars have noted that such social categories, Marxist or otherwise, are in any case rooted in European history and do not match the social system of pre-1951 Tibet, let alone the very different arrangements found among the people of eastern Tibet.

These scholars do not disagree with the Chinese claim that Tibet had a particular form of social relations that differed from those later found in democratic and Communist countries. What is contested is whether later scholars or politicians should use terms that imply a value judgment about the moral quality of these relations. This is a matter of intense dispute, because the Chinese claim about serfdom, on the surface a factual account of social relations, in fact depends for its effects on its linkage to two other elements, which are highly contestable—feudalism and extreme oppression. It is taken for granted that these are inseparable from serfdom. A conscious effort of the intellect is required to recall that one does not follow from the other.

There is no question but that Tibet was an extremely poor society for most of its members, or that the poorest were the most liable to exploitation and abuse. This was true of most sectors of any society in Asia and elsewhere until recently, including China, and is still true today in many areas. So even if it were agreed that serfdom and feudalism existed in Tibet, this would be little different other than in technicalities from conditions in any other "premodern" peasant society, including most of China at that time. The power of the Chinese argument therefore lies in its implication that serfdom, and with it feudalism, is inseparable from extreme abuse.

Evidence to support this linkage has not been found by scholars other than those close to Chinese governmental circles. Goldstein, for example, notes that although the system was based on serfdom, it was not necessarily feudal, and he refutes any automatic link with extreme abuse. "I have tried to indicate that the use of the concept of 'serfdom' for Tibet does not imply that lords tortured and otherwise grossly mistreated their serfs. . . . There is no theoretical reason why serfdom should be inexorably linked to such abuses," he writes, noting that extreme maltreatment was unlikely since it would have been against the interests of landowners, who needed the peasants to provide labor (1988: 64–65).

There seems to be limited evidence of the systematic savagery described by Chinese writers, at least since the late nineteenth century. There was a famous case of mutilation as a punishment in 1924, but the officials involved were themselves punished by the 13th Dalai Lama for this action; he had banned all such punishments in a proclamation in 1913 (Goldstein 1989: 123–26, 61). A case of judicial eye gouging in 1934 as a punishment for treason was clearly exceptional, since no one living knew how to carry it out (Goldstein 1989: 208–9). On the other hand, there are hundreds of reports, many of them firsthand accounts, of Tibetan political prisoners being severely tortured in Chinese prisons during the early 1990s, as well as almost ninety cases of suspicious deaths in custody (see, e.g., TCHRD 2005), none of which have been independently investigated.

The more important question is why Chinese officials raise the issue of conditions in pre-1959 Tibet at all. They are entitled to argue that these might tell us something about the views of the Dalai Lama and other Tibetan rulers at that time, although this would ignore the efforts of the 13th and 14th Dalai Lamas to ameliorate the social system (in 1913, for example, the 13th Dalai Lama declared an amnesty for all serfs who had run away from their landlords and gave all vacant land to whoever was working it), let alone the attempts of senior officials like Lungshar and Künphel to reform the system. But the issue is hardly relevant, since a country is not entitled to take over a neighbor merely because social or political conditions there are backward. In addition, human rights are not usually judged by improvement, as if they were economic statistics, but by whether or not they meet current international standards. A regime does not normally argue that its abuses are justified because they are less than those of a regime half a century earlier; racism in contemporary America would not be considered acceptable even if it were in a form less odious than, say, lynchings in the 1950s. The social practices of a previous regime are only of marginal relevance to the human rights practices of its successor.

In any case, China made no claims at the time of its invasion or liberation of Tibet to be freeing Tibetans from social injustice. It declared then only that it was liberating them from "imperialism" (meaning British and U.S. interference). The issue of freeing Tibetans from feudalism appeared in Chinese rhetoric only after around 1954 in eastern Tibet and 1959 in central Tibet (Goldstein 1986: 109n2). Its justification then became that it was freeing them from class oppression. In the 1980s, this also changed: it now claims to be freeing them from "backwardness," or lack of modernization.

Chinese references to preliberation conditions in Tibet thus appear to be aimed at creating popular support for Beijing's project in Tibet. These claims have particular resonance among people who share the assumption—based on nineteenth-century Western theories of "social evolution" that are still widely accepted in China—that certain forms of society are "backward" and should be helped to evolve by more "advanced" societies. This form of prejudice converges with some earlier Chinese views and with vulgar Marxist theories that imagine a vanguard movement liberating the oppressed classes or nationalities in a society, whether or not those classes agree that they are oppressed. Moreover, the Chinese have to present that oppression as very extensive, and that society as very primitive, in order to explain why there were no calls by the Tibetan peasantry for Chinese intervention on their behalf.

The question of Tibet's social history is therefore highly politicized, and Chinese claims in this respect are intrinsic to the functioning of the PRC, and not some free act of intellectual exploration. They have accordingly to be treated with caution. From a human rights point of view, the question of whether Tibet was feudal in the past is irrelevant. A more immediate question is why the PRC does not allow open discussion of whether Tibet was feudal or oppressive. Writers and researchers in Tibet face serious repercussions if they do not concur with official positions on issues such as social conditions in Tibet prior to its "liberation," and in such a restrictive climate, the regime's claims on this issue have little credibility.

20

WHAT RIGHTS DO THE TIBETAN PEOPLE ENJOY? [QUESTION 92, 2001]

Tibetans enjoy "all the rights as stipulated in China's Constitution": the right to administer "state affairs, economic and cultural enterprises and social affairs; and the freedom of religious belief, speech, publication, assembly, association, and demonstration." Moreover, they enjoy particular rights linked to the status of regional autonomy for ethnic minorities such as the right to establish autonomous organs and "the freedom to develop their own spoken and written language, and the freedom to keep and reform their own customs and habits."

[The 2001 edition gives considerable detail about the rights to self-government (Questions 14–16) and the freedom of religious belief

(Questions 85–89). But it makes no reference to the existence of any other civil or political rights or freedoms in Tibet. Instead, in answer to Question 92, it says only, "Tibet was one of the most backward areas in the world" until 1959 when "feudal serfdom was abolished," thus showing that "the situation of human rights in Tibet has improved significantly." No further indication is given concerning individual rights apart from statement that after 1959, "Tibetans began enjoying their rights of personal freedom, as stipulated in China's Constitution."]

Robert Barnett

The Chinese constitution of 1982 guarantees all Chinese citizens a number of rights, including freedom of speech, assembly, opinion, religious belief, and publication. However, these appear to be viewed in China as a set of aspirations, not as legally enforceable rights that people can claim at will. Indeed, these are described as "freedoms," not as rights. The word "freedom" usually refers to an occasional privilege granted by a state when it sees fit, and the use of this term here suggests that Chinese citizens do not have the right—in the sense of an inalienable privilege owed to human beings by virtue of their humanity, which a state is not normally entitled to withdraw—to exercise these freedoms.

The PRC's constitution and criminal code make it clear that a citizen or a people can enjoy these "freedoms" only if they do not infringe various norms, such as "the socialist road," the Marxist-Leninist-Maoist system, the leadership of the Communist Party, and the "democratic dictatorship of the proletariat" (or, more commonly nowadays, of "the people"). These and similar "cardinal principles" have been written into the latest version of the criminal code (1997) as part of the definition of crime in China, which covers "all acts that endanger the sovereignty, territorial integrity, and security of the state; split the state; subvert the political power of the people's democratic dictatorship and overthrow the Socialist system."[1] The 1997 code established another overarching crime, "endangering state security," thus setting up an-

---

1. Article 13 of the PRC criminal law, amended on March 14, 1997. See Xinhua 1997. A similar list is given in article 2, describing the purposes of the criminal law. Acts against social and economic order, damage to state and private property, and so on are listed secondarily in both articles. Article 1 of the Chinese constitution (1982) reads: "The socialist system is the basic system of the People's Republic of China. Disruption of the socialist system by any organization or individual is prohibited." Article 4 reads: "Any act which undermines the unity of the nationalities or instigates division is prohibited."

other inviolable norm open to wide interpretation and used by officials to override any "freedoms" offered elsewhere in Chinese legislation.

The later edition of *100 Questions* does not even refer to any individual rights in Tibet apart from "the right to freedom of religious belief" (see Part V below).

Freedom of speech, publication, and assembly are similarly conditional in the PRC—they are allowed only if the activity does not threaten the Communist Party, the state, socialism, China's territorial claims, the "unity of nationalities" *(minzu tuanjie)*, state security, and other variable political criteria. In the 1980s, for example, it was permissible to criticize the Communist Party's economic strategies; by 2000, it had become unsafe for any Tibetan to criticize the policy of constructing a railway to Lhasa, let alone policies encouraging Chinese migration into the region.

The issue of publications and news sources is addressed in Question 73 of the 2001 edition, which gives the number of printing presses, TV stations, newspapers, and cinemas in Tibet, without mentioning that all forms of media and publication are controlled and vetted by the state. As a result, no contrary views of important policies are published or broadcast in Tibet, and no outside publications or media are allowed distribution. The Internet is widely available in towns, but access to a vast number of foreign web sites is forbidden (with increasing assistance from foreign firms like Google), identity cards have to be shown before using a public terminal, sites and messages with critical content are routinely blocked, and several people have been imprisoned as a result of information given about their computer use by foreign firms like Yahoo (see Alme and Vågen 2006).

The legal and political systems in China do not offer due process, and there is no independent judiciary. Decisions in important cases are made by Party officials, and forced confessions are routinely accepted as evidence. Fewer than 2 percent of cases in China end in acquittal, and the number is certainly much lower in Tibet. A large proportion of custodial sentences— those of "reeducation through labor" *(laojiao)*—are decided arbitrarily by administrative committees. The Chinese political system allows citizens the right to vote, but there is only one ruling Party, candidates for all positions are chosen by the Party, and each governmental, police, judicial, or military office is run by an embedded Party group or cell.

The Chinese authorities do give citizens significant economic and social rights, including access to educational and health facilities, and Tibetans, as one of the fifty-five "minority nationalities" recognized in China, have the right to autonomy or self-governance (see Part VI below). In practice, these rights are severely limited and ineffectual—to give one example, since 1992, criticism of PRC policies allowing Chinese migration into Tibet has been outlawed as a form of "narrow nationalism, . . . feudal ideas and the xenophobic mind-set," even though such flows are controlled in certain other areas of China and the Minority Nationality Regional Autonomy Law of 1984 allows each nationality to regulate migration into its area. "Historic experience tells us that keeping a long stable core of officials of the Han and other nationalities in Tibet is . . . needed to defend national unity," it is contended (*Tibet Daily* 1998).

21
SOME PEOPLE HAVE SAID THAT TIBET HAS SEVERAL HUNDRED PRISONS HOLDING MANY THOUSANDS OF POLITICAL PRISONERS. OTHERS HAVE CLAIMED THAT TIBET HAS 73 PRISONS WITH 80,000 PRISONERS. WHAT ARE THE FACTS? [NOT INCLUDED IN THE 2001 EDITION]

The TAR has only one prison and two reform-through-labor teams. There are some 900 prisoners, and all are guilty of criminal acts. All those who were involved "in the 1959 rebellion have already been released."

ROBERT BARNETT

At the time when these statements were made, Chinese officials used the term "prison" only to describe a facility confining people formally convicted of a crime by a court. However, most people serving a custodial sentence in China have received it from an administrative or police committee, not a court. Places of detention holding people who have not been given the right to a trial are not recognized as prisons by the Chinese government. These "nonprisons" include "reeducation through labor" camps (Chin. *laojiao*), detention centers (*kanshousuo*), juvenile holding centers, and, until June 2003, shelter and investigation centers (*shourongsuo*). There are also police lockups, People's Armed Police prisons, and military prisons (see Human Rights Watch 1996). To say that there is only one prison in Tibet ignores these other institutions and is therefore disingenuous.

There are at least seven of these "nonprisons" in the Lhasa inner urban area (the *chengguanqu*) alone, including those known locally as Gutsa, Trisam, Sangyip, and Seitru ("Unit 4"), and one detention center in each of the seventy-four counties in the TAR, as well as in each of the sixty-five Tibetan counties outside the TAR. There is almost certainly one "reeducation through labor" camp in each of the seven prefectures in the TAR and the nine Tibetan prefectures outside the TAR. There are additional "reform through labor" camps in Qinghai and Sichuan, which hold prisoners from other parts of China (see, e.g., Marshall and Cooke 1997).

The single prison referred to in the 1989 edition of *100 Questions* is "TAR Prison No. 1," known more commonly as Drapchi, after the area of Lhasa in which it is located, with about 900 prisoners. In 1998, the Chinese authorities first admitted the existence of two further prisons (in their sense of the word) in the TAR, with 1,400 inmates: "TAR Prison No. 2" in Powo Tramo, about 250 km east of Lhasa, and "TAR Prison No. 3," apparently opened to serve the Lhasa municipal area in 1997 (Xinhua 1998; TIN 1998). Another prison, specially for housing long-term political prisoners, was established in Chushül, just to the west of Lhasa, in 2006.

The total number of prisoners in broader Tibet is unknown; the Chinese authorities said in 2001 that the three official prisons held 115 prisoners sentenced for "subversion" (*People's Daily* 2001), but they have never given numbers for other prisons. In 1995, independent sources compiled the names of at least 700 political prisoners in custody throughout Tibet, and in 2001 Tibetan exiles presented a list of 252 such prisoners (Marshall 2001; TCHRD 2001), believed now by some observers to be around 150.

The number of Tibetans detained after the 1959 rebellion or uprising is unknown, but is believed to have run to many thousands (see Question 22). Most of those who survived were released only in 1978 or 1979.

22

SOME FOREIGN NEWSPAPERS HAVE CLAIMED THAT THE CHINESE KILLED MORE THAN 1 MILLION TIBETANS. IS THIS TRUE?
[QUESTION 56, 2001]

No. This is a lie concocted by the Dalai clique. In 1953, the local government of Tibet headed by the Dalai Lama reported that the local population was 1 million. The whole Tibetan population would have been wiped out if 1.2 million people were killed after the peaceful liberation of Tibet in 1951. According to the fifth national census in 2000, the population of Tibet was 2.6163 million, with Tibetan people accounting for 92.2 percent. [from the 2001 edition]

R O B E R T   B A R N E T T

The Tibetans in exile have not said that a million or so Tibetans were killed by the Chinese. They have said that this number of Tibetans died of un-natural causes as a result of the Chinese invasion. They allege that 680,000 of these were killed in conflict or were executed between 1950 and 1979; some 500,000 deaths, they claim, occurred as a result of famines, suicides, and other factors resulting from Chinese policies.

The claim that Tibetan exile figures for these deaths exceed the population at the time is based on a linguistic manipulation of the meaning of the word "Tibet" (see Question 8 and, for a discussion of the figures, Question 43).

The exile claims about these unnatural deaths between 1950 and 1979 are unverified. The methods by which these figures were compiled remain unclear, and these claims are not used by most scholars or researchers. How-ever, there are credible indications of very severe loss of life among Tibetans. The U.S. government reported that "tens of thousands" of Tibetans were killed in conflict in the 1950s (Tofani 1996); an important Chinese history of the conflicts, later banned for this disclosure, reported that 93,000 Ti-betans in the rebel forces alone were killed, wounded, or imprisoned in central Tibet during the three years from 1959 to 1961 (Ji Youquan 1993). Internal documents obtained by the CIA in the 1960s are said to have re-ferred to 81,000 deaths among Tibetan rebels in 1959–60 (Knaus 1999). On the other hand, an Australian-Chinese demographer for China's Plan-ning Commission, Yan Hao (2000: 11–36), using gaps in the population counts between 1953 and 1964—which he emphasizes were themselves only estimates—guessed that the number of "missing" Tibetans in this twenty-year period could be placed between 768,000 and 152,000, with the lower figure (which would include the 70,000 or so who fled to India) be-ing in his view the most likely.

Since the exile figures include the Tibetan areas now in Qinghai, Gansu, and Sichuan, it is necessary to include the catastrophic deaths in those areas that resulted from policy-induced famine during the ultra-leftist period known as "The Great Leap Forward" (1958–62). The Chinese authorities have never released census figures for the relevant ten-year period (Dom-enach and Richer 1987: 1: 177), which some researchers have said may have led to 27 million deaths in China (one researcher found documentation showing that 900,000 died from the famine in Qinghai and 9 million in Sichuan, with Tibetans among the worst affected [Becker 1996]).

The most important evidence comes from an official report written to

Premier Zhou Enlai in 1962 by the late Panchen Lama, then head of the Tibetan government. The report noted that "there has been an evident and severe reduction in the present-day Tibetan population" due to the fact that "many people were lost in battle," "many people were arrested and imprisoned [which] caused large numbers of people to die abnormal deaths," and "many people died of starvation or because they were so physically weak that they could not resist minor illnesses" (Barnett 1998a: 103). In a speech delivered in 1987, the Panchen Lama estimated the number of prison deaths in Qinghai at around 5 percent of the total population of Tibetans in the area. "In Qinghai, for example, there are between one to three or four thousand villages and towns, each having between three to four thousand families with four to five thousand people. From each town and village, about 800 to 1,000 people were imprisoned. Out of this, at least 300 to 400 people of them died in prison. This means almost half of the prison population perished. . . . Most of these people were completely innocent" (Dharamsala 1991). Five percent of the then Tibetan population in Qinghai would have been approximately 20,000–28,000 people.

Although precise figures are unclear, there is thus extensive evidence that the number of executions and prison and starvation deaths in some Tibetan areas was extremely high during this period.

23

IN 1987, TWO MEN WERE EXECUTED IN TIBET. WERE THEY POLITICAL PRISONERS? [NOT INCLUDED IN THE 2001 EDITION]

The two men executed in September 1987 had been sentenced to death by the People's Court of the TAR and were common criminals who had murdered two other Tibetans in June that year. One was called Gesang Zaxi [Kelsang Tashi]: he had robbed and killed Bianba Renci [Penpa Rinchen?] on June 14; the other one, Chilie Jiancan [Thrinley Gyaltsen] had killed Luosang Yixi [Lobsang Yeshe] on June 7. These were absolutely not political prisoners as claimed by the Dalai Lama and certain people in the United States.

ROBERT BARNETT

Two executions carried out in Lhasa in September 1987 led to rumors among Tibetans in the city that these events were intended to intimidate Tibetans opposed to Chinese policies. There was also a rumor that the two victims were political prisoners. It has not been possible for outside researchers to assess the latter claim, but the sentences were clearly announced in a provocative manner: a special rally at which the prisoners were paraded was held in the Lhasa Sports Stadium, and some 14,000 Tibetans were required to attend, including those who had committed minor workplace offenses in the previous six months. The rally signaled a more aggressive stance by Chinese policy makers toward the Dalai Lama, and any form of Tibetan opposition, in response to a visit earlier that month by the Dalai Lama to the U.S. Congress. Thus, although the details of the cases remain unclear, it seems that the way in which the executions were announced was intended to deliver a political message to the Tibetan populace.

The rumors in Lhasa surrounding this case were partly based on other Tibetan prisoners who were paraded and humiliated at the sentencing rally in the Sports Stadium, but not executed. One was Migmar Tashi, who was given a suspended death sentence at the 1987 rally for a murder he had committed. The details of that crime are unclear, but Migmar's subsequent history proves that executions in Tibet are sometimes falsely attributed by the authorities to common criminal offenses when in fact they are for political acts or beliefs.

Migmar Tashi was executed, along with a Tibetan named Dawa, on May 18, 1990. The authorities declared publicly that the two men had been executed for trying to escape from prison. However, even public announcements stated that the death sentences were handed down for "holding counter-revolutionary views," among other offenses (*Tibet Daily,* May 18, 1990). Internal documents show that two men had formed a secret pro-independence group within Drapchi prison, led by a famous student activist called Lobsang Tenzin, who had a popular following in Lhasa and so was not executed, although he was judged by the court to be the "ringleader" in this case. Migmar and Dawa were minor accomplices and so should not normally have been executed according to Chinese law (Lhasa People's Procuracy Document No. 2, 1989; Lhasa Intermediate People's Court Document No. 13, 1990). Similarly, in neighboring Sichuan province in 2003, an illiterate Tibetan farmer was executed for pro-independence activities and causing explosions, on unclear evidence and without Supreme Court review, while the supposed "ringleader," a prominent lama called Tenzin Delek, again without any publication of significant evidence against him, was given a suspended death sentence, later commuted to a life sentence (see Spiegel 2004). These episodes illustrate the sometimes deceptive political nature of execution decisions by the Chinese authorities in Tibet.

24

WHAT IS THE TRUE STORY OF GESHI LUOSANG WANGZHU,
A SO-CALLED IDEOLOGICAL CRIMINAL THE U.S. CONGRESS HAS ASKED
TO BE RELEASED? [NOT INCLUDED IN THE 2001 EDITION]

There are no "ideological crimes" in the Chinese criminal code and therefore there is no possibility of a person being sentenced for such a crime. This "Geshi" was arrested on September 21, 1960 for having taken part in the counterrevolutionary rebellion and sentenced to ten years in prison. After release, in 1979 and 1980, "he posted reactionary leaflets and concocted so-called history of Tibetan independence," and was rearrested on October 26, 1981. He died from disease, despite receiving "proper medical treatment."

ROBERT BARNETT

Geshe Lobsang Wangchug was a famous Tibetan activist and historian who died from illness in 1987 after being imprisoned for writing and putting up posters about Tibetan independence some seven years earlier (260 copies of another historical essay by him, "Twenty Years of Tragic Experience," were printed in 1981 by Shöl Dawa, a Tibetan, who received a two-year sentence for the offense [see Dharamsala 1995] and died in Drapchi prison in 2000, reportedly as a result of maltreatment [TIN 2000e]).

The account in *100 Questions* does not say that when he died, *Geshe* Lobsang Wangchug was still serving the 18-year sentence imposed on him in 1981 for putting up the posters; or that he was only moved from the prison to a Tibetan hospital four days before he died. According to accounts by people involved in the efforts to save his life, his doctors said that he could have been saved if he had been moved to the hospital earlier (TIN 1989). The attendants who prepared the body for sky burial said that his liver was severely damaged—he had said in the hospital that prison officials had only given him cough mixture to treat this long-standing ailment—and that three of his ribs had been broken some time earlier, probably as a result of a beating by a prison guard. There are no reports of any postmortem carried out by the authorities, or of any investigation into the claims that the elderly scholar had been beaten.

His fellow prisoner Palden Gyatso, who in 1980 had helped put up the posters, wrote after his escape to India that the authorities had been particularly hostile to *Geshe* Lobsang Wangchug and that they "treated him with a special hatred. Even at the age of seventy-five his hands and feet were shackled and he was made to do hard labor" (Palden Gyatso 1997).

It is true that there are no crimes in the Chinese criminal code described specifically as "ideological." However, all crimes relevant to Tibetan political cases until 1997 were described in the code as "acts of counterrevolution," which is clearly an ideological concept. The term was changed to "acts endangering state security" in the revised code of 1997, which included "all acts that . . . subvert the political power of the people's democratic dictatorship and overthrow the socialist system" (Article 13 of the PRC Criminal Law, amended March 14, 1997). *Geshe* Lobsang Wangchug was not accused of any action by Chinese officials apart from "attempting to split the motherland" by putting up posters and writing a book. Since the posters did not call for violence, in international law writing or distributing them could not be considered a crime, and he was therefore a political prisoner incarcerated because of his peacefully expressed opinions.

25

IT HAS BEEN CLAIMED THAT THE CHINESE HAVE TRIED PRISONERS
IN TIBET AT MASS RALLIES, AFTER WHICH THEY WERE IMMEDIATELY
KILLED. IS IT TRUE? [NOT INCLUDED IN THE 2001 EDITION]

China is a unified state and all courts follow the same laws and procedures, according to the Criminal Code of the PRC. Criminals who are convicted are judged by a court and not at a mass rally, but sometimes executions are carried out at a mass rally "because of the serious nature of their crimes and the desire of the people to see justice done."

ROBERT BARNETT

Until approximately 2000, the Chinese authorities in Tibet typically paraded prisoners in front of the public before taking them away to an execution ground to be shot. The international community deems the practices of public sentencing and public execution to be humiliating and degrading to prisoners and therefore illegal in international law. The Chinese government said some years ago that it would discontinue public executions, and there are few or no reports of prisoners being publicly executed in Tibet in recent times. However, the practice of public sentencing, and in particular the parading of condemned prisoners through the streets, was commonplace in Tibet and in China until recently, particularly before sensitive anniversaries when unrest is expected. The prisoners' heads are shaved, they are tied in a manner that forces them to lower their heads, and they are festooned with boards around their necks displaying their names and alleged crimes. On December 2, 1998, for example, a number of prisoners were paraded in a convoy of trucks through Lhasa, eight days before the anniversary of the awarding of the Nobel Peace Prize to the Dalai Lama in 1989. The prisoners were driven through the city in open trucks escorted by soldiers in combat gear with machine guns mounted on the trucks, suggesting that the treatment of the prisoners was intended to intimidate the public, and that the event had a primarily political purpose.

26

SOME PEOPLE HAVE ACCUSED CHINA OF CARRYING OUT "RACIAL SEGREGATION" AND "RACIAL DISCRIMINATION" IN TIBET. WHAT IS THE REALITY? [NOT INCLUDED IN THE 2001 EDITION]

This is not true. Equality between the fifty-six nationalities in China is a political guarantee of the Chinese Communist Party. The central government has given great support to Tibet for its economic development and the improvement of the standard of living of the population. It respects the religious beliefs, customs, and habits of the Tibetans. "It has helped Tibet to achieve regional autonomy and to train tens of thousands of Tibetan cadres, who represent 61 percent of the cadres in Tibet" [from the French edition]. These cadres can be found at all levels of the government organizations, and all prefecture, county, and township leaders in Tibet are Tibetans.

ROBERT BARNETT

The Chinese system promises equal representation for Tibetans and their culture in the political system. It has extensive legal commitments that endorse this, and it has spent vast amounts on development in non-Chinese areas. But these concessions are significantly undermined by two notions used by the state as reasons for exemption from this offer of equality: first, any view or activity that might question such principles as the supremacy of the socialist system, or the policy of "national unity" is forbidden. Second, affirmative action in favor of non-Chinese nationalities does not apply to the Communist Party or the military. Since many Tibetans and others disagree with some Party policies, and since all power in the Chinese system resides with the Party and the military, these two exceptions make the theoretical attempts to procure equality between nationalities in China of largely cosmetic value.

The Chinese state has made intensive efforts to improve the statistical equality of Tibetan officials since 1980 and has trained thousands of Tibetans to work as cadres, to the point where they constituted 72 percent of the TAR cadre force by 2000. This was some 20 percent below the officially recognized proportion of Tibetans in the population, which the Chinese government put at just over 92 percent that year, even though this figure for Tibetan cadres included all levels of government employees, including technicians and cleaning and facilities staff. Only a small percentage of these cadres work in the administration, and even fewer of them have senior positions. Many of those who enjoy higher-level positions are in posts that are largely ceremonial, such as the People's Political Consultative Conference or the People's Congress (Conner and Barnett 1997). In addition, nominal heads of offices are often less powerful than one or other of their deputy leaders, of whom one is frequently Chinese.

In any case, since all government offices are in fact run by the Party, the significant distribution of power depends on membership of the upper ranks of the Party and the military, not on government or congressional positions. Between 1950 and 1987, 489 Tibetans held leadership positions in the Party in the TAR, compared to 1,826 Chinese; 69 Tibetans held such positions in the TAR military, as against 528 Chinese (see PRC 1993). The significant proportion of Tibetans in the cadre force at that time, judged by these figures, was thus 21.1 percent in the Party and 11.6 percent in the military.

It was true that most leaders of county governments in the TAR were Tibetans during the 1990s, but even then two leaders of each county were normally Chinese, and each county had at least one deputy leader who was Chinese (Conner and Barnett 1997). Since then, there has been a policy of sinicization of the rural leadership—for example, in 1995, the leader of the Lhokha Prefectural Government in southern Tibet was replaced by a Chinese official. In 2001, Tibet University began three-year training courses for an average of seventy Chinese a year, each of whom on graduation has become a leader at the township *(xiang)* level in the TAR. It is believed that there were never Chinese leaders at this level in the TAR until the first graduates from this group were appointed to their positions in 2004. This new appointment policy will make little difference to aggregated statistics but will radically transform the nature of rural leadership in Tibet and raise doubts about the seriousness of official claims concerning ethnic equality and self-governance at the grassroots level.

China's record on racial discrimination is far better than that of many states, particularly in terms of its legislation, which promises equality between ethnic groups. But these admirable concessions are undermined by the government's ideological position on these questions. The official Chinese view of Tibetans and other non-Chinese nationalities is that they are backward; this is stated openly, in line with the Marxist theory of economic and social determinism. Tibetans are regularly described as leftovers from a society with feudal characteristics that is to be improved by Chinese society, openly declared to be more advanced. The official view depicts this relationship as one of exchange between the two peoples and does not acknowledge that it involves domination—the Chinese provide civilization and economic advancement to the lesser nationalities, and in return the lesser nationalities provide natural resources, such as minerals and land space, to their Chinese compatriots (see, e.g., Ma Yin 1989: 3). This classification of nationalities as "backward" is inherently discriminatory.

Furthermore, Chinese policy since at least 1992 has ruled that it is in the interests of the Tibetans, as of other non-Chinese peoples, to have an unrestricted flow of ethnic Chinese migrants into their areas in order to advance Tibetan society. This practice, which Tibetans are apparently not allowed to contest, tends to produce a major imbalance in the urban economy and in government in favor of non-Tibetans. This means that the "affirmative action" practices that were developed in the early 1980s are now largely ineffective other than in certain cultural or scholarly domains.

Thirdly, since at least the time of the Third Tibet Work Forum, a policy meeting held by Chinese leaders in July 1994, the Chinese state has ruled that certain aspects of Tibetan culture and religion are not "compatible" with socialism and must be eliminated (see Question 49). Most significantly, there is continuing failure to introduce Tibetan as the language of teaching in secondary schools and colleges in the TAR, despite a legal commitment to do that given by the government in 1987. The views that generate these controls are not intended to be racist, but they produce policies that, except in periods of liberalization such as the early 1980s, undermine theoretical rights established in the constitution or in Chinese law and strongly disadvantage Tibetans and other non-Chinese nationalities. The practical outcome of these policies may be seen from the fact that in 2000, three times as many copies of local newspapers were printed in the TAR in

Mandarin as in Tibetan, although Chinese are only one-twentieth of the population (PRC, *TSY,* 2001: table 16-25). This was a marked drop from 1989–95, when the number of Tibetan copies had equaled 75 percent of Chinese copies.

27
SOME PEOPLE HAVE SAID THAT TIBETANS CANNOT ACT
FREELY IN TIBET, AND THAT TIBETAN CADRES AND CHILDREN
AGED UNDER 18 CANNOT TRAVEL ABROAD. IS THIS TRUE?
[NOT INCLUDED IN THE 2001 EDITION]

It is false. Tibetans enjoy democratic rights and freedoms assured by the constitution. They can travel freely within Tibet and foreigners are allowed to come to see the actual situation. The number of Tibetans going abroad to give lectures, study, or visit relatives increases year by year. Several Tibetan art troupes have also gone abroad to give performances. However, the TAR government has been forced "to take some precautions" because separatists in exile attempt to lead children out of the country with the aim of indoctrinating them with reactionary ideas about "Tibetan independence."

ROBERT BARNETT

It is true that an increasing number of Tibetans with financial resources or official connections can obtain travel papers, and in the 1990s, a significant number were for the first time allowed to go abroad as individuals for study, business, or tourism. (However, most of these travel papers do not allow the bearers to visit India, where the exile community is based.) Government employees in the TAR usually have to return their passports between each journey and to seek permission for each trip, whether it is for private or official purposes. Most concessions on travel apply only to the elite: Tibetans without connections or large funds are often refused passports without any reason being given, or are made to wait for several years. This is clear from the fact that since 1985, some 2,000 to 3,000 Tibetans have fled from Tibet each year to Nepal and India without legal papers, at great personal risk, indicating that it is difficult or dangerous for ordinary Tibetans to obtain legal travel papers from the Chinese authorities. The "precautions" taken to counter exile indoctrination increased markedly in 1994, when officials in Tibet were banned from allowing their children to attend any exile school. Since then government offices have not been allowed to employ Tibetans who have made unauthorized visits to India (see TIN 1995a, 1995b, and 1997).

As for art troupes, the Chinese government has continued to send these abroad, but they are in most cases strictly regimented, and are threatened with serious punishment if they leave their group unaccompanied, speak with exiles, visit Buddhist temples, or express unapproved views during their travels. For example, the first of a set of five regulations given to the members of one art troupe, sent to the West in 1992, was "strictly preserve the unity of the Motherland, preserve the dignity of the state and of the nationality, do not do anything that is not beneficial to the Motherland, and do not say anything that is bad about the Motherland." Rule number three was: "Strictly carry out the system of reporting and asking for permission [before going out anywhere] and move about collectively. . . . No one is allowed out without permission" (TIN n.d.). The situation has changed little for Tibetans traveling in official art troupes, although some artists can now get permission to travel as individuals.

28

THE DALAI LAMA AND OTHERS SAY THAT TIBETAN CHILDREN HAVE BEEN DEPRIVED OF THE RIGHT TO EDUCATION AND THAT TIBET HAS BECOME AN AREA OF ILLITERACY. IS THIS TRUE? [QUESTION 65, 2001]

Before 1951, there were no schools in Tibet, except for some private courses with no more than 600 students. By the end of 1986, Tibet had 148,000 pupils, of whom 121,000 were in primary schools, and 109,000 of them were Tibetans, or 90 percent of the total. Out of 21,950 secondary pupils, 14,200 were Tibetans. Of the 2,860 students in tertiary institutions, 1,900 were Tibetans [from the 1989 edition]. In old Tibet, education was backward, and there were no modern schools. Only some 2,000 lamas and children of noble families were eligible to study in old-style official and private schools. By 1998, Tibet had built four modern colleges—Tibet University, the Ethnic University, the Agricultural and Animal Husbandry Institute, and the Institute of Tibetan Medicine, as well as sixteen secondary specialized schools of teaching, agriculture and animal husbandry, health-care, Tibetan medicine, economy and finance, sports, arts, posts and telecommunications, ninety middle schools and 4,251 primary schools. In 1998, the school enrollment rate for children was 81.3 percent, and the registered number of pupils was more than 370,000, with Tibetan students as the majority. The number of teaching staff stood at 16,000, two-thirds being Tibetan teachers. Over the past fifty years, there have been 18,000 university graduates and 510,000 primary-school and middle-school graduates in Tibet, of whom 40,000 are graduates of secondary specialized schools, senior middle schools, and vocational schools, and 15,000 cadre-training-course graduates [from the 2001 edition].

ROBERT BARNETT

The Chinese authorities have improved education significantly in Tibet since they arrived in 1951, and the number of children registered in schools has more than doubled between 1990 and 2000, according to official figures. This trend is not unique to China and is true of many developing nations in Asia over this period.

Despite some positive developments during the 1990s, a number of significant problems in education exist in the TAR that are not addressed by the figures presented by *100 Questions*, particularly the 2001 edition, which discloses less information than the earlier edition. For example, the school enrollment rate in the TAR (which dropped markedly in the early 1980s and only began to recover in 1987) remains the lowest in China; some experts believe that the enrollment figures may only show those who attend the first day of a term; by 2001, only five of the seventy-four counties in the TAR had been able to implement the nine year compulsory education program (Li Xiao 2002).

The larger problems are structural, and are concealed by aggregated statistics: as a UN assessment put it, there is "a striking difference" in education levels between the sexes, ethnic Chinese residents have higher education levels than Tibetans, and people in rural areas of the TAR have a much lower educational level than people in towns or cities. This was partly due to a surge in enrollment after the Cultural Revolution, but Catriona Bass, a British researcher, noted as late as 1999 that "according to official statistics . . . enrolment in primary schools is . . . lower than 10 per cent in some rural prefectures" (TIN 1999a).

As for the urban-rural discrepancy, Bass found that in 1990, when primary school enrollment was 67 percent for the whole TAR, in rural areas it was only 17 percent (Bass 1998, § 4.1.3), a pattern that is not known to have changed greatly since then—as of 1999 there was only one rural secondary school in Tibet. Primary school dropout appears to be a significant area of difficulty—UNICEF estimated in 2004 that the rate in the TAR was 30–35 percent, compared to 0.55 percent in China as a whole.[2] Official statistics indicate that it might be higher, or that some schools may not yet offer the full six years of primary education: of 52,700 children who entered TAR primary schools in 1992, only 30,700 graduated six years later, a 41.7 percent drop (PRC, *TSY*, 2001: tables 16-6 and 16-7). Teaching quality is reported to be low, and in one county in 1995, only 31 out of 208 rural teachers had been educated beyond junior secondary school level (personal source). The figure given in *100 Questions* for 4,251 primary schools is incorrect—there were 842 primary schools in the TAR in 2000. Some official newspaper articles refer to some 3,000 "teaching centers," but it is not known what these are, and they do not appear in official statistics.

The secondary school sector in Tibet is small and predominantly urban. Of those students who completed primary school in the TAR in 2000, only 55 percent went on to middle school (plus a small number who went to schools in China proper). This was a significant drop, since the average for the previous ten years had been 66 percent. In the same year, there were only 212 middle school students per 10,000 people in the TAR, compared to 660 in the PRC as a whole—39 percent of China's school students are in secondary schools, compared to 16 percent in the TAR. Tibet has four tertiary level colleges, but there are only 21 college students per 10,000, half the equivalent number for China as a whole, and in 2000, only four out of 813 teachers in Tibet's tertiary-level institutions had doctorates, and only 37 had master's degrees (PRC, *TSY*, 2001: table 16-16).

The secondary and tertiary sectors face an additional problem in Tibet: an increased proportion of Chinese students. The 1989 edition of *100 Questions* gives figures that show that already by 1986, some 33 percent of secondary and college students in the region were not Tibetan, although only 4 percent of the population at the time were listed as non-Tibetans. In 1994, only 29.2 percent of students at the Tibet College of Agriculture and Animal Husbandry and 19.5 percent of the students at the Tibet Nationalities Institute were Tibetans; the proportion of Tibetan graduates was even smaller (PRC, *TSY*, 1995). These figures reflect a pattern of non-Tibetan students from China being sent to Tibetan schools: this is because the lower standards give them a much better chance of getting into a university and

2. UNICEF 2004; PRC 2001. According to UNICEF, 92% of primary school students in China reached fifth grade in 2003.

of obtaining government positions subsequently, since college graduates in Tibet, alone in the PRC, still get automatic job placements (this was true at least until 2007). They also reflect a much wider pattern of Tibetan students being trained in arts and humanities subjects, often regarded as inferior for future work prospects, while the majority of science and technical students are Chinese.

The presence of Chinese students in Tibetan classrooms exacerbates the difficult issue of the Tibetan language, which appears to be less and less an educational priority in Tibet other than for specialist classes (see Question 75). There is no mention of any commitment to Tibetan-medium or to bilingual education in the 2001 edition of *100 Questions,* which says only that "the Tibetan language is a major item on the curriculum of schools at all levels in Tibet" (Question 66). The Tibetan education system is improving, but at the cost of marginalizing the Tibetan language, and with limited reach to rural and poorer Tibetans (see Question 61).

29

IT IS REPORTED THAT THERE ARE SERIOUS PROBLEMS OF UNEMPLOYMENT AND CHILD LABOR AMONG THE TIBETANS. IS THAT TRUE? (NOT INCLUDED IN THE 2001 EDITION)

The problem of unemployment does not exist in Tibet. In fact there are not enough Tibetan workers to fill available vacancies. The great majority of workers are Tibetans who enjoy the same conditions as the Han in terms of salaries, welfare, and work protection. Child labor is forbidden and has never been a serious problem in Tibet, although in the countryside, children often work with their families in farming and herding.

ROBERT BARNETT

Employment conditions overall in Tibet are probably broadly similar to those in other societies where a government is trying to mechanize rural labor to produce a surplus of rural workers and boost the resources available for urban development: there is a surplus of unskilled rural workers with little opportunity for employment in the expanding, largely urban, economy.

This strategy, which is anyway regarded by some economists as flawed, faces two major problems in Tibet. First, it usually requires industrialization—

which brings its own problems—to absorb labor and generate wealth. But few industries have developed in Tibet apart from agriculture, and those that have (such as mining) prefer to import Chinese labor. So employment prospects for unskilled Tibetans are not promising. The construction industry is a major source of local employment, because of government investment in infrastructural expansion, but almost all but the least skilled jobs go to migrant Chinese laborers. Tibet's major construction project in recent years, the Golmud to Lhasa railway, for example, employed an estimated 27,000 workers, of whom only 7,800 were Tibetans. (A senior TAR official said that "most of the work units on the railway come from inland . . . but we do employ some local people to do manual work, like digging" [Gittings 2002].)

The second problem is that, especially since 1992, when intra-provincial checkpoints were removed, Chinese governmental policies have favored the migration of non-Tibetans into the region, creating a large body of Chinese laborers who are relatively more skilled in urban work than their Tibetan counterparts. As a result, Tibetans face huge competition in the two major sectors of the economy that offer employment in the TAR—the service sector, which produces opportunities for those such as traders, shopkeepers, drivers, and tour guides, and the administrative or governmental sector. Both sectors require skilled or semi-skilled labor, leaving few opportunities for rural Tibetan migrants, and unskilled Tibetans are often likely to lose out to migrant Chinese job seekers in the service sector. In the administration about one quarter of all government employees are Chinese; the authorities claim that this is because Tibetans lack the skills to carry out these functions, but there may also be political factors involved.

The most evident example of the severe lack of employment opportunities in Tibet is the proliferation of Tibetan women involved in prostitution, hostess work, and other forms of the sex and leisure industries (TIN 1999b, 2000c). Prostitution creates extremely high health risks from AIDS and other sexually transmitted diseases. In addition, an increasing number of school-age Tibetan girls from the countryside are taking work as domestic servants in towns. These professions involve no skill development, attract extremely low wages, and have no workplace protection or security.

The disparity between Tibetan and Chinese skill levels is due to a failure by the Chinese authorities to develop training and "human capital" in Tibet before the late 1990s ("A lack of investment in the TAR education system as a whole has led to the perception that the TAR is unable to provide sufficient numbers of well-trained personnel for the economic development of the region and this, in turn, has led to the transfer of large numbers of Han Chinese from central China" [Bass, quoted in TIN 1999a]). For skilled Tibetan workers, and especially those in the government sector, the situation is complicated by the fact that almost all white-collar positions require fluency in Mandarin. There were affirmative action policies to compensate for this requirement during the 1980s, but since the late 1990s, such policies have been reduced throughout the country, and in most areas, government positions and promotions are awarded through open examinations. This is likely to further disadvantage even educated Tibetans, most of whom are less qualified than their Chinese competitors, particularly in Mandarin. In the 1990s, Chinese officials pushed for Tibet to be "fully integrated" into the Chinese economic system, increasing the competition that Tibetans have to face in the marketplace without having had significant opportunities to develop the skills for survival in that system (see also Question 86).

Independent research on child labor has not been carried out in Tibet, although tourists and others frequently report seeing young children working on building sites or begging in the streets.

30
PEOPLE AT THE SIDE OF THE DALAI LAMA ALSO SAID THAT THE HOSPITALS IN TIBET ONLY SERVE THE HAN PEOPLE. IS THAT TRUE? [QUESTION 59, 2001]

This is false. It is well known that in the 1950s, the PLA sent medical teams everywhere who gave free medical care to Tibetans, who are still the only people in China to get free medical care. Over the past thirty years, the majority of patients in the hospitals of the TAR have been Tibetans. The mortality rate has dropped by two-thirds since 1959, and the population growth rate is now 21.15 percent. This could only have happened thanks to the improvement in medical provision [from the 1989 edition]. Farmers and herdsmen in Tibet enjoy free medical services, while urban residents share medical costs with the state. In old Tibet, there were only two official hospitals, both small and poorly equipped. A medical and health network now covers all urban and rural areas. In 1998, there were 1,324 medical institutes in the region, with 6,246 hospital beds, averaging 2.5 beds per 1,000 people. There were also 1.84 doctors and 3.57 medical workers per 1,000 people in Tibet, higher than the national average. The average expected life span has risen from 36 to 65 years in Tibet [from the 2001 edition].

ROBERT BARNETT

Provision of medical care, life expectancy, and the mortality rate have improved dramatically in Tibet since the 1950s, as they have in almost all countries in the world over the past half-century. It is unlikely that anyone has ever claimed that hospitals in Tibet only treat Chinese patients, but it is the case that the best hospitals and the best treatments are unavailable for ordinary people, whether Tibetan or Chinese. This is because the medical system is structured hierarchically and usually only Communist Party leaders and senior officials have access to the best facilities. In Lhasa, the only hospital regarded as having a very high standard of medical treatment, the Military Hospital at Sera, usually only accepts officials at the prefectural level or above.

Extensive concerns have, however, been expressed about the quality of medical care available in Tibet, which remains basic, especially in rural areas, despite the number of facilities. Based on discussions with health officials in Tibet in 2000, an American diplomatic source reported having been told that 3,600 of Tibet's rural "medical workers" probably had little or no training and existed in name alone (U.S. Embassy, Beijing, 2000). In 2005, only 50 of the 119 medical facilities in Lhokha prefecture in southern Tibet were equipped to handle childbirth; a *xiang*- or township-level clinic serving a community of 7,000 people in Lhokha had "only one bed, bought in the 1980s, two pairs of scissors, and one set of obstetric forceps for midwifery," and the midwife at the clinic said standards of sanitation were so low that no one would dare have a child delivered there, according to an official PRC source (*China Daily* 2005).

At the county level, hospital conditions are also reported to be elementary, and the U.S. Embassy report cited above said that "one in five county-level hospitals reportedly cannot conduct simple surgery, and there is only one CT scanner in all of Tibet." Concerns have repeatedly been expressed about standards of hospital care and hygiene even in the Tibetan capital, and in 2000, a team of junior British doctors working at the top public hospital for emergency facilities in Lhasa reported seeing a patient die because doctors had stitched up his stab wound without checking to see whether his airway had been pierced (Hulme et al. 2000).

Medical services were largely free to Tibetans at the time the 1989 edition of *100 Questions* was written, but in the 1990s, the social welfare system in China was replaced by a market-oriented system. Since then only government employees and rural inhabitants can claim (but may not necessarily receive) free treatment, and then probably only in their local facility, if approved by local officials. In all other cases, substantial fees have to be paid for any treatment, making most medical facilities inaccessible to poorer sectors of the community. The British team who worked as observers in the main hospitals in Lhasa and Nagchu in 2000 wrote that in their experience, the healthcare system in Tibet "is in fact a completely private system where even the most basic investigations and treatments are paid for in cash and on the spot." The doctors reported that "unconscious patients had their pockets searched for enough money to pay for an x-ray film, or they simply did not receive one at all. The prices of some of these interventions were often in excess of what a rural worker would earn in six months, and so many could not afford even the most basic levels of care necessary to keep them alive in the department. Half of doctors' pay comes directly from prescribing and carrying out procedures, and many patients with seemingly trivial illnesses were admitted to the ward at Rmb200 a night (US$25), with intravenous antibiotics at extra cost, which would drain the resources of a family for weeks. This may explain why many Tibetans seek help from traditional herbalists in Lhasa" (Hulme et al. 2000; see also Question 74 on Tibetan traditional medicine).

31
How long is the average life span of Tibetans living in Tibet? How is it compared with what it was before the peaceful liberation of Tibet?
[not included in the 2001 edition]

Life expectancy has increased from 35.5 years before 1950 to 63.7 years in 1989, and the population has increased from 1.2 million to 2 million in the same period.

ROBERT BARNETT

There is little reason to doubt that life expectancy has increased in Tibet over the past fifty years, or that it will continue to improve. This statement, however, conceals some other questions. These improvements might have come to Tibet even if the Chinese had not intervened in the running of Tibet in 1950; Tibet might then have been spared some of the catastrophic loss of life associated with Beijing's extreme policies. Some scholars query the exact figures given for life expectancy before 1950, since there were no independent studies of health conditions in Tibet in that period, and it is widely acknowledged that Chinese statistics about Tibet before the 1980s were largely estimates. Reports of severely impoverished rural conditions in Tibet in 1980 suggest that there was little progress in Tibetan health among the rural masses in the first three decades of Chinese rule; advances came mainly from 1980 on. So the progress in health and population may have been uneven. Nevertheless, there is wide agreement about the recent improvement in the overall health of the population, partly because of improvements in nutrition, even though medical care is increasingly expensive.

There is, however, concern about the relatively high death rate among young children and mothers during childbirth. In 2004, UNICEF reported that, despite notable recent improvements, the infant mortality rate in the TAR was 53 per thousand live births and the maternal mortality rate "was over 400 per 100,000 live births, up to eight times higher than the national rate" (UNICEF 2004). Melvyn Goldstein and his colleagues put the infant mortality rate at 12.9 percent in their 2002 survey, although they describe this as low compared to certain communities in Nepal (Goldstein et al. 2002). Infant mortality in China as a whole was officially rated as 3.1 percent in 2003. In 2005, official sources put infant mortality in the TAR at 3.1 percent in 2004 (*People's Daily Online*, March 31, 2005) or 2.6 percent, lower than in China (Feng Jianhua 2005). Other Chinese official publications put the maternal mortality rate in Tibet in 2001 at 327.3 per 100,000, compared to 43.2 per 100,000 in China as a whole, according to Ministry of Health figures. One NGO survey put the rate in one area at nearer 700 per 100,000 (Tibet Poverty Alleviation Fund n.d.: 5). The high rate of perinatal deaths among both mothers and children as late as 2000–2001 and the relative rapidity with which these have since been improved suggest that rural health conditions may have remained retrograde until the 1980s, when figures first become reliable. (For the increase in Tibetan population over the past fifty years, see Question 43.)

The 2000 U.S. Embassy report pointed to other indicators of inadequate progress in health care, including the high prevalence of tuberculosis and hepatitis B in Tibet. One foreign survey found that 51 percent of rural Tibetan children were small because of malnutrition (Harris et al. 2001:

341–47). Only 39 percent of households in Tibet have iodized salt, compared to 95 percent throughout China, a deficiency that leads to severe incidence of mental retardation and goiter (UNICEF 2004).

32
SOME PEOPLE HAVE CLAIMED THAT CHINA PRACTISED FORCED STERILIZATION AND THE KILLING OF INFANTS IN TIBET. IS THIS TRUE? [QUESTION 57, 2001]

The claim is "sheer nonsense" and birth control has been encouraged in Tibet only among Tibetan cadres, workers, and government staff, but in a more lenient way than among Chinese. Tibetans in rural areas have not been asked to practice family planning [from the 1989 edition]. At present 88 percent of Tibetan farmers and herdsmen are not subject to the family-planning policy, but are encouraged to practice birth control in order to give their children a better quality of life. The government of the TAR has, since 1984, advocated a family-planning policy among Tibetan officials, encouraging each couple to have one to two children over several years' span. But there is no restriction on the number of children in Tibetan farming and herdsmen's families. Forced abortion in any form is prohibited in implementing the family-planning policy. In addition, birth control propaganda has not even found its way into the sparsely populated frontier regions of Tibet [from the 2001 edition].

ROBERT BARNETT

The announcement made in the 1989 edition of *100 Questions* probably represented the first official admission that China had imposed population controls on Tibetans working for the government in Tibet. Previously, Chinese officials had implied that there was no birth control policy for Tibetans, although in fact an initial birth control law had been introduced in the TAR in 1985, which was reissued in a stronger form in 1992.

The rules for Tibetans in the TAR are indeed more lenient than for Chinese people, and Tibetans in the countryside are not subject to the same regulations as those imposed on government employees in the TAR. This is clear from table 1, compiled from internal regulations on birth control, which shows that Tibetan cadres can have two children, while their Chinese colleagues can have only one, and that fines for "above plan" children are higher for Chinese couples living in the TAR than for Tibetans. Rural Tibetans in the TAR did not face any limit until the 1992 rules and, as far as is known, are still not threatened with a fine for exceeding that limit (Goldstein et al. 2002). *100 Questions,* however, wrongly implies that only government employees in the TAR are subject to controls. These apply to all urban Tibetans, some 12 percent of the population.

However, rural Tibetans were under significant pressure—even by 1991, the Five-Year Plan issued by the TAR government stated that "the farmers and nomads must self-consciously support and practice the methods of preventing pregnancy," and it had earlier "encouraged" them to have no more than three or four children (TIN 1992d). Although systematic controls have not been implemented in rural areas of the TAR, there have been occasional reports of excessive use of pressure. These reports usually relate to "pilot campaigns" where the authorities have experimented with more aggressive policies in some communities (TIN 1994b; an example of a pilot campaign is given in TIN 2000c). It remains unclear to what extent these operations were forced or how widespread they were. There is no question that the laws in the TAR mandate forced sterilization in certain circumstances, such as for "mobile" or unregistered migrants who become pregnant, and that these laws are implemented in inland China. Yan Hao rejects accusations about excesses against Tibetan women, but affirms that in China sterilization is "routinely suggested to, or forced to a certain extent on, women who already have two or more children," and that of the "nearly 100 million Chinese women [who] have undergone sterilization . . . for most of them it is not a voluntary choice" (Yan 2000: 26–28). It is not known whether or how often these rules are implemented in the TAR.

But Yan also notes that "individual cases of abuse cannot be dismissed completely, particularly in the neighboring provinces of Qinghai and Sichuan, where not only are local regulations different, but policy enforcement is less lenient." Yan does not regard those accounts as significant, but his remarks confirm scholarly findings that most refugee claims of abuses are from areas to the east of the TAR, where birth control laws were introduced in the early 1980s that were stricter and earlier than those in the TAR. As table 1 shows, in the TAP of Kandze (Chin. Ganzi), which covers most of traditional Kham, an urban Tibetan who has a third child has to pay a fine of 15 percent of his or her income for seven years, as does a rural Tibetan who has a fourth child. In Qinghai, the single document obtained so far (most local regulations are secret) orders a "birth prevention operation" for one of any couple with excess children, although it is not clear whether

TABLE 1. Number of Children Allowed to Different Population Segments in the TAR and Kandze (Ganzi)

Group	TAR Regulations 1985		Kandze Regulations 1989		TAR Regulations 1992	
	Number of Children	Fine for Excess Children	Number of Children	Fine for Excess Children	Number of Children	Fine for Excess Children
Urban Chinese	1	500	1	15% of salary for 7 years	1	3,000
Intermarried	2	150	2	ditto	2	500(?)
Rural Chinese[c]			2	15% of salary for 7 years	1	3,000
Mobile Chinese			0	1,000	0	8.000
Tibetan (cadre or worker)	2	150	2	ditto		500
Urban Tibetan	2(?)	150	2	ditto		500
Rural Tibetan			3	ditto		
Mobile Tibetan			0	1,000		8,000

SOURCES: First published in TIN 1994b. The figures are taken from official documents giving regulations for each area, published in translation in TIN 1994a, 46ff.

[a]The 1985 TAR fines are for failing to observe the correct interval between births (three years), not specifically for having an extra child. It is unclear whether they cover all urban Tibetan residents or only those in government offices.

[b]Fines in yuan for first unauthorized child; $1 = 7.73 yuan.

[c]Chinese living in rural areas of Kandze can have two children if they are market gardeners, farmers, or nomads or if they have lived in a high remote area for eight years. If they also live in an isolated place, they can have three children. People in all categories (except "mobile" people and genetically disabled people) can have one extra child under special conditions, such as when a previous child is seriously handicapped with a nonhereditary disease.

[d]"Mobile" people are those without registration papers for the areas in which they are living. They are forcibly sterilized in the TAR if they have a child out of plan unless they return to the place where they are registered.

this meant forced sterilization or if the regulations were carried out (Dharamsala 1993).

Most of the definitive reports of forced sterilizations of Tibetans thus come from the eastern Tibetan areas outside the TAR, where we know that Party officials were set quotas that they had to meet, and where teams of surgeons were sent round villages in the 1980s to implement those policies by force. A number of serious incidents involving the use of force have been documented from that period (TIN 1994b: 46ff.). It remains unclear how widespread these practices were at that time and for how long they continued.

PART THREE

Policies toward the Dalai Lama

In this section, the questions and answers reflect the position of China before 1989, the year of the Nobel Peace Prize award to the Dalai Lama. The
position of the Chinese government hardened as soon as the Dalai Lama acquired an international status and his supporters became more numerous.
But if, over the years, the question of Tibet became a leitmotiv in discussions with China on human rights, most Western countries now have softened their language in order to gain access to the Chinese economic market. Per Kvaerne, who answers the first questions of this chapter, chose to
group together Questions 33 and 34, which deal with the possible return of
the Dalai Lama "in China."

The 2001 version of *100 Questions* insists more on the present positions
of the Dalai Lama.

33
What policy has the central government adopted toward the Dalai Lama? [Question 97, 2001]

34
If the Dalai Lama returns, can he settle in Tibet? [not included in the 2001 version]

"All patriots belong to one big family, whether they rally to the common cause early or late." The Dalai Lama is welcome to come back. China's policy includes five points:

1. "China has entered a new period of political stability and economic prosperity in which all the nationalities" are united and help each other. The Dalai Lama must understand this.

2. "The Dalai Lama and his envoys to the central government should speak frankly and sincerely." They should not bargain or recall the history of 1959.

3. The Dalai Lama is welcome if he wishes to contribute to the country's unity and modernization.

4. "After returning, the Dalai Lama may enjoy the same political treatment and living conditions as he had before 1959." He could be elected a vice-chairman of the National People's Congress, or a vice-chairman of the National Committee of the Chinese People's Political Consultative Conference. "It's unnecessary for him to hold a post in Tibet, because younger Tibetans have taken office. . . . Of course, the Dalai Lama can often make tours to Tibet." His followers also would be treated well.

5. When he decides to return, the Dalai Lama has just to issue a press statement; "It is up to him what to say." An appropriate welcoming ceremony will be organized and the news will be published.

Per Kvaerne

The Chinese authorities have consistently viewed the question of the Dalai Lama's return as a question of his personal status. The Dalai Lama has equally consistently insisted that it is not a question of his personal functions, status, or welfare but of finding a solution to a political situation.

Taken at face value, the Chinese position would seem to be singularly naïve. Even the briefest acquaintance with the statements of the Dalai Lama should suffice to convince one that the Chinese terms are not acceptable to him. It is also far from clear what the Chinese position vis-à-vis the Dalai Lama actually is. Thus, in connection with the Nobel Peace Prize award in 1989, he was branded "an international gangster" by the Chinese authorities (*People's Daily*, October 11, 1989)—hardly a characterization appropriate for someone who at other times is offered high positions of honor (although not of influence).

Likewise, there is ambiguity regarding the question of the Dalai Lama's place of residence after his return. The 10th Panchen Lama declared that the Dalai Lama was entirely free to live in Tibet if he wished (*People's Daily*, April 5, 1988), and *100 Questions* dismisses the entire question as being of small consequence. The official position is, however, less open. The Dalai Lama will not, so it is asserted, be burdened by political functions in Tibet, although it is admitted that "from time to time" [French edition] he may be allowed to visit Tibet. Here again, there is a basic inconsistency, for it is formally stated that "after he has returned and installed himself, the Dalai Lama will be treated *in all respects* [emphasis added] as he was before 1959" [French edition]—in other words, as he was when he was resident in Lhasa and a Tibetan government and a Tibetan army still existed.

Underlying this apparent ambiguity and confusion, however, there is a basic position on which the Chinese authorities have never been willing to compromise, namely, "the unity of the country" and the "union of Tibetans and Han." This position was very clearly expressed in the statement made by the Panchen Lama on April 4, 1988: the only condition for the return of the Dalai Lama to China and Tibet, is that he renounce the claim for the independence of Tibet and defend the unity of the motherland. This remains the heart of the matter. The overriding aim of the Chinese government is to ensure the unity of the state, including strategic, economic, and political control of Tibet. The rites of welcome and the political honors offered to the Dalai Lama are intended to underscore this unity. Furthermore, the Chinese authorities cannot but be aware that the driving force behind the continual unrest in Tibet is a nationalistic commitment, not least among the young generation. If the Dalai Lama were to take up permanent residence in Lhasa, this would immensely encourage those struggling for independence, no matter how conciliatory the Dalai Lama's statements on this issue have been in recent years.

This is, understandably, something that, seen from the Chinese point of view, must be avoided at any cost. The Chinese reluctance to engage in real dialogue with the Tibetan exile government is no doubt the reason why the Dalai Lama thinks now that he may not see his homeland again and may die in exile (WTN, May 6, 2007).

35
WHAT IS THE ATTITUDE OF THE CHINESE GOVERNMENT TOWARD THE DALAI LAMA'S VISIT TO OTHER COUNTRIES? [QUESTION 99, 2001]

The Chinese government considers that "the Dalai Lama is not only a religious personage but also an exile who engages in political activities aimed at splitting the motherland. Therefore the Chinese government resolutely opposes his visits to other countries . . . to deliver reports distorting Tibet's history . . . or advocating 'Tibetan independence.' It also opposes any country that takes advantage of the 'Tibet issue' to interfere in China's internal affairs."

PER KVAERNE

The Chinese authorities condemn any move made by other countries or international bodies that they regard as intervention "in internal Chinese affairs." Such expressions of righteous indignation are particularly strong with regard to international protests against Chinese breaches of basic human rights. On the other hand, China does not hesitate to exert direct pressure on other governments in order to further its own policy. This contradictory position is particularly acute with regard to the Dalai Lama. The reason is not difficult to see. The Dalai Lama symbolizes the aspirations of all Tibetans, both inside Tibet and in exile, to national independence, as well as to personal freedom and dignity. He enjoys great international esteem and is received by heads of state and government representatives all over the world. Although no government has, so far, formally recognized the Tibetan claim to independence, there has been no lack of expressions of concern regarding the human rights situation in Tibet. Tibet is invariably highlighted in the media and in public awareness as an international issue during the Dalai Lama's frequent international tours.

The Chinese government has repeatedly issued threats before the Dalai Lama's travels abroad. Thus, when he received the Nobel Peace Prize in 1989—an award that was particularly resented by the Chinese authorities, perhaps, in the end, because no Chinese had at that time received the Nobel Prize in any field—Beijing made it clear to the Norwegian government that if the Dalai Lama were received in the manner customary for the Nobel laureates, including an audience with the king of Norway, this would not remain without consequences for the relationship between Norway and China. The Dalai Lama was nevertheless received in the normal way, and the Chinese threats were not put into effect.

Soon afterwards, Václav Havel, newly elected president of Czechoslovakia, invited the Dalai Lama to visit his country. Once again, the Chinese protested—and again the Dalai Lama's visit took place as planned. This was also the case in the United States. President Bill Clinton received him in 1998. George W. Bush met him in the Oval Office prior to a presidential visit to China in 2005, but he received him not as a political leader but to pay homage to him as Nobel Prize winner. Other Western nations, fearing the consequences, have cancelled visits by the Dalai Lama, as Belgium did in 2005 and 2007, when the Belgian king was soon to visit China. Most Western nations, however, have not objected to the Dalai Lama's invitation. The situation has been different in Asia, where in recent years such visits have often been cancelled, as in Thailand and Mongolia. In 2000, the South Korean authorities declared that it was not appropriate to allow the Dalai Lama's visit after the Association of Korean Buddhists invited him. Moreover, UN Secretary-General Kofi Annan asked the organizers of the Summit of Peace (August 28–31, 2000) not to invite the Dalai Lama when one thousand spiritual leaders gathered at UN Headquarters in New York, a decision that led to much protest. The reason put forward by the secretary-general, without naming China, was that the summit organizers were "compelled to take into account the sensitivities of the state members of the United Nations" (*Le Monde*, August 27, 2000, our translation). The refusal to receive the Dalai Lama at the United Nations or to authorize pro-Tibetan associations to speak has continued over the years. Nevertheless, in 1987, the European Parliament Tibet Inter-group (EPTI) was founded to create opportunities for members of the European Parliament (MEP) to discuss the situation in Tibet and to provide information on Tibet to their colleagues and the general public (TibetInfoNet, March 3, 2006).

A change in the attitude of some leaders of Western countries occurred in the late 1990s. In January 1993, the British foreign secretary said that the government of the United Kingdom favored negotiations without preconditions. In April 1998, Tokyo allowed the Dalai Lama to visit Japan for the First World Buddhist Propagation Conference, despite intense Chinese pressure. During his official visit in China in November 2005, President

G. W. Bush asked the Chinese authorities to invite the Dalai Lama to Beijing in order for them to be convinced that his aim is not the separation from Tibet but a peaceful solution of the Tibetan question within the Chinese state (Tibet News Digest, January 7–20, 2006).

36
WHAT IS THE BASIC DIVERGENCE OF VIEWS BETWEEN THE DALAI LAMA AND THE CHINESE GOVERNMENT AND PEOPLE?

The main point is "China's territorial integrity and the unity of all its nationalities." Abused by "certain separatists," the Dalai Lama attempts to split Tibet from China, hoping for the aid of some foreign powers. "This is what the Chinese government and people, including Tibetans, can never accept." However he should be remembered for "his contributions made in upholding the national unity in the 1950s [i.e., by signing the 17-Point Agreement incorporating Tibet into the PRC]"; it is to be hoped that he will understand the situation and "stop his separatist activities."

PER KVAERNE

The primary concern of the Chinese government, repeated several times by *100 Questions*, is "to protect the territorial integrity of the country and the union of the different ethnic communities of China." Obviously, this concern is not compatible with aspirations to national independence or even with aspirations to real autonomy on the part of Tibetans (see Questions 37 and 38).

The Dalai Lama has repeatedly called for a referendum among Tibetans to settle the question of what the real aspirations of the Tibetan people are with regard to the issue of independence. In fact, in June 1994, in talks with Belgian officials in Brussels, the Dalai Lama said that he intended to organize a referendum on the future of "the Himalayan region," with the following questions:

1. Would you favor the non-violent path supported by the Dalai Lama for a dialogue on obtaining autonomy and peaceful cohabitation with China?

2. Would you favor any action, violent or not, to achieve total independence?

3. Would you favor another type of solution?

While contending there would be little problem in putting such a referendum to Tibetan exiles, the Dalai Lama was evasive on the question of how people in Tibet would be polled (WTN 1994).

But for the Chinese (Question 11, 2001), any attempt to hold a "plebiscite" of this kind would be just another calculated political move by the "Dalai clique" to win support from the international community in the name of "democracy," thereby internationalizing the Tibet issue. By insisting on Tibetan independence, they are "advocating and instigating separatism."

The Dalai Lama has emphasized that there is no conflict between himself and the Chinese government, but that he is distressed by a situation in which great unhappiness and frustration prevail among the Tibetan people.

As early as the Strasbourg Proposal (1988), the Dalai Lama withdrew the demand for independence in favor of a "genuine autonomy." This course, though controversial among expatriated Tibetans, has remained the official policy of the Tibetan government in exile ever since. Nevertheless, the Chinese position has not changed. As was explained by an official of the Foreign Affairs Committee of the National People's Congress (NPC), China's top legislature, "China's policy towards the Dalai Lama is consistent and explicit. We hope that he could renounce his separatist stand of 'Tibetan independence' and come back to the position of patriotism" (*People's Daily Online*, October 28, 2001). When the Dalai Lama visited Russia in 2004, the Chinese Foreign Ministry spokeswoman Zhang Qiyue accused Tibet's spiritual leader of attempting to split China, and she insisted on the need for him to "genuinely abandon his position of advocating Tibet independence and make public statement acknowledging that Tibet and Taiwan are inseparable parts of China" (Reuters, October 20, 2004).

During the process of "dialogue" between the Tibetan government in exile and the Chinese authorities, which began in 2002 and has continued on a yearly basis since then, the position of the Chinese authorities has been unclear. On the one hand, official statements have maintained that a dialogue with the Dalai Lama is welcome, but, on the other hand, a Chinese Foreign Ministry spokesman refused in 2006 to confirm any talks between a Tibetan delegation and Chinese officials and said the Tibetans were visiting in a "private capacity" (UNPO 2006).

The basic problem underlying the dispute between the Chinese authorities and the Dalai Lama is that the Tibetan people have not had the opportunity of publicly expressing their preferences through a process of democratic consultation, whether in the form of a referendum or otherwise. There are, in fact, fundamental contradictions in the respective positions of the Chinese authorities and the Dalai Lama. On the one hand, if the Chinese authorities were confident that the vast majority of Tibetans were happy with the economic and social situation and political institutions in present-day Tibet, it is difficult to see why they should not allow the issue to be put to the test of a referendum, if it were not—and this, of course, is the crucial factor—for the fundamentally undemocratic and elitist nature of the Chinese state. On the other hand, the Dalai Lama has received no mandate whatsoever from the Tibetan people to state that the independence of Tibet is no longer at stake, and to limit, on their behalf, his demand to that of "autonomy"—which the Chinese government is in any case not prepared to grant. It may be worth recalling that in its official statement, the Nobel Peace Prize Committee explicitly pointed out, "the Committee has attached particular importance to the fact that the Dalai Lama in his struggle for the liberation of Tibet consistently has opposed the use of violence." He did not receive the Nobel Prize as a supranational messenger of universal peace and individual happiness and success, but as a spokesman of his people. Neither side having a strong case in terms of legitimacy, the principle of "might is right" is, unfortunately, likely to prevail.

37
What is the Chinese government's attitude toward the "five-point proposal" put forward by the Dalai Lama in the United States during September 1987?

This proposal is nothing new. "In essence, it continues the advocation of 'Tibetan independence', which both the Chinese government and people resolutely oppose."

Per Kvaerne

100 Questions criticizes the Five-Point Peace Plan for Tibet presented by the Dalai Lama on September 21, 1987, in the course of a statement to the U.S. Congress, claiming that it insists on "the independence of Tibet." The authors of the Chinese booklet did not, however, choose to quote the text of the Five-Point Plan, thus enabling readers to form an independent judgment of its contents, so the text is given below in full:

1.   Transformation of the whole of Tibet in a zone of peace;

2.   Abandonment of China's population transfer policy, which threatens the very existence of the Tibetans as a people;

3.   Respect for the Tibetan people's fundamental human rights and democratic freedoms;

4.   Restoration and protection of Tibet's natural environment and the abandonment of China's use of Tibet for the production of nuclear weapons and dumping of nuclear waste;

5.   Commencement of earnest negotiations on the future status of Tibet and relations between the Tibetan and the Chinese peoples.

Clearly, there is absolutely no demand in this proposal for independence. There is however, a demand for respect for "the Tibetan people's fundamental human rights and democratic freedoms," and one cannot but suspect that the Chinese government fears that if such rights and freedoms were granted to the Tibetan people, they would opt for independence.

The Five-Point Peace Plan should be seen in its proper context, which is that of regional peace and stability. The central point is the transformation of Tibet into "a zone of peace." This is not an original concept. Nepal likewise proposed that it be proclaimed a peace zone, and this initiative received the declared support of China (*People's Review* [Nepal], January 9–15, 2003). Traditionally, Tibet has been a neutral "buffer state" between China and India. With the Chinese occupation of Tibet, the massive Chinese military buildup there has created a state of permanent tension in the region, punctuated by outbursts of armed conflict along the border with India.

Likewise "the restoration and protection of Tibet's natural environment" is a matter of regional concern. In the absence of reliable statistical and other data, it is difficult to assess the consequences of deforestation, overgrazing, pollution, and manipulation of water resources accurately, but there is no doubt that the vast Tibetan plateau plays a crucial role in shaping the climate of large parts of Asia, and that deforestation and erosion have had grave consequences in terms of floods and silting up of waterways in neighboring countries like Bangladesh, not to mention in China itself. The Chinese authorities realized the importance of acknowledging ecological problems, at least on paper, as seen in the 2001 version of *100 Questions* (see here Question 84).

38
How does the Chinese government view the Dalai Lama's "New proposal" on Tibet he put forward in Strasbourg, France, in June 1988?

The Dalai Lama distributed copies of this "new proposal" at a press conference. Although it varies in some detail from the previous Five-Point proposal, "there are no substantial differences." It still rejects Tibet status as "an inalienable part of China's territory" and it aims "to internationalize the Tibet question. The Chinese government and people will never accept this 'new proposal' or other similar suggestions. . . . The Chinese government has solemnly declared that neither independence nor semi-independence or disguised independence of Tibet will do."

The Dalai Lama said that he was ready to send his representatives to hold discussions. He or his representatives are welcome: "the channel is always open for dialogue," in China or at any Chinese embassy abroad, or at any other place. "But no foreigners can be allowed to attend. Any issue is open for discussion except the question of 'Tibetan independence.'"

Anne-Marie Blondeau

The European Parliament had invited the Dalai Lama to Strasbourg in 1988, but China threatened to cancel the imminent visit to Beijing of the president of the Parliament, then Lord Henry Plumb of Coleshill, if the Dalai Lama's invitation was maintained. Members of Parliament decided then to invite the Dalai Lama on a private basis. The press obviously grabbed the affair and gave it a much greater publicity than if the Chinese had not made such a scandal. During his "private" visit to the European Parliament on June 15, 1988, the Dalai Lama gave an "Address to the Members of the European Parliament" with his proposals "to solve the problem of Tibet," a document that was, the same day, relayed in a press conference. Globally, the Dalai Lama reiterated his Washington proposals of the previous year, but developing several points. Recalling the territory division instituted by the Yuan, he proposed that "the whole of Tibet known as Chölkha-sum ["the three districts," Ü-Tsang, Ngari, and Kham-Amdo] should become a self-governing democratic political entity . . . in association with the PRC." In exchange, Tibet's claim to independence would be abandoned. The government of this political entity "should be comprised of a popularly elected chief executive, a bicameral legislative branch, and an independent judicial system. Its seat should be in Lhasa." This government would be responsible for everything concerning Tibetans, but foreign policy would continue to be determined by China. The country should, after consultation, be declared a "zone of peace," but for defense purposes, "China could have the right to maintain a restricted number of military installations in Tibet."

During the press conference, the Dalai Lama admitted that this proposal would no doubt disappoint many Tibetans. Tsering Shakya (1999: 423 and n. 88) briefly describes the shock that the Strasbourg Proposal—the contents of which the Dalai Lama's government in exile had known only a few days before—provoked in the exile community: to the nationalists, abandoning Tibet's claim to independence seemed like treason, and they have said and continue to say ever more clearly that the nonviolent path chosen by the Dalai Lama is a dead end.

As for the Chinese reaction, it was equally negative. The Chinese government rejected the Tibet status proposed by the Dalai Lama—to Beijing, a disguised independence—in the same words reproduced in *100 Questions*: "Neither independence nor semi-independence or disguised independence of Tibet will do." Beijing also condemned this "internationalization" of the Tibetan question. Moreover, the Dalai Lama's proposal of an "association" between Tibet and China implied that he was still thinking of the two countries as separate states, something quite inadmissible to the Chinese government. On September 23, 1988, the Chinese Embassy in New Delhi released Beijing's formal response to the Dalai Lama's proposal, which is accurately summarized in *100 Questions* (and quoted in full by Shakya 1999: 425–26).

Beijing's response shows that the Chinese government remained unyielding and was still willing to talk only about the possible return of the Dalai Lama. Any proposal by the latter regarding Tibet's autonomy within the PRC was viewed as an attempt to achieve the independence indirectly. Despite the apparent deadlock, the Tibetan government in exile announced, however, that talks would take place in January 1989 in Geneva, and that its delegation would be led by a group of officials from Dharamsala and advised by Michael van Walt van Praag, a Dutch lawyer well known for his pro-Tibet position.

Interpreting this as ridiculing the conditions it had laid down for any dialogue, the Chinese government accused the Dalai Lama of lack of sincerity and violation of the most basic diplomatic rules in publishing a meeting date without consultation. It unofficially let it be known that it did not wish to pursue the talks, and even the unofficial dialogue between the two parties seems to have been cut off for several years (it has been officially resumed since 2002, but without any tangible results). On the other hand, the Strasbourg proposal was officially withdrawn by the Dalai Lama and his government in 1992 "because of the closed and negative attitude of the present [Chinese] leadership."

39

HOW DOES THE CHINESE GOVERNMENT VALUE THE IDEA OF A "GREATER TIBETAN AUTONOMOUS REGION" SUGGESTED BY SOME PEOPLE AROUND THE DALAI LAMA?

"It is an unrealistic idea." Tibetan ethnic groups also inhabit parts of Sichuan, Qinghai, Gansu, and Yunnan provinces, but "these areas have never been a unified administrative region. Nor have they formed an economic unity." [Question 1, 2001, adds that the Dalai Lama has never had jurisdiction over those areas.] When delimiting the autonomous regions, the Chinese government took into account "their economic and cultural development and the regions' administration." Administering the TAR, with 1.2 million square kilometers, is a hard task. "Therefore, the idea of a 'greater Tibetan autonomous region' is neither realistic nor scientific."

ANNE-MARIE BLONDEAU

100 Questions here touches on one of the most sensitive problems with respect to Tibet: supposing the Chinese authorities grant the Tibetans their autonomy—or that they end up recovering it—should this autonomy be limited to the TAR or extend to the old political and cultural frontiers of Tibetan territory, as demanded by Tibetans in exile? One may choose whether or not to believe the assertion that the dismemberment of the two eastern provinces of Tibet, Kham and Amdo, and their incorporation into four Chinese provinces, was merely in the interests of economic and administrative efficiency (see Questions 16 and 66). But it must be admitted that up to 1950, these regions formed an ethnic and political mosaic that was more or less controlled and controllable in theory, under the central administration of Lhasa. Kham and Amdo were two neighboring entities that differed greatly in topography, dialects, and ways of life, and each was jealous of its own identity. Moreover, these regions have known almost continuous movements of population from the time of the arrival in the seventh century of the first Tibetan "colonists," former soldiers of Songtsen Gampo, to that of different groups of Turks, Mongols, and, since at least the eighteenth century, Chinese settlers. Politically, these regions were highly diverse and included independent "kingdoms" (e.g., Derge and Nyarong [Samuel 1995: 77]), territory enfeoffed to Lhasa through great Gelugpa monasteries (Kumbum, Labrang), but always under the jurisdiction of lay Mongol patrons, and de facto independent nomadic or sedentary ethnic groups (e.g., the Sharwas in Amdo [Karmay and Sagant 1998]), whose religious obedience was often other than Gelugpa. These regions have also at all times been coveted by China and regularly the scene of wars and skirmishes between Tibet and the Chinese empire, since the seventh century. From the eighteenth century on, at the height of its power, Qing China sought to "nibble" at traditionally Tibetan zones and incorporate them into the empire, but it then returned part of them to Lhasa (see Question 5). After the Chinese revolution and the instauration of the Nationalist Republic of China, border conflicts became ceaseless, and territories changed hands constantly; in 1949, the Yangtse was the frontier. This "nibbling" was accompanied by an insidious colonization by Chinese farmers, who, especially in Amdo, occupied the valleys, pushing the Tibetans into the highlands. Needless to say, PRC policies have done nothing but increase this colonization, and the Tibetan percentage of the populations of the present so-called TAPs and municipalities is continually diminishing (see Question 44). Regarding this sensitive problem, even if a hypothetical frontier could be agreed upon, one must not forget the hostility to the Lhasa government before 1950 of several chiefdoms or tribes of Kham, which dreamed of an independent Kham state. Therefore, although there are still numerous pilgrims to Lhasa from Kham and Amdo, it cannot be said that, were they given the choice, a majority of their inhabitants would decide to unite with central Tibet.

In any case, the Chinese government remains inflexible on this matter. It argues that "the former government of Tibet had never ruled the

Tibetan-inhabited areas outside today's Tibet Autonomous Region" (Yedor 2006).

Whatever the case may be, the distinction drawn by Melvyn Goldstein (1997) and others between "political Tibet," namely, the TAR, and "ethnic Tibet," or what some call "historical Tibet," however convenient, seems reductive and unhelpful for solving the Tibetan question, because, like the Chinese government, these categories separate the issue of the TAR from that of the eastern Tibetan regions.

40
WHY DOESN'T CHINA AGREE TO APPLY THE "ONE COUNTRY, TWO SYSTEMS" CONCEPT TO TIBET? [QUESTION 11, 2001]

This concept was formulated for the Hong Kong, Macao, and Taiwan issues, in order to reunify the motherland. The question of Tibet is quite different. Tibet was given autonomy in the 17-Point Agreement (1951), and the TAR was set up in 1965. The regional autonomy of Tibet and other areas "has helped these regions, under the unified leadership of the Central People's Government and in line with their own characteristics."

ANNE-MARIE BLONDEAU

The Dalai Lama's Strasbourg Proposal contained in the background the idea of modeling the status of Tibet on Hong Kong's after its return to the PRC: defense and foreign policy under China's control and civilian affairs managed by a Tibetan government. Later, the Dalai Lama expressly adopted the "one country, two systems" formula devised by Deng Xiaoping to describe the status envisaged for Hong Kong and to reassure businesspeople.

But as the *100 Questions'* answer shows, the Chinese government has not budged. It considers the integration of Tibet into China and the socialist system a fact since 1965, meaning since the creation of the TAR, and there is no going back for it—while Hong Kong and Macao continue to follow their previous capitalist system. "He [the Dalai Lama] wants to integrate Tibetan settlement areas in the provinces of Sichuan, Yunnan, Qinghai, and Gansu into Tibet. He wants to be in charge of this 'Greater Tibet' and he demands that the PLA be withdrawn from the region. Besides, he wants to see a return to an earlier, theocratic feudal realm. . . . And he wants even more autonomy for Tibet than has been given to Hong Kong and Macao. That is splittism," the current secretary of Tibet's Communist Party has insisted in an interview (Zhang 2006).

41

WILL THE CHINESE GOVERNMENT PERMIT THE TIBETANS WHO FLED
ABROAD WITH THE DALAI LAMA AND HAVE ACQUIRED FOREIGN
CITIZENSHIPS TO RETURN? IF SO, WHAT FORMALITIES SHOULD
THEY GO THROUGH BEFORE THEIR HOMECOMING VISIT?
[NOT INCLUDED IN THE 2001 VERSION]

All Tibetans are welcome if they want to come back to visit their relatives and friends. The condition is that they "not take part in separatist activities." They only need to apply for a Chinese visa in the country where they are.

KATIA BUFFETRILLE

Before answering this question, it seems important to underline some crucial aspects of Chinese governance. In China, the rule of law is merely theoretical, and a distinction needs to be made between laws, which in principle apply countrywide and might be relatively liberal on the paper, and their often-restrictive implementation. Additionally, regulations that at the time are not even publicly disclosed are subject to diverse interpretations, sometimes only at a local level (see also Question 58).

That said, the Chinese answer asserts that Tibetans with foreign passports are allowed to go back to Tibet. Only those Tibetans who obtained a foreign nationality after escaping are concerned. In this sense, the answer given by *100 Questions* is accurate: numerous Tibetans, both lay and clerical, go back to Tibet every year and spend various lengths of time there. Religious masters can visit their monasteries and even give teachings, but such visits are strictly regulated and take place under surveillance by the authorities. High lamas are generally hosted by the United Front, the organ of the Communist Party that deals with ethnic and religious affairs. Moreover, the condition laid down for such travel is that they "not take part in separatist activities harmful to the national unity." What exactly "separatist activities" means escapes clear definition, since, as said above, government instructions are subject to various interpretations according to who applies them, where, and when. Naturalized Tibetans benefit from the protection of their country of adoption, and it does not appear that, so far, any naturalized Tibetan has ever been subject to direct repression. Still, in many instances, Tibetans have effectively been barred from entering Tibet, when current events, mostly official celebrations, made the Chinese authorities prefer to avoid any risk of disturbance. For instance, in 2005, the year of the fortieth Anniversary of the foundation of the TAR, hardly any Tibetans with foreign passports could get visas.

But what of Tibetans who have only an "identity certificate" or a temporary permit issued by the receiving nation, and hence do not enjoy foreign protection while traveling in Tibet? In order to be allowed to enter Tibet, they have to obtain a document specifying that they are overseas Chinese from the Chinese embassy in their country of residence. The case of the ethnomusicologist and music teacher Ngawang Chöphel is revealing. Born in Tibet, he was taken to India by his parents as a refugee at the age of two and came to study in the United States in 1992, thanks to a Fulbright scholarship. In 1995, he decided to visit Tibet again in order to make a movie about vanishing Tibetan musical traditions. Carrying only a certificate of Indian nationality, he was traveling in Tibet with the papers of an overseas Chinese as required by the Chinese authorities. Arrested and charged in September 1995 with "separatist activities and spying," he was sentenced to eighteen years imprisonment. He was released only in January 2002, under pressure from the international community and, not coincidentally, during the visit of U.S. President George W. Bush to China and just before the UN Commission on Human Rights was to hold a session to investigate China's human rights records.

Ngawang Chöphel's story sheds some light on the insecurity many Tibetans face when traveling to Tibet and helps explain why so many of them renounce the idea of doing so. Hence, it appears that, while *100 Questions'* answer is in principle accurate, and Tibetans living in exile can visit Tibet, they are obviously considered potential threats to the established order. Also, by obliging refugees to carry an "overseas Chinese" pass, the Chinese authorities take advantage of their comparatively weak position. It is worth remarking, too, that such Tibetans will appear in Chinese statistics as "returning" to China. These simple facts show that, despite Beijing's public assertions, the freedom of movement that *100 Questions'* answer suggests is still far from being a reality.

42
WHAT RELATIONS DOES THE SELF-EXILED DALAI LAMA MAINTAIN WITH THE BAINQEN LAMA? [NOT INCLUDED IN THE 2001 VERSION]

On September 29, 1988, *China Daily* published an interview in which the Bainqen [Panchen] Lama said that he had had a telephone conversation with the Dalai Lama on April 4. They had talked about the Lhasa riots in March. The Bainqen Lama said that "it was not in the interests of the Tibetan people . . . and he hoped that the Dalai Lama would use his influence to stop such violence. The Bainqen also hoped that the Dalai Lama would not instigate disturbances from abroad." He also told reporters that he and the Dalai Lama were still good friends and "maintained contact through correspondence and telephone exchanges."

ANNE-MARIE BLONDEAU

The life of the 10th Panchen Lama and the role that the Chinese wanted him to play after the escape of the Dalai Lama in 1959 have been described above (Question 13). In the eyes of many, especially outside of Tibet, he was judged a traitor, or at the very least a collaborator. The courage he displayed in addressing a long critical report to Mao Zedong as early as 1962 was only known much later. After his death, the Dalai Lama for his part also revealed the correspondence and the telephone calls they had never ceased to exchange, but he did not disclose their contents. In any case, the declarations of the two top Tibetan leaders sufficiently reveal the artificial nature of the so-called opposition between them.

It must be noted that the Chinese question and answer were written when the 10th Panchen Lama was still alive and had been reinstated in his functions but was compelled to reside in Beijing. He unexpectedly died on January 28, 1989, when visiting his Tashilhünpo monastery. The search for and recognition of his reincarnation opened a new crisis between the Dalai Lama and the Chinese government. On May 14, 1998, after an active and unusually long search by a Sino-Tibetan team sponsored by the Chinese government, the Dalai Lama suddenly announced that he recognized as the new Panchen Lama a boy born in northern Tibet on April 25, 1989, named Gedün Chökyi Nyima. Presented with this fait accompli the infuriated Chinese government hastened to recognize and enthrone another boy, Gyaincain Norbu (Gyeltsen Norbu), arguing that, since the Qing dynasty, the reincarnations of the Dalai and Panchen Lamas had been selected by drawing lots from a golden urn under the authority of the Chinese government (as explained in the Question 90, 2001). At the same time, Chinese police removed the boy recognized by the Dalai Lama and his parents from their home and, to this day, nobody knows their whereabouts, in spite of insistent demands from the Tibetan government in exile and international human rights organizations. The head of the search team, Chadrel Rinpoche, the abbot of Tashilhünpo monastery, was jailed for having communicated with the Dalai Lama. Although he was released in 2002, after campaigns for his liberation, he is still under house arrest.

PART FOUR

Population

Demography is well known to be a key political weapon. It is thus not surprising that population is one of the areas where the assertions of Tibetans living in exile differ most from those of PRC government sources, as noted in connection with Questions 22 and 32.

43

HAS THERE BEEN A DECREASE IN THE NUMBER OF TIBETANS
SINCE THE PEACEFUL LIBERATION OF TIBET IN 1951?

On the contrary, it has increased. The Tibetan population has varied
a lot over the centuries. According to historical records, Tibet's population was estimated at more than 4.6 million in the seventh century.
Incessant wars reduced this number to 560,000 in the thirteenth century; by the eighteenth century, it recovered to 940,000.

The following assumes the numbers and percentages already supplied in Question 22 to be known: Tibet, including the prefecture of
Chamdo, had 1,270,000 inhabitants in 1953; there were 1,892,000 inhabitants, of whom 94.4 percent were Tibetans, in 1982. In other words,
in twenty-nine years, there was an increase of 40 percent, an unusual
rate of demographic increase in the history of Tibet.

*[Question 54, 2001, reiterates several of these questions in modified
form, along with questions relating to population transfer (Question
55), the 1.2 million Tibetan deaths (Question 56; see also Question 22
earlier in this book), and forced sterilization and abortion campaigns
(Question 57; see also Question 32 earlier in this book). Updating the
population statistics, Question 54 of the new version notes:*
According to the fifth national census of 2001 [actually November
2000] . . . the total population of Tibet is [2.6163] million, an increase
of 420,300 over the 2.196 million figure recorded in 1990, which denotes
an average increase of 40,700 annually, and an annual population growth
rate of 1.7%.

Of the total 2.6163 million inhabitants of the region, 2.4111 million
are Tibetan, making up 92.2% of the total. The remainder comprises
155,300 Han, making up 5.9%, and 49,900 [persons of] various other
ethnic groups, making up 1.9%.]

ANDREW M. FISCHER

The Chinese government's response to this question, and to the series of
related questions in the 2001 version, relates to three issues: estimates of
the Tibetan population before 1950; the increase in the Tibetan population
since the 1950s; and, a response to exile accusations that Chinese occupation, or what the Chinese government calls the "peaceful liberation" of Ti-

bet, has caused a reduction in the Tibetan population owing to numerous deaths up to 1978 and policies to limit population growth.

In the first case, the response yet again chooses to confuse the territorial designation of Tibet. In the first part of their answer in the old version, the population of 4,600,000 Tibetans in the seventh century refers to the territory controlled at the time by the Tibetan empire. This empire covered all of the Tibetan areas currently divided among the TAR and four Chinese provinces (Qinghai, Gansu, Sichuan, and Yunnan), that is, the territory often recognized as "ethnic Tibet," and it also included non-Tibetan territory, such as Khotan in present-day Xinjiang and Dunhuang in present-day Gansu. The thirteenth- and eighteenth-century populations cited in the same paragraph presumably refer to central Tibet only, while the second paragraph refers to the area that is currently under the administration of the TAR. Beijing's response therefore compares vastly different territories, making it appear as if there was a dramatic decline in the number of Tibetans between the seventh and thirteenth centuries.

Furthermore, it is not clear whether the figure of 4,600,000 refers to the total number of residents within the territories occupied by the seventh-century Tibetan empire, which would have included Chinese and other ethnic groups, or whether this figure refers specifically to those of Tibetan ethnicity. In theory, an empire would be mostly concerned with the former figure—that is, the number of subjects in its domains—because this would determine the population liable to taxation, tributes, military and labor service, and so forth. Also, the constructions of ethnicity that are currently used to categorize populations in China are relatively young in Chinese history, codified only in the mid twentieth century. Indeed, the conception of a pan-Tibetan community itself was only at a very early formative stage in the seventh century. It is therefore doubtful whether these historical references to a "Tibetan" population of the Tibetan empire are in any way comparable to modern census figures.

Following the breakup of the Tibetan empire in the ninth century, about half of the ethnic Tibetan areas, most of Amdo and a large part of Kham, were never again ruled by a centralized authority until the 1950s, and any capacity to conduct regional population censuses would have been very weak or nonexistent. During certain periods of Mongol overlordship, censuses were conducted in all of Tibet, but these counted "fires" (i.e., households), rather than people, for the purpose of collecting taxes (and thus probably only counted taxable households). Many monasteries and other landholders also kept accurate and regularly updated lists of persons under their jurisdictions (i.e., "serfs" and others who belonged to them or owed services or taxes).

These records, where available, constitute micro-censuses of certain areas, although, again, they may not have represented the entire population in question. Therefore, population estimates for the whole of the ethnic Tibetan areas are bound to be very inaccurate up until 1953, when Chinese rule allowed for the first comprehensive population census over all of the Tibetan areas since the breakup of the Tibetan empire. Moreover, the earlier 1953 and 1964 censuses conducted by the PRC in Tibetan areas are generally considered to have been estimates involving a large degree of guesswork.

With regard to the thirteenth- and eighteenth-century populations, it is unlikely for similar reasons that these population estimates are comparable. For instance, the response does not specify the exact territory to which these population estimates refer, but it may be presumed that they refer to the territory controlled by the Sakyapas in the thirteenth century and the Gelugpas in the eighteenth century, both representing high points of centralized rule in central Tibet. Nonetheless, the boundaries of these kingdoms were constantly shifting over time. Differences between thirteenth- and eighteenth-century populations provided by the response thus probably reflect these changes in territory as much as actual population changes. In other words, even in central Tibet, comparing these historical population estimates cannot be taken seriously as an indicator of actual changes in the Tibetan population over time within a fixed and defined territory.

Due to the questionable reliability of these historical population estimates, many of the claims about population growth or decline prior to the modern era are quite simply nonsense. We simply do not know, with any degree of accuracy, what the population of the entire Tibetan plateau might have been prior to the 1950s. Whether from the PRC or the Tibetan exiles, any definite claims can be easily discounted as politically motivated rhetoric, rather than the result of any honest scholarly inquiry.

To further confuse issues, *100 Questions* (Question 22) estimates the population of "Tibet" (i.e., the TAR) at one million in 1953. This estimate was supplied by the Tibetan government in Lhasa, at the time headed by the Dalai Lama. This 1953 population of one million is then compared to the TAR population in 1964 of 1,250,000, implying a substantial population growth of 250,000 people (Questions 55 and 56, 2001). Yet it is specified in Question 22 that this population of one million excluded the prefecture of Chamdo, which the answer stipulates was placed under the jurisdiction of Tibet (i.e., the TAR) in 1956. Therefore, the population of one million does not refer to the TAR but to a smaller territory, given that the TAR includes Chamdo. In the same question, the Chinese authors further specify that the 1953 population of the region including Chamdo was 1,270,000. This is the appropriate comparison to the 1964 population and surprisingly reveals that the population of the TAR, properly defined with the inclusion of Chamdo, actually fell by 20,000 people between the 1953 and 1964 censuses. Obviously, even this observation, if it is to have any significance, again depends on whether any of these estimates can be considered reasonably accurate. The estimate provided by the Tibetan government in 1953 was not based on a proper census but was the result of informed guesswork. Most of the statements of the PRC on the nature of population changes in the TAR up to the 1960s are similarly based on such guesswork.

This leads to the second issue addressed by the response: the increase in the Tibetan population since the 1950s. As background to this issue, the government insists that population growth was slow if not stagnant up until the 1950s, at least during the last several hundred years of Gelugpa rule in central Tibet, in contrast to relatively rapid growth since the 1960s. However, this is not surprising if considered in light of modern demographic transitions. In almost all premodern societies across the world, Europe included, population growth was relatively slow over time, given that, on average, death rates were almost as high as birthrates.

This slow momentum was accentuated in Tibet by what is generally considered to have been a high proportion of celibate ordained men and women in the society. Population control via monasticism, polyandry, or other practices can be further understood in economic terms, given the scarcity of arable land.

These historical demographic factors are discussed in related government publications, although they are ignored in this section of both the old and new versions of *100 Questions*. The old version only stipulates that incessant wars led to stagnant population growth, apparently an attempt to reinforce the hypothesis that pre-1950 Tibet was a feudal tyranny. Ironically, the same stylized "fact" of population decrease is often used in Tibetan textual and oral traditions as proof that Buddhism tamed the wild, warlike Tibetans over the same period; by the beginning of the second millennium C.E., Tibetans' piety presumably affected their birthrates. Both arguments are dubious.

In contrast to this historical context, the old version of *100 Questions* stipulates that the population increase of 40 percent in the TAR between 1953 and 1982 was exceptional in Tibetan history. In light of the dynamics of modern population growth, which will be explained below, this comparison to earlier historical periods is inappropriate. More appropriate would be a comparison to other ethnic groups in China over the same time period, particularly those indigenous to the regions surrounding the Tibetan areas.

For instance, whereas the Qinghai Tibetan population increased 48 percent between 1952 and 1978, the Qinghai Hui Muslim population increased 93 percent over the same period (*QSY*, 2003: table 3-5). In China overall, the population increased 70 percent between 1953 and 1982 (*CPSY*, 2003: table 3-4), a rate that accounts for the massive losses of Chinese life during the famine of the Great Leap Forward. Furthermore, the slowing effect of monasticism no longer applied to the Tibetan areas, given that this heritage was wiped out in the 1950s and monks and nuns were forced to marry. In other words, the Tibetan population was actually growing slowly in comparison to other groups or the national average, at least up to the beginning of the reform period in 1978.

Relatively slower population growth over this period can be explained by one of two causes: either Tibetan women had comparatively lower fertility (i.e., on average they were not bearing as many children as Han or Muslim women), or else Tibetans experienced comparatively higher death rates. In particular, higher death rates could be related to the uprisings, from 1956 on in the Sichuan parts of Kham, in 1958 in Qinghai, and in 1959 in the TAR, and their subsequent suppression, as well as the effect of the famine of the Great Leap Forward, from 1958 to 1962. Official government statistics show that the birthrate and accrual rate in the TAR have been above the average national level since the 1964 census. Independent demographic field studies by Goldstein et al. (2002) also confirm that fertility rates among women who were bearing children in the 1960s and 1970s were quite high. In light of these insights, the comparatively slower population growth from 1953 to 1982 was probably due to a disproportionate loss of life during the peak of violence and famine in the Tibetan areas from the mid 1950s to 1962.

Nonetheless, this changed in the early 1980s following the strict imposition of the one-child policy on the Han, which was leniently applied to minority areas, Tibetan areas included, as argued in Question 57 (2001). Tibetans have since become one of the youngest and fastest-growing ethnic groups in China. Thus, by the 2000 census, the Tibetan population in the TAR and in other Tibetan areas had close to doubled since the early 1950s, recouping in the 1980s and 1990s the lag in population growth over the previous thirty years. Specifically, between the 1982 and the 2000 censuses, the Tibetan population in the PRC as a whole increased by 40 percent. Tibetans in the TAR increased by 36 percent between 1982 and 2000; in Sichuan, they increased 38 percent; in Qinghai, 44 percent; in Gansu, 46 percent; and in Yunnan 34 percent (PRC, National Bureau of Statistics 2002: table 1-6; data from Question 43). Over the same period, the total population in China increased by only 26 percent (*CPSY*, 2003: table 3-4). In other words, the Ti betan populations in both the TAR and Qinghai increased almost as much in eighteen years as they had over the thirty previous years.

Using a slightly different population tabulation (i.e., one that appears to have been adjusted for errors following the 2000 census), the local comparison of groups in Qinghai is interesting, because the Muslim community in Qinghai is widely considered to be growing rapidly. The Qinghai Hui population, which accounts for about 80 percent of Muslims in Qinghai, increased 54 percent between 1982 and 2000, although some of this would be due to in-migration from neighboring Gansu. The Qinghai Tibetans, according to this source, increased 50 percent, of which in-migration would account for very little. In other words, the Qinghai Tibetan population was increasing about as fast as the Qinghai Muslims since 1982. In contrast, the Qinghai Han population grew by only 20 percent over this same period. Note that these calculations of population growth aggregate together both natural population change and changes due to in- and out-migration (QSY, 2003: table 3-5).

Although these Tibetan rates of population growth started to slow in the late 1990s, the TAR still stands out as having the highest rate of natural population increase (i.e., birthrates minus death rates) in the PRC. In 2002, this rate was 1.28 percent a year in the TAR, with the fastest-growing population of all the provinces in the PRC, versus a national average of 0.65 percent. In Sichuan, it was 0.39 percent (PRC, CSY, 2003: table 4-3). It should be noted that Chinese population surveys only sample permanent residents, most of whom are Tibetans in the TAR.

Furthermore, rural Tibetan communities generally have young population structures, a sign of a growing population. For instance, according to the 2000 census, 31.2 percent of the TAR population was under the age of fifteen, whereas in China, it was only 22.9 percent and 22.6 percent in Sichuan. This not only confirms that birthrates have been higher over the past fifteen years but also implies that this larger cohort of young people will maintain a stronger momentum of population increase over the next twenty to thirty years as they enter reproductive age groups, particularly because they are officially allowed two children, versus one for the Chinese.

Exiles often regard these population statistics with incredulity, particularly in light of their own evaluation that Tibetans number six million, which is higher than even the 2000 census, which counted only 5,416,021 Tibetans in all of the PRC. Nonetheless, these increases in Tibetan population before and after 1978 appear to be accurate according to all of the available information. In other words, population statistics corroborate with a cross-referencing of different demographic data over the same period, such as birthrates, death rates, age structures, and so forth, as discussed above. They also corroborate the field observations of a variety of independent scholars, which consistently confirm that Tibetan households in many Tibetan areas, particularly in remote pastoral areas, often have three, four, or more children, even within currently reproductive generations. These observations obviously vary from locality to locality, depending on the degree of strictness in the application of family-planning policies (see Question 32). Even in the Tibetan areas outside the TAR, to which many of the reports of forced family planning refer, it appears that strict family planning is inconsistently applied, despite being officially endorsed by provincial governments. For instance, in the pastoral areas of Golok TAP and Yushu TAP, both in Qinghai, the policy appears very lax, if implemented at all, because large families are still commonplace. In essence, at the aggregate level, most survey results confirm the broad trends observed in the official statistics.

However, the Chinese government uses these facts of population growth as proofs of the positive impact of "peaceful liberation" and its beneficial development of the Tibetan areas. This is equivalent to saying that rapid population growth in Africa has been caused by successful development. Indeed, population has more than doubled over the same period in neighboring Nepal and India, as well as in countries in the midst of war and social upheaval such as Afghanistan. In fact, the two processes—population growth and development—are not necessarily causally related.

Rapid population growth is an attribute of the demographic transition, experienced all over the world. The demographic transition is a modern process that is catalyzed by a drop in death rates. This is then followed by a much slower and lagging drop in birthrates, which may actually increase in the initial stages of the transition. Rapid population increase results from the gap between the two rates during the transitional period. Pre-transitional situations are characterized by high birthrates and death rates, resulting in slow rates of population increase, as mentioned above. The transition ends in a situation of low birthrates and death rates, which also results in slow if not negative rates of population increase, as observed in many rich countries today, as well as in Shanghai.

This transition took place slowly in Europe. However, it was sudden in most areas of the developing world, starting later in the twentieth century, particularly following the huge international effort in the postwar period of the 1950s to extend basic public health measures throughout the world. Because death rates dropped much more suddenly than in the earlier European cases, the gap between birthrates and death rates has been much more accentuated, resulting in the sudden surge in population growth that has been characteristic of developing countries since the 1950s. Attention to controlling birthrates has therefore become the dominant issue of population policy in the developing world, as stipulated in Question 57 (2001).

Tibetans have clearly entered the demographic transition, contrary to simplistic explanations sometimes given for their poor economic development. This has been well established in the literature on Tibetan demography and amply confirmed by field observations. Suffice it to say that Tibetans inside and outside the TAR had definitively entered the demographic transition by the 1960s. Presumably, death rates would have started to fall in the 1950s with the expansion of modern health care, although the exact timing is difficult to ascertain, given poor data and the high death rates and fertility suppression that would have accompanied the period of uprising, repression, famine, and social upheaval in the late 1950s and early 1960s. Tibetans are currently well advanced into the transition, to the extent that total fertility rates are now below replacement levels. In terms of population structure, demographic momentum generally reached its peak among all Tibetans in China in the mid to late 1980s. In terms of natural population increase, the Tibetan population was growing considerably more slowly than the Han up to the mid 1960s, then at about the same rate in the 1970s and 1980s, and then considerably faster since 1989 (see, e.g., Childs et al. 2005; PRC, CSY, 2004: table 4-2; TSY, 2004: table 3-2).

Current demographic differentials between Tibetans and Han are partially explained by differences in the strictness of family planning, rather than by any intrinsic demographic behavior or backwardness on the part of the Tibetans. The official birth limit for minorities in China is two children, rather than the one-child limit applied to Han, and even this two-child limit is only applied to urban dwellers in many parts of Tibet, as indicated in Question 32 in the old 100 Questions and Question 57 in the new. These limits nonetheless contribute to the falls in Tibetan fertility and crude birthrates, particularly with increased enforcement since the mid 1990s, as analyzed by Goldstein et al. (2002) and Childs et al. (2005). As a result, fertility transition among Tibetans has accelerated since the late 1980s, albeit with a lag behind the Han and thus more rapid rates of natural population increase.

A variety of sociological factors also contribute to falling fertility, such as increasing family sizes as more children survive to adulthood, female education and participation in the workforce, urbanization, and so forth. These patterns observed in Tibet are similar to those elsewhere in the world, albeit conditioned by the institutional environment of imposed national family-planning policies. Indeed, Geoffrey Childs et al. (2005) note that the demographic trends among Tibetans in the TAR and Tibetan refugees in South

Asia are remarkably similar in both timing and magnitude despite the fact that the two groups now live under completely different political, economic, and social conditions, and even though the outlook of the refugee community is pro-natal. More generally, fertility rates were already falling in China well before the introduction of strict family-planning legislation in 1978. The one-child policy basically accelerated this modern demographic trend.

Therefore, the relatively rapid population growth in the Tibetan areas since the 1960s has been the result of these transitional demographic processes. It is true that China can be commended for its extension of basic public health-care measures to the Tibetan areas following their "peaceful liberation," which would have had the effect of lowering death rates and increasing life expectancy before and after the periods of widespread violence or famine. Nonetheless, anything other than this would have been a complete aberration in terms of the international standards of health policy that emerged in the postwar period, and to which the ideology of the socialist PRC strongly adhered. Also, similar advances were taking place across the developing world and would conceivably also have taken place in the context of an independent Tibet, as they did in neighboring Himalayan countries.

Population growth per se cannot be taken as a measure of the success of Chinese rule and development in the Tibetan areas. More appropriate considerations include comparative health indicators. For instance, life expectancy in the TAR in 2002 was the lowest in the PRC, at 64 years, versus 71 years nationally (*CPSY*, 2003: table 3-5). This improved from just less than 60 years in the 1990 census, but it corresponds to the international average for all developing countries in 1998, which was 65 years according to the World Bank. It is also similar to life expectancy in Bhutan, estimated by the United Nations at 62 years for males and 64.5 years for females in the period of 2000 to 2005. In India, the respective rates were 63.2 and 64.6 years. Even in conflict-ridden Nepal, one of the most impoverished countries in Asia, the rates were 60.1 and 59.6 years (UN Population Division 2002).

Unofficially, many health workers in the TAR estimate that rates of infant and maternal mortality as given in Robert Barnett's answer to Question 31, are much higher, perhaps more than double these official rates, placing them in the range of many sub-Saharan African countries. Comparatively, infant mortality in China in 2000 was 35 per 1,000, and maternal mortality, 56 per 100,000. The estimated rates for Bhutan in 2000 were 56 and 420 respectively, and for Nepal, 64 and 740 (UN Population Division 2002). The differences between the rates of the TAR and China are partly related to the remoteness of the rural Tibetan areas, making it difficult to provide health services to a dispersed population. Nonetheless, the poor and neglected quality of rural health services in the Tibetan areas has been noted by many observers as an important additional factor. In this regard, the comparison to Bhutan is interesting, because conditions there are comparable to those in the TAR, and similar health indicators have been achieved under an entirely different political framework, although the country is heavily subsidized by India, just as the TAR is by Beijing.

Finally, the third issue indirectly addressed by this question refers to exile accusations that the Chinese invasion and subsequent occupation resulted in 1,200,000 Tibetan deaths up to 1978. The enumeration of deaths has been dealt with earlier in this book (Question 22). Here it is useful to clarify some of the standard misconceptions regarding these population estimates. Tibetan exiles typically claim that there are (or were) six million Tibetans. If the Chinese government was only able to count 3,870,000 Tibetans in all China during the 1982 census (Question 45), would this then not imply that the Tibetan population had fallen from its previous figure of six million under the first thirty years of Chinese rule, due to enormous losses of Tibetan life, population-control policies, and so forth? This reasoning bolstered exile allegations of genocide in the 1980s, which have since been toned down.

In its response, the Chinese government conveniently overlooks the issue of population loss that occurred throughout the Tibetan areas during the period of violent upheaval in the late 1950s and early 1960s by treating the totality of the period between 1953 and the 1982. Beijing further sidesteps the issue by treating the TAR as Tibet, although some of the worst and most drawn-out violence during the uprisings occurred in the Tibetan areas outside the TAR. In other words, the Chinese government dodges the allegations, relying on the ignorance of the uninformed reader.

On the other hand, much of the confusion embedded in these questions relates to the population claims of the exiles, which have attained an almost mythical status. The figure of six million Tibetans is definitely meant to refer to their population in all of the Tibetan areas, although it is often not clear whether this is meant to refer to a historical population or to the population now. In any case, this population claim has not changed over time, which is completely unrealistic in light of the evident signs of population growth mentioned above.

Moreover, in the past as in the present, there has been no way for the exiles to know the population of all Tibetans within all Tibetan areas, given that Lhasa controlled less than half of these areas in the last half century of their independence in the twentieth century. As discussed above, the first comprehensive modern attempt to estimate the Tibetan population throughout all of Tibet was made in 1953 by the PRC. Most of central Tibet was not directly enumerated in the 1964 census. Even in the 1982 census, some remote areas of the TAR were only indirectly enumerated, although by then the Tibetan areas outside the TAR were being directly enumerated. As a result, the 1982 census is the first broadly accurate record that we have available of the size of the Tibetan population, and its findings must be accepted given the lack of any alternative enumerations. The exile estimate of six million Tibetans, whatever its origins, must therefore be treated as a symbolic rather than factual number.

Nonetheless, it is interesting to note that population records from Qinghai are candid about the disproportionate loss of Tibetan population in the late 1950s and early 1960s relative to equivalent Muslim or Han losses. For instance, the Tibetan population of Qinghai fell sharply from 513,000 in 1957, the year before the widespread uprisings in Qinghai, to 478,000 in 1959, and then again to 408,000 in 1963, although this population was apparently growing before and after these years (*QSY*, 1991: 163). Notably, mortality rates in Qinghai were among the highest in the country during the famine of the Great Leap Forward, only surpassed by those of Guizhou and Anhui (D. L. Yang 1996: 33).

In other words, these statistics show a loss of 105,000 Tibetans over six years, or just over 20 percent of the 1957 population. Considering lost population growth over these years, it is conceivable that the actual population shortfall was over 150,000 Tibetans over this period of uprisings and famine, or over 30 percent of the 1957 population. This is probably a more realistic measure, given that the 1963 population of 408,000 includes replacements, namely, the children who were born in the midst of the mayhem. Refugee exoduses of Tibetans from Qinghai, first to central Tibet in 1958, where many were killed in the ensuing uprising in 1959, and then on to India, would account for a small but significant part of the shortfall. In a broader comparison, excess loss of life due to the famine in China overall is generally considered to have been less than 5 percent of the population, that is, less than 30 million deaths in a population of 600 million (see Question 22).

Qinghai Muslims, who also rebelled in 1958, were similarly repressed, and likewise faced the famine, did not experience a drop in population between 1957 and 1959. They did experience a smaller but significant drop in population during the years of famine between 1959 and 1963. Overall, as discussed above, the Tibetan population of Qinghai grew at almost half the rate of the Qinghai Hui Muslims between 1952 and 1978. The much slower Tibetan growth up to 1978 is suggestive of the severity of repression, incarcerations, executions, and famine that were experienced by Tibetans in this province.

In light of these insights, it is very likely that Tibetans were in fact disproportionately discriminated against by such events, due in part to the intensity of their revolts once things got rough in the mid to late 1950s. Their losses were definitely higher than those experienced by other rebelling groups. And had these events not taken place, one thing is certain; the total population of Tibetans today would have surpassed the six million mark.

44
DALAI AND HIS FOLLOWERS CLAIM THAT 7.5 MILLION HAN
HAVE BEEN EMIGRATED TO TIBET, AND THAT TIBETANS HAVE BECOME
A MINORITY NATIONALITY IN THE REGION. IS THAT TRUE?
[QUESTION 55, 2001, DRAWS ON THIS QUESTION]

It is an unfounded affirmation. In reality, "educated and technically trained Han people go to work in Tibet to help develop the local economy and culture. But because of the highland climate" and altitude, "most of those people take turns to working there. Usually they return to the hinterland provinces after a few years." According to the census figures, in 1964, 37,000 Han worked in Tibet; in 1982, 92,000, accounting for 4.8 percent of Tibet's total population. By the end of 1986, the Tibetans were greatly the majority, accounting for 95.68 percent (1.937 million), the Han for 3.62 percent (73,000). The remainder, 0.7 percent (14,000), were ethnic minorities: Loba, Monba, Hui, and Naxi.

[Question 55 in the 2001 edition answers this question similarly by giving an enumeration of Tibetan population shares in the TAR from the 1950s on.]

ANDREW M. FISCHER

This question refers to allegations of "demographic invasion" made by the Tibetan exiles, namely, that Tibetans have become a minority in Tibet due to policies of population transfer, and that the intention of Chinese policy is to populate the Tibetan areas with Han, sinicizing the region by force of numbers. The models for such population colonization strategies are the historical experiences of Inner Mongolia, where Mongolians are currently a small minority, and Xinjiang, where the Han are close to becoming a majority.

In its response to this question, as in the preceding one, *100 Questions* again employs the tactic of treating Tibet as the TAR, rather than all of the Tibetan areas in the PRC. Regardless of the nomenclature used, the exile allegation of 7.5 million Han refers to all of the Tibetan areas in China. In particular, the Tibetan areas outside the TAR play an important role in this calculation, given that they border Han areas and are thus more susceptible to population dominance. The Chinese government response therefore ignores the exiles' actual polemic.

However, on the exiles' side, the reference to 7.5 million Han is also vague. Like the claim of six million Tibetans, it has not changed over time, despite changing population patterns among both Chinese and Tibetans. In reality, it is difficult to come to an exact agreement about the numbers of Chinese in Tibetan areas, because certain pockets that were once Tibetan areas are now densely populated by Han. The question therefore arises of whether these pockets should be included in a counting exercise that is meant to portray the overall situation in Tibet more generally. As such, it is as much a political battle over the representation of the crisis as a more straightforward statistical procedure.

For instance, the government in exile rightly includes the districts of Xining and Haidong, located in the northeast corner of Qinghai, in its own delineation of Tibet. Most of this territory was predominantly Tibetan up until the late nineteenth century, although it was interspersed with important concentrations of Chinese Muslims, along with some concentrations of Han, based mainly in Xining City and along the Huangshui River valley, which runs between Xining and Lanzhou. Presumably, the exile government includes this area in its population tally.

However, Xining and Haidong have been the main destinations of Chinese migration to the province, particularly following the creation of Qinghai Province (in its current form) in 1928 and especially during the 1950s and 1960s. Today, these two districts have been effectively rendered Han, as well as urbanized and industrialized, and account for about two-thirds of the population of Qinghai, more than three million people, in about 2.8 percent of the provincial land area. They also account for most of the provincial Muslim population and a sizeable proportion of the total Tibetan population of Qinghai.

Therefore, the exclusion of Xining and Haidong from the exile population count would lower the exile estimate of the Han population in Tibet to under 4.5 million (presuming that this number is accurate in the first place). Again, the bulk of this remaining Han population is concentrated in several strategic pockets of Chinese interest, such as the mining towns of Tsonub and Tsochang Prefectures, also in Qinghai, the counties of Kangding and Luding in the Kandze TAP of Sichuan, Lhasa, and a handful of cities and towns in the TAR.

The exercise is complicated by the fact that populations in borderland areas are often mixed within a single county, although segregation might still remain very distinct. For instance, in Xunhua Salar Autonomous County of the Haidong District in Qinghai, the birthplace of the 10th Panchen Lama, Tibetans account for about one-fifth of the population. However, this Tibetan population remains very homogeneous in the higher-altitude townships of the county to this day, while Salar Muslims dominate the lower-altitude townships and towns, and this pattern of segregation predates the twentieth century. The population dominance of the Salar reflects a much higher population density in the lower-altitude areas of these counties rather than migration into the higher-altitude areas, where, if anything, out-migration is the dominant trend.

Considered in this way, Tibetans are definitely not a minority in most Tibetan areas. If anything, they are a large majority, albeit one that is predominantly rural and thus not very visible. In contrast, Han in the Tibetan areas are mostly concentrated in cities and towns and thus they are very visible. The PRC answer to this question is therefore partly correct, although it refers only to the TAR. The government could further support its position by referring to many Tibetan areas outside the TAR, such as Malho, Golok, and Yushu Prefectures in Qinghai or most of the counties of Kandze and Ngawa Prefectures in Sichuan.

Although some Tibet scholars may differ with this opinion, it might actually be the case that the Han share of the population in the Tibetan areas outside the TAR has been decreasing since the 1980s. This is not the case in the TAR, where their share has been definitely increasing, although from very low levels, as indicated in the government response to this question. The reason for this apparent incongruity with exile claims has to do with a variety of complex factors, such as the demographics and distribution of the Tibetan population versus the characteristics of Chinese migration since the 1980s.

In this regard, important features differentiate the experience of the Tibetan areas from that of Inner Mongolia, Xinjiang, and the northeast core of Qinghai. Han migration to Inner Mongolia was largely agrarian and took place as early as the eighteenth century, at a time when rural wealth was still coveted by migrants in China. Mongolians were already in a minority position in Inner Mongolia by the end of the nineteenth century, when population transfer for the purpose of land colonization became official policy under the Qing dynasty. The agrarian focus of such policies meant that Han migrants settled in the countryside and became dominant in rural as well as urban populations. By 1947, Mongolians only accounted for about 14 percent of the population of Inner Mongolia. This proportion further dropped to 11 percent by 1964 during the peak of the Maoist transfer policies, but the proportion slowly regained ground to 13.5 percent by 1985 (Burjgin and Bilik 2003: 55–56). Similarly, the large-scale population transfers that transformed the Han share of the total population in Xinjiang from 6 to over 40 percent, and from around 50 percent to over 60 percent in Qinghai, took place entirely during the heyday of radical Maoism in the 1950s, 1960s, and early 1970s.

However, agrarian colonization in most of the high-altitude rural areas of Tibet (Kham and Amdo included) in the 1950s and 1960s was marked by widespread failure. Indeed, it exacerbated the effects of the famine of the Great Leap Forward and led to desertification in many areas. Thus, despite the government's plan for a massive population transfer to Qinghai, with the goal of ten million by 1967, large exoduses followed the famine of the Great Leap Forward, and in-migration during the Cultural Revolution was for the most part balanced by out-migration over the same period (Goodman 2004: 386–88). The failure of population transfer was evidenced by the fact that the population of Qinghai had only reached 3.65 million by 1978, far below earlier goals (*QSY*, 2003: table 3-1).

Tibetan rural areas have therefore remained mostly Tibetan, with few exceptions outside strategic or borderland locations. In contrast, the Han have been almost entirely concentrated in towns and cities in most Tibetan areas. The destination of new Han migrants is equally urban. There is little or no incentive for this to change, given the poverty of the Tibetan rural areas, the harshness of the conditions (in the eyes of lowland Chinese) and the fact that most land is already fully used by the Tibetans themselves, with little potential for commercial farming or ranching, given the ecological sensitivity of the region. This is a critical difference with Inner Mongolia, Xinjiang, and even Xining and Haidong in Qinghai, where Han populations were already well entrenched in the rural areas by the advent of the reform period.

With the advent of the reform period, the concept of transfer (i.e., organized, large-scale movements of population from one region to another) became antiquated, given that it only applied in a strict sense up to the end of the Maoist period, when population movements were closely controlled and managed by the state. Since 1978, this control has been gradually lost or liberalized, with the result that the principal trend in population movements has been away from rural areas and poor peripheral regions, and toward towns, cities, and the coastal areas of China. This trend has been reinforced, as in most countries of the world, by the gradually declining economic importance of agriculture, together with rapid population growth, which rural economies, particularly in poor peripheral areas, have been unable to absorb fully.

Furthermore, given that the Tibetan areas are some of the most remote, rural, and poor in the PRC, the tendency for both Han and Tibetans alike is to move out of the region, not in. The tendency would be stronger among Chinese, given that they are not indigenous to the region, that they maintain family connections to other areas of China, and that many of them were forced to move there in the first place. Moreover, as the old version of *100 Questions* stipulates, many leave because of climate and altitude. A fair share of Tibetan refugee migration to India can also be understood as young Tibetans leaving in search of better opportunities, which are perceived to exist in the exile community.

Consequently, since the beginning of the reform period, outflows of population have consistently exceeded inflows in Qinghai from 1986 to the present (*QSY*, 2003: table 3-3). The same applied to the TAR in every year from 1981 to 1992 aside from three. The greatest outflows from the TAR took place in 1981 and 1982 because of a change in cadre policy, allowing many Han cadres to return home and increasing the representation of local Tibetan cadres, but they continued at a steady pace nonetheless up to the early 1990s (Iredale et al. 2001: 151).

The main factors counteracting this trend are the opportunities that have ridden in the wake of increased subsidization of the Tibetan areas. For instance, a return to net inflows in the TAR would have only taken place following the sharp increase in subsidies that accompanied the Third Tibet Work Forum in 1994, which stimulated economic growth after many years of recession. Similarly, the sharp increases in net in-migration observed in the TAR since 2000 have been stimulated by the massive increases in subsidies that have accompanied the Western Development Strategy, which started in 2000 (see Fischer 2005: chaps. 2, 3, and 5). To a lesser extent, recent increases in subsidies to other Tibetan areas outside the TAR have also stimulated in-migration, although, compared to the TAR, these areas have been much less privileged by Beijing.

Chinese migration to the Tibetan areas is thus best described as a churning of inflows and outflows, the net balance of which is largely determined by economic conditions. On the other hand, demographic factors (i.e., birthrates, death rates, and fertility) would not count for much among the Chinese migrants. Surveys in the TAR in the mid 1990s indicated that Han migrants were disproportionately male and that they did not tend to bring their families with them, leaving them at home and concentrating on economic activities in the Tibetan areas for a temporary period, perhaps five to six years on average (Iredale et al. 2001: 156). Furthermore, many Chinese migrants in the TAR have been seasonal migrants, particularly since the late 1990s, when tourism began to boom. Finally, the Chinese who reside long-term in the Tibetan areas tend to have an urban Chinese demographic profile, that is to say, only one child. While these demographic characteristics would tend to amplify the demand for alcohol and prostitutes, they produce little increase in the existing Han population, whose growth mostly depends on net inflows of migration.

In contrast, the rural Tibetan population holds the upper hand in the demographic momentum. Net inflows of Han are thereby counterbalanced by higher Tibetan rates of natural population increase. For instance, the faster rates of population increase among the Tibetan population of the TAR imply that a sustained net inflow of at least 25,000 Han a year would be required merely to maintain the Han population share, let alone increase it. Such net inflows might be sustained so long as the economy is booming, but if the province were to follow a boom-bust cycle following the completion of a megaproject, the balloon of Han migration could equally deflate.

In Tibetan areas outside the TAR, net Han inflows are probably not even enough to maintain their population share. This is confirmed by changes in the ethnic composition of provinces containing Tibetan areas between the 1990 and 2000 censuses; only in the TAR has the share of the Tibetan population been decreasing over the 1990s. In Qinghai, it has been slowly edging upward since the 1980s (Fischer 2004: 14).

The common rebuttal to this observation is that Han migrants are underestimated in the Tibetan areas because of a variety of considerations, such as the sensitivity of their presence, particularly in the TAR, their "floating" character, and the fact that the military are not included in any of the provincial population data. For instance, the 2000 census recorded only 158,570 Han in the TAR (PRC, National Bureau of Statistics 2002: table 1-6). This number is treated with incredulity by most observers.

The Han census count in the TAR was obviously an underestimate. Arguments of statistical manipulation aside, there may be several reasons why the Han count was low. Temporary migration is not necessarily one of them. There is much confusion in this regard, because many believe that the census did not record temporary migrants. In fact, the 2000 census did attempt to record all types of migrants, down to those who were temporary or had not yet resolved their residency status (Fischer 2004: 11).

Whereas temporary migration is less of an issue in the 2000 census, timing is critical. The census was conducted in November, when most of the seasonal Han migrants would have already left for the winter. The figure of 158,570 may therefore represent a reasonable count of the number of non-military Han who were actually residing in the TAR all year round in 2000. Han presence is also swollen by tourism during the summer months. In 2005, government sources estimated the number of Han tourists at close to 1,700,000, most of whom visited between May and September, along with many of the seasonal migrants who arrive specifically to service this tourist trade. The Han presence would therefore oscillate greatly between summer and winter months.

The military population is not known, but estimates in the 1990s from various sources ranged from 40,000 to 200,000 or more, the upper end during military exercises and other shows of force (UNPO 1997: 70). If a very rough guesstimate of 130,000 were taken, this would be equivalent to about one soldier for every twenty residents in 2000. Nationally, the equivalent measure would be one soldier for every 4,500 residents. Such a presence would almost double the year-round Chinese population estimated in the 2000 census and would have a vital impact on the visual presence of Han, particularly in Lhasa and other cities and towns.

In other words, although there has been a definite increase in Han migration to the TAR since the mid 1990s, particularly during the summer months, such migration is not stable outside the resupply of military personnel and civil servants. The churning component of Han migration would therefore be very susceptible to changes in economic conditions.

Nonetheless, in-migration to the Tibetan areas is an urgent issue that needs to be addressed, but not necessarily because of its effect on overall ethnic population shares. Because Tibetans are mostly rural and Han mostly urban, the key issue is not whether the population balance has shifted toward the Tibetans or the Han, but that the latter have dominated urbanization. Furthermore, rapid urban expansion can give the visual impression that the more urbanized groups are becoming more dominant notwithstanding that they are only maintaining or even losing their share in the overall population. Because the towns and cities hold the levers of economic and political power, the relevant concern is economic and political dominance, not population dominance.

For instance, while the underestimated Han population of the TAR might only represent about 6 percent of the TAR population according to the 2000 census, given that Tibetans were only 15 percent urbanized in 2000 and the Han 80 percent urbanized (in the TAR), the Han share represents about one-third of the city population. A more accurate appraisal of the Han population in the TAR would raise this share even further, probably surpassing 50 percent in the cities year around. Again, it would be much higher during the summer months, precisely when urban economic opportunities are at their peak due to tourism. Therefore, whereas an increase of net inflows of Han migration might have a small impact on the Han population share of the TAR and other Tibetan areas, the impact would be enormous, amplified many times over, in the urban or nonagricultural economy.

In this sense, current Chinese migration is critical in terms of its exclusionary impact on economic opportunities outside agriculture, marginalizing the average Tibetan from the dynamic areas of modern development in Tibet, which are mostly concentrated in cities and towns. The Chinese government response emphasizes that population transfers to the TAR (and we can assume other Tibetan areas) have mainly involved educated Han and technical experts who have gone to help in the effort of developing Tibet, and that aside from these, the itinerant migrants are few in number. Yet, while the numbers of both might be relatively small in population shares, they are large in terms of urban employment, with the effect of crowding out local Tibetans.

In this way, migration fuels resentment among local Tibetans. This is portrayed by the exiles as a "demographic invasion," which the Chinese government easily refutes, given the population dominance of Tibetans in most Tibetan areas, particularly the TAR. Yet if this is expressed in social and economic terms, it remains as one of the most critical issues concerning contemporary development in the Tibetan areas. The way that the government deals with migration is therefore pivotal to how the average Tibetan experiences inclusion or exclusion within development, given his vast disadvantage to the average Han migrant in terms of education or job skills adapted to the urban economy.

45
What is the Tibetan population? How is it distributed?

The third census of 1982 indicates that there are 3,970,000 Tibetans in China: 0.2 percent are "scattered in 24 other provinces" while 99.8 percent "live in compact communities in the TAR, and in Sichuan, Qinghai, Gansu and Yunnan provinces." In these five regions they are distributed as follows: TAR, 1,786,544; Sichuan, 922,024; Qinghai, 754,254; Gansu, 304,540; Yunnan, 95,915.

ANDREW M. FISCHER

This question and its answer appear to serve as a statistical check, perhaps intended as a response to the exile claims that there are six million Tibetans. The 2001 version ignores this question, focusing instead on the Tibetan population of the TAR. As a result, these statistics have not been updated in the new version.

According to the 2000 census, there were a total of 5,416,021 Tibetans in all of China. There were 2,427,168 in the TAR, 1,269,120 in Sichuan, 1,086,592 in Qinghai, 443,228 in Gansu, 128,432 in Yunnan, and 61,481 elsewhere in China (PRC, National Bureau of Statistics 2002: table 1-6). In the 1990 census, there were a total of 4,593,000 Tibetans in all of China, which represents an increase of about 17.9 percent in the total population of Tibetans in China between 1990 and 2000, or about 1.8 percent a year.

46
HOW MANY MINORITY NATIONALITIES ARE THERE IN CHINA?

China has fifty-six nationalities. Apart from the Han (93.3 percent), the 1982 census indicated that fifteen nationalities had a population of over 1 million [list given]. Among them, the Tibetans came seventh, with a population of 3,870,068, accounting for 0.39 percent of the total population of China.

ANDREW M. FISCHER

This question and its answer appear to be an effort to give perspective to the relative significance of Tibetans in China by pointing out that they are simply one among many ethnic groups and not the largest. While this is true, Tibet itself is Tibetan and is distinct from the rest of the PRC, regardless of the historical and political polemics. The fact that it is also part of the PRC is an outcome of the empire-building efforts that the Nationalist republicans and Communists inherited from imperial China. The size or the importance of other ethnic groups in China does not invalidate in any way the concerns of Tibetans in Tibet and their struggles for self-determination, even if these are to be handled within the context of Chinese sovereignty over Tibetan areas.

47
How many minority ethnic groups are there in Tibet?
[Question 58, 2001]

"Apart from the Tibetans, Moinbas [Mönpas], Lopas [Lhopas], Naxis and Huis live in Tibet. There are also communities of Dengs and Xiaerbas [Sherpas], whose population has yet to be fully ascertained."

The Moinbas mainly live in the Monyul district of southern Tibet. "They have their own spoken language, but no script, and can also speak and write in Tibetan. For many generations they have intermarried with Tibetans, and they share many economic, cultural and religious customs and habits."

The Lopas are scattered in the Loyul area of southern Tibet, but the majority live "in the Indian occupied [area] south of the 'McMahon line.' They have their own spoken language but no written form." They are farmers and hunters and good archers.

"The Naxis live around Markam in eastern Tibet. They have their own spoken language. But [they] usually use Chinese." They are mainly farmers, a small minority being cattle breeders, craftsmen, or merchants.

"The Huis [Muslims] live in towns such as Lhasa, Xigaze [Shigatse], Qamdo [Chamdo] and Zetang [Tsetang] and speak both Tibetan and Chinese. They mainly work in commerce, handicraft trades and animal slaughtering. In Lhasa, they have their own mosques."

"The Dengs live in the Zayu [Dzayül?] area of southeastern Tibet. They have their own spoken language, but no written form." They mainly are farmers.

"The Xiaerbas [Sherpas] live in the region around Zhangmu and Dinggye [Dingri] County in southwestern Tibet." They generally speak and write Tibetan. "Before the 1950s, they mainly engaged in barter trade and portering. Now, most of them cultivate crops and raise animals."

ANDREW M. FISCHER

This question and its answer focus on ethnic groups within the TAR. It appears as if the government wishes to demonstrate its awareness of and attention to minority cultures and rights. As with the preceding question, a line of reasoning is implicit in the response; Tibetans are not the only ethnic group in the TAR, and it is therefore unreasonable for them to be making special claims for themselves. In particular, all citizens are equal under the law in China, and no person should be given preference or else discriminated against because of his or her ethnicity. Therefore, the Chinese state presumably defends the position of these minorities within the TAR, as it defends that of Tibetans within the PRC in general.

The only point to add to this description of the various minority ethnic groups in the TAR is that they are all minuscule. For instance, in the 2000 census, there were 8,481 Moinbas, 2,691 Lhobas, and 9,031 Huis, and the Naxis, Dengs, and Sherpas are included among the 3,610 people belonging to a collection of these three and other tiny groups. Together, these groups accounted for about 0.9 percent of the total 2000 census population of the TAR, or about 1 percent of the total indigenous population of the TAR. Their mention therefore does not take away from the fact that the TAR remains the most homogeneous ethnic region of China, a tribute to the fact that Tibet is Tibetan, albeit with a small degree of diversity along its fringes or, in the case of the small pockets of Muslims in Lhasa and other cities up to the 1950s, inherited from its past relations with South Asia and northwestern China.

Furthermore, the categorization of these minuscule groups stems from efforts in the twentieth century by the Chinese state itself to classify the members of its nation into fifty-six nationalities. While the Moinbas, Lhobas, and Sherpas might be distinct from Tibetans, they associate closely with the larger Tibetan Buddhist culture of this region. For instance, the Sherpas, a group that are mostly concentrated on the other side of Mount Everest in Nepal and that might in fact be descended from Tibetan traders who migrated from eastern Tibet, were closely integrated into the monastic system in central Tibet, sending monks to the main monasteries and having lineages of reincarnated lamas recognized by the same authorities. In this sense, one wonders why the Chinese state, in its efforts to classify ethnicities, did not also subdivide the Tibetans into Üpa, Tsangpa, Khampa, and Amdowa ethnicities, doing away with the term "Tibetan" altogether, because the differences between these regional Tibetan identities are probably as great if not greater than those between the Moinbas, Lhobas, and Sherpas and the Tibetans of the south of the TAR. This certainly would have served the purpose of weakening the emergence of a pan-Tibetan national identity, which is astutely avoided in these questions and answers by their constant and singular reference to the TAR as Tibet.

Moreover, the difference between the Cantonese and the people of northeastern China is immense, with different dialects, customs, and so forth. Yet all of these diverse Chinese identities were classified as Han, with the purpose, stemming from the nationalism of Sun Yat-sen, of forging a national identity among them. Presumably, the classification of "Tibetan" was also kept intact, given that Sun Yat-sen himself declared that Tibetans were one of the five great nationalities of China. Although this categorizing of ethnicities postures as a form of scientific anthropology, it is steeped in politics.

Thus, this question and its answer in fact reveal the factitiousness and perversion of the official Chinese argumentation. The fact is that intra-Tibetan cleavage is almost limitless. Where the boundary is drawn depends almost exclusively on the motivation of the ethnographic cartographer. There is extraordinary diversity within Tibet, which Tibetans themselves will readily emphasize. The elevation of specific sub-Tibetan categories to full minority status under Chinese minority law usually occurred due to very specific local political reasons, dictated primarily by the state. We therefore have to be very careful of the political motivations that underlie such ethnic terminology.

PART FIVE

Religious Belief

To the Western public, the religion of Tibet is probably the most visible and spectacular aspect of the culture of the "Land of Snows." It is an exaggeration to say that all Tibetans are devout Buddhists, busy telling their beads and turning their prayer wheels, let alone mystics with supernatural powers spending their lives in meditation. However, Buddhism has effectively shaped the Tibetan civilization (which also contains many other aspects), and religious activities of all types were the real fabric of daily life. A few questions in this section attempt to describe Tibetan religion, but the majority concern Chinese policy in religious matters. The *100 Questions'* answers are ahistorical and occlude the Cultural Revolution's persecutions, as well as the constant fluctuations of this policy between liberalism and repression.

In this section of *100 Questions*, the thesis is that although the Cultural Revolution caused regrettable excesses, freedom of worship in Tibet (always understood as the TAR only) since 1986 has been total, and that Tibetan Buddhism enjoys the government's protection. Of course, the Tibetans in exile argue the contrary and publish stories of recent exiles that report arrests, torture, and discrimination. The scholar who seeks to be impartial has no choice but to compare the comforting affirmations of the Chinese government with Western and Tibetan testimonies, which can always be accused of bias. Here, we strive to identify the suppositions and implications of the official Chinese documents, while offering some relevant facts and individual observations made in the field.

To give a complete picture of the religious situation in Tibet is very difficult for various reasons: (1) the extreme fluidity of the situation since the liberalization of the 1980s to the present; there has been a succession of periods of relaxation and constraint, based, not only on events in Tibet itself (e.g., demonstrations), but on changes in policy stemming from the general situation in China; (2) the Chinese information covers only the TAR and ignores the sociological and religious phenomena of Tibetan populations incorporated into different Chinese provinces; (3) we do not know the story of the various uprisings that, according to the Tibetans, occurred before 1987. Starting with the great protest of September 1987 in Lhasa, the first with Western witnesses, the majority of the endemic protest movements has always been led by monks or nuns, drawing along with them a great number of demonstrators. While the protests often originate in a demand for the release of prisoners, it is impossible to unravel the role of nationalism and that of devotion to the Dalai Lama. Arrests and jail sentences that Chinese government depicts as legal punishment of a handful of "separatist" troublemakers are seen as religious persecution by the government in exile.

48

WHAT POLICIES HAS THE CHINESE GOVERNMENT
ADOPTED TOWARD RELIGIOUS BELIEF IN TIBET?

*[The beginning of Question 85 in the 2001 version, which noticeably
does not give more space to religion proper.]*

Freedom of religious belief is clearly stipulated in Chinese constitution. It applies to the Tibetans as well as every citizen. Everybody is
free to believe or not. "All citizens, religious or atheistic, are equal
politically. . . . All religions are equal, and the state treats them
equally."

ANNE-MARIE BLONDEAU

The Chinese answer is put at the constitutional level, which in fact guarantees freedom of religion but does not answer the question of specific policy;
this will arise out of the following questions. One can only acknowledge this
declaration of principle. The authors might have added that for Tibet, the
17-Point Agreement of 1951 reconfirmed this principle of freedom of religion and stipulated: "The religious beliefs, customs and habits of the Tibetan
people shall be respected, and lama monasteries shall be protected. The central authorities will not effect a change in the income of the monasteries"
(article 7). We explore this below.

Furthermore, although freedom of religion is guaranteed in the PRC's
constitution, many constraints block it. The Party can decree that such religious activities, movements, or their leaders are subversive and harm the
unity and stability of the country. Several such decrees, broadly reported
by the press, have been issued against Catholics, the Falun Gong sect,
Moslems in Xinjiang, and even unregistered Taoist "parishes," which have
formed again throughout China. In reality, China officially recognizes only
four religions: Buddhism, Taoism, Christianity (Catholicism and Protes-
tantism), and Islam; everything else is outlawed. It is in this context that
one should understand the assertion that "regular religious activities are
protected by the state" in the Chinese answer to the following question.

49

SOME PEOPLE CLAIM THAT THE CHINESE COMMUNIST PARTY HAS
ELIMINATED RELIGION IN TIBET. IS THIS TRUE? [QUESTION 85, 2001]

Everyone going to Tibet can see that it is not true. "There are now 1,142 active monasteries and religious centers [more than 1,700 in the 2001 version]. Incense smoke can be seen everywhere curling up from the monasteries. Lamps in front of Buddhist statues burn day and night. There are always continuous streams of worshippers. . . . Most Tibetan families have niches for Buddhist statues, and colorful sutra streamers are openly displayed."

"Chinese Communists are atheists," but they let other people practice: they know that religion cannot be suppressed by force. The Chinese constitution stipulates, "No state organs, social groups or individuals are allowed to interfere with or discriminate against the religious beliefs of others. In fact, regular religious activities are protected by the state."

"In the past 10 years, the Chinese government has allocated more than 36 millions yuan . . . to rebuild and renovate monasteries in Tibet that were destroyed during the 'cultural revolution.'" . . .

"The Tibetan branch of the Buddhist Association of China and Buddhist associations in all prefectures and cities in the region have been reinstated. A Tibetan Buddhist College has been established, and all monasteries have opened sutra-learning classes." Two ceremonies suspended during the Cultural Revolution have been revived: the display of Amitâbha Buddha's image in 1985, and the Monlam [Great Prayer] in 1986.

"Leftist errors" during the Cultural Revolution have caused serious destruction among Tibetan temples and monasteries, "[b]ut this problem was not exclusive to Tibet." Now, "the Party's policy of religious freedom is being fully implemented."

ANNE-MARIE BLONDEAU

One of the most important of the stated principles of the Chinese Communist Party is that its members are atheists, which implies they *must* be atheists. This principle does not appear to allow exceptions in China proper, but the Party itself acknowledged in 2005 that about 20 million of its 60 million members believed in a religion. In Tibet, the situation is more blurred, and we have only isolated observations to go by. After the Cultural Revolution and until the 1990s, it does not seem that the Party strictly controlled the private religious activities of Tibetan members; a good number sent their children to exile Tibetan schools in India. An anthropologist observed that in Tsang villages in central Tibet (TAR), it was the (Tibetan) secretary of the local Party organization who organized the yearly great festival of the local god. A series of events—the Tibetan protests since 1987, that of the Chinese students on Tiananmen Square in 1989, and the acceleration of reforms for economic development—have hardened Chinese policy, as will be seen in detail below.

The declaration of atheism by the Chinese Communist Party is as significant as the elusive manner in which the present religious policy is evoked. The failure of forced eradication of religions during the Cultural Revolution has been publicly acknowledged, but official tolerance is purely strategic; it takes into account the "backwardness" of the masses who have to be led to reject their "superstitions" thanks to material progress and socialist education. The essential document establishing this policy is a Party instruction to the cadres of the Party and the government in 1982, known as "Document 19" (translated in MacInnis 1989: 8–26; for its application in Tibet, see the official documents quoted and translated in *Defying the Dragon: China and Human Rights in Tibet* [TIN 1991]: 7–8, 108–14). This policy is not specific to Tibet (on Buddhism in China, see Vandermeersch 1989: 27–36, and Wang-Toutain 1997). But regarding Tibet, where religion was inseparable from cultural and social life, there is in fact a discrimination between those who express their beliefs and those who, having rejected their beliefs, retain power. Decision-making power rests in the hands of Party members, who are obliged to be materialists and atheists. Tibetans who seek higher education or a government position must therefore refrain from expressions of religious belief. Even for those without such aspirations, there is discrimination against many beliefs and practices, since the state protects only "normal" religious activities. In this, the PRC is only continuing the policy of the empire, in which "deviant" religious practices were always condemned. On this point, it is instructive to quote the missions of the Buddhist Association of China, created in 1953:

> To unite all the nation's Buddhists within the norms of the socialist state.

> To contribute to the application of government religious policy under the control of the Bureau of Religious Affairs.

To identify and give examples of the best Buddhist traditions. (Vandermeersch 1989: 27)

What these best traditions are is illustrated by the topics studied in the Buddhist Academies in China: the *sûtras* (Buddha's sayings, on which the Small
and Great Vehicles are based), monastic rules *(vinaya),* and exegetic treatises *(shâstras).* The study of *tantras* and tantric traditions is absent, although these have historically been important in China. In Tibet, normal-
ity seems to be defined in the same terms. *Defying the Dragon* mentions
the interdiction of certain rituals registered in the liturgical calendar of
monasteries (TIN 1991: 10). These include prayers or rituals written by the
Dalai Lama and prayers for his long life and also propitiatory rituals to
wrathful deities *(kangso).* These are all tantric rituals, but they also serve
to strengthen Tibetan nationalism. The prohibition may arise from the long-
standing suspicion of the Chinese state of practices judged irrational and
magical—catalogued as "superstitions"—and its desire to channel religious
phenomena into a controllable institutional framework. At least two facts
seem to corroborate this hypothesis: the ban on popular mediums and the
generalized disappearance of oracles attached to some great monasteries (see
Diemberger 2005), and the acknowledgement of the Gelugpa School as the
"official" church of Tibetan Buddhism. From a purely political point of view,
this preference cannot be explained, because this is the Dalai Lama's school,
in power since the seventeenth century and, consequently, a symbol of the
ancient order that must be destroyed. One must then see this as the choice
of the school known to represent the most intellectual trend of Tibetan Buddhism and to most favor "ethical" rules. Here again, the official analyses of
the Chinese researchers in the social sciences illustrate the usefulness of a
Buddhism reduced to only ethical laws to help the state in educating the
masses: "Buddhism is not separate from the world. . . . Everyone . . . must
contribute to the edification of socialism. . . . The first director of the Buddhist Association of China, Yuan Ying, thought that activities in the interest of the country, safeguarding world peace, the people's well-being, and
also love for and protection of the motherland were priority tasks that believers had a duty to accomplish" (Shanghai Academy of Social Sciences,
"Religious Questions in the Era of Chinese Socialism" [1987], from French
trans. in Vandermeersch 1989: 30).

The document notes religion's power to rally the people and provide
social cohesion and observes that because "ethics rule life in society," it is
useful to rely on the Buddhist faith, which draws its strength from the idea
of retribution for one's deeds, promised in this life or a future life. Buddhism

can thus be used to combat the decline of morality that resulted from the ten years of trouble during the Cultural Revolution (Vandermeersch 1989: 32–33). Finally, the last benefit of associating Buddhism with socialist construction is as an instrument for unifying the different Chinese "nationalities," including Tibetans. The "Report on Six Years' Work of the Buddhist Association of China" (Beijing, 1987, from trans. in Vandermeersch 1989: 33–36) notes the constant support of the Panchen Lama during the survey, the association's attention to the problems and questions of Buddhists belonging to the minority nationalities, as well as its role in external relations with Hong Kong, Taiwan, and Japan.

The Chinese government thus protects a state Buddhism, under state control, which does not include all forms of Buddhism. This is reminiscent of the "state" Catholicism recognized since 1953, while Roman Catholicism remains banned.

Later in their response, the Chinese authors dismiss the irreparable damage, not only to religious life, but to the Tibetan cultural heritage with which it was so closely associated: temples and monasteries were destroyed with all their contents—not only murals, paintings, statues, and religious objects but also libraries and xylographic printing blocks. According to an estimate of the Dalai Lama's government in exile, 80 percent of the Tibetan cultural heritage has vanished. These ravages cannot be ascribed only to excesses of the Cultural Revolution. They began to be committed as soon as the "Liberation Army" entered eastern Tibet, where monasteries paid dearly for their resistance. Refugees attest that, as early as 1960, specialized Chinese teams looted monasteries, sending objects of value to China to be sold on the antique market via Hong Kong (Avedon 1984: 119). But in 1982, the Lhasa Bureau of Religious Affairs announced that Beijing had decided to return the objects of religious art to their former places. According to the International Campaign for Tibet's 1990 report *Forbidden Freedoms,* the Tibetans sent to Beijing found proof that hundreds of tons of metal religious artifacts had been taken to various Chinese smelting works (ICT 1990: 14). More than 13,000 ancient statues were recovered and shipped back to Tibet, but there is no way of knowing how many art objects stayed in private Chinese collections or were smuggled onto the black market.

The answer in *100 Questions* opens with a description of religious life in Tibet, like the travelers' accounts prior to 1950: incense smoke, butter lamps, prayer wheels, circumambulations and prostrations, numerous icons, multicolored prayer flags flapping in the wind on mountain passes and above houses. It is true that the traveler in Tibet in the 1990s had the superficial impression, outside of cities, of a Tibet identical to that described in the old stories he or she had read. The vigor with which the Tibetans resumed their traditional religious activities once they were again authorized to do so at the beginning of the 1980s, after years of daily Maoist indoctrination and the decade of destruction and persecution of the Cultural Revolution, surprised all Western observers, and probably the Chinese as well. But what in fact occurred?

As has been noted, the relatively relaxed policy of the 1980s was significantly rolled back in the following decade. At the Third Tibet Work Forum (1994), it was decided that: "some aspects of Tibetan culture and religion" were not compatible with socialism and had to be eliminated. A broadscale campaign of "patriotic education" was launched, involving not only the monasteries, where monks and nuns had to sign a document disavowing the Dalai Lama and stating that Tibet was an integral part of China, but laypeople as well. Homes and monasteries were systematically searched for pictures of the Dalai Lama, from then on forbidden everywhere, and Party cadres were ordered to destroy family altars and not to allow any religious book or image in homes. Likewise, those who had sent their children to Tibetan schools in India were warned to bring them back under the threat of losing their jobs and of being forbidden to be employed in a government office or enterprise. In 1998, it was decided to extend the campaign to eastern Tibetan regions absorbed into the provinces of Qinghai, Sichuan, and so on, which until then had paradoxically enjoyed much greater freedom of religion than in the TAR. A campaign to spread atheism was launched in January 1999 and renewed for four years during a political meeting in Chengdu in April 2000. In that year, limitations on religious practices, police controls, and threats were taken to a scale previously unknown, to the point that a Tibetan from Lhasa said that it was "like a second Cultural Revolution" (TIN 2000f). According to this source, confirmed by several scholars who were in Lhasa in the summer of 2000, house searches were intensified, not only for photos of the Dalai Lama but also for religious paintings *(thangka)* and fumigation hearths (from then on burning juniper as an offering to the gods and sticking prayer flags on the roof were forbidden). In addition to Party members and government employees, these restrictions were also imposed on merchants and businesspeople and Tibetans working for foreigners. Pupils and students were forbidden under the threat of expulsion to visit monasteries, to attend religious ceremonies, and even to perform the ritual circumambulation of Lhasa *(lingkor)* during the anniversary festival of Buddha's birth, illumination, and death *(Sagadawa)* in June.

A front-page article in *Tibet Daily* on July 4, 2000, threatened government employees with penalties if they took part in religious activities, giving a phone number to report violations. "Young children should be educated in atheism in order to help rid them of the bad influence of religion," it recommended (TIN 2000f).

This virulent anti-religion campaign seems to be officially linked to the development plan for western Tibet, for which social stability is necessary (see Part VIII, "Economic Development," below). But the hardening of this policy in Tibet is probably also a consequence of the campaign to spread atheism launched in China, in response to the religious problems mentioned above, including problems inside the Party. In any case, we are far from the Chinese constitution's second principle: "No state organization . . . can adopt a discriminatory attitude toward the believing citizen."

In January 2000, the astonishing escape, widely publicized by the Western press, of the young Karmapa hierarch, who had been raised as a "patriot," was a serious setback for the Chinese government and was followed by arrests and expulsion of monks from his monastery. But, as further testimony to the great variability of Chinese politics, since the arrival of a new Party secretary, Guo Jinlong, in October 2000, the drastic anti-religious measures seem to have been softened, at least as regards some widespread popular practices, such as circumambulation, prayer flags on roofs, fumigations, and so on. However, the "patriotic education" campaign was intensified in Tibetan regions outside the TAR. In June 2001, a huge religious community of about 10,000 persons, including both Tibetans and Chinese, which had gathered at Larung Gar near the town of Serthar in Sichuan province around a charismatic figure, Khenpo Jigphün, was dispersed by the army, and its buildings were partly destroyed, while the residents were ordered to return to their original provinces. (Khenpo Jigphün subsequently died in a Chengdu hospital, but the community has formed again under his niece, a nun.) Another important monastic encampment in Sichuan, Yachen Gar, met the same fate in October 2001.

To prove that religion is protected by the Chinese state, the answer in *100 Questions* reports the amounts of money allocated by the Beijing government to the restoration of "monasteries and temples damaged during the Cultural Revolution" (a subject treated several times in *100 Questions* and developed in our response to Question 71). It must be first noted that it was the same vigorous Tibetan faith that made possible the reconstruction in record time of the "1,142 monasteries and places of worship" that were counted by *100 Questions* in 1989 (more than 1,700 in the TAR in 2006, according to *People's Daily*, May 10, 2006); the majority were rebuilt by Tibetans who gave their time and money, and also with the funds collected by Tibetans in exile. The Dalai Lama's government in exile asserts that before the destructions of the 1950 invasion and then of the Cultural Revolution, there were about 8,000 monasteries in all of Tibet. For the TAR, the figures given by *Forbidden Freedoms* from Chinese sources speak for themselves: there were more than 2,463 monasteries in 1959, and 553 were active in 1966, but by 1976, only 10 were still standing (ICT 1990: 33). From 1982 on, the TAR government made the decision first to repair 53 of them, then more in the following years, and in 1989, the number of 1,142 monasteries and religious centers was reached, as *100 Questions* reports.

That the Chinese government committed huge sums to restore certain temples and monuments cannot be denied, with the most to date in Lhasa, including the Potala Palace and the main temple, the Jokhang. However, it is impossible to determine which monasteries in fact receive this aid for reconstruction. Since the "liberalization," Tibetans have rebuilt their religious buildings at incredible speed, as identically as possible to the old ones as remembered by old surviving monks. Year after year, photos show new religious buildings where there were once only ruins. But aside from the elaborate restoration of the most prestigious monuments—a must for Western, Japanese, and Chinese tourists—who paid for this work? The answers gathered in situ are contradictory. In Eastern Tibet (today Qinghai), for example, in any case, the Kumbum monastery received subsidies via the Buddhist Association of China, but the reconstruction of lesser-known temples, notably the non-Gelugpa ones, relied entirely on contributions from the faithful, according to the testimony of researchers who were able to go there. The official Chinese press admits that the majority of the reconstructions are done with private funds. Thus, in 1989, the restoration of 200 monasteries benefited from public funds, while 700 others were renovated by the local population (*Beijing Review,* April 24, 1989, quoted in ICT 1990: 35). Furthermore, in several cases, although the government has only very partially contributed to the work, it controls the monastery and registers it among those it financed. Tsurphu, seat of the Karmapa hierarchs, received about 100,000 yuan from the Chinese government in 1984 and a smaller amount later, while more than $2 to 3 million were spent by 2000, money coming mainly from Taiwan, Hong Kong, Malaysia, and Singapore (personal communication from Ward Holmes, president of the Tsurphu Foundation). This case is not unique: especially in what used to be Kham and Amdo, more and more Chinese—from China proper, Taiwan, and Hong Kong—are becoming disciples of Tibetan lamas and contributing to the reconstruction or the improvement of monasteries and other religious buildings.

However, the PRC authorities never viewed this massive restoration favorably, seeing it as a waste of "a lot of manpower, materials and funds" (*Nanfang Ribao*, June 5, 1983, quoted in ICT 1990: 31). In fact, an authorization must be requested from the administration to undertake a reconstruction or construction. The conditions for this authorization have been precisely stated in the "New Religious Regulations" (article 14) promulgated by a decree of the State Council of the PRC on July 7, 2004, and effective as of March 1, 2005:

1. The religious site is established for a purpose not in contravention with the constitution, laws, regulations, and rules (safeguarding unification of the country, unity of all nationalities, and stability of society, and being not subject to any foreign domination).

2. "Local religious citizens have a need to frequently carry out collective religious activities."

3. There are religious personnel or other qualified persons to preside over the religious activities.

4. "There are the necessary funds."

5. The site must be located "without interfering with the normal production and livelihood of the neighboring units and residents."

Tibetans generally seem to have disregarded these conditions: *Forbidden Freedoms* gives the example of a county to the north of Shigatse where, in 1990, thirty monasteries were under reconstruction, of which only one had requested authorization (ICT 1990: 34). But the same source and Ronald Schwartz (1994) mention several cases of the arrest of monks on the site itself for "illegal religious activities."

50

DID THE CHINESE GOVERNMENT APPROPRIATE MONEY
FOR RENOVATING MONASTERIES IN TIBET IN ORDER TO
ATTRACT MORE FOREIGN TOURISTS?

Those funds were allocated "in order to satisfy the people's religious desires. At the same time, renovations are meant to safeguard the nation's historical and cultural heritage, not to solicit foreign tourists." Tibet is praised for its natural beauties: snowcapped mountains, lakes, and rare wild animals, as well as for its customs and handicrafts. "All this attracts people to come here for sightseeing, mountaineering, hunting and adventure. If foreign tourists are willing to visit temples in Tibet, they will certainly be accorded a warm welcome."

ANNE-MARIE BLONDEAU

As discussed in the answer to the previous question, the Chinese government has spent huge sums to preserve and restore certain monasteries and monuments—listed officially as the "Nation's Historical and Cultural Heritage." Here, "nation" refers to China, not Tibet. A "Regulation for the Protection of Relics" issued in 1990 by the People's Congress of the TAR, specified that "all religious relics belong to the state" (ICT 1990: 17). In the Chinese answer to Question 71, it is said that "13 of Tibet's monasteries and palaces have been listed as key cultural treasures under state protection, and 11 have been put under the protection of the [Tibet] autonomous region," which is a small number compared to the 1,142 monasteries and places of worship counted in the previous question. It is difficult to know what criteria were used to select those to be restored. Other Chinese declarations state that the choice went to the monuments of great historical value. Yet the reconstruction of the Samye monastery, the first Buddhist monastery in Tibet and thus a place of great historic and symbolic value, was undertaken thanks to the perseverance of a great master in exile, Khyentse Rinpoche, and the money he collected outside of Tibet. (We would note that the information gathered in situ is often contradicted by the Cultural Relics' Administration in Lhasa, which maintains that aid from the state or the region was used for Samye; see Buffetrille 1989: 389–92).

The intentions of the Chinese government cannot always be inferred, but doubts are raised about its alleged preoccupation with saving the culture when one sees that the tourist circuits include precisely the monuments restored with Chinese funds: in Lhasa and its region, the Potala, the Jokhang, and Norbulingka, and the three great monasteries of Drepung, Sera, and Ganden; and in Tsang, Tashilhünpo, the monastery of the Panchen Lamas. Let us note that all these monuments and monasteries belong to the Gelugpa school. The official Chinese documents are very explicit on this point: the famous "Document 19," mentioned above, recommends "painstaking efforts to safeguard" monasteries and keep them in good condition "so that the surroundings are clean, peaceful, and quiet, suitable for tourism" (quoted in ICT 1990: 75).

One of Tibet's main resources at present is tourism, and there should be no objection to China's wish to contribute to its development by restoring the most prestigious buildings. But it is disingenuous to suggest that foreign tourists come to Tibet to admire the scenery and immerse themselves in the wilderness. The majority of the tourists are attracted by the myth of Tibet, the land of high spirituality, and the first things they wish to see are religious monuments and, if possible, their rituals. At the same time, it is also true that they wish to contemplate the impressive beauty of the landscape. But unrestricted travel in Tibet, whether for climbing or hunting, is not permitted, as *100 Questions* implies (see Question 82).

There is typically a charge for the warm welcome in monasteries and temples; one must buy entrance tickets (in 2006, 100 yuan for the Potala) and, when not forbidden, photos are authorized according to the place (125 yuan for the 10th Panchen Lama's reliquary in Tashilhünpo in 2007). These revenues go to the monastery, according to the Drepung case study by Goldstein (1998) and the Chinese answer to Question 54. In these "state-protected" places, the monks in charge of ticket collecting and watching tourists sometimes behave like fierce watchdogs, offering a welcome very different from the warmth shown in more modest monasteries that have not benefited from government generosity.

51
Are Tibetans free to take part in religious activities?

"Tibetan lamaists" can practice freely. "They can set up shrines at home. . . . They can also go to monasteries everywhere to worship and give alms" and to attend religious ceremonies. In Lhasa, "lamaists from different places can be seen kowtowing [prostrating] in front of the Jokhang Monastery. Inside, halls are crowded with people adding butter oil to the burning lamps and bowing before Buddhist statues." Thousands of people attend the annual Monlam. In 1986, the Bainqen [Panchen] Lama came from Beijing to participate in it. "He touched believers' heads and gave them blessings."

ANNE-MARIE BLONDEAU

This question reiterates Question 49, whose answer has already been commented upon. Let us only recall that this freedom of practice—within the limits of authorized religious and worship activities—varies from one moment to another and from one place to another. In the summer of 2000, such freedom seemed to be a thing of the past, but at the end of 2000, some interdictions were cancelled (see too Question 41). On the other hand, the practices listed in the Chinese answer are individual acts that do not require the clergy's intervention. But it is the very interaction between the clergy and the laypeople that Tibetans are deprived of. Their attendance at authorized ceremonies in monasteries is limited, and it is illegal for them to ask fortune-tellers, priests, and mediums for assistance in confronting the vicissitudes of life. The "Temporary Measures for the Administration of Places of Religious Activity in the Municipality of Lhasa" promulgated in February 1999 even forbid any act aimed at "improving someone's health" by "religious personnel" (quoted in TIN 2001: 48), which means the resort of the faithful to the benediction of a great lama and to the traditional rituals pertaining to medical practice.

Finally, the Chinese answer mentions neither the popular cults to the chthonian deities, individually or collectively (see Question 89), nor the countless apotropaic rituals geared to propitiate, appease, or ward off the invisible entities that populate the Tibetan universe. Though the annual cult to the mountain deity protecting every region is still very much alive in former Kham and Amdo, all those beliefs and practices are stigmatized as "superstitions" linked to the former feudal regime.

———

52
HOW ARE TIBET'S MONASTERIES ADMINISTERED?

———

"Every monastery has its own democratic administrative committee (or group) composed of a director, one or several deputy director[s], and several committee members. The committee, elected by all monks in the monastery on the basis of full consultation, is responsible for overseeing the monastery's Buddhist activities, its repair and upkeep, selecting administrative personnel, and any work that goes on. The committee receives guidance and support from relevant government departments in charge of religious affairs [see Question 57], and keeps them informed of any problems in implementing state policies."

ANNE-MARIE BLONDEAU

Those democratic administrative committees are a creation of Communist China and did not exist in Tibet in the past; they were established in the most important monasteries after the 1959 uprising. Their role is defined in the "Regulations for the Democratic Administration of Temples" promulgated by the People's Congress of the TAR and regularly updated. Originally, their members were chosen from the monks of the "poor" class. Nowadays, depending on the monastery, the community elects them, or some members are elected and others are nominated by the Bureau of Religious Affairs. In several committees, former monks who married during the Cultural Revolution play an important role, but their presence and that of their families is problematic for the monastic community. The smallest monasteries had no committee; instead, someone designated by the local authorities acted as their liaison agent (ICT 1990: 25).

In the Chinese answer, it is easy to read between the lines that, in fact, these committees control the monasteries. Their assigned duties are rather vaguely described here; in fact, they are substitutes for the classic administration of monasteries, which dealt with such matters as curriculum, ritual calendar, acceptance of postulants, and so on. They also manage the buildings and finance (what *100 Questions* calls "production" is the remunerated work now demanded from the monks who do not follow the program of studies; see also Question 54). The testimony of monks who fled Tibet describes the strong role of the police on those committees and of the mistrust they often inspire in the monastic community. They are more or less repressive, depending on the monastery and local administration: *Forbidden Freedoms* illustrates this variation of attitudes through the examples of four monasteries, Drepung, Sera, Ganden, and Shelkar (ICT 1990: 27–30). Goldstein's study on Drepung (1998) clearly describes the daily activity of the committee, but does not mention any mistrust of the monks, contrary to *Forbidden Freedoms,* a further sign of the difficulty of obtaining reliable information on Tibet.

One can infer, however, that the committees control the list of monks registered in the monastery and are ready to report the unregistered at the slightest provocation. They also help organize sessions of political education and control of the monks' "correct" thoughts; those sessions are led by "work teams" composed of civil servants and cadres (including researchers from the Academy of Social Sciences) whenever troubles arise or upon the launching of a political campaign. The democratic administrative committees are under the direct jurisdiction of the local branch of the Bureau of Religious Affairs, which pays their members. They must present a report to the bureau and follow its directives, and they also submit requests to enter the monastery to the bureau.

53
ARE THERE ANY PROFESSIONAL SCHOOLS FOR TRAINING RELIGIOUS WORKERS IN TIBET?

Yes. The Tibet College of Buddhism was established in Lhasa in 1980, preparing the students "for future religious work." Classes "for learning sutras" exist in "various large temples and monasteries." In Beijing, a "high-level Tibetan Buddhist institute" trains the Buddhist Tibetans; its president is Bainqen Erdini Qoigyi Gyaincain [the Panchen Lama], "one of the two highest living Buddhas in Tibet."

ANNE-MARIE BLONDEAU

Traditionally, the only "theological schools" in Tibet were monasteries, some of which were famous for their excellent "theological" studies, meaning philosophy, epistemology, and metaphysics. After the Cultural Revolution, monasteries tried to renew the tradition by reinstating the program of classical studies. They succeeded only with difficulty because of the lack of *geshes* (learned scholars), whose numbers had been decimated by the Cultural Revolution, the diaspora, the suppression of teaching structures, and the late age at which a boy is officially authorized to enter a monastery; we shall return to this in the next question.

The Institute of Buddhism created in Lhasa and mentioned in *100 Questions* is a secular institute under the TAR's Bureau of Religious Affairs and, according to different sources, was founded in 1980, 1982, or 1985 in Nechung, the ancient monastery of the state Oracle, situated below Drepung; similar institutes were founded at Kumbum and Labrang, in Amdo, and at Khandze, in Kham. The reason for their existence is clearly stated in the directive on the policy of religious matters ("Document 19"), addressed by the central Government to all Party and state cadres: in 1982 "the task of these seminaries is to create a contingent of young religious personnel who . . . fervently love their homeland and support the Party's leadership and the Socialist system and who possess sufficient religious knowledge" (quoted in ICT 1990: 48).

In Nechung, in 1990, about 180 students were supposed to obtain their diploma of *geshe* in ten years (half the time required in the monastic program), and the courses included Chinese history, law, and religion. The dean was a Tibetan Party member, former Red Guard, and proclaimed unbeliever (ICT 1990: 49). However, at least one student of this institute in 1992 had registered because he could not be officially accepted into one of Lhasa monasteries, where the quota had already been reached.

The Superior School of Buddhism in Beijing—the Chinese Academy of Tibetan Language for Superior Buddhist Studies (Zhongguo Zangyuxi Gaoji Foxueyuan)—was created in 1987 by the Panchen Lama, not "to train Tibetan Buddhists," as *100 Questions* says, but to provide an education both classical and "modern" to children and young people recognized as "rein-carnations" (*trülkus*). In addition to courses on Buddhism, the teaching provides courses in "religious policies, state decrees, [and] religious theory, as well as scientific and cultural knowledge" (Xinhua, September 5, 1990, quoted in TIN 1991: 9–10). The political advisor of the academy and direc-tor of the Education Bureau of the State Council, Ren Wuzhi, declared that "the Academy must strengthen its education in the fields of patriotism, na-tional solidarity and opposition to separatism" (TIN 1991:9–10). The ref-erence to classes "for learning sutras"[1] inside temples and monasteries may simply refer to studies of texts in the program of each monastery, but it may also mean the authorized yearly sessions—two, for example, in Drepung—for public teachings, which laypeople are allowed to attend. It is in fact for-bidden to teach religion outside of dedicated places; this means that laypeo-ple can at best invite a lama to their home, but they are not allowed to ask him for teachings and initiations as was done in the past (Goldstein 1998).

54
PLEASE GIVE A BRIEF ACCOUNT OF THE LAMASERY LIFE. DO LAMAS SUFFER MANY PRIVATIONS?

Nowadays [in 1989] there are more than 20,000 "lamas" in Tibet; most of them are young, around 20, with the youngest being 16 years old. "They spend about four hours a day learning the Buddhist su-tras, and debating what they have learned. During the rest of the day, they engage in business services or work in the orchard. Some of them service Chinese and foreign tourists, and some clean the halls of the temple."

They lead a comfortable life because, in addition to funds allocated

---

1. Chinese—and often sinologists—use a terminology drawn from Chinese Bud-dhism that does not have direct equivalents in Tibetan Buddhism. For example, they refer to the "sutra hall" instead of "assembly hall."

by the state, they receive alms given by worshippers and earn incomes from their work or from tourism. In Tashilhünpo, for instance, "the average monthly income of a lama . . . is more than 100 yuan, more than double that of the local farmers." Democratic administrative organizations have been set up in many monasteries, "the leaders of which were democratically selected by the lamas."

ANNE-MARIE BLONDEAU

One must start with the abusive use of the term "lama" by the Chinese authors in general. In Tibet, not all clerics are monks and not all monks are lamas. Tibetan clergy are of two types. First, there are ordained monks living in monasteries and obeying the rules of Buddhist discipline as transmitted from Indian Buddhism; they take many vows, including vows of celibacy, poverty, abstinence from alcohol, and so on. These are apparently what *100 Questions* calls "sedentary lamas." The second type is less homogeneous and includes wandering storytellers *(manipa)*, village priests living with their families, anchorites, and clerics living together in monasteries, sometimes alongside a monastic community. What differentiates them is that they do not take monastic vows—they can consequently marry, drink alcohol, and so on. They may or may not take all the vows of a "lay disciple" *(genyen,* Sanskrit, *upâsaka)*, but they all take the bodhisattva vow, the vow of one who aspires to enlightenment in order to benefit living beings. Most are also tantric practitioners, and, depending on their birth, personal inclination, and education, they can reach high spiritual levels, bringing them fame and attracting many disciples, both ordained and lay. Among them, as among monks, the lama (Sanskrit *guru)* is the spiritual master holding a tantric transmission, authorized to confer the teachings and initiations of the tantric path.

100 Questions only describes—rather succinctly—the life of monks in monasteries, a description that requires substantial comment. (One should note that nuns are completely ignored. Their number has always been smaller than that of the male clergy and their role more modest, but they have recently led protests and independence demands, giving them a new stature, both in Tibet and in exile [see Barnett 2005].)

Let us go back to the Chinese answer. The figure of 20,000 monks in 1989 cannot be verified; it is unclear whether it is for the TAR only or all of the Tibetan regions, for monks duly registered or for the monastic population as a whole (totaling 46,000 Buddhist monks and nuns in the TAR according to *People's Daily,* May 10, 2006). If compared with pre-1959 Tibet, the data given by the Dalai Lama's government in exile again differ considerably from the Chinese estimates; there were over 592,000 monks in Tibet prior to 1959, according to Dharamsala, and from 100,000 to 200,000 afterwards, according to the Chinese, but perhaps this was only in the TAR (ICT 1990: 64). In any case, the current figure of 20,000 monks represents the approximate monastic population of the three largest Lhasa monasteries before 1959. Much larger published numbers can be found, but a reasonable estimate indicates that there were about 9,000 monks in Drepung, from 5,000 to 6,000 in Sera, over 3,000 in Ganden, 4,700 in Tashilhünpo, and, in Amdo (eastern Tibet), 4,000 in Labrang (Dorje 1996). One can compare these numbers with those given in the following question: 200 monks in Ganden, 750 in Tashilhünpo. In 1995, Drepung had 540 "official" monks, 396 "irregular" ones, and a hundred from outside the TAR, while the authorized maximum number at that time was 600 (Goldstein 1998: 45). Based on in situ information in October 2000, Drepung had 500 (registered?) monks.

In effect, the government severely limits the number of residents in each monastery. The criteria are unclear, as is the branch of the administration setting the quotas; it seems that the Bureau of Religious Affairs plays an important role. The result of this limitation is that, in addition to "official" monks regularly admitted to and registered in a monastery, there is an "irregular" monastic population, of greater or less significance depending on the strictness of local authorities. Those monks residing without authorization in monasteries are not allowed to attend ceremonies or teachings and must provide for their own sustenance. They are also the first to be expelled if there is trouble. The quasi-autonomous colleges of the most important monasteries—themselves subdivided into "houses"—have been abolished. It was in those colleges that students from all over Tibet, as well as Mongolia and China, were trained. When they returned to their home monasteries, they trained local students. Administration and the discipline are now in the hands of the democratic administrative committee, which cannot supervise the monks as closely as was done in the past by the masters and elders of each college. In principle, it is forbidden to enter a monastery outside of one's home region (Drepung, where authorities have agreed to allow nonresidents to pursue their studies, is an exception [Goldstein 1998: 163n63]). Thus, the whole monastic structure is disorganized, which explains why so many monks flee to India to receive a traditional education in monasteries reestablished in exile.

The following section of the answer of *100 Questions* is easy to verify: any traveler to Tibet in the 1990s was struck by the absence of middle-aged monks in monasteries, where one instead met young monks and a few very old ones. The reason is clear: the Cultural Revolution emptied the monasteries before destroying them; monks were denounced in public and humiliated as the people's "oppressors." Submitted to "reeducation" sessions, they had to defrock, marry, and work like any layman (even the 10th Panchen Lama had to marry a Chinese wife). Those who resisted were tortured and sent to prison or "reeducation through work" camps, where many died. The testimony of survivors who were able to flee to India is very instructive in this regard. During the same period, no new monks were ordained; reordination started again in 1976 at the earliest, at the end of the Cultural Revolution or, more probably, with the "liberalization" following the 1980 visit of Hu Yaobang (on that subject, see Shakya 1999: 381). The consequences of this demographic "hole" have been catastrophic: the elaborate system of intellectual and spiritual training, in which elders were guardians, tutors, and teachers, has been annihilated. Assuming that in 1989, the majority of monks were twenty-year-olds and had entered monasteries around 1976–78, they would have been ten to twelve years old at that time; in fact, they were probably much older, because entering a monastery before the age of sixteen or eighteen is officially forbidden, (although one often encounters much younger monks). In the traditional system, boys could enter a monastery at about eight years of age.

The monastic schedule that is described cannot remedy this lack of initial training and of qualified teachers: four hours a day would be devoted to "the study of the holy scriptures and debating Buddhist questions." (However when the "work teams" mentioned in our answer to Question 52 come to monasteries for sessions of political "reeducation," lasting from several weeks to several months, all religious and teaching activities are suspended.) To properly compare this to the traditional system, it is important to note that the monastic population was not homogeneous and that great differences existed from one school to another, from one monastery to another, and within each monastery. The Gelugpa and Sakyapa schools generally offered a more intellectual training compared to other schools, where meditation and ritual were more important. But depending on its size too and on its founder's rules, each monastery stressed a particular aspect of monastic life. The religious society generally reflected the hierarchy of lay society with, at the top, great lamas (reincarnations of prestigious personages) and abbots, each at the head of a "house" of greater or lesser size and wealth, run by bursar monks, treasurers, and secretaries. Next were less well known "reincarnations" (*trülkus*), then scholars and monks involved in studies leading to the eminent rank of *geshe* and, finally, what could be called the lower clergy, by far the greatest number, who performed menial tasks and rarely went beyond learning how to read, write, and count. When their duties allowed, these monks would participate in prayer assemblies and rituals.

It is therefore difficult to briefly depict the "lamasery life" as asked by the question. The interested reader might refer to Georges Dreyfus's *The Sound of Two Hands Clapping* (2003) and to autobiographies of exiled monks describing the cycle of studies and monastic life in different monasteries. In the great monastic universities of the Gelugpa School, the young monk divided his time between his master's service and studies, entirely based on memorizing texts: first, prayers, and then various scholastic treatises according to the program of each monastery or college. Several hours each day were devoted to memorization and then recitation. For those who committed themselves to studies, the program of study lasted twenty years, encompassing metaphysics, logic, and epistemology. The year was organized in individual study sessions, interrupted by organized debates within the colleges and the entire monastery, sometimes between two monasteries. A student's day began before dawn and often ended close to midnight. Those who judged it necessary for their studies could be excused from obligatory daily prayer assemblies, although this created hardships for poor monks, since they were then deprived of distributions of food and money from laypeople during those assemblies.

In most cases, there are insufficient data to evaluate the percentage of monks authorized to pursue their studies. In Drepung, in 1993, there were 137 students out of a total of 427 monks (Goldstein 1998: 36), but at an unspecified date, a Sera monk reported that in his monastery, only ten students were exempt from work to pursue their studies full-time (ICT 1990: 47). All the others had to work for money for the community or for themselves in the jobs listed in the Chinese answer: trade, gardening, and welcoming tourists, not to mention monastery reconstruction. Labor was the fate of the majority of monks in the great monasteries of old Tibet, but strict working hours, eight hours per day, six days a week (ICT 1990: 47), are new; consequently, a great number of rituals and collective prayer sessions have been removed from the liturgical calendar.

This brings us to the income of monasteries and monks. In the former Tibet, monasteries were the largest landowners, and the most important constituted wealthy and powerful monastic estates. Having lost their lands, they have had to develop substitute means of income, using monks as manpower: from agriculture to various forms of manufacturing, of incense sticks, for instance. The wealth of monasteries did not necessarily redound to the benefit of individual monks. In the traditional system, there was a huge disparity, not only between the high and low clergy, but also between monks whose families could support them financially and those who had to find their own sustenance or donors, because their families were too poor or too far away. If we are to believe the Chinese answer, the monks' present situation seems much better, since they enjoy a comfortable income. In fact, although there are no extremely wealthy lamas any more—the disparity still exists: first, between the registered monks, who in fact receive part of the monastery's revenues, and the unregistered, who must find their own means of support; second, between the different categories of residents (students, old monks, members of the democratic administrative committee, and "merchants"); and, finally, also between monasteries. The Tashilhünpo example given here is misleading, for this monastery has always been favored on account of the Chinese policy toward the Panchen Lama. It is here, apparently, that the monks' authorized quota is the highest (see the figures given in the following Chinese answer). As noted (Question 49), the authorities tolerate building reconstruction and the reconstitution of monastic communities, as long as they are self-sufficient. In monasteries with a democratic administrative committee, it manages the finances. Monks form a kind of cooperative in which all the revenue is redistributed according to the "work points" accrued by each monk. Very young, very old, and sick monks cannot earn enough points to live. Goldstein (1998) shows that in Drepung at least, a sophisticated system allows minimal support, however insufficient, to all registered monks. Contrary to Chinese allegations, only members of committees and monks in charge of precise official functions receive a direct salary from the government. In fact, as in the past, the family must provide for the needs of their son or sons in the orders, and sometimes of his master. But more than in the past, the gifts of laypeople are an indispensable complement in the sustenance of the clergy.

55
WHICH MONASTERIES ARE FAMOUS IN TIBET?
AND WHAT IS THE SITUATION THEY ARE IN NOW?

The most famous are:

- The Jokhang Monastery, "worshipped by the Tibetans as a holy place," belongs to "the Yellow (or Gelug) Sect," and was built in the seventh century by the two princesses, one Chinese and one Nepalese, who became the wives of Songtsan Gampo. The main statue is one of Shâkyamuni, "which was brought by Princess Wen Cheng from Changan [present X'ian], the capital of the Tang dynasty. In front of the monastery stands a stone tablet marking the Tang-Tibet alliance."

- The Zhaibung [Drepung] Monastery, the largest monastery of the "Yellow Sect," was built in 1416. It contains "many Buddhist classics and cultural relics. In 1653, when the fifth Dalai Lama was entrusted by Emperor Shunzhi of the Qing Dynasty to become the local political and religious ruler of Tibet, it began to serve as a traditional office for the local government."

- The Sera Monastery, built in 1419, is also one of the largest monasteries of the "Yellow Sect." It contains many historical relics and books, including the "Tibetan Tripitaka (a series of Buddhist learning) written in powdered gold and the calligraphy and painting scrolls of the Ming and Qing dynasties."

- The Gahdan [Ganden] Monastery, the oldest of the "Yellow Sect," was built in 1409 by Tsongkhapa, the founder of this sect. It was destroyed during the Cultural Revolution but is in repair. More than 200 lamas are living in it.

- The Tashilhünpo Monastery, built by the first Dalai Lama between 1447 and 1459, "is the major monastery of the Yellow Sect in the inner Tibetan region" [? in Tsang province]. It was repaired and expanded by the successive Bainqens [it is the Panchen Lamas' residence]. "It houses numerous Buddhist classics and historical artifacts" and a huge statue of Champa [Jampa] Buddha. "There are more than 750 lamas in residence."

- The Sagya [Sakya] Monastery, the main monastery of the Sagya Sect, stands 150 kilometers southwest of Xigatse [Shigatse]; it includes two sections: the northern section was built between 1079 and the "mid-13th century when Pagba [Phagpa], the leader of the Sagya Sect, was entrusted the power to administer the political and religious affairs in Tibet by the Yuan emperor." This part was "severely destroyed during the 'cultural revolution.'" The southern section, built in 1268, is well preserved. Its architecture reflects "a blend of Tibetan, Han and Mongolian" styles. Its "hall for sutra chanting" can hold an assembly of up to 10,000 lamas. Here are kept a great number of books, "as well as gifts and tokens given by the emperors of the Yuan Dynasty." There is also "a large mural painting depicting the scene of Pagba being received by Kublai Khan, the founder of the Yuan Dynasty."

- The Palkor Monastery was originally built by the Sagya Sect but later it pertained to various other sects. "The Palkhor (Octagon)

Pagoda . . . is an 11-storey construction with a base space of 2,200 square meters. It houses many fine sculptures and murals."

- The Tshurpur [Tsurphu] Monastery is situated in the Doilung-deqen [Tölung Dechen] County northwest of Lhasa. Built in 1187, it is "the leading monastery of the Karma sub-branch of the Kargyu Sect. . . . Karma Batsong [?], the abbot of the monastery, was conferred with the title of 'The Great Treasure Prince of Dharma' by an emperor of the Ming Dynasty. The monastery houses many cultural relics of Ming and succeeding dynasties."

ANNE-MARIE BLONDEAU

The seven monasteries briefly described here are all in the TAR. The important monasteries—by size or history—of the ancient eastern provinces of Kham and Amdo are ignored.

Even regarding the TAR only, one must note that the monasteries chosen by *100 Questions* are those on the tourist circuits. These also often include the important sites of Samye and Zhalu for their history and art. The authors of *100 Questions* reveal a certain ignorance, since these two sites are also recognized for their heterogeneous nature: the juxtaposition and combination of Tibetan, Nepalese, and Chinese styles. They could have illustrated one of the chief preoccupations of *100 Questions:* evidence of Chinese influence on Tibet's art and history.

Space does not permit a more detailed description of the seven temples or monasteries chosen by *100 Questions*, and we shall not add to its list; art books and cultural and tourist guides do so well. We shall limit ourselves instead to some remarks and corrections.

First, the places do not have the same status: the Jokhang temple, around which Lhasa has been established, is the spiritual center of Tibet, the site of pilgrimage that every Tibetan dreams of visiting. It is not a monastery, like the other places mentioned, but a temple of impressive proportions, with multiple chapels. Only a small monastic community lives there. The "pagoda" of the Pelkor Chöde monastery in Gyantse—the Kumbum—is itself a fifteenth-century temple in the shape of a monumental stupa and is a unique architectural compound both because of its size and the quality of its sculptures and paintings. Finally, it is important to note that the 5th Dalai Lama had come to power ten years before the Shunzhi emperor of the Qing dynasty "put him . . . at the head of the religious and political power in Tibet."

56
WHEN DID TIBETAN BUDDHISM COME INTO BEING?
HOW MANY SECTS DOES IT HAVE?

"Tibetan Buddhism, commonly known as Lamaism, is a branch of Buddhism practiced mainly in areas inhabited by Tibetans and Mongolians. It came into being in the late 10th century. During the mid-13th century, with the support of the central government of the Yuan Dynasty, Lamaism became inter-twined with political power in Tibet, explaining how it spread to areas inhabited by Mongolians."

"It comprises many sects, the major ones being the Ningma, Kargyu, Sagya and Gelug."

"The Ningma [Nyingma] Sect, commonly known as the red sect (red hats, French version), was formed in the 11th and 12th centuries." Its name, which means "Old School" in Tibetan, comes from its adhering to the older Buddhist teachings, as opposed the sects that developed "new interpretations."

"The Kargyu Sect [Kagyü], commonly known as the white sect (white hats), was established in the 11th century. Its practice centers on the oral teaching of the Buddha's 'secret teachings'. Many of the leaders of its numerous sub-branches had titles conferred upon them by the Yuan and Ming imperial courts, making the sect a major political force in Tibet." But they lost their influence during the Qing dynasty, with the Yellow Sect winning favor.

The Sagya [Sakya] Sect, also founded in the eleventh century, is named after the place, Sagya, where its first monastery was built. "Its influence peaked during the Yuan Dynasty," when Kublai Khan gave Phagpa "the power to supervise administrative and religious affairs in Tibet. At the end of the Yuan Dynasty, it was gradually replaced by the Kargyu Sect. Since then, its influence has been limited to the Sagya region."

"The Gelug Sect, commonly known as the yellow sect (yellow hats), was founded by Tsongkhapa in the 14th century. Its lamas were not allowed to marry and its belief in reincarnation gave rise to the two grand Living Buddhas system of Dalai and Bainqen [Panchen]. In the 17th century, the fifth Dalai Lama received a title of honor from the Qing imperial court and thus became the overall religious leader in areas inhabited by Tibetans and Mongolians. In the mid-18th century, the Qing court ordered the seventh Dalai Lama to assume political leadership, and ever since, the Gelug has been the major Lamaist sect in Tibet."

ANNE-MARIE BLONDEAU

The editor of *100 Questions* prides himself in having benefited from the help "of experts in the history of Tibet." They do not appear to have been experts in religious history, however, because the above answer displays a dismaying ignorance, alternating between errors and approximations. It is also distorted by the Chinese obsession to prove the dependence of Tibet on China. As a result, one learns very little about Tibetan Buddhism itself.

We shall not dwell on the term "Lamaism," "commonly" used, it is true, by some of the best specialists. It is a convenient appellation but totally unjustified for Tibetan Buddhism. We have already dealt with the impropriety of the generalized use of the term "lama." To call Tibetan Buddhism "Lamaism" implies that it is not a form of Buddhism. Tibetan Buddhists thus strongly condemn the use of this term, insisting that their religion simply be called *chö* (Sanskrit *dharma*, "the order of things, law, etc."), or *Sangye ki chö*, Buddha's law, inherited from Indian Buddhism. Buddhism, born in India in the sixth century B.C.E., went through variations and local adaptations in all the countries where it was established, and Tibet is no exception. But no one would invent a specific name to designate Buddhism in Sri Lanka, in China, or elsewhere. D. S. Lopez Jr. (1998: 15–45), in pages as savory as they are instructive, traces the history of the term "Lamaism" from the eighteenth century on, and the ideological implications of its adoption by Europeans.

To end with this first sentence of the Chinese answer, let us say that Tibetan Buddhism is not only found "in areas inhabited by Tibetans and Mongolians." In the course of history, it has spread much more widely, all along the Himalayan arc, to Ladakh, to the high valleys of the north of India and Nepal, to Sikkim (now Indian), and to Bhutan. In the north, it has been adopted in all of Mongolia—and not only in Inner Mongolia—and it has influenced China proper, an influence that grows every day in both China and Taiwan.

Rather than undertaking a word-by-word correction of the Chinese answer, we shall instead roughly sketch the history of Tibetan Buddhism and its subdivision into schools. Buddhism appeared in Tibet around the seventh century, and not at the end of the tenth, and was imposed as the state religion by the sovereign Trisong Detsen in the middle of the eighth century, in an edict preserved in Tibetan history (see Part I of this volume). It is important to emphasize the similarities in the ways that Buddhism has been introduced to nations across Asia. Initially supported by kings, princes, or emperors, it followed the fate of their dynasties. In Tibet, the collapse of the Yarlung dynasty in the middle of the ninth century marked the decline of monasticism, at least in central Tibet, to such a point that in its rewriting of imperial history, the later tradition invoked a persecution of Buddhism—for which there is no documented evidence—by the last sovereign, which is said to have caused its near disappearance for a hundred years. Succession struggles and the parceling out of the empire suffice to explain the absence of sources for that period. In any case, small tantric communities survived and developed throughout the country.

The thread of history reappears again at the end of the tenth century, at a time Tibetans call the later propagation of Buddhism *(chidar).* Compared to a dying fire suddenly flaring up, it occurred almost simultaneously in central and in western Tibet, but in different ways. In central Tibet, religious individuals sought ordination from Tibetan and Chinese monks in the Dunhuang region and restored monastic communities on ancient sites. Claiming an uninterrupted transmission since the introduction of Buddhism in Tibet, they formed one of the groups later classified as "Ancients" (Nyingmapas). In the West, descendants of the imperial dynasty had founded a kingdom. One of the kings, a devout Buddhist, troubled by the deviations he witnessed in the religion practiced by the Tibetans, decided to restore the ancient custom of exchange with Indian Buddhism. He sent young men to Kashmir for training and invited Indian pandits to Tibet; this marked a new era of intensive translation of canonical texts—including some that had been translated during the imperial time but that were judged incorrect—and of building temples and monasteries in western Tibet. A little later, the most famous Indian pandit, Atisha (982–1054), was invited. It was he who reestablished the doctrine and monastic rules, especially for the school created around him, the Kadampas, "those who follow oral instructions." At the end of the fourteenth century, Tsongkhapa's preaching, a striking success in central Tibet, was presented as a new exegesis of Atisha's works. The most recent school of Tibetan Buddhism based on his teachings took the name "New Kadampas," or Gelugpas, "the Virtuous," since, in their turn, they would strictly follow the monastic code.

The religious revival of the tenth and eleventh centuries inspired tantric adepts to go to India in search of a guru who could teach and initiate them. Upon their return, empowered with the prestige of this direct transmission, they attracted more and more disciples, which rapidly forced the initial hermitages to develop into monasteries on lands donated by the faithful laity. Some of these establishments became the seats of the various schools named after the mother monastery, for example, the Sakyapas, "those of Sakya." The case of the Kagyüpas, "those of oral transmission," is slightly different; it was not the first master, Marpa, who founded the school, nor even his famous student Milarepa, but a disciple of the latter. In their turn, his many disciples founded monasteries, which were to become the seats of the different Kagyüpa branches: Drigungpas, Phagmodrupas, Karmapas, and so on. These schools' hierarchs often belonged to the noble families they relied upon. Wealthy, powerful, and venerated, they filled a political void, and some imposed their schools' hegemony, at least for a time, often with Mongol assistance, as explained in Part I above.

Because those groups only accepted the validity of the new translations of the tantras and claimed a direct Indian transmission, they were called "the New," in contrast to the faithful adepts of texts and teachings transmitted from the imperial period, called "the Ancients." One sees that the *100 Questions* answer is a simplification; although the appellation "Ancients" appeared in the eleventh or twelfth centuries, their tradition in fact goes back to the Tibetan empire.

The Chinese authors persist in attempting to distinguish the schools of Tibetan Buddhism by the color of their dress or their hats. This habit, inherited from the Qing imperial court (see Question 6), is a source of confusion, because the shapes and colors of religious hats are very diverse, even in a single school. Thus, "red hat" *(zhamar)* probably designates the Karmapa hierarch, second in importance after the "black hat" *(zhanag)* Karmapa, for Tibetans, rather than a Nyingmapa cleric. Also, schools other than the Gelugpa wear yellow hats.

We shall not return to the historical distortions noted throughout this volume but only attempt to provide some precision to what *100 Questions* calls "succession by the incarnation system." First, contrary to what the Chinese answer implies, this system did not begin with the Gelugpas but with the Karmapas in the twelfth and thirteenth centuries. This system replaced that of succession from uncle to nephew as head of the school or of the monastery, probably because it provided more stability. It derives from two Buddhist beliefs: of the reincarnation of beings and the capacity of buddhas and bodhisattvas to "emanate" bodies in order to save those beings. What is called a "reincarnation"—a "living Buddha" for the Chinese—is an "emanation body" *(trülku)* and the rebirth of his human predecessor. It is because of their transcendental nature that *trülkus* enjoy such veneration, and, with time, this succession system has been adopted by all schools, with *trülku* lineages multiplying inside each school and even in each great monastery. For the Gelugpas, the Dalai and Panchen Lamas form only the two most prestigious lineages, and hundreds of *trülkus* have been counted.

Faithful to the ideological line at the time when *100 Questions* was published, the Chinese authors ignore another important religious school on the fringe of Buddhism, the Bönpo. For Tibetans, this school—presented by them as a different religion—is the continuation of pre-Buddhist beliefs, the Bön, whose priests violently opposed Buddhism when it was introduced. For this reason, the Bönpos have been ignored, denigrated and sometimes persecuted by Buddhists throughout history. The origins and history of Bön are much more complex and still not well understood. When Bön appeared as an established school around the end of the tenth century, it had adopted the totality of Buddhist beliefs and practices—including monasticism—while showing original characteristics, notably in its myths and rituals, which seem to be inherited from old Tibet.

What is of interest in the context of our work is the sudden Chinese change in attitude toward this school, until recently classified as "superstition." This change accompanied a political change toward the Dalai Lama in 1994, at the Third Tibet Work Forum. From that point, he was accused of fueling Tibetan "splittism," and Buddhism was stigmatized as a religion "foreign" to Tibetans. In a speech given in 1997 in Lhasa, Chen Kuiyan, the TAR Party secretary until October 2000, said that to assimilate Tibetan culture to Buddhist culture is "totally absurd," because it existed a thousand years before the introduction of Buddhism; and that this view "belittles the ancestors of the Tibetan nationality and the Tibetan nationality itself" (Kvaerne 1998: 72–73). The future will tell if this unexpected support of the Bönpos' affirmations of their antiquity will restore their image in the eyes of Tibetan Buddhists or if it will ferment new domestic discord. (In exile, the Bönpos have already recovered their respectability in the Dalai Lama government, which gives them equal representation to that of the Buddhist schools in its various organizations.)

57
IT HAS BEEN REPORTED THAT CHINA WILL SET UP A "TIBETAN BUDDHISM GUIDANCE COMMITTEE." WHAT WILL BE ITS TASKS?

This committee "is a special organization under the Buddhist Association of China to oversee the practice of Tibetan Buddhism in Tibet,

Qinghai, Gansu, Sichuan and Yunnan. Its main tasks are: to unite monks and laymen . . . and help the government implement stipulations on religion included in the Constitution, and state laws and policies; to educate monks and nuns to be patriotic and law-abiding." It is also responsible for protecting freedom of believing, the legitimate rights of monasteries and clergy, for training "Buddhist intellectuals," for giving guidance and exercising "supervision over the management of lamaseries . . . and [to] raise the living standards of monks and nuns."

ANNE-MARIE BLONDEAU

We have found no trace of the creation of a "Tibetan Buddhism Guidance Committee" in the documents at our disposal. When *100 Questions* was published in 1989, there may have been a plan to establish the new Bureau of Religious Affairs at the regional level. In 1986, this had merged at the central level—in Beijing—with the Commission of Affairs of Nationalities to form the Commission of Nationalities and Religious Affairs (which Tibetans continue to call the Bureau of Religious Affairs, the appellation that we have also used previously). However, to our knowledge, the Tibetan branch does only manage the TAR and not the TAP incorporated in various Chinese provinces, as *100 Questions* suggests.

Nevertheless, it is not useless to present the organizations for religious control in China with their TAR branches here.

The first is the Buddhist Association of China, also mentioned in Question 49, which was created as early as 1952. The government, for which it holds the role of official advisor, appoints its members, who included eminent Tibetan lamas in the early years. The Tibetan branch was established in 1956 (Conner and Barnett 1997) or 1957 (ICT 1990: 20), and later it opened specific branches in several cities (the Lhasa branch in 1984). The Tibetan Buddhist Association has no power, and its role is limited to transmitting carefully screened claims of Buddhists to the Bureau of Religious Affairs and to collecting and writing biographies of great lamas and the history of monasteries. Cleansed of its "anti-revolutionary" members after the 1987 and subsequent protests, it is more and more politicized, and its currently assigned priority is "to strengthen the links between the government and the practicing religious faithful" (ICT 1990: 21–24).

At the government level, the most important organization is the former Bureau of Religious Affairs under the Party's authority via the Department of the United Front Work. According to "Document 19" (see Question 49), "all places of worship are under the administrative control of the Bureau of

Religious Affairs" (quoted in ICT 1990: 19). Its Tibetan branch was established in 1956. The bureau was abolished during the Cultural Revolution, reinstated in 1978, and transformed in 1988 into the Commission of Nationalities and Religious Affairs, as previously mentioned. In the TAR, a delegate administration exists in each prefecture and some municipalities. The "New Religious Regulations" promulgated in 2004 empower (article 19) local departments to "supervise and inspect the sites for religious activities in terms of their compliance with laws," to develop and implement the management systems, to control "the alteration of registered items [i.e., religious artifacts registered in a monastery], the conducting of religious activities and activities that involve foreign affairs."

Everything to do with religion in Tibet, including building restoration, entering orders, monk quotas in monasteries, festival celebrations, and pilgrimages, has to be authorized by the Commission of Nationalities and Religious Affairs, which supervises the democratic administrative committees in monasteries and the "work teams" in charge of the political "reeducation" of monks and nuns. Moreover, if we are to believe the examples provided in *Forbidden Freedoms*, the local cadres responsible, who are sometimes former Red Guards, are not concerned with respecting freedom of religion; they may even be openly opposed to religion (ICT 1990: 20–21).

PART SIX

Right to Autonomy

The reader who has been patient enough to follow us this far must have by now a clearer idea about what "autonomous rights" are in the Tibetan context. The analysis offered here by Thierry Dodin explains why the Chinese government definitively refuses any discussion about the "autonomous rights" of its minorities and turns a deaf ear to the Dalai Lama's proposal to grant Tibet true autonomy within the PRC (Questions 37–38).

58

WHAT POLICIES HAS THE CHINESE GOVERNMENT ADOPTED IN REGARD TO MINORITY NATIONALITIES?

"Apart from the Han nationality, which accounts for 93.3% of China's total population, there are 55 minority nationalities comprising about 6.7% of the total population." The principles and policies toward them are as follow:

- National equality. "National discrimination and oppression are prohibited."
- "National unity and mutual assistance."
- "Freedom of developing their own spoken and written languages, of keeping or reforming their own customs and habits, and of religious belief."
- National regional autonomy for the areas "where minority nationalities live in compact communities."

According to these principles, the government has formulated a series of decrees and policies since 1949: In 1951, it "gave instructions to prohibit or change all antiquated expressions bearing discrimination and insult towards minority nationalities." In 1952, "the Decision on the protection of all dispersed Minority nationality components for the Enjoyment of National Equal Rights" was issued, which gave the minorities the same rights as the local Han people, and the right "to make legal appeals and defenses in their own national spoken and written languages; and to lodge complaints with the government when they are discriminated against and oppressed." The same year saw the promulgation of "the General Program for the Implementation of National Regional Autonomy to guarantee minority nationalities the right to administer their own national affairs." The 1953 electoral law, amended in 1959, provided for each minority "living in a compact community"—even with a few people—"to have its own deputies to the local people's congress at various levels."

Beside the Inner Mongolia Autonomous Region created in 1947, there are 4 autonomous regions, 30 autonomous prefectures and 103 autonomous counties.

Ten nationality colleges have been established, "and nearly one million minority cadres have been trained."

Concerning the spoken and written languages of minority nation-alities, a guiding committee was established in 1951 "to help nation-alities without written languages create them and nationalities with-out perfect written languages develop them." "Those languages . . . should be used in elections of representatives to the people's congress in autonomous areas. It was further provided that these areas use their own national spoken and written languages for local administrating, teaching, publishing and broadcasting."

"Minority nationalities have been helped to develop their economies and cultures. . . . The state grants huge financial subsidies to national autonomous areas every year. It provides these areas with many industrial and agricultural products, machines and transporta-tion vehicles. The state also sends scientists, technicians, teachers and medical personnel, as well as experienced managers . . . to help work there."

THIERRY DODIN

Historical Remarks

The PRC's political mythology has not only pronounced contemporary China a multi-ethnic state, it has also projected this modern concept into the past, thus providing a convenient, legitimizing reading of history. In-dependent historical research however, presents a more accurate and differ-entiating view (see Sperling in Question 1 and Chayet in Question 5).

With the end of Manchu/Qing rule in 1911, the emerging "New China" saw itself inheriting a by then largely nominal suzerainty over populations who had neither considered themselves to be Chinese nor were considered as such by the Chinese. As was the case with many other modern nation-alist movements, Chinese nationalists not only developed a homogenizing perception of their own people (which hardly acknowledged the wide scope of intra-Chinese diversity, in particular the linguistic and cultural gap be-tween north and south), they also viewed themselves as the political heirs of the Manchu empire they had overthrown. Non-Chinese people were per-ceived to be "natural" subordinates of the new regime and became part of the nationalist project without being asked.

Perhaps surprisingly, the Chinese Communist Party (CCP), with its Marxism-inspired social-revolutionary agenda, showed comparatively less interest in the non-Chinese population in territories outside China itself. In fact, in the early years of its existence (i.e., the 1920s), the Party even acknowledged, at least in principle, the right of these people to choose their own status, including independence. However, this was only temporary, and once it became more important in China's political life, the CCP swiftly adopted the mainstream call for the "reintegration" of non-Chinese ethnic groups. This change was likely impelled by the fact that most tributary states sought to sever themselves from the new Chinese republic soon after the collapse of the Qing dynasty. Tibet declared its full independence, the core Mongolian lands formed an independent state (but soon became a satellite of the USSR), and there were strong moves toward autonomy in East Turkestan (Xinjiang). The Kuomintang Nationalist government laid claim to these territories, as the CCP did later, and strove to establish its dominance there both by diplomacy and by force. It continued to maintain the bureaucracy established by the late Qing empire for the administration of "various ethnic groups," in particular the Bureau for Tibetan and Mongolian Affairs, even though most of the territories in question had effectively lapsed from its control.

Even before the advent of the PRC in 1949, the Communists went a step further by drafting a modernized vocabulary and a theoretical framework inspired by Soviet models. China's neighboring nations and ethnic groups became "national minorities," all of which were given Chinese names (where these did not already exist). The Chinese themselves were officially denominated as "Han," and the word "Chinese," in the sense of "citizen of China," was translated as *Zhongguo ren* (lit. "People of the Middle Kingdom"), thus neatly separating ethnic identity and citizenship. The meaning of the term "motherland" was enlarged to include the whole territory over which sovereignty was claimed, whereby the actual Chinese/Han core land was understood to be the "inner land" and the rest as the "borderland" (although the area to which this applied was much larger than under the empire). The PRC's population is thus understood to consist of "various ethnic groups," all expected to strive toward the "unity of all nationalities." These politically correct proclamations of multi-ethnicity should not mask the fact that a significant shift had occurred. The "Old China" of the Qing empire matched the definition of a multi-ethnic state rather well. The Manchus, a very small ethnic group, ruled it and attributed different roles within the empire to different ethnic groups. For example, Koreans and Mongols played a predominant role in the military; the Chinese held a strong position within the bureaucracy; and, because the Manchus were followers of Tibetan Buddhism, Tibetans played a prominent role in the religious life of the empire. Most official documents were written in Manchu, followed by Mongol, Tibetan, and Chinese translations. The Chinese (Han), although representing the enormous majority of the empire's population, were in all regards subjects of the emperor just like any other ethnic group.

The "New China" paradigm, however, saw the country's population in terms of a Han majority/"national minorities" dichotomy, whereby, although in principle (and specifically by law) all ethnic groups are equal, deep-rooted ethnocentric categories and structural facts place the Chinese majority in a "more equal" position. This is best reflected in the official and widespread popular portrayal of all the nationalities as "brothers" in the one "family," but with the Chinese being the "elder brothers."

Basic Principles

Most regions within the borders of the PRC where "national minorities" live have been given a special status that can apply to different levels of the country's administrative subdivisions, that is, province level, prefecture level, county level, or lower subdivisions. Such subdivisions are termed "autonomous." The Regional Ethnic Autonomy Law states that China's government has an obligation to "[respect] and [protect] the right of every minority nationality to manage their own internal affairs." However, the exact meaning of the terms "autonomous" and "management of internal affairs" (referred to, for instance, in Question 60) requires clarification. Although the existence of a nationality minority population is the determining factor in designating a given territorial unit as autonomous, this implies neither any prerogative on the part of the national minority in question nor an inalienable entitlement of the minority to this territory. Autonomous territories are not acknowledged as any kind of "homeland." Under Chinese law, the central government exerts full and unlimited control over each and every square centimeter of the country's territory. Territorial units labeled autonomous are not strictly determined by the extent of the linguistic or cultural features of a given nationality. Rather, these autonomous areas are established where ethnic minorities live "in compact communities," as the Chinese answer phrases it (hence they need not even form the majority of the population in a given territorial unit). The need for "autonomy" is defined by the perceived necessity to adapt policies formulated in Beijing to local "characteristics," that is, to optimize their mode of implementation to the mentality, traditions, history, and also sensitivities of local minorities. The answer to Question 14 (2001) clarifies this by stating that "special implementation methods with Tibetan characteristics" are adopted, and that local regulations must be "within the ambit of certain national laws." This distinction might seem academic, but it is crucial in understanding how the PRC autonomy system is meant to function. Hence, "autonomy" is in no way a departure from the top-down approach of the Chinese authorities toward the "masses." No autonomous area is expected or permitted to define its own policies, but the authorities posted in such areas still have the duty to figure out how centrally defined policies can best be implemented in a non-Chinese context. To that extent, the answers given to Question 60 about the specific "rights" granted the TAR are, at best, misleading.

An ethnic and cultural perspective provided by the United Front complements this essentially territory-based approach. The United Front is the organ of the CCP devoted to forming broad "alliances" with non-Party and non-Chinese social groups within the country. Its role is to involve the "patriotic upper strata," that is, high religious or ethnic dignitaries who are deemed loyal to the regime, in an *advisory* position in the decision-making structures of the state. Ethnic affairs are thus dealt with using a dual system: policies are drafted by the central government and its organs based on the recommendations of the United Front. These are then applied in autonomous territorial units with ethnic populations, taking into consideration which mode of implementation best fits the local ethnic settings. Consequently, the same laws and regulations may be applied differently, for instance, in two different autonomous prefectures or counties, whether located in the TAR, Qinghai, or Sichuan, even though both might be declared Tibetan autonomous areas. Tibetan autonomous areas, or those attached to any other minority for that matter, are not controlled by the central government in any more relaxed or flexible a manner. In fact, due to political tensions, they are often under tighter control by the central authorities than core Chinese lands.

In any case, whether in autonomous areas or any other territorial unit of the PRC, the actual power lies exclusively in the hands of the Party. The Party secretary of a given territorial unit, although often not the highest-ranking member of the local administrative hierarchy in ceremonial terms, always decides. His is the last word, and he is only answerable to the higher echelons of the Party hierarchy that appointed him. He and the Party secretariat under his direction entertain a tight network that parallels and effectively supervises all political and administrative work. As a result, even if the local administration in autonomous areas is in local ethnic hands (which is often the case in Tibet) and some kind of locally elected administrative leadership is in place, as long as the nod is effectively given from outside the region, autonomy is only theoretical. Moreover, even in autonomous areas, the Party secretary is usually Chinese. In the TAR for instance, no Tibetan has ever made it higher than to the position of deputy Party secretary (the answer to Question 67 acknowledges this, but cynically explains it in terms of the "equality" of all ethnic groups), whereas, as the answer to Question 14, 2001, emphasizes, all other major posts, including those of "chairman of the Standing Committee of the People's Congress of the TAR, chairman of the People's Congress of the TAR, [and] chairman of the government of the TAR . . . are all occupied by Tibetan residents." However, the answer does not mention that these individuals have no actual decision-making powers, or at best, very few, and all of them are subordinate to the directives of the Party secretary. Hence, although the answers to Questions 63 and 64 correctly list the heads of the TAR government and chairmen of the TAR People's Congress and rightly specify that all were Tibetans, this in no way corroborates the substantial devolution of power to Tibetans it suggests.

In autonomous areas, a semblance of ethnic participation is provided by the involvement of a great number of ethnic personalities as members of the local chamber of the Chinese People's Political Consultative Conference (CPPCC). However, the Party handpicks the CPPCC's members from among "patriotic" individuals, and its role, as the name indicates, is of a purely advisory nature, or as the answer to Question 16, 2001, puts it, to "participate in discussions of state affairs." In reality, its members are generally clients of the Party, and it is unlikely that their "advice" will ever extend beyond the framework established for them by the Party. There is also a sizeable ethnic participation in CPPCC branches in autonomous areas, but this local "parliament" is in fact a ceremonial organ exhausted by rubber-stamping Party policies and whose members, as is the case with the CPPCC, are Party-selected. Beyond that, in the TAR, for instance, Tibetan membership of the CPPCC is far below the percentage of ethnic Tibetans in the region, even though the TAR is one of the most ethnically homogeneous territories in the country. Even so, the answer to Question 60 does emphasize the limitations of their competency by specifying that "autonomy regulations and specific regulations in accordance with local political, economic and cultural characteristics" only become effective "after ratification by the National People's Congress Standing Committee," and that modifications to nationwide rules are possible "provided that they have the approval of a higher-level government department." Effectively, a law or regulation applied in the TAR, for example, will be decided, at least in its general features, at the highest level of the Party in Beijing and then passed down to the TAR Party secretariat (a full wing of the TAR government building in Lhasa is dedicated to central-regional "communication"). The Party secretary will then ensure that the law or regulation is handed over to the TAR Congress, where Party-selected parliamentarians will "discuss" it. At some point, the Party-designed CPPCC will advise the Congress about the law or regulation after its deliberations, which will then be formally passed by the Congress. Finally, it will be implemented by the local government (mostly Tibetans), but under the supervision of the Chinese Party secretary. Considering this, the answers given to Question 61 about "decrees on self-government . . . formulated by the Tibet Autonomous Region" are in effect entirely irrelevant.

59
WHEN WAS THE TIBET AUTONOMOUS REGION FOUNDED? HOW MANY AUTONOMOUS REGIONS ARE THERE IN CHINA?

It was founded in September 1965. Preparations had begun in 1956, the Dalai Lama being the chairman of the preparatory working committee. After the 1959 "armed rebellion" and the flight of the Dalai Lama, the central government "dismissed the Tibetan regional government" and "the working committee functioned as the local government of Tibet, with Bainqen Erdini Qoigyi Gyaincain [the Panchen Lama] as chairman."

There are five autonomous regions: Tibet, Inner Mongolia, Xinjiang Uygur, Ningxia Hui, and Guangxi Zhuang.

[This factual answer needs no comment.]

60
AS ONE OF THE AUTONOMOUS REGIONS, WHAT RIGHTS DOES TIBET HAVE?

These rights include:

- "Enforcing national laws and policies in accordance with the actual situation in Tibet;
- Formulating regulations in accordance with the political, economic and cultural characteristics of Tibet. The regulations go

into effect after ratification by the National People's Congress Standing Committee;

- Administering local finance and planning local economic development;

- Administering local education, science, culture, public health, and sports, protecting and caring for local cultural relics, and developing local culture;

- Establishing local public security forces with the approval of the State Council;

- Using one or more local languages in government affairs. The prevailing languages in Tibet are Tibetan and Chinese.

- China's Constitution stipulates that the chairmanship and vice-chairmanships of the autonomous areas shall include a citizen or citizens of the nationality or nationalities exercising regional autonomy in the areas concerned; and the administrative heads of the autonomous areas shall be citizens of the nationality, or of one of the nationalities exercising regional autonomy in the areas concerned."

[On the illusory character of those "rights," see Question 59.]

61

How many decrees on self-government have been formulated by the Tibet Autonomous Region?

"Since 1979, the People's Congress of the TAR has worked out 21 legal decrees and 14 decisions bearing the nature of legislation." Among them, the adaptation to the TAR of the Law of criminal procedure and of the Marriage Law; the "Rules on the procedures of election of the People's Congresses at various levels in the TAR, the Regulations on the protection of forests, the Resolution on the study, use and development of Tibetan language and writing."

Thierry Dodin

We have underlined in our answer to Question 59 that the local powers are not the actual decision makers and that the decrees they may issue merely rubber-stamp decisions taken at the central level. Here, we shall only add a few words on the language issue (see also Question 75).

Language is rightly acknowledged as a primary element of cultural or ethnic identity. The degree to which cultural autonomy within a given polity is achievable is reflected by the extent to which a cultural or ethnic group is supported in the use of its own language, and the way in which that language is allowed to develop. It is therefore not surprising that *100 Questions* praises the PRC's language policies in Tibet. As is common in such official literature, the statements made here are general declarations of intention but hardly reflect the reality on the ground. The Chinese authorities have undeniably paid great attention to the language issue since their arrival in Tibet in the early 1950s, and many of the Tibetans who in the early years of Chinese rule were inclined to support the authorities were often among the few educated people and intellectuals who resented the conservatism of Tibetan society, mainly exerted by the clergy. The Tibetan written language had essentially become a fossilized instrument used to convey an institutionalized sense of religion, rather than a lively idiom suitable for expressing individual views and feelings in the modern sense. It was certainly in the nature of the CCP to try and use existing reformist circles for political purposes, but this also set clear limitations on their activities. Although the regime supported essential reforms of the Tibetan language, it did not allow for the writers to freely develop material whose content may have been at odds with its political purpose (see Question 70).

After the failed attempt of the Tibetans to free themselves from Chinese domination in the late 1950s, and during the Cultural Revolution, the Tibetan language was almost totally suppressed, as was anything differentiating Tibetan from Chinese culture. At times, children were prohibited from speaking Tibetan in classrooms. These policies were reversed in the 1980s and, under the influence of the Panchen Lama, a pro-active support program for the Tibetan language was drafted. It was decided that the Tibetan language would progressively get the same status as Mandarin in public life; court cases would be held in Tibetan, and the administration would not depend on being able to read rules and regulations in Mandarin. Equal stress was to be given to Tibetan and Mandarin, with the greater emphasis on the former. While this policy, formulated in the "Regulations Concerning the Study, Use and Development of the Tibetan Language" quoted in the Chinese answer (and Question 14, 2001), remains on the statutes up to the present day, in practice it has never really been implemented. Following the death of the Panchen Lama in 1989, and in the repressive atmosphere of the 1990s, even its principles were watered down. Today, the political and economic reality makes Tibetan at best a language of secondary importance. Most administrative work is carried out in Mandarin, whether by Tibetans or by

Chinese. Other than in the case of propaganda, which for obvious reasons must reach as many people as possible, Mandarin dominates all aspects of public life.

Even when the Tibetan language is used in propaganda, the impact of Chinese language and culture on Tibet is apparent: news reports on Lhasa TV are read in Tibetan by Tibetan presenters. The Chinese obsession with modernity and "development" has determined that these Tibetans needed "modern" training in their own language. The Tibetan speakers are therefore sent to China proper for speech and pronunciation training. As a result, they speak to viewers with pronounced Chinese accents, provoking horror among Tibetans in exile and derision from Tibetans in Tibet. The full irony and absurdity that lies at the heart of Tibetan cultural autonomy becomes apparent here—propaganda material written in Mandarin is translated into Tibetan and read to a Tibetan public by Tibetans speaking in a Tibetan with Chinese phonetic characteristics. No better statement could be made about the realities of language and cultural autonomy in today's Tibet. Language, as with many other aspects of Tibetan culture, is often not suppressed as such, but the value the regime assigns it is bound to its political functionality in the first instance. Moreover, rather than being allowed to freely develop, it is pressed into presumed "modern" moulds meant to "develop" it, but inevitably it ends up as a pale copy of Chinese models (which are themselves often a pastiche of Western practices).

A key issue for the future of the Tibetan language is ultimately its relevance. There are regions of Tibet where school education in Tibetan is, in principle, satisfactory (for example, in parts of Qinghai), but no matter how brilliant students are, they will probably be unable to use their language professionally.

62
What is the proportion of Tibetans to Han in the Tibet Autonomous Region's civil service?

[In 1989] "there are more than 53,000 government employees in Tibet. Of these over 33,000 are Tibetans, or more than 60%. Some 83.9% of the leaders of the autonomous regional Party committee, the standing committee of the people's congress, the people's government and the autonomous regional committee of the Chinese

People's Political Conference are Tibetans. Hans account for 15.9%, with the remaining 0.2% coming from other minority ethnic groups."

THIERRY DODIN

100 Questions rightly acknowledges that a requirement of autonomy is effective local government in the hands of local staff. It is therefore unsurprising that in the past fifty years, the issue of local cadres has been a central one. The 17-Point Agreement forced by China on Tibet did not predict the suppression of the traditional Tibetan administration, but it was "attended" by contingents of Chinese cadres to "support" it, that is, effectively to supervise it. Through all political upheavals, this has remained the basic reality of autonomous administration in Tibet. There seems to have been a serious attempt in the 1980s to create an indigenous cadre class, and people from the upper strata of old Tibetan society, or rather their offspring, were able to reach relatively high positions within Tibet. This policy was effectively stopped in the 1990s with the realization that local cadres would have more local, and broader Tibetan, interests at heart, rather than national loyalties. A combination of mistrust of Tibetans and the failure of the education system to produce enough qualified local cadres have recently led to new strategies. Chinese cadres are given incentives to come to Tibetan regions for a few years and take over key positions in these areas. Apart from their general cultural incompetence and lack of interest in Tibet, these cadres tend to be motivated primarily by a desire for an easy life. Spending a few years in Tibet is also materially advantageous for them and provides them with a record of nationalist devotion and social concern useful for their future careers in China proper. They appear to lack the dedication and dynamism necessary in a region with such low development indicators. Very recently, under the influence of the Party leader Hu Jintao, there have been efforts to provide Tibet with more competent cadres. Chinese cadres who have spent some years in Tibet and have proved efficient there (in the sense of the facilitating the regime's strategies) were given opportunities to pursue their careers by moving from one Tibetan region to the other. The phenomenon of a Tibetan career for Chinese cadres is new. This might indeed make the administration in Tibet more effective, but it also demonstrates how half a century during which a modern Tibetan leadership could have been put in place has simply been wasted. Today, as in the decades before, although Tibetans are numerous in absolute numbers among cadres, most of them are employed at the lower levels of administration; the higher the level, the smaller their participation. At the contrary, the higher the level of administration, the higher the percentage of Chinese employed (see also Question 26). The diminishing contingent of Tibetan cadres despite a swelling total number of cadres is, by the way, at least in the TAR, fully confirmed by official Chinese statistics. Thus, whereas the total number of cadres grew from 69,927 in 2000 to 88,734 in 2003, the number of Tibetan cadres shrunk from 50,039 (or 72 percent of the total) to 44,069 (or less than 50 percent).

63
WHO WERE THE HEADS OF ALL PREVIOUS GOVERNMENTS OF THE TIBET AUTONOMOUS REGION? WERE THEY ALL TIBETANS?

"Since the establishment of the TAR in 1965, four people have headed its government: Ngapoi Ngawang Jigme, Tianbao [Sangye Yeshe], Dorje Cedan [Dorje Tsetan], and Dorje Cerang [Dorje Tsering]. They are all Tibetans."

[Dorje Tsering occupied the position until 1991; he was succeeded by Gyeltsen Norbu until 1997, then by Legchog, elected for the period 1997–2003 (China Directory), *then by Jampa Phuntsog, who was still in office in 2007.]*

64
WHO HAVE SERVED AS THE STANDING COMMITTEE CHAIRMEN OF THE TIBET AUTONOMOUS REGIONAL PEOPLE'S CONGRESS? WHAT NATIONALITY WERE THEY?

Since the founding of the TAR in 1965, the chairmen have been Ngapoi Ngawang Jigme and Yang Dongsheng, both Tibetans.

[Yang Dongsheng (Tib. Sherab Döndrub) is the Chinese name of one of the first Tibetans who joined the CCP. According to China Directory, *he doesn't seem to have been the president of this committee; Ngapo kept the position until 1992 or 1993. Raidi (Ragdi) succeeded him in 1992 or 1994 and was himself replaced by Legchog.]*

65
How many counties and cities does the Tibet Autonomous Region have under its jurisdiction? What are the nationalities of the county magistrates and mayors?

"The Tibet Autonomous Region has 75 counties and two cities—Lhasa and Xigaze [Shigatse]—under its jurisdiction. The county magistrates and mayors are all Tibetans."

[The Chinese territorial and administrative divisions within a province are, in decreasing level: prefecture (Chin. di qu; Tib. sakhül); municipality (Chin. shi; Tib. drongkyer); county (Chin. xian; Tib. dzong or shan [transliteration from Mandarin]).

Municipalities have different statuses: Lhasa is at a prefecture level; Shigatse is at the county level (Conner and Barnett 1997: 210). In 1997, there were seventy-nine counties and not seventy-five, following boundary changes implemented by the government (Conner and Barnett 1997:210)

Questions 26 and 58 have dealt already with the increasing number of Chinese cadres at the county level.]

66
Are there any other Tibet autonomous areas in China apart from the Tibet Autonomous Region?

"Besides the Tibet Autonomous Region, there are ten Tibetan autonomous prefectures and two Tibetan autonomous counties in China." They are: in Sichuan, the TAPs of Ganze and Aba, and the Muli Tibetan autonomous county; in Yunnan, the Deqen TAP; in Gansu, the Gannan TAP, and the Tianzhu Tibetan autonomous county; in Qinghai, the TAPs of Golog, Yushu, Hainan, Huangnan, and Haibei, and the Haixi Mongolian-Tibetan autonomous prefecture.

Thierry Dodin

Although Tibetans are acknowledged in the PRC as an ethnic group of their own, the territory where Tibetans live has been structured in different territorial units with various administrative statuses. A look at the ethnic map of the PRC will reveal that the distribution of the Tibetan population within the country is strikingly homogeneous. Almost the entire area is covered by constituencies with autonomy status, although these currently belong to different provinces. A list of these constituencies is given in the answers to Questions 65 and 66 (it includes neither all constituencies in which Tibetans are not the sole titular ethnic group, however, nor constituencies that were once part of the territory of ethnic Tibet but, due to recent populations shifts, were attributed to diverse non-Tibetan ethnic groups). Their unification under one single autonomous administrative unit does not seem to figure on any current PRC agendas, but it would, in theory, be feasible. It is often assumed that this current policy reflects the PRC leadership's intention to divide and rule Tibet, but this assumption is not wholly accurate. To a large extent, the various statuses of Tibet's administrative subdivisions and their integration into diverse provinces follow a pattern drawn from its history over the past few centuries (see Question 39). The PRC cemented the status quo by keeping Amdo/Qinghai as a separate, multinational province and placing Kham under the control of Sichuan province, since Chinese influence in the region was mostly exerted from Chengdu, the capital of Sichuan. Two further portions of Tibetan territory were attributed to other provinces. One, belonging to Kham in the south, was integrated into another multinational Chinese province, Yunnan, and the other, the region around Labrang, culturally belonging to Amdo but, under strong Chinese political influence in the nineteenth and twentieth centuries, was absorbed into Gansu province. Thus, the current partition of Tibet reflects the inner Tibetan political cleavage as it existed on the ground in recent history.[1] But it also reflects another theme in Chinese ethnic policies; although it in principle respects and reflects the ethnic situation by according autonomy status to most ethnic Tibetan areas, China does not reverse perceived territorial acquisitions. Hence, all territories that escaped the domination of Lhasa in recent history remained attached to the neighboring Chinese con-

---

1. Since the advent of the PRC, there have been some adjustments of the inner Tibetan borders, possibly in order to accommodate either geographical features or the integrity of local subgroups (nomads, etc.). For instance, a part of Kham, which was under the Lhasa government in the 1950s, was attributed to Sichuan, and the southern part of Amdo, which was also controlled by Lhasa, came under Qinghai. Both these rectifications made for a slight reduction in the pre-1951 Lhasa-controlled territory. However, on the other hand, plans in the late 1950s and early 1960s to create a province covering almost the full area of Kham, under the name Hsikang, were finally abandoned, despite efforts in Beijing and among local nationalist Khampas to create it.

stituencies they tended to be under the influence of. This again underlines the fact that autonomous status is conceived of as an instrument for appropriately managing ethnic affairs at the local level, not as an instrument for Tibetans as a distinct nationality to exert stronger influence over the territories they populate. The notions underlying the inner-Tibetan territorial cleavage and the reluctance to modify it were once more reflected by a Chinese government official speaking to reporters in Beijing on May 26, 2006, who said that the Dalai Lama's proposals to establish a "Greater Tibet" and allow Tibetans living in that area to exercise "high-level or real autonomy" (see Question 39) were "not consistent with the history of Tibet."

67

WHY ARE NONE OF THE FIRST SECRETARIES OF
THE TIBET AUTONOMOUS REGIONAL COMMITTEE
OF THE CHINESE COMMUNIST PARTY TIBETANS?

"Until now, there have been no Tibetan first secretaries. . . . This is nothing strange in China, because there is no difference in nationality in the organizations of the Chinese Communist Party. Any Party member of any nationality can be a Party cadre, provided he or she has the qualifications as stipulated by the Party Constitution."

[For the background to this answer and the cynicism behind it, see Question 58.]

PART SEVEN

Culture and Education

Some aspects of the Tibetan culture are particularly well known in the West through movies, TV, and illustrated reports. What is most striking to the Westerners is the importance of religious life in Tibet, and consequently of religious art and also of the monumental architecture of which the Potala Palace is the emblematic example. However, there are other aspects of Tibetan culture that are just as important, if not as well known, among them a notable scholarly literature and a rich and colorful popular culture, in which orality plays a great role. Here, too, the Chinese government prides itself on its achievements, while the exiles assert that the Tibetan civilization is seriously threatened by sinicization. This is unquestionable in the case of urban culture, and the process is now beginning in the countryside too. One of the main problems encountered by the people in the countryside is access to education, and the statistics cited in this section and the following one (Part VIII, "Economic Development") show Tibet to be among the lowest-ranked developing countries.

68

WHAT IS THE POLICY ADOPTED BY CHINA REGARDING TRADITIONAL TIBETAN CULTURE?

The Red Guards' vandalism during the Cultural Revolution must not be confused with "the correct policy carried out by the people's government during the greater part of the post-liberation period. Respecting and protecting the traditional cultures of all minorities is the policy of the Chinese government. . . . The world-famous Potala Palace, for example, has been listed on the register as a national historical relic, under special protection by the government." Works of art and books held there are all "well preserved."

The government also encourages the development of Tibetan medicine and medical science. As far as Tibetan literature is concerned, "by 1987, more than 43 million copies of 600 books written in Tibetan had been published in China." The world-famous epic *King Gesar* has been "saved and edited and published." Tibetan dramas, dancing, and operas are being encouraged, and "traditional repertoires" have been developed.

AMY HELLER AND ANNE-MARIE BLONDEAU

Government policy toward Tibetan culture has varied considerably during the period of occupation since 1951. One must distinguish between the official policies, their implementation, and how the general population perceive these policies in their daily lives in the TAR.

During the Cultural Revolution (1966–76), everywhere in China, cultural values were overthrown, but rampant destruction of temples and monasteries, with their treasures of art and literature, was particularly widespread in Tibet. Red Guards, often Tibetans, not only destroyed monuments but often also forced local villagers to do the same. It is true that the official policies encourage the notion of a "unified and multi-ethnic" China, according to government declarations (PRC, Information Office of the State Council, 1999: 1), yet at the same time, the "Chinese constitution stipulates that there must be broad opposition to chauvinism, whether it concerns the Han population or major ethnic groups, and also oppose[s] local nationalism" (PRC:12; our translation). In fact, practically speaking, this means "first and above all, training totally sinicized Tibetan citizens" (Tournadre 1999), with the objective of reinforcing unity among the diverse ethnic groups. This applies to Tibetans living in the eastern provinces of Qinghai, Gansu, Sichuan, and Yunnan, as well as to the inhabitants of the TAR. The problems resulting from this policy are obvious: in Tibet, "culture" was intrinsically linked with religious values, principally Buddhist values; it was also linked with social structure dependent on religion (the predominant role of the clergy, the national religious festivals and ceremonies, village rituals, etc.). Thus, the destruction and limitations imposed on religious practices, as well as the suppression of traditional social structures resulted in the disappearance of a relatively large proportion of festivals and cultural events—or else, the basic meaning of these gatherings was distorted to align them with official policies.

Moreover, the clergy is no longer the sole depository of knowledge, and the aim of the Chinese government is as always the "laicization" of Tibetans, which is completely out of harmony with traditional Tibetan cultural values (this also applies to Question 70). That is why "popular" gatherings are in theory authorized, but are sometimes so estranged from their initial intention that they become pure "folklore" rather than religious celebration. And such festivals become tourist attractions. For example, there is a Jyekundo "fair" that now has thousands in attendance, watching horse races, participating in various competitions, and attending a giant commercial bazaar. Originally, this "fair" took place during a weeklong celebration for local deities, with rituals to honor them. This intent is now totally disguised, and unknown to many who attend. Describing a similar "popular cultural festival" in Amdo at the end of the 1980s, Per Kvaerne (1994: 180–82) emphasizes the aspect of masquerade and the artificial character of the ritual, as well as the political message of peace, harmony, and unity among all the nationalities of China conveyed by such a festival. For the same reasons, village rituals—which are conceived of as beyond the sphere of Buddhism, since they occur outdoors and unconfined by temple walls—are on the whole favored. This despite the fact that to the foreign observer, such festivals would appear to reinforce local identity to the detriment of the process of construction of national identity as citizens of the "motherland" (Karmay 1994). Here, too, the PRC is heir to the policies formerly maintained by the empire, whereby the notion of "folklore" is applied to local customs, songs, and popular dances, making them, as such, innocuous and easy to integrate into Han culture. (On this subject, see Trebinjac 1990, which demonstrates the policy of control of popular gatherings in process since the Han dynasty.)

In Tibet under control of the PRC, for example, the singing of the Gesar epic—given here as an example of protection of culture—has become an "official competition," with prizes for the best singer (see also Question 70). The traditional contest of the butter sculptures *(torma)* made by the monks of Lhasa and Kumbum monastery as part of the month-long New Year celebrations (see Richardson 1993: 27–30) is now advertised in the mass media.

The Chinese authors give several other examples, such as the architectural restoration of the Potala and the encouragement of Tibetan medical techniques and pharmacology, which will be discussed later. Here, we shall say a bit about Tibetan opera—or theater—and songs and dances.

It is true that these arts have a protected status "in a Chinese way," which is to say that both in the TAR and in China, institutes have been founded to train *professional* actors, singers, and dancers. In the old Tibet, there were professional touring theater companies, but on the whole, their performances were unsophisticated. They were either traveling companies or people who pursued agricultural activities outside of the "theater season," when they had to perform first for the Dalai Lama, then for Drepung monastery, for aristocratic families, and finally in the Norbulingka, where the entire population of Lhasa was in attendance. This was the festival called "The Yogurt Feast" *(zhotön)*, which in fact marked the end of the monks' summer retreat. This festival still exists, but paradoxically, the plays are also performed in theaters. And (as the Chinese answer to Question 70 tells as well), the religious origin of this festival has been all but effaced, because it is now called "The Festival of Tibetan Opera." The actors' and singers' training has been in great part sinicized, and their makeup and singing style have been altered to suit Chinese theatrical tastes. This is also true of the so-called popular troupes of singers and dancers that go on stage and are sent on tour abroad. The contrast with villagers' performances of the same songs and dances—which may not be as pretty but are at least authentic—is striking.

100 Questions praises the development of the traditional theater repertoire. In all, formerly, there were about ten plays, all related to moral or religious themes, except for one whose theme was the marriage of Songtsen Gampo with a Chinese princess and a Nepalese princess *(Gyaza Belza)*. However, what the authors neglect to mention is that except for the creation of a theater play from the Gesar epic, the majority of the new creations are directly inspired by Communist ideology: the themes are those of the liberation of the oppressed serfs from their evil masters, the patriotic sacrifice of the hero for the good of the nation, and so on. Censure of other themes can sometimes be quite strong; in 1996, a play called "The Secrets of the Potala

Palace" was simply forbidden both in theater and on film, because there was no performance of the kowtow (Chinese protocol prostration) by the 5th Dalai Lama when he met with Emperor Shunzhi.

69

SOME FOREIGN NEWSPAPERS HAVE CLAIMED THAT CHINA
HAS PAID NO ATTENTION TO TIBET'S HISTORY AND CULTURE.
WHAT ARE THE FACTS?

The regional government has made great efforts to maintain and develop Tibetan historical culture. A wide range of institutes and schools, as well as research institutes, have been created: the "Nationality education research institute," the "Tibetan language teaching research society," the "Tibetan language teachers training centre." Language textbooks and training materials for students at primary and secondary schools are translated [from Mandarin] and published. A Tibetan medical school and a medical department in Tibet University have been set up. Tibetan history and religion are studied in specialized institutes, while the Academy of Social Sciences focuses its research on history, religion, and culture.

Since 1980, the central government has spent huge sums of money for the restoration and preservation of Tibet's cultural and historical sites. For instance, since 1981, state expenditure on the maintenance of Potala Palace alone has exceeded 4 million yuan, and more will be given in the future.

AMY HELLER

The Chinese reply to this question is extremely vague. It combines culture (Questions 68–69) with the subject of restoration of buildings (Question 71) and with teaching of language, history, and traditional medicine; instead, here, culture and history will be discussed as a direct reply to the question. We refer the reader to Question 74 on Tibetan medicine. One must emphasize that since *100 Questions* was initially published in 1988 (in French), there have been several years of work on the restoration and renovation of the Potala (see Question 71).

As regards the importance attributed to Tibetan history and culture, it is essential to note that for the Han, culture is by definition Chinese culture, conceived as a central and centrifugal force, all other cultures being regarded as "exterior" and peripheral, in short, barbarian and viewed as curiosities. In Tibet today, this is the mutual perception of both the crowds of Han tourists and the inhabitants of Tibet: who is mocking whom in the game of masquerading as a Tibetan nomad for a souvenir photograph in front of the Kumbum monastery, in Qinghai, or in front of the Potala in Lhasa? The recent intense interest in Tibet by Chinese results in the high percentage of Han tourists in Tibet. But it is not Tibet's art treasures but rather the Disneyland effect that dominates.

That said, it is true that certain traditional cultural activities are protected and encouraged, but, as indicated in the previous answer, in a very selective way. In line with the declared goal of achieving the secularization of Tibetan society, the areas that will be encouraged are purely secular, such as horse races, dances, and open air theater, in which the clergy hardly participated in traditional Tibet. Those activities linked with religion are either forbidden or officially limited to such an extent that their impact is virtually nil, and in any case, the government does not patronize them. For example, pilgrimage to holy places was certainly one of the Tibetans' most widespread religious activities. Currently, the policies about pilgrimage vary from year to year, and pilgrimages are sometimes tolerated, sometimes discouraged, either by economic sanctions or political restrictions.

In short, as long as "culture" is defined as that of lay society, Tibetan culture is officially protected (PRC, Information Office of the State Council, 1999). But as soon as "culture" is related to the clergy, the concepts of feudalism and social exploitation are used to devalue and discourage religious practices.

The subject of religion is certainly a vexed question in a Communist society, which by definition is atheistic. But, in the case of Tibet, it is clear that the official hostility to religious culture is reinforced both in the sense of opposition to the previous regime of government by the Dalai Lamas as religious leaders, and by the aristocracy, and because of the strong attachment to this religious culture that Tibetans still frequently express.

On another level, the Chinese reply to this question describes the creation of schools, research institutes, and so on, responsible for the study of Tibetan language and history, and encouragement of such studies. This is indeed a concrete achievement (on which, however, see Questions 61 and 75). As far as history is concerned, the way of studying it reflects the political ideology, that is, the study of history is oriented toward the proof of the subordination of Tibet to China and the justification of Chinese sovereignty over Tibet. The political history of Tibet has been systematically "re-arranged" to correspond to these claims and to the "just cause" of the Chinese occupation of Tibet since 1951. The ideology only recognizes the Chinese version of Tibetan history, whereby Tibet has been an integral part of China since the thirteenth century, but the far more complex historical reality is silenced. Certainly, the idea of a vast Tibetan empire from the seventh century to the ninth is accepted, but any notion of Tibetan political independence in the twentieth century is officially denied, as shown in Part I of this book.

70

WHAT IS THE CHINESE GOVERNMENT'S ATTITUDE TOWARD
TRADITIONAL TIBETAN LITERATURE AND ART?

In order to show the great importance attached by the Chinese government to this topic, which is "an important component of China's traditional culture," three examples are given:

1. The collection, collation, and publication of the King Gesar epic, the longest epic in the world. It is also "a valuable historical document of the three or four centuries of war that followed the collapse of the Tubo Dynasty, with much information about the religious rites, social mores, marriage system, customs, and habits of the period." This epic is "one of the state's key academic research projects. Research institutions on King Gesar have been set up across the country," bards are invited, their singing is recorded, and the written versions are collected and published.

2. The spreading and development of the Tibetan opera. "A wide-spread popularization program has led not only to the establishment of full-time troupes in the TAR and other areas, but also the organization of amateur opera groups in many villages," more than twenty in Medu Kongkar [Meldro Gungkar] county, near Lhasa. "The Sour Milk Drinking Festival [*zhotön*] in July–August was originally purely religious. Now, Tibetan opera is its main component, hence it has been renamed the 'Tibetan Opera Festival.'"

3. The new development of tangka [*thangka*] religious art. These painted scrolls are hung both in the temples and monasteries,

and in the homes of many Tibetans. Exhibitions in Beijing in May 1986 and in Paris during summer of 1987 have been highly praised.

Moreover, various publications on Tibetan opera, folk songs and folk-tales, proverbs, and folk dances are in preparation. Since 1983, a dozen or so Tibetan cultural and art troupes have toured in many Asian and Western countries.

AMY HELLER AND ANNE-MARIE BLONDEAU

One cannot deny that in the past fifty years, thanks to the impetus of the Chinese, there have been considerable strides forward in publication of oral and written Tibetan texts and research on various aspects of Tibetan liter-ature, and a modern literature has developed on a vast scale among young Tibetan writers. Here, as in the general conception of culture, it is secular literature—at least as far as the Chinese understand it—that is esteemed. Much of the literature produced in Tibet during the past 1,300 years is re-ligious: philosophical, and ritual, of course, but also hagiographical, historio-graphical, and poetical. Even what the Chinese consider "secular" or "popu-lar" literature—such as the Gesar epic, the opera, and medical literature—was written by the clergy and served to transmit the values of Buddhism to the general populace. In other words, a complex interaction evolved between forms of literature that probably had popular origins, like the Gesar epic, and the learned literary production where religion, whether Buddhist or Bönpo, is omnipresent, often forming the principal theme.

This interaction has also influenced modern bards, whose songs reflect or sometimes reproduce written versions of the Gesar epic. So, while it is true that the wars Gesar must wage against his adversaries are the main-spring of all the episodes, which are full of battles, sorcery, and intrigue, they are incorporated into what is now a completely Buddhist framework, in which Gesar, as the incarnation of a Buddha, fights against incarnations of demons who threaten to destroy his kingdom and the world. It is thus to-tally delusory to think, as the Chinese seem to do, that this epic saga is the reflection of a society where the clergy had not yet developed a strong influence, and to attempt on that basis to exploit it ideologically against the former Tibetan social system.

But in discussing the Gesar epic, which is the first example cited by the Chinese as proof of their "attachment" to Tibetan literature, it is neces-sary to recognize the systematic research accomplished on this topic and praise the results, even if their outcome may be deleterious in the long run to Tibetan culture. As *100 Questions* emphasizes, this epic is probably the longest in the world, and it is still in a process of creation and transformation: even today the bards are inspired to create new episodes. First introduced to the Western public by Alexandra David-Neel's publication in 1930, the Gesar epic has been relatively little studied in the West, and preponderantly in written rather than oral form, as scholars were unable to hear it in situ. It is to the credit of Chinese and Tibetan scholars that they succeeded in locating living bards and recording their versions of the epic saga. There are literally thousands of hours of such recordings (Yang Enhong 1999). They have thus documented a living tradition that, without their efforts, would have inevitably been lost in the present context of modernization.

Besides, this interest in the epic has had an unexpected effect among the Tibetan population. Traditionally forbidden in the big Gelugpa monasteries, the epic was a declining tradition before the 1950s, except in eastern Tibet; but, as the mass publication of the Gesar episodes has exploded in the low-price market, a new appreciation of their literary monument has arisen among Tibetans. Moreover, Gesar has become the representative of a glorious, free, and powerful Tibet and the emblem of the Tibetan nationalism (Karmay 1994: 115). It is ironic to think that for the Chinese, the study of the Gesar epic was encouraged because it "is a valuable historical document of the three or four centuries of war that followed the collapse of the Tubo Dynasty," which means for them till the period of the integration of Tibet into China by the Yuan dynasty.

As a second example, *100 Questions* stresses the spread and development of Tibetan opera, already discussed in Question 68. What the Chinese authors describe here illustrates our earlier remarks: the creation of professional theater troupes, the secularization of the "Yogurt Feast" *(zhotön)*, which has become an opera festival.

The discussion has hitherto been based on traditional forms of Tibetan literature, essentially, as noted, stemming from the clerics, who were the bastion of knowledge; even though literate people were to be found among the nobility, they left few writings. Only one early novel is known that does not take religion as its central subject, and whose plot is based on laypeople's lives. Dokhar Tsering Wangyal, the author of this "romantic adventure," titled "The Tale of the Incomparable Youth," was an eighteenth-century Lhasa aristocrat who derived much of his inspiration as regards both style and content from Indian epic literature such as the *Râmayana* (Shakya 2000).

The dismantling of traditional monastic education means that the literati are no longer trained in the monasteries, and classical literary production has virtually ceased (except among the Tibetans in exile, of course). On the other hand, a new phenomenon has arisen under the influence of Chinese schools and universities. This is a secular literature, written by laypeople, in nontraditional forms, notably short stories and novels, and also poetry in free verse (on these new literary genres, see Shakya 2000). There are many new literary reviews in the TAR and in the former Kham and Amdo. One must remark, however, that a good many of the young Tibetan authors write in Mandarin rather than Tibetan.

As for the themes dealt with, they obviously are different from those of classical literature, and writers are slowly freeing themselves from the political correctness that was de rigueur in early novels and short stories. Following contemporary Chinese models, the new literary forms that have become popular in Tibet are plots proselytizing for the Communist Chinese regime. Tsering Shakya shows the ideological framework in which "lay" Tibetan literature has been encouraged, and the political constraints hanging over it. The first magazine devoted to modern Tibetan literature, *Bökyi tsomrig gyutsel* (Tibetan Literary Art), published in 1980 by the TAR Writers' Association, contained four short stories by Tibetan writers written in Mandarin and then translated into Tibetan. The goal was to make the Chinese public empathize with the sufferings of the Tibetan people during the ancien régime and furnish a moral justification for the liberation of Tibet. Consequently, these stories tell about "Tibetan serfs" questioning the feudal system (Shakya 2000). This magazine was followed by several others devoted to modern literature, but the fact that the subject had to include some kind of social commentary was evident, although the choice of what is politically correct changes with the various political phases inside and outside the TAR.

Publication in literary reviews imposed the genre of the short story. When the first novel written in praise of the PLA, "An Auspicious Flower *[kelzang metog]*," appeared in 1982, it won a prize as "best national minority groups" novel but did not sell well. However, the second modern Tibetan novel to appear, "The Turquoise [Ornament] of the Crown of the Head *[Tsug yu]*," published in 1985, which denigrated the old society in politically correct fashion, was a bestseller. The style of these two works, especially the latter, constituted a major innovation in literary expression, and even if the themes are predictable, the language is lively and vivid.

Modern Tibetan poetry, which was first published in a magazine called *Drangchar* (Gentle Rain), as of 1981, deserves special mention. The leader of the movement was Döndrup Gyel (1953–1985), who defended a modern Tibetan nationalism without arguing for either the ancien régime or the official Communist Party line. He committed suicide at the age of 32 (Stoddard 1994a; for translations of some of his poems and novels, see Shakya 2000, Virtanen 2000, and Thöndrupgyäl 2007).

To conclude on the subject of Tibetan literature, one must add a comment on publishing. Chinese government policy encouraged mass publication of cheap paperback editions, especially of the works of Marx, Lenin, and Mao and other political and ideological writings. The "Text of the Government Policy on National Minorities" was published in Tibetan in Beijing as early as 1952, and the constitution of the PRC was available in Tibetan in 1954 (Stoddard 1994b: 129). The Chinese answer to Question 68 rightly boasts about the volume of publications: already in 1987, more than 600 titles in Tibetan were available, amounting to 43.5 million books; these figures probably include large numbers of textbooks, technical and agricultural manuals, and propaganda translated from Chinese into Tibetan. Still, the spread of Tibetan literature was encouraged by this government policy. Apart from the Gesar epic, there are also other forms of classical literature reprinted in these inexpensive paperback editions or, in some cases, where the woodblocks survived, in the traditional Tibetan format of individual rectangular pages. Whatever the Chinese motivations may have been, it has resulted in a popularization of Tibetan literature that had never before been conceivable. For example, the collected works of Gedün Chöpel, a most prominent intellectual of the first half of the twentieth century, well known for his "progressive" opinions (see Stoddard 1985; Lopez 2006), were reprinted in Lhasa and sold out in just a few days.

Unfortunately, after the political change of the 1994 Third Tibet Work Forum, the budget devoted to academic and literary publications was severely reduced in 1996: magazine circulation was almost cut in half. Today, an author who wants to be published has to assume the cost of the publication of his own work, which can be as much as 20,000 yuan (U.S.$10 in September 1997 was equivalent to 75.52 yuan).

The third example cited in the Chinese reply as a proof of the protection guaranteed to Tibetan art is the "new development of the art of *thangka*." The meaning to attribute to this "new development" is rather obscure, because the authors merely cite two exhibitions, in Beijing and Paris, following a very summary description of the *thangka*, portable Tibetan paintings on fabric, which are used in meditation rituals or as a didactic tool, depicting, for example, scenes from the life of the Buddha. Here we shall examine the present situation of Tibetan art in more detail.

Tibetan traditional art, whether painting or sculpture, was essentially religious and has been made famous in the West by numerous exhibitions.

Although there are now conservation and restoration projects (see, e.g., the Tibet Museum, Question 71), for many years, Tibetan traditional art was not really encouraged in official training programs or by commissioning of new works of art in traditional style. This is starting to change, and Tibet University's Department of Art in Lhasa now gives courses in traditional painting, although traditional sculpture is not taught at present. There is a gallery, the Gedün Chöphel Artists' Guild, situated on the northeastern corner of the Barkor, which shows their paintings, mixing both modern and traditional styles. Few masters of the preceding generation are still teaching individual students; their work may be seen in the restoration projects of monasteries and temples. Officially, however, the Chinese esteem and encourage the "new art" of lay Tibetan or Chinese painters living in Tibet, who either reinterpret traditional art or are influenced by Western modern art. The Kandze district school (in Kham), which rapidly became famous for its reinterpretations of traditional *thangka,* came into being at the end of the 1980s. But if the esthetic style of Kandze *thangka* creates an illusion of traditional painting, the subjects treated are purely secular. These paintings are very subtle means of conveying specific new political myths in a form familiar to Tibetans: the heroic grandeur of the period before Buddhism was dominant in Tibet; friendship between the Han and the Tibetans; and the attraction of consumer products (Kvaerne 1994). It is not yet clear what impact these messages have on the public, and if a painting "commissioned" for these purposes will find a supportive echo. Nonetheless, among the new artists, there are some who are very gifted, and whatever subject they are required to paint—whether patriotic or pastoral—they show real originality and talent (Stoddard 2000). As for sculpture, everyone sees the pair of monumental yaks in gilded concrete commemorating the fortieth anniversary of the "peaceful liberation" of Lhasa, exemplifying how art is exploited for political purposes today in Tibet. In fact, a yak would never have been the principal subject of a traditional Tibetan sculpture.

Following the Cultural Revolution, in accordance with the new policies of restoration and economic restructuring, some artists and artisans were authorized to work in their traditional techniques. However, the economic priorities and lack of practitioners make transmission of these problematic, because the traditional apprenticeship system, both in art and in building techniques, has been done away with. Tibetan and foreign architects have worked to reestablish such apprenticeships since 1995, but these programs are still limited to the urban center of Lhasa for now, and the outlying communities do not have access to such training (see also Question 71).

71
WHAT WORK HAS BEEN DONE TO PROTECT CULTURAL RELICS
AND HISTORICAL SITES IN TIBET?

It is repeated that "the protection of patrimony is the constant policy of the Chinese government," stating that much has been restored since Tibet and the rest of China were devastated by the Cultural Revolution, and that the protection of patrimony has been reinforced with attention to restoration of historic monuments "as much as possible." The amounts cited in previous answers are repeated: in Tibet, public funds totaling 36 million yuan were spent on restoration of "important temples"; thirteen are under central government protection as cultural treasures, and eleven have been designated as TAR-protected. In March 1980, Lhasa created a construction company specialized in restoration, which repaired eleven famous temples and monasteries, including the Daipung [Drepung], Sera, Gahdan [Ganden], the Jokhang, Norbulingka, and Tashilhünpo (the names of the other five restorations are not listed). "[M]ore than 10,000 m² of buildings and 1,500m² of murals" were thus restored.

Other, secular historic sites have also benefited from special credits, such as the tombs of the Tibetan kings and the fortress of Gyantse, "witness of the 1904 Tibetan resistance there against the British invaders."

Last, the Tibetan Cultural Relics Administration Bureau, created shortly after the foundation of the TAR, "is now staffed with many professional specialists to ensure all renovation is carried out authentically."

AMY HELLER

Even if the statistics on the destruction of temples and monasteries during the Cultural Revolution can be contested, it is hard to name a single city or village where any of the religious and historical buildings were left intact indicating how widespread the destruction was. It is true that the central Chinese government and the government of the TAR subsequently established a policy of protecting Tibet's cultural heritage, administered by the Tibetan Cultural Relics Administration Bureau, whose offices were until recently housed in the outbuildings of the Norbulingka. The bureau chiefly employs archeologists, but it is not known what training they have received. Surviving historical archives are also conserved, in a building especially constructed for this purpose, and the invaluable library and artistic treasures accumulated over the centuries in the Potala have been preserved. An inventory of Tibet's artistic and historical patrimony has been undertaken. In 1999, the Tibet Museum was opened in Lhasa, and several rooms in it present artistic treasures, even if one of them is exclusively devoted to the demonstration that Tibet has been part of China since the Yuan dynasty. The desire to protect Tibet's cultural heritage is quite obvious, and the conservation and restoration of cultural monuments has indeed begun. This will undoubtedly take years. The resources for restoration—whether human, financial, or technical—are limited, and sometimes the "best intentions in the world" bring sad results. Examples abound of inadequate or inappropriate restoration techniques that have actually damaged, rather than restored, the artwork on which they were used: for example, varnish applied to wall paintings in the fifteenth-century Gyantse stupa in a government restoration program in the 1980s attacked the pigments underneath the surface, resulting in irreversible loss of ancient pigment (Heller 1993; Lo Bue 2004). In 1994, during roof restoration by a foreign NGO using Tibetan traditional techniques to preserve eleventh-century wall paintings in the Dratang temple, inadequate supervision resulted in water seepage and mud spilling all over the ancient paintings. Other problematic restorations have occurred when local communities of monks, acting without consultation with regional cultural relics authorities, whitewashed or repainted the ancient mural paintings using acrylic paint that compromises any future restorations.

The most important example of the protection of cultural heritage is the Potala Palace, which is now a museum (the monastery that it sheltered is still inhabited by about sixty monks, who are the guardians of the rooms visited by tourists). The Chinese reply to Question 69 indicates that vast amounts of money have been devoted to restoration of the Potala. Indeed, since the publication of *100 Questions* in 1989, it has been restored several times, at great expense. However, a large section of the exterior wall collapsed in 2001 after the restoration had been completed, and work on the roof and structural repairs were still ongoing in 2006.

On the other hand, beside the interest shown in Tibetan cultural heritage, the government has also undertaken a series of major urban development plans for Lhasa, with the creation of giant avenues and an undeniable disregard for architectural context; despite the creation of "protected historic zones," the immediate periphery of the monuments has been divested of many of the ancient constructions, which have been replaced by incongruous modern ones (see Barnett 1998b, 2006). In 2004, there were small boutiques bordering the esplanade in front of the ancient Jokhang temple, where there are now stable paving stones and bright streetlights; this represents an improvement, because previously, from around 1995 until 2000, there were two giant fountains in front of the Jokhang, a total architectural anomaly in the dry climate of Tibet. The nomination of the Potala to the World Heritage List of UNESCO in 1995 was expected to bring enforcement of the concept of the "architectural buffer zone" according to the UNESCO principles, calling for respect of the integrity of the historic zone (MacLean 1993). Instead, in 2001, to celebrate the fiftieth anniversary of the "peaceful liberation," a concrete "mountain" was built in front of the Potala, to the despair of urban conservationists and architects. After consultation with UNESCO experts in 2004, the Lhasa cultural relics authorities announced a competition for architects to propose a new monument and urban project to replace the "mountain," which was, however, still there in 2007.

One must also consider secular architecture. Historians of Lhasa city development have documented the disappearance of numerous ancient buildings in the residential section in the center of Lhasa. From 1993 until 1998, an average of thirty-five buildings were demolished every year. In 1998, a moratorium on demolition of traditional buildings in the center of Lhasa was declared, and seventy-six buildings were targeted for restoration as residences by the Lhasa municipality, which consulted with the residents to determine contemporary needs, especially as regards sewers and drainage (Alexander and de Azevedo 1998; Alexander 2005; THF 1999). The Tibet Heritage Fund (THF), a European NGO that was responsible for many restoration projects, in collaboration with 270 Tibetan architects, masons, and artisans, as well as for training in Tibetan traditional building skills, was obliged to leave Lhasa in 2000, but there are now several other construction companies specialized in traditional Tibetan architectural techniques adapted to current needs. Awareness of this issue was demonstrated by an international seminar in Lhasa in 2004 on conservation of architecture and mural paintings in Tibet, co-sponsored by Lhasa Tibet University, and Trondheim Norwegian Technical University. Fifty urban planners, architects, painters, sculptors, painting restorers, Tibetologists, cultural relics authorities, and engineers attended. Such a seminar shows understanding of the need for concerted interdisciplinary efforts to implement good conservation strategies for secular and religious architecture in Tibet, but just beyond the protective zone and buffer zones, high-rise buildings are still being constructed, such as the 13-storey Public Security building towering above the Jokhang and Ramoche temples. The situation is far from a stable and consistent policy to promote preservation of Tibet's architectural heritage.

Finally, it should be noted that the "encouragement of Tibetan traditional culture" includes the construction of modern concrete buildings "in Tibetan style," which is truly absurd, both esthetically and technically, in relation to traditional Tibetan architecture (on which see Chayet 1994).

72
WHAT IS THE SITUATION OF TIBETAN STUDIES IN CHINA?
[QUESTION 70, 2001]

The Tibetans "have a long history and brilliant culture. The field of Tibetan studies is a comprehensive science. China's study of Tibet began before the Tang Dynasty (618–907), and thousands of works in the field have resulted from research done in various periods of history."

"In recent years, Tibetan studies have developed further. Remarkable progress has been made in training professional researchers and gathering historical data and reference materials." Institutes of Tibetan studies have been established in various areas. In May 1986, the China Tibetology Research Center was founded, which has "pushed the country's research in this field to a higher level."

[The 2001 version speaks of more than fifty institutes of Tibetan studies, some thirty periodicals, in Tibetan, Chinese, and English, and developing academic exchanges.]

AMY HELLER AND ANNE-MARIE BLONDEAU

Let us start by saying that the Chinese definition of Tibetology is quite different from the usual definition in the West, that of a modern discipline that uses all the tools of the humanities and the social sciences for the study of Tibet and its civilization. The Chinese present official documents, encyclopedia articles, and travelers' and pilgrims' accounts that have appeared since the Tang era as "research," supporting the notion that Tibetology has long been a discipline in China. However, in practice, the Tibetan and Chinese Tibetologists work in very similar manner to Western Tibetologists, aside from the inevitable ideological givens, the exclusion of certain politically sensitive subjects, and weakness in critical methods. They also lack exposure to foreign publications in the field and may thus be unaware of previous work by other scholars, which sometimes limits the scope of their research. However, Chinese Tibetology is a relatively young field, and it is all too easy to criticize these weaknesses, which are rapidly being corrected by the Tibetologists themselves.

Tibetology has been officially encouraged as a discipline. One example is the creation in 1989 of the Center for Tibetan Studies at Sichuan University, Chengdu, to conduct archeological research in Tibet, as a complement to the Institute of Nationality Studies of the Chinese Academy of Social Sciences in Beijing, which focuses mainly on current cultural, economic, political, and social aspects of Tibet. It is said that there are about 2,000 Tibetologists in China, 1,000 of whom are of Tibetan nationality, primarily working in Lhasa, Xining, Beijing, and Chengdu (but this figure includes translators, political scientists, publishers, and so on). There are indeed fifty Tibetology institutes, located throughout China, although some of them have only one or two members (Tan Hongkai 2000).

In Tibetological research, certain subjects are particularly favored, as we saw earlier in connection with Tibetan literature and protection of Tibet's cultural heritage. Ethnology and study of nomad life are recognized as economically useful as well as culturally appropriate. However, if research on ancient Tibet and archeology has great official encouragement, subject to the limitations and political imperatives mentioned earlier, the study of modern history is undoubtedly subject to close supervision. "While the Dalai Lama clique actively distorts current realities in Tibet in the name of Tibetologists, Chinese Tibetologists have an obligation to tell the world what Tibet was and is like," Lhagpa Phuntso, current director of the Beijing Tibetology Research Center, asserts (quoted in Tan Hongkai 2000; see also Barnett 2003). Tibetologists in the PRC are also charged with translating Chinese classics and literature into Tibetan as a way of culturally integrating Tibetans into the "Han" motherland.

Curiously—perhaps a repercussion of Chinese ethnocentrism? —*100 Questions* focuses on the creation of the Beijing Tibetology Research Center, to which the following Question 73 is devoted, and avoids mentioning any of the other institutes, some of which are quite active and maintain a high level. In particular, the Tibetan Academy of Social Sciences in Lhasa has reprinted many rare works, some from the Potala library, and also publishes two journals, one in Tibetan and the other in English, both of which are less politically oriented than *China Tibetan Studies*, published by the Beijing Center.

73
WHAT DOES THE CHINA TIBETAN STUDIES CENTER DO? WHO RUNS IT?

Its mandate is "to organize and co-ordinate Tibetan studies in China, to collect, collate and publish Tibetan literature and other Tibetan writings, to train Tibetan studies personnel, and to further academic exchanges on Tibetan studies with other countries." Its general secretary [in 1989] is the Tibetan scholar Dojie Caidan [Dorje Tseten], former chairman of the people's government of the TAR.

Work in progress includes the collation and publication of the *Tripitaka* ["Three Baskets," the Buddhist scriptural canon] in Tibetan, the study and classification of Sanskrit manuscripts preserved in Tibet, and the study of "the relations between the Tibetan local government and China's central government since the Yuan Dynasty, and the Tibetan serf system." The center also publishes a quarterly, *China Tibetan Studies*, in both Chinese and Tibetan.

AMY HELLER

Since its creation in 1986, the Beijing Tibetology Research Center has evolved considerably. Even if the scholars are not free in their choice of subject, they do good work. The results—both in research and publications in the fields of Tibetan religion, history, and literature—are quite noteworthy. Several departments, such as those dealing with linguistics, the Gesar epic, and Bönpo religion, are very strong.

Dorje Tseten, a longtime high-ranking TAR official, formerly headed the center. Since 2000, its director has been Lhagpa Phuntso, a former president of the Tibetan Academy of Social Sciences, then vice president of the TAR from 1992 to 1997 (Conner and Barnett 1997: 241).

In addition to the activities indicated by the Chinese answer, the Beijing Tibetology Research Center organized international congresses on Tibetology in 1986, 1991, 1997, and 2001, in the social sciences, history, archeology, anthropology, and literature. In 2002 and 2004, in collaboration with the Chengdu Tibetan Center, the Beijing center organized seminars on Tibetan art and archeology, bringing together some fifty scholars from many parts of China and foreign countries. In October 2006, the Institute of Sino-Tibetan Buddhist Art at Capital Normal University (Beijing) convened the Third International Conference on Tibetan Art and Archeology.

74

IT IS SAID THAT TRADITIONAL TIBETAN MEDICAL SCIENCE
IS VERY SPECIAL. WHAT HAS CHINA DONE TO DEVELOP IT?
[QUESTIONS 59–62, 2001]

Tibetan medical science is "an important part of Chinese medical science. The Chinese government has paid great attention to developing" it and "has adopted a policy of inheriting, encouraging, systematizing and improving it." Some important classical and modern books have been published. "Many specialists have graduated from the Tibetan Medical Science Department of Tibet University and from the training classes run by the Lhasa Tibetan Medicine Hospital. A Tibetan Medical Institute has been established in Lhasa."

"Before liberation," there were only a few medical centers, including the "Menzikang" [Mentsikhang] and "Yaowangshan" [Cagpori] in Lhasa, and the "Gejina" [?] clinic in Tashilhünpo monastery. "All of them were exclusive clinics for the privileged." In 1998 [from the 2001 version], "there were 1,324 medical institutes in the region, with 6,246 hospital beds. . . . There were also 1.84 doctors and 3.57 medical workers per 1,000 people in Tibet, higher than the national average." Pharmaceutical plants produce Tibetan medicines. Farmers and herdsmen enjoy free medical services.

FERNAND MEYER

Before 1950, biomedicine was virtually unknown among Tibetan-speaking populations, except for medical care liable to be dispensed by rare diplomatic or commercial British missions. Those regions were also lacking any formal health organization. On the other hand, a large array of therapeutic offers were available, in various local proportions, ranging from domestic care to traditional scholarly medicine, and including production of religious merit, prayers and reading of holy books, pilgrimage, shamanic cures, and therapeutic rituals. Tibetan medicine, one of the traditional sciences based on a written corpus, was itself dispensed by practitioners with very different standards of knowledge and practice, because they did not constitute a professional group and their activity was not subject to any control (see Meyer 1981).

Medical training was mainly provided, often along with religious teachings, in family lineages or within a master-disciple relationship. The Cagpori medical college in Lhasa, founded at the end of the seventeenth century by the Tibetan government, was probably the first institution specifically dedicated to medical teaching. However, it took over the traditional model of monastic organization. Thereafter, some large monasteries opened similar institutions. The foundation, by the 13th Dalai Lama, of the Mentsikhang ("Center for medicine and astrology") in 1916 in Lhasa, answered his wish to develop a medical teaching freer from the monastic model and more directed toward practice. The recruitment of the students, through a network of monasteries all over Tibet, can be considered a first step toward a national health system. Each Tibetan practitioner used to collect the needed ingredients and processed his own medicines, the number and sophistication of which were very variable. Only a few institutions, such as the Mentsikhang in Lhasa, had a collective organization for processing remedies, which, however, were not objects of trade.

We are lacking data that would enable us to evaluate, even roughly, the epidemiology of Tibet before 1950, the number of traditional doctors, or the respective share of the various therapeutic offers available for the care of patients. Epidemics, like smallpox, were frequent, and most of Western travelers reported the very poor health conditions of the people.

The entry of the Red Army into Tibet in 1950 marked the beginning of deep social, political, and cultural disruptions. They were accompanied by the introduction, first under very rudimentary forms, of new modes of health organization and cures, which were then current in China and derived mainly from the biomedical model. The first Chinese dispensaries and hospitals were established in a few administrative headquarters in 1954. It was also at that time that the first Tibetan health workers were trained. Among them some traditional practitioners thus got acquainted with rudiments of biomedicine. The Cagpori medical college was destroyed in 1959, during the repression of the Tibetan uprising by the PLA. The new administration, set by the Chinese authorities, who closely controlled it, integrated the remaining Cagpori doctors into the staff of the Mentsikhang (about eighty persons), which was then placed under the authority of the Lhasa municipal Health Bureau. In the larger frame of a policy clearly henceforth claiming its intention of a radical rupture with the old social order, the Mentsikhang was ordered to develop primary health care for the formerly underprivileged masses. However, the establishment was doomed to stagnate for lack of financial resources, and certain authorities eventually contested its very existence. Besides, the disintegration of the religious system, due to massive confiscations and active campaigns against the so-called "superstitions," drastically reduced the traditional range of therapeutic recourses in all the Tibetan regions.

In 1961, the Mentsikhang eventually gained the official support of the Lhasa authorities after profound changes implying its complete secularization and adoption of certain biomedical standards: creation of specialized departments, wearing of white coats and caps, use of some modern diagnostic and therapeutic techniques, and so on. It was also allowed to resume the teaching of traditional medicine in 1963 with a class of forty-five pupils, who had been intentionally recruited from formerly underprivileged families, and which for the first time included a noteworthy proportion of women. Even if the memorizing of the basic texts remained as fundamental as before, the new framework of teaching was that of a modern study class. The following year, a drug-manufacturing unit was created within the Mentsikhang. The 1963 recruits could not complete their degree course because of the enormous upheavals caused by the Cultural Revolution and its hysterical condemnation of everything evocative of traditional culture. The masters were persecuted and younger staff had to leave to work in rural popular communes. Any traditional medical activity, even in the remotest areas, exposed the practitioners to Maoist aggression. The Mentsikhang was thus reduced, during many years, to the state of a ruined vestige, apparently doomed to final collapse.

At the beginning of the 1970s, with the ebbing of the Cultural Revolution, the surviving Tibetan practitioners, on whom political suspicion did not weigh, were requested, whatever their training level, to take part in the restoration of an incipient public health service. The medical situation was horrendous, and the human and economic resources available to confront it were extremely limited. Recourse to local skills and the indigenous pharmacopoeia, which was easily available and cheap, was essential. Rudimentary training in "Tibetan medicine" was thus resumed around 1975. However, those teachings, formalized in small handbooks in modern format, and expurgated of any religious or even traditional reference, were mainly directed at the empirical use of a restricted range of simple medicines, on the model of the "barefoot doctors" then promoted all over China. They also included the rudiments of biomedical anatomy, physiology, and therapy. The qualifications thus obtained, which are those held by a number of practitioners still active today on all levels, remained very poor.

The socioeconomic reforms introduced in China by Deng Xiaoping from 1976 on had significant repercussions in the TAR only after 1980. Tibet then knew a relative economic and political liberalization, as well as a certain opening to the outside world, with, in particular, the development of tourism and the help proposed in various fields by international institutions and NGOs. This new orientation, which also allowed the revival of certain aspects of the traditional culture, including medicine, has been maintained since then, with setbacks imposed by the slogans of the Chinese national or regional policies. The health-care and teaching institutions of Tibetan medicine, integrated into the health system entirely managed by the state, benefited from substantial financing by the central government and the local authorities.

In 1980, the Mentsikhang, which was still a health-care establishment of the Lhasa municipality, was placed under the direct authority of the Health Bureau of the TAR, thus becoming a central institution of the health organization, alongside its biomedical equivalent, the People's Hospital. Important extension works then endowed the Mentsikhang with new buildings meant to accommodate an outpatient clinic, a new teaching course in Tibetan medicine recruiting from high schools, and two small research departments, one in medicine and the other in astrology and computing of each year's calendar. The unit manufacturing traditional drugs was also equipped with new premises and machines in order to increase production, now intended to be widely distributed. Their production became almost industrial in 1995, with the shifting of the factory to the vast complex of buildings that is today the Tibetan drug factory of the Mentsikhang. These developments still reinforced the influence of the biomedical model. But at the same time, Tibetan medicine could again officially acknowledge a great part of its heritage, including some of its religious components. The teaching was again based on the unexpurgated fundamental treatises, ancient medical texts were reprinted, the traditional medical iconography (see Parfionovic and Dorje 1992) was reintroduced, and the statues of the founding figures of Tibetan medicine were installed beside the samples of materia medica in the exhibition hall of the new Mentsikhang. Besides, toward the middle of the 1980s, the Mentsikhang became a regular destination for organized tours, an attractive showcase where the authorities could show off their dedication to public health and their patronage of Tibetan culture to foreign visitors. Lastly, the then acting director of the Mentsikhang, a scholar who had formerly studied with the old masters of the institution, occupied a high-level position in the government of the TAR for many years.

In 1985, buildings erected on a new site endowed the Mentsikhang with the hospital infrastructure (150 beds) it had hitherto been lacking. That same year, the state teaching of Tibetan medicine was shifted from the Mentsikhang to a specific institute founded, with a class of approximately seventy students, within the recently created Lhasa University. This reference institution gradually developed, then it was endowed with its own campus and promoted in 1995 to an administrative level equal to that of the medical faculties of China. This new Tibetan medicine faculty could consequently recruit students at the level required for admission to Lhasa University, which, however, lacked a biomedical equivalent. It trained the young traditional practitioners who served in the health-care organization of the TAR, both in Lhasa and in prefecture and county seats. Basic or more advanced training courses, intended in particular to train basic health workers, were also organized in some prefectures. Lastly, health-care institutions similar to the Lhasa Mentsikhang, some of them also providing teaching courses in Tibetan medicine, were established outside the TAR, in various Tibetan areas of Qinghai, Sichuan, and Yunnan provinces.

The current health-care system of the TAR is a state-administered pyramidal organization, headed by the Health Bureau under the authority of the TAR government, and closely linked with the different levels of the territorial administration: prefectures *(sakhül)*, counties *(dzong)*, townships *(shang)*, and administrative villages. Branches of the central Health Bureau in charge of the implementation of the sanitary policy, of the administration of health services, and of the distribution of medicines and state subsidies are found at prefecture and county levels. The size and equipment level of the hospitals, in terms of material and staff (number and qualification), decrease according to their place within the territorial hierarchy.

At the prefectoral level and in many county headquarters, a Tibetan medicine health-care establishment has been set up independently of the biomedical hospital. On a lower level than that of the counties, the peripheral ramifications of the public health system do not extend beyond the township headquarters, where they are restricted to poorly equipped dispensaries generally staffed by two or three health workers who have received a basic training. In certain villages, modestly paid volunteers provide primary health care after brief training. Most of the staff of the health system are civil servants, but their number is currently decreasing in favor of contract employees. The health services are very largely subsidized by the state, especially in rural areas where, provided the assigned stock has not been exhausted, medicines are dispensed at low prices or even free of charge. In the wake of the Chinese policy of economic liberalization, the TAR authorities have recently begun to undertake a reform of the health-care system, of which the shortcomings are now acknowledged. It aims in particular at a relative decentralization in favor of the counties, which are urged to institute health insurance contributions and to gradually develop a private health sector. Moreover, for about fifteen years, under strict control of the authorities, various international or nongovernmental organizations have been able to set up health programs (training, prevention, infrastructures, health care), some of them involving Tibetan medicine.

Practitioners with more or less thorough training in Tibetan medicine, sometimes in addition to elementary biomedical instruction, are thus found at all levels of the public health system. In the TAR, the total number of medical staff acquainted, to various degrees, with Tibetan medicine, seems to amount to approximately 1,500 persons, and thus must represent nearly 30 percent of the total. Besides, about this same proportion of the subsidies allocated by the state to the drugs distributed by its health services goes to Tibetan remedies. However, it is generally admitted that a biomedical prescription is on average two to three times more expensive than a traditional treatment. In fact, Tibetan populations, even in rural areas, are now used to resorting to the modern pharmacopoeia, of which one can often observe an inadequate use, especially in terms of antibiotics and injections, which are viewed as fast-acting panaceas, whereas, paradoxically, the long eclipse of traditional Tibetan medicine has made it relatively alien to younger people. It thus appears today that, generally speaking, patients desire free access to both types of medicine, according to the respective advantages they ascribe to them. Besides, it frequently happens that health-care providers, especially those less qualified, combine the two therapeutics.

For all the practitioners of Tibetan medicine in China, the Mentsikhang and the traditional medicine faculty of Lhasa are still the institutions of reference.

The Mentsikhang, which has steadily developed over the past twenty years, today employs approximately 450 persons, including about 30 doctors in charge and more than 70 qualified practitioners. It is divided into twelve departments, including internal medicine, maternal and infant health, and ophthalmology, and has two research units (medicine; astrology and calendar computing), and has integrated certain biomedical techniques, especially diagnostic aids such as radiology and ultrasound, for example. The number of outpatients has steadily increased and currently exceeds 260,000 patients per year, whereas its inpatient department has a total of 300 beds available. The Mentsikhang's unit manufacturing Tibetan drugs, the world's largest of its type, nowadays employs roughly 190 persons on the production side and has a vast sales network, with approximately 180 agents. It manufactures more than 200 types of traditional preparations almost industrially and has recently started the production of several new formulas with modern packaging intended for the Chinese national market. The Mentsikhang is now comparable, in terms of size and number of patients, to the five biomedical hospitals of Lhasa.

The Lhasa Tibetan medicine faculty now has more than 300 students, divided into eight classes and engaged in three- or five-year courses, each followed by one or two years of practical training. Admission, which is by examination, testing for command of literary Tibetan, in particular, takes place at the high school level for the short course and at the entry level to the university for the long course of thorough study. A few students go on to higher training involving research work.

Each prefecture (sakhül) chief town is endowed with an establishment similar to the Lhasa Mentsikhang, and locally known by the same name. It comprises an outpatient clinic, an inpatient sector, a unit manufacturing traditional Tibetan medicines, and often a small research department. The Mentsikhang of Nagchu prefecture, for example, employs a staff of about 150, and nearly 70,000 people attend its outpatients' clinic each year. It produces some 200 traditional drug preparations, which are locally distributed. Some of those establishments also hold courses, generally short, to train basic health-care workers.

At the level of nearly all county headquarters (dzong), a Tibetan medicine establishment, often independent of the biomedical hospital and sometimes having a small inpatient ward, is staffed by a small team of practitioners in which at least the doctors in charge have received a relatively thorough training. A growing number of these establishments is now planning to develop its local production of Tibetan drugs in order to better meet local needs.

Finally, it often happens that one among the two or three health workers who usually staff township dispensaries, sometimes equipped with a rudimentary inpatient ward, has received a basic training, exclusively or not, in Tibetan medicine.

As previously mentioned, the Chinese health system, including to a lesser degree in the Tibetan areas, has started to allow the development of a private sector. Foreign NGOs have thus recently been requested to finance, in various places, basic training in Tibetan medicine for young villagers recruited in regions still badly served by the public health system. After completing their training, they are intended to return to their villages and work there either in private practice or as contract employees of the public health service. The past few years have also seen an increase in the number of companies, either semi-public or private, manufacturing so-called Tibetan drugs because of the profits expected from the growing Chinese and international demand for them. This process of privatization of a part of the health system will soon raise the problem, notably for Tibetan medicine, of the qualifications and practice standards required, at regional or national levels, for official registration as a medical practitioner.

Tibetan medicine has been the object of a significant number of publications in China during the past twenty years. According to a nonexhaustive estimate, more than 150 books and 400 articles in Tibetan bear testimony to the vitality of this field and the interest it arouses. These publications—which are of unequal quality and sometimes repetitive, although some are excellent—are very varied in nature: they include new editions of more than forty classical texts and corpuses (some of which, such as the fundamental treatise *Gyüshi*, have been translated into Chinese), teaching handbooks, monographs and commentaries on classical texts, pharmacopoeias and pharmaceutical formularies, dictionaries, historical studies, critical essays, and clinical research articles.

Tibetan medicine thus appears to be one of the components of the country's cultural heritage that have best survived the deep disruptions of the past fifty years. This is probably due to several factors: the place conceded to traditional medicine in China itself, its local availability at a low cost, its pragmatic, rational orientation, which is liable to be promoted at the expense of its religious aspects, and its ability, easily controlled, to exemplify a Chinese policy eager to show itself concerned with the promotion of the well-being and the cultural heritage of the Tibetans. This last factor, and the economic prospects opened up by the growing interest in Tibetan medicine on the world market of alternative therapies, including in urban China, were probably instrumental in the planning of the large international congress on Tibetan medicine held in Lhasa in July 2000. Over the same decades, biomedical concepts and techniques were introduced, even under rudimentary forms, down to the most remote administrative headquarters, while the range of the traditional therapeutic offers was largely deprived of what the new authorities assiduously fought as "superstitions." Tibetan medicine was integrated into the public health system at the cost of an evolution that draws some of its aspects from the biomedical model: institutional training sanctioned by official diplomas; secularization; professionalization; a more exclusive focus on the somatic nature of disease, at the expense of its psychological or social dimensions; more impersonal encounters between patients and healers in the formal medical setting of a dispensary or a clinic; reappraisal of certain traditional concepts and practices with reference to modern science; relinquishment of drug processing by practitioners in favor of a specialized production by pharmaceutics companies; joint resort to certain biomedical diagnostic or therapeutic techniques, and so on. Some of these trends also mark, to various degrees, the recent evolution of Tibetan medicine beyond China's borders, driven by the communities in exile. At the same time, Tibetan medicine permits a number of practitioners and patients to assert their cultural identity and express the sociopolitical tensions and frustrations they feel without exposing themselves to political repression in Chinese Tibet.

75
HOW ABOUT THE USE OF THE TIBETAN LANGUAGE?
[QUESTION 66, 2001]

"The Chinese Constitution stipulates that each ethnic group has the freedom to use and develop its own language." Since the "peaceful liberation" of Tibet, Tibetan-language specialists have been trained, and the number of newspapers, such as *Tibet Daily*, and magazines published in Tibetan has continuously increased. "In both rural and urban areas, most primary schools use Tibetan. In all middle schools and colleges, there are special courses in the language, and the Tibet University has a Tibetan language department." The TAR government has set up many language research institutions and published textbooks, and so on, for primary and secondary schools.

"All the regional government's official documents are written either in Tibetan or both Tibetan and Chinese." According to the regulations adopted in 1988, as of 1990, "every unit can refuse to accept official documents if there are no copies in Tibetan; and all official seals, certificates and the proper names of public institutions must use both Tibetan and Chinese." The implementation of these regulations will certainly develop the use of the Tibetan language.

[The 2001 version adds that local TV and radio use both languages, that "a major principle of local employment and school enrollment" is to give "priority to Tibetan language users," and that "the Tibetan Codes and characters for Information Technology, formulated by Tibet, have been adopted by the International Organization for Standardization, ISO."]

AMY HELLER AND ANNE-MARIE BLONDEAU

The Chinese response was optimistically written in 1989, but the situation was rather different in 2006.

As far as media are concerned, there is a newspaper in Tibetan, *Tibet Daily*, but it is hard to find it, even in Lhasa. Regarding radio and TV, the language issue has been addressed in Question 61. They are good tools for sinicizing, as are cheap cassettes, which can even be heard in nomads' tents. The advent of portable telephones and text-messages, which are as popular in Tibet as elsewhere on our planet, constitute another challenge to the Tibetan language, because so far, only Mandarin can be used for text messages. However, Tibet University's Engineering Department is working on producing a Tibetan-language option for text messages (2004).

Concerning education (on which see Question 28), primary school is indeed taught in Tibetan, or was until 1997, with progressive introduction of Mandarin, which is required in secondary studies. As the *100 Questions* reply states, the People's Congress of the TAR adopted a series of rules in 1987 concerning the study, use, and development of Tibetan language, which imposed Tibetan as the language of instruction in early school, with Mandarin introduced as of nine years of age. From 1993, Tibetan was to be used in conjunction with Mandarin in secondary school, and Tibet University courses were to be taught in Tibetan as of 2000.

However, as discussed by Catriona Bass (1998; see also Question 61), the intentions of the 1987 regulations were undermined as a result of the Third Tibet Work Forum, which resulted in realignment of Tibetan economic development with other provinces and suppression of any Tibetan "separatism." Bass explains how the 1980 policies to promote teaching of the Tibetan language were abandoned during the 1990s in conjunction with the priority given to economic development. The policy of primary education in Mandarin or Tibetan fluctuated over the years.

The utilization of Tibetan in secondary education and university was suppressed, and professors had to purge their courses to eliminate religious content (Dharamsala 2000: 19). Tibet University in Lhasa now offers studies in humanities, fine arts, computer science and engineering, twenty-seven teaching research offices, twenty-one laboratories, and one research institute. The eighteen departments include the Department of Tibetan Language, the Department of Language, the Department of Political Science and History, the Department of Mathematics, the Department of Chemistry, Biology and Geology, the Department of Economic Management, the Department of Art, and the Department of Tibetan Language Teachers. However, all scientific disciplines are taught in Mandarin.

Far more serious, however, is the level of illiteracy. The official statistics are bleak in this regard: according to the 1990 census, 44.43 percent of Tibetans over fifteen years of age were illiterate. A PRC publication, *China's Tibet* magazine, reported that only 0.57 percent had studied at the university level; 2.12 percent had high-school diplomas, 3.85 percent had undergone secondary education, and 18.6 percent had attended primary school.[1] Independently, Bass found similar statistics (1998: 11). Nicolas Tournadre (1999) observes: "The total primacy of Chinese in education and the media divides Tibetan society in two: the highly sinicized urban groups, who have access to secondary education, and the nomads and farmers (about 80 percent of the population), who speak only Tibetan and are often illiterate. . . . When the younger generation come to the cities, they feel like complete foreigners."

As an attempt to remedy this situation, in 1987, a Tibetan-language high school was founded in Beijing that recruits some 70 percent of its students from families that are not on the payrolls of government offices and factories, and even from among nomads. In 2000, there were said to be twenty-four such high schools located throughout the country, with an annual recruitment of 1,300 Tibetan teenagers (*People's Daily*, July 1, 2000).

After a slight improvement in the percentage of illiteracy (43.8 percent in 2002), this percentage sharply increased (see Question 87). Anyway, in the context of the present policy of encouraging academic associations linking Tibet University with other universities in China and the policy of encouraging students, scholars, and technicians from the best Chinese universities to "head west," whether to Xinjiang, Gansu, or Tibet, it seems unlikely that a genuinely bilingual educational system will be created in Tibet (TIN 2000b).

1. *China's Tibet* 1995, no. 2: 36.

PART EIGHT

Economic Development

In this section, we depart from the plan generally followed through the book, namely, taking the Chinese questions and answers one after the other. Andrew Fischer, who analyzes economic development in Tibet, begins with general and historical outlines, then discusses Questions 77 and 76, 78 and 83, and 79 and 81 respectively in tandem. Question 82, about Tibet's tourism resources, is answered by Katia Buffetrille, and Question 84, dealing with nuclear waste and the environment, by Thierry Dodin.

The series of exchanges on economic issues in *100 Questions* exudes a certain confidence. Whereas the Chinese government has been on the defensive concerning most other issues, it feels exemplary in its economic achievements, particularly since the mid 1990s. This confidence is engrained with a Marxist outlook, in that the priorities of social and economic "democracy" are seen to supersede the formalistic practices of political and legal democracy. Therefore, social and economic transformations are evoked to legitimize its rule of the TAR.

Rapid transformations started with the arrival of the Chinese Communists in the 1950s. Before this time, the starting point in Central Tibet and to which these questions refer was characterized by a Tibetan form of serfdom (see Questions 19 and 85). As in most premodern settings around the world, life expectancy was low and health indicators were poor (by modern standards). Education levels were very low; given the lack of modern schools, the monasteries were the mainstays of literacy and learning. Aside from a few small pioneering efforts in the first half of the twentieth century, most aspects of any modern economy were absent.

The outcome at the turn of the twenty-first century offers a contrast to this earlier period. Five decades of Communist rule have resulted in a heavily subsidized modern urban economy transposed onto rural areas that remain largely subsistence-based. However, even these rural areas have also undergone huge transformations; traditional patterns of landownership were replaced by collectivization, from the mid 1950s on, outside the TAR, and from the late 1960s on, in most of the TAR, and communes were in turn replaced by the reallocation of land to individual households in the early 1980s. Intensive subsidization paralleled the integration of the Tibetan areas into Chinese regional economic planning. Thus, public education and health care are now widespread in the Tibetan rural areas, although they are undersupplied and often of very poor quality relative to the rest of China. There are roads and other infrastructure that did not exist before, although some of the technology referred to in the 2001 version of *100 Questions*, such as the Internet and satellite television, did not, of course, exist anywhere in the world in the 1950s. Notably, following a huge government effort in the TAR over the past few years, there is now solar-powered television reception in all townships and most villages, even those without electricity or running water (on the broadcast programs, see Question 61).

The Tibetan areas today can thus be described as two economies—the rural subsistence economy, based on individual landholdings and accounting for

about 85 percent of Tibetans in the TAR (2000 census), and the urban modern economy, based largely on government administration, services, military,
construction, and, increasingly, tourism. In both cases, manufacturing industries play a very limited role. Mining and other natural resource industries
have been developed in pockets, although mainly outside the TAR, such as in
the Tsaidam (Qaidamu) Basin of western Qinghai. Once the effects of inflation
are taken into account, the rural economy has been largely stagnant throughout the 1990s, contributing little to the rapid growth experienced since the
mid 1990s. Growth has been mainly concentrated in the urban modern economy or in a few large-scale construction projects, such as the railroad, which
passes through rural areas but has few economic linkages with them.

Economic growth in these modern areas has been almost entirely driven
by subsidies from Beijing. Or, rather, investment and subsidy programs decided in Beijing more or less determine the fate of growth in the TAR. For
instance, by the beginning of the reform period, which started in 1978, direct subsidies from Beijing to the TAR were equivalent to about 60 percent
of the TAR economy. This proportion slowly fell up to the mid 1990s to about
45 percent, during which time, the TAR economy as a whole was effectively
in recession once inflation is taken into account. Various development
strategies for the western PRC adopted since the mid 1990s have led to the
proportion of direct subsidies and investment to gross domestic product
(GDP) edging up and stimulated rapid growth in the TAR from 1995 on.
Subsidies, investment, and growth further increased sharply with the Western Development Strategy (xibu da kaifa), or WDS, launched by Beijing in
2000 and supported by the tenth national Five-Year Plan. The TAR has been
since achieving some of the highest provincial growth rates in China, mostly
concentrated in urban areas or in large-scale construction projects.

Because of these rapid changes since the mid 1990s, it is important to
consider the 2001 version of 100 Questions. The old version was written in
the 1980s, when the TAR economy was stagnant. Most of the arguments therefore referred to changes over the three decades from the late 1950s to the
late 1980s, avoiding the fact that the TAR was one of the worst provincial
performers in China during the 1980s. In contrast, the 2001 version of 100
Questions was released in the midst of a subsidy- and investment-induced
bonanza. It therefore refers to changes since the mid 1990s, along with numerous new references to the pre-1959 economic system.

However, as usual, both new and old versions treat the TAR as Tibet, ig-
noring the economic situation in the other Tibetan areas outside the TAR.
Here, some examples will be drawn from the other provinces containing Tibetan areas, although the economic data for Qinghai, Sichuan, Gansu, and

Yunnan refer mostly to the Han areas of each province where people and economic activity are concentrated. The TAR is the only province-level jurisdiction that is made up entirely of Tibetan areas, and it is thus the only one where the Tibetan experience can be deciphered from the macroeconomic data.

In this regard, the main differences between the TAR and the other Tibetan areas are their respective places in the fiscal pecking order. No doubt due to its politically sensitive status, the TAR is much more heavily subsidized than the other areas. The Tibetan areas outside the TAR receive subsidies via their respective provincial capitals (i.e., Xining, Lanzhou, Chengdu, and Kunming), which are considerably poorer than Beijing and are themselves recipients of central government subsidies. In this sense, local governments in the Tibetan areas outside the TAR find themselves at the bottom of a fiscal hierarchy that is much more austere and with many more levels of intermediation than are faced by the TAR.

Nonetheless, subsidies, whether great or small, mostly relate to the modern economy, that is, urban areas, construction projects, and so forth, whereas most Tibetans outside the TAR are as rural as those in the TAR, if not more rural. The difference in the intensity of subsidization is therefore mostly seen in the rapidity and opulence of urban development. It can also be seen in the salary levels of those who have access to jobs in the state or para-state sector, who are again mostly concentrated in the urban areas. For instance, the average salaries of staff and workers in the TAR (mostly state-sector) were the highest in China in both 2002 and 2004, even surpassing those of Shanghai and Beijing and almost double the national average. In contrast, average salaries in state-owned units in Qinghai, another hardship placement for cadres and other professionals, were only 8 percent higher than the national average in 2004, while those in Sichuan were 12 percent lower than the national average (*CSY*, 2005: table 5-21). Furthermore, these salaries in the TAR have been increasing rapidly since the late 1990s, beyond levels that can be justified by the "hardship" pay scales and accounting to a great extent for the subsidies, economic growth, and urban affluence in the TAR over these years.

These differences in state-sector salaries lead to the perception in China that Tibetans in the TAR are spoiled, although such complaints relate mainly to comparisons among cadres or professions, not to Tibetans overall. For instance, while average urban household incomes in the TAR were the seventh-highest in China among thirty-one provinces in 2001, average rural incomes were the lowest in China in the same year, even lower than those of Guizhou, the poorest province of China in terms of GDP per person (*CSY*, 2002: table 10-21).

In this sense, Tibetan rural areas inside and outside the TAR exhibit a remarkable similarity, reflected in a variety of indicators such as education levels, health indicators, or average rural household incomes. This indicates that conditions in Tibetan rural areas are more or less independent of the relative intensity of subsidization in each province. Thus, the rural areas of the TAR can be taken as representative of the experience of most Tibetans in other Tibetan areas.

There has definitely been a subgroup of Tibetans who have been profiting well from current growth. Drawing a rough line, this would account for the 15 percent of Tibetans with secondary education or above in 2002. Obviously, there are cases of some people with less education yet who are successful in business, or conversely, some who have secondary education but are unemployed. The two probably cancel themselves out, leaving a 15 percent to 85 percent split among Tibetans in terms of those who are riding the subsidized boom and those who are struggling in the margins. This split does not follow the urban-rural divide, because more than one-third of the permanently resident adult city population in the TAR (mostly Tibetans) was illiterate in 2002, an exceptionally high level in urban China, with no parallel in any other province.

The 85 percent with no education or only primary education are possibly making a bit more money in petty trade or unskilled labor, yet they are also faced with the inflationary pressures induced by subsidies, urban affluence, tourism, and so forth. It is notable that inflation in the TAR in the 1990s was the highest in China, whereas the prices of the main commodities produced by Tibetan farmers and pastoralists have fallen sharply over the same period. Those rural families who have some off-farm employment definitely tend to be better off than those without. But it is hard to evaluate whether net changes in the post-inflation livelihoods of even these families with diversified employment have been positively affected by recent developments. For every example of a family that has been enriched by current policies, there might equally be one that has been impoverished, whether because of mounting tuition fees or hospital bills, or loss of employment due to some shift in the economy away from certain sectors or regions. There are winners and losers within growth, and the averages belie an increasing gulf between the haves and have-nots. It cannot be automatically assumed that "a rising tide lifts all boats."

The current challenges of development in the TAR, and to a lesser extent in the other Tibetan areas, are found in this polarization of the economy and its exclusionary dynamics, that is, the marginalization of a large majority of Tibetans from participation in and benefit from the dynamic sectors of the economy. These challenges are further exacerbated by the presence of Han and Muslim Chinese migrants in the cities and towns, who arrive from much more competitive conditions elsewhere in China, with better connections and with much higher levels of education on average. Thus, with each passing day, the majority of Tibetans are faced with increasingly mounting barriers to take part in the economic boom. Tibet has certainly changed since the 1950s; this ethnically exclusionary dynamic within growth is as new as the growth itself.

The exclusionary dilemma is combined with a loss of local agency within development, which exacerbates a feeling of alienation despite all of the monumental change and pockets of affluence. Given the extreme level of subsidy dependence, the policies that guide development in the TAR have been essentially promulgated from Beijing as top-down dictates, following the trends of national development policy. Policies are then, effectively or ineffectively, implemented by local authorities, themselves appointed by Beijing, with the assistance of a corps of professionals and cadres from around the country on terms of duty that usually last two to three years. Tibetans did make up about 70 percent of local government employees within this system up to 2000, although their share of public employment fell sharply between 2000 and 2003, to less than 50 percent in the case of cadres. Such local Tibetan officials mostly toe the line set out from above, given Beijing's fiscal monopoly, the political and security paranoia that grips the Tibetan areas, and the increasingly high salaries that reward their obedience.

The fact remains that local initiatives and locally generated investment and accumulation play a very minute role in the overall processes of economic change in the Tibetan areas. In the tense political environment, they may even have been discouraged. The TAR economy has been changing rapidly, but the local Tibetan population has been rendered more or less redundant to factors causing the change. The agency and ownership of development is largely outside Tibetan hands, and thus, in a certain sense, development in the present carries continuity with the Maoist years, in that a meaningful decentralization of political and economic decision-making has not taken place in the TAR the way it has in most other areas of China.

Historical Comparisons

In the 2001 version of *100 Questions*, several of the questions refer to social and economic conditions in the "old society." The 2001 version is not given here, although some comments on it are useful.

While it is true that Tibet more or less embarked on modern development following the Chinese takeover in the 1950s, this is not to say that it would have remained static in the absence of Chinese rule. Probably, like all other Asian countries, it would have embarked on its own process of modernization, about which we can now only speculate. The only certainty is that the Tibetan economy of the late 1940s and its elites would have served as a starting point for an autonomous economic transition, possibly aided by China or other countries, much as Bhutan has been heavily aided by India in its own development.

Based as it is on Marxist theories of ethnicity that were adopted and elaborated by Stalin in the 1930s and later adapted to China by the Chinese Communist Party, *100 Questions* offers little insight into the realities of premodern Tibet, which it depicts as a feudal society most of whose population were chattel serfs and slaves. Minority nationalities were categorized by Maoism according to their stage of economic development, ranging from slave societies, as in the case of several of the Yi and Yao tribes in southwestern China (see, e.g., Harrell 2001: 7), right up to feudal, advanced feudal, and even nascent capitalist stages of development in the case of various Han regions. Tibet was categorized as a theocratic feudal system. Ethnic and religious identities were accordingly considered to be manifestations of these lower stages of historical material development. They would therefore eventually recede under the material and scientific progression of a society, best achieved in the Tibetan areas by opening them up to the more advanced regions of China and allowing for the dissemination of rationality, technological capabilities, and so forth.

Such simplistic theories of modernization, whether derived from Marxism or from mainstream economics, are problematic in that they impose categories and classifications from the outside, often with little relation to local realities or indigenous systems of reference. The Marxist lineage also leads to a conflation of ethnicity and religiosity with material conditions, despite the fact that even some of the most advanced economies of the world today, such as the United States, are still very ethnically stratified and very religious, as evidenced by recent elections. Unfortunately, most studies of the historical Tibetan economy coming from within China and Tibet are heavily constrained by official ideology.

Furthermore, it is in fact very difficult to make any qualified comparisons between poverty in the old economy and poverty now. Not only are data lacking from the past and present data of poor quality, but the old and new economic systems are also completely different, meaning that processes of impoverishment have changed substantially over time. If the notion of "absolute" poverty is considered, that is, the ability of households to produce enough output or earn enough income in order to supply their essential food needs (2,100 calories a day per person) and non-food needs, absolute rural poverty in the TAR was as high as 25 percent in 1999, according to the most recent publicly available official statistics and national poverty lines (for more details on these poverty measures, see Fischer 2005: 96–110). These rates of absolute rural poverty were among the highest in the PRC, and they are supported by the high rates of stunting observed and measured among Tibetan children by health workers in the TAR in the 1990s (see, e.g., Harris et al. 2001).

In this sense, it is conceivable that absolute poverty might be as high today as it was in the past—when the population may have been quite effective in providing for its own basic food needs, even if it did not have roads, airports, telecommunications, modern cities, Internet cafes, and karaoke bars—or even higher. Indeed, the economic system up to the 1950s was largely subsistence-based, with wool as one of the main internationally tradable goods. The main poverty consideration would have been the ability of households to feed themselves based on their own production or on barter and trade. However "backward" the old economy of Tibet was, there is no reason to assume a priori that one quarter of its population was unable to provide itself with basic subsistence food needs (i.e., the absolute rate of poverty measured in 1999). The high rates of poverty today are due to a variety of factors, such as population growth on limited land resources and falling agricultural prices, many of which are not necessarily the direct intention or result of government policy specific to the TAR since the 1950s. Nonetheless, the validity of any comparison of poverty between the old and new economies requires serious questioning.

Furthermore, certain aspects of the old economic system functioned with an efficiency that the modern state still has a difficult time matching, particularly in rural areas with dispersed, low-density populations. For instance, the sheer pervasiveness of the monastic system, while it to a certain extent impeded the development of a strong centralized state in Tibet in the first half of the twentieth century, nonetheless played a key distributive role in the dispersed rural economies and an integrative role throughout the Tibetan areas that functioned parallel to the state and far exceeded the reach of the Tibetan government based in Lhasa. In particular, monasteries acted as the dominant financial institutions, providing for an impressive accumulation of capital via non-state channels, channels that were to become the main object of attack and expropriation in the Communist occupation of Tibetan areas.

For instance, the Chinese government estimated that just prior to the dissolution of Drepung Monastery in Lhasa in 1959, the monastery had outstanding loans worth 10 million yuan in cash (worth five million 1959 U.S. dollars, or equivalent to about a quarter of a billion yuan in 2000) and 130,000 tonnes in grain (Goldstein 1998: 23). Other monastic institutions, such as Sera and Ganden, would have had outstanding loans of similar financial magnitude. Question 19 (2001) stipulates that bank deposits in the TAR in 2000 were valued at just over four billion yuan. In other words, in the premodern and unsubsidized conditions of the 1950s, a few monastic institutions in Lhasa alone would have accounted for a significant proportion of the entire financial system in the TAR today, defined in terms of deposits.

When the thousands of large and small monasteries spread out across the Tibetan ethnic areas are considered, the extensive breadth and depth once sustained by the indigenous financial sector can be appreciated. Given the tendency for every family to have had a relative in a monastery or nunnery and for every populated valley to have had a monastery or nunnery of some sort, the outreach, accessibility, and efficiency with which these indigenous financial institutions would have been able to operate is indeed striking. They would have been able to perform functions from providing for microcredit to the smallest of peasants right up to financing large trading companies in Lhasa, the government, and a wide range of social functions. This system would have been essential for the financing of dispersed mountain agriculture and herding, and of the extensive trade networks both within Tibet and abroad with Nepal, India, and even England, such as the wool trade. Indeed, the monasteries or reincarnate lamas often played central roles in trade as well as finance, particularly in Kham and Amdo.

The Communists typically portray this role of the monasteries in the economy as very exploitative. These assertions are evidently imbued with ideological concerns, as explained above. Furthermore, there is no reason to assume that the current state-run financial system is any less exploitative. For instance, it has been generally observed in China that the financial system drains resources away from the rural areas by lending or investing a large part of rural savings outside of the rural areas (on the rural-urban divide in China, see Knight and Song 1999). This is reinforced by the fact that rural dwellers, more than half of whom are illiterate in the Tibetan areas, have great difficulty accessing the formal state-run banks. As a result, rural lending in the Tibetan areas tends to be monopolized by officials or other wealthy and well-connected people. Thus, whether corrupt or not corrupt, the formal system tends to soak savings away from the rural economy, while the monasteries tended (and still tend) to retain them and may even bring in savings from elsewhere (for instance, from wealthy Chinese sponsors from Shanghai, Hong Kong, or Taiwan).

In any case, events related to the radicalization of Maoism in the 1950s eventually brought about the destruction of this monastic system. The main landholding groups (the monasteries, the aristocracy, and the Tibetan government in central Tibet) were eliminated by the 1960s both inside and outside the TAR, and most of their assets were expropriated. This started earlier outside the TAR, that is, in 1955–56 in the Kham areas of Sichuan, while it was postponed until 1959 in the TAR. The closure, expropriation, and eventual destruction of the vast majority of monastic institutions in the period leading up to the advent of the Cultural Revolution in 1966 therefore had the effect of wiping out the entire indigenous financial basis of the Tibetan economy. Loans were cancelled, estates and granaries were confiscated, the valuables and collateral of the monasteries, such as gold and precious metals, were largely sent to China, and the physical infrastructure of the monasteries was either disassembled, destroyed, or vandalized. Much the same happened all across the Tibetan areas.

The ensuing collapse of the financial sector would have wreaked havoc in the other sectors of the economy dependent on this finance, such as agriculture or trade. In this sense, the "democratic reform" involved not only an expansion of the Chinese state into the Tibetan areas and consequent infrastructure and social services, but also a forced de-capitalization of the indigenous Tibetan economy. Furthermore, a large proportion of those Tibetans who were skilled in business (i.e., monastery officials or aristocrats, along with the "Tibetan Muslims" of Ladakhi origin) escaped into exile or were ruined, incarcerated, or killed. Thus in a matter of years, the wealth and elites that could have served as the basis for an indigenously driven modernization in Tibet were effectively wiped out.

Thus it comes as no surprise that the Tibetan economy was entirely dependent on funding from the central government of the PRC by the advent of the reform period, because a financial void was created in the wake of occupation. Wang Xiaoqiang and Bai Nanfeng (1990: 73) note, in fact, that TAR government revenue fell sharply into deficit *and* the level of subsidy started to increase sharply precisely in 1968, in the midst of the Cultural Revolution and just before the onset of broadscale collectivization in the TAR. In other words, the pattern of heavy subsidization in the TAR effectively began in the late 1960s. This legacy is vital to understanding development in Tibet ever since.

Obviously, the legacy was the result of the radicalization of Maoism under occupation rather than occupation per se. During the first decade of Communist rule, state ideology became progressively more hostile to the indigenous socioeconomic system, which in the end was simply not allowed to coexist with the new rule and was obliterated over the course of the Maoist period. Instead, the Chinese state took over the management of a distant and distinct region through administrative means on all levels, from the micromanagement of the rural economy all the way up to provincial government finance. This involved a huge security and military dimension, given that Communist China fought a war with India in 1962 from two locations within the TAR itself.

Had Maoism not been radicalized in the mid 1950s, it is conceivable that the Tibetan elites and their sources of wealth would have played a significant role in developing a modern Tibetan economy, even in the context of Chinese occupation. In particular, had moderate land reform been undertaken, as was done elsewhere in China in the early 1950s, without engaging in a wholesale attack on the monastic institutions, it is conceivable that having lost their traditional sources of wealth—landed estates—Tibetan elites would have transferred their wealth into a variety of new activities in the emerging economy. In fact, this is precisely what many of these elites did in exile, using the wealth that they escaped with along with their "human capital" to successfully integrate into the modernizing economies of their host societies. In contrast, collectivization and animosity toward the monasteries from the mid 1950s on resulted in the major Tibetan uprisings in Kham and Amdo from 1955 on, often organized around some of the most prominent monasteries in each region (see Shakya 1999: 136–44). The economic dimensions of these conflicts cannot be underestimated.

Of course, Maoism was radicalized in both Tibet and China, and the social structure was turned upside down in each. However, this revolutionary zeal was an indigenous process in China, while it was imposed from the outside in Tibet, in accordance with political trends evolving in the Han areas of China. The reform period similarly originated in China and was imposed on the Tibetan areas from the outside. Moreover, despite the demise of Maoism, the legacy of Chinese nationalism has been maintained as a central part of state ideology, whereas Tibetan "ethnic" nationalism has been treated with suspicion and as counterrevolutionary. As a result, once the reform period began in the late 1970s, many elements of the Chinese elite who survived the Cultural Revolution quickly reemerged as leaders in the new market economy, whereas the suspicion of these classes in Tibet remains as a predominant legacy even to the present and is compounded by the fact that many of these Tibetan elites are now in exile. As a result, the reversion of the social order has been much slower and much more entangled by paranoid politics.

The Legacy of State Intervention in the Tibetan Areas over the Past Fifty Years

77
WHAT POLICIES AND ASSISTANCE HAS THE CENTRAL GOVERNMENT
PROVIDED IN REGARD TO ECONOMIC DEVELOPMENT IN TIBET?

A series of flexible measures have been taken, in order to "initially overcome the region's poverty and backwardness." State assistance includes:

1. Financial subsidies: more than 12 billion yuan from 1952 to 1986
2. Investments in capital construction: 3.43 billion yuan from 1952 to 1987
3. Other subsidies: 5.91 billion yuan from 1979 to 1986
4. Tax breaks: since 1980, agriculture and animal husbandry have been exempted
5. Aid in goods, for instance, tea: 484 million yuan from 1979 to 1983
6. Favorable credits granted to farmers and herders
7. Construction of roads everywhere
8. Creation of schools, colleges, and university establishments
9. Sending of medical and sanitary teams, building of hospitals and clinics
10. Subsidies for the upkeep of temples and monasteries: more than 36 million yuan from 1980 to 1987

Tibet doesn't repay anything to the central government, which, moreover, pays for defense.

76
WHAT IS THE STATUS OF ECONOMIC DEVELOPMENT IN TIBET?

"Since the democratic reform and especially since 1978, the economy has developed rapidly and outstanding achievements have been made. Industry has gradually climbed from zero to more than 250 medium-sized and small enterprises. . . . Handicrafts, agriculture and animal husbandry have also developed." Then statistics showing an economic boom are given, taken from 1987 sources. "The economic development has improved the living standards of the people. Every person has an average of 300 kilograms of grain a year, and the per-capita income of 1987 was 361 yuan. Many families have television sets, refrigerators and washing machines. By May 1987, the people's savings deposits were 1.54 billion yuan."

[Similar updated answers are found in the 2001 version. See Questions 17 (economic changes since the Democratic Reform); 18 (policies implemented); 20 (exile argument that China has gained more from Tibet than it has given, with amount of subsidies given); 21 (assertions that the WDS will lead to the colonization of Tibet and ecological deterioration); 23 (onset of modern industries); 27 (sixty-two aid projects of the Ninth Five-Year Plan); 28 (Three Rivers Comprehensive Agricultural Development Project); 39 (strategic points for development); 40 (growth rate of economy in 2000); and 41 (development goals for the next fifty years).]

ANDREW M. FISCHER

Question 20, 2001, refers to the exile argument that China has gained more from Tibet than it has given. This argument derives from a belief that one of the main motivations for Chinese rule, particularly under recent developments, is their desire to exploit Tibet's abundant natural resources, such as mining and forestry, in order to supply the voracious appetites of China's coastal industries.

This belief is based on a misunderstanding of the economic importance of the Tibetan areas for China. There are certain pockets of intensive resource exploitation in the Tibetan areas, such as the Tsaidam (Qaidamu) Basin in Qinghai, hydroelectric projects along the Yellow River in Qinghai, or logging in Kham (up to 1998; see Question 84). There is also some speculation that the Golmud-Lhasa railway will open up the potential for large-scale gold and copper mining in the TAR, although none has been realized as of yet. However, outside of these pockets, mining is quite minor for most Tibetan areas in terms of both GDP and employment. In the TAR, mining and industry have actually been shrinking as a share of GDP since 1997, to only 7.3 percent of GDP in 2004 (*CSY*, 2005: table 3-10). This reflects a shift away from resource-based industries within the development strategies for this region.

Even the pockets of mineral exploitation may not be as profitable as they appear. Tibet may be rich in certain natural resources, but most of these are remote and often very difficult to access. As a result, the costs of exploitation are many times higher than elsewhere in China. Without massive support and intervention from the central government, most of these resources are unprofitable to exploit and private businesses are not willing to get involved without substantial subsidies from the state. Therefore, even the profits of operations in places like the Tsaidam Basin may not necessarily outweigh direct and indirect subsidies. While this might explain part of the rationale behind subsidized government infrastructure projects, it is difficult to argue that China has received a net profit from the Tibetan areas.

The Chinese strategies in these areas are not so much based on the profitability of such ventures but rather on the demands of diversifying industrial development around the country, allowing certain regions, such as Xining and Lanzhou, to specialize in the industries in which they should, in principle, have the best comparative advantage, given their position in the national industrial structure. The generation of employment is also another important consideration. However, the Tibetan areas, already very marginal to the Chinese economy as a whole, have become increasingly so in the reform period, when the liberalization of international trade has allowed coastal industries to supply themselves with natural resources and raw products from abroad. Ironically, the exile thesis would have pertained most during the heyday of Maoism, but it is far off the mark in the present context.

Instead, subsidization policies of the Chinese government, especially in the TAR, are more likely guided by strategic and security/military concerns. The past five decades of subsidization of the Tibetan areas have been part of an effort to secure their integration into China and to build up the infrastructure necessary for maintaining control over both the local population and the remote borderland areas. In particular, military interests in the TAR cannot be underestimated, as noted above. Obviously, the high ratio of military personnel in the TAR (see Question 44) is in part due to a vast border area, requiring many troops, compared to a small population. Nonetheless, the relative presence of the military in the TAR is enormous and carries a heavy weight in the economy, even if this is disguised in the statistics.

These considerations are reflected in the main drivers of economic growth in the TAR over the past decade. To start with, the tertiary sector has become by far the largest sector, with its share of total GDP increasing from 34 percent in 1995 to over 50 percent in 2002, and stabilizing around 52 percent by 2004. In terms of their contribution to annual growth, tertiary activities were contributing on average well over 50 percent of total GDP increase in each year throughout this period, reaching high points of 80 percent in 1996 (i.e., 80 percent of GDP increase came from the tertiary sector), 87 percent in 2002, and remaining at 54 percent in 2004 (for sources and more detailed analyses of these and following data, see Fischer 2005: chap. 3).

Construction has also played a strong role as a share of GDP, increasing from around 11 percent in 1996 to almost 20 percent by 2004. However, in light of the de-industrialization mentioned above, the surge in construction has been utterly divorced from secondary productive activities, unlike in all other provinces in China. The TAR is the only province in China where construction has been consistently larger than industry, with the ratio of construction to industry/mining rising from 1.1 in 1997 to 2.7 by 2004, surpassing an earlier construction boom in 1995, when the ratio reached 2.3. Furthermore, the TAR is the only province in China where the primary sector (farming and herding) is larger than industry and mining (still by more than two times in 2004), despite the fact that the TAR has experienced the sharpest decline in primary share in the country, from 42 percent of GDP in 1995 to 21 percent in 2004. The combined secondary sector only surpassed the primary sector in 2003 due to a surge in construction activity, which was in large part related to construction of the Golmud-Lhasa railway. Notably, the construction boom accounted for 56 percent of GDP increase in 2003.

Within the tertiary sector itself, the TAR again contrasts with the experiences of all the other provinces in China. In particular, the share of "government and party agencies and social organizations" in the total tertiary sector of the TAR, which has always been the highest in China, surged at the beginning of the WDS from around 20 percent of the tertiary sector in the late 1990s to over 26 percent in 2000 and 2001, becoming the largest component of the tertiary sector in those two years. Considering that the tertiary sector in the TAR had surged to almost 50 percent of GDP in 2001, government and party agencies had come to account for over 13 percent of total GDP, or almost twice the entire mining and industrial activity in the same year, and close to the total construction activity as well (construction has since outpaced government administration). In comparison, government agencies accounted for only 2.7 percent of total GDP in China and 7.7 percent in Qinghai.

Government and party agencies were also the fastest-growing large category in the TAR in the opening years of the WDS, growing by 47 percent a year on average between 1998 and 2001 and accounting for 22 percent of total GDP growth over those years, which was more than the contribution of construction. The category accounted for 49 percent of total GDP increase in the year 2000 alone, and almost all of the total tertiary increase. This extreme case of government administrative expansion in the opening years of the WDS petered out by 2003, when tertiary expansion was largely based on sharp increases in the categories of transport (36 percent of GDP increase) and finance and real estate (8 percent). This would seem to indicate that a massive expansion of the government administrative apparatus was seen as a necessary precondition for the various subsequent projects under the WDS, such as the railway.

Moreover, this exceptional administrative expansion, which is completely out of sync with the needs of the local economy, indirectly implies a probable military or security buildup under the WDS. Although the military is not included in any of the provincial economic statistics, if it were included, it would show up in this component (like policing and jails). Inversely, the military requires the support of a parallel public administration. Therefore, a military buildup would be reflected by an expansion in public administration beyond local needs, such as in the TAR. This inference is supported by people who have been living in or have visited Lhasa repeatedly over the past ten years and have noted the expansion of military facilities around Lhasa and along the highway leading to the Gongkar Airport. The railroad project can also be best understood in this context, given that arguments concerning its economic viability simply do not stand the test of logic. Therefore, as in the past, military concerns probably guide and indirectly soak up much of the subsidies allocated to the TAR.

In this light, it is equally incorrect to say that the subsidization of the TAR and other Tibetan areas has been a philanthropic endeavor. In many cases, as with tied development aid from rich countries to poor countries, much of it is self-serving. China seeks to legitimize its rule over Tibet by citing the money that it spends there. While it is probably true that China has not gained more from Tibet than it has given, this calculus misses the point. Instead, the relevant inquiry is: what are the impacts of subsidies, how and why did the policies of subsidization arise, and who actually benefits? This inquiry is slightly different, because it pertains to China spending money on itself via Tibet. This will be analyzed in three parts.

1. ARE SUBSIDIES BEING USED EQUITABLY AND EFFICIENTLY TO PROMOTE LOCAL DEVELOPMENT?

In summary, most of the growth generated in the TAR since the mid 1990s has derived from an alternating sequencing between tertiary activities and construction, both resulting from policies of subsidized spending and investment determined by Beijing and with little relation to the local productive economy. These outside subsidies and investments are enormous relative to the local economy and to locally generated revenue, as asserted in all of these questions and answers. As a result, changes in the provincial economic structure have been much less gradual, much more volatile, and much more radical than anything observed elsewhere in China, including the next most resembling province of Qinghai.

Despite (or because of) the intensity of subsidies and investment, the TAR exhibits an extreme level of subsidy dependence, which has not abated over time. Local government expenditure remained over 90 percent funded by direct budgetary subsidies throughout the 1990s and up to 2004. As a proportion of GDP, such direct budgetary subsidies rose from just under 50 percent of GDP in 1990 to a peak of 81 percent in 2002 (i.e., subsidies were equivalent to 81 percent of all economic activity in that year). The subsidy/GDP ratio then fell sharply after 2002, to 59 percent in 2004, although this fall was achieved only because the government spent much less money in that year, rather than through a substantial increase in its revenue.

Falling public expenditure since 2002 was nonetheless compensated for by continuously increasing levels of investment, which reached an all-time high in 2004, equivalent to 77 percent of GDP in that year. Provincial aid projects to the TAR (62 in the Ninth Five-Year Plan—Question 27, 2001—and 70 in the Tenth Five-Year Plan) mostly show up in investment and construction data, along with investment funding from Beijing for various construction projects (117 in the Tenth Five-Year Plan, worth 31.2 billion yuan—see TIN 2001). The railway, which started in 2001 and was initially projected to cost 25 billion yuan, no doubt accounts for much of this recent investment boom (as many had speculated, the costs of this project have been greater than expected).

In comparison, investment in China in 2004 was equivalent to about 50 percent of national GDP, which is still considered very high by international standards and was the highest ever achieved in China ever since the beginning of the reform period. However, an important distinction is to be made: in China, most of this investment is domestically generated, whereas local revenues or capital in the TAR cannot finance such high levels of investment. As in the case of government expenditure, most medium- and large-scale investment in the TAR is subsidized through outside government sources, particularly through state-owned enterprises, which accounted for 84 percent of all investment in 2004 in terms of sources of ownership.

As a result, the most effective reflection of subsidy dependence in the TAR would include both direct budgetary subsidies and investment. Together, they increased from 74 percent of GDP in 1990, to a peak of 121 percent in 1995, back down to around 90 percent in the mid to late 1990s, and then surging to a remarkable 147 percent of GDP in 2003. In other words, in 2003, the government spent or invested in the TAR one and a half times the total official value of economic activity in that year. The fact that the strategy has achieved above national average growth rates since the late 1990s and the highest of the western provinces is hardly surprising with such intensive subsidization. The mere injection of cash at such volumes will inevitably create expansion. It also helps to explain why government administration and construction have been the two fastest-growing components of the TAR under the WDS, given that these two areas receive a disproportionate share of subsidies.

All of these figures support the fact that China is making a huge effort to generate growth in the TAR. However, the TAR has been heavily subsidized now for almost forty years. The strategy since the mid 1990s represents a return to previous strategies of heavy state subsidization rather than an entirely new approach to development. The form is different, cloaked in a new ethos of the market economy, but the essence is the same, that is, large construction projects, mostly run by state-owned enterprises from other parts of China, which in turn capture most of the outside investment and a large share of the direct subsidies. In this context, has the new strategy been successful at breaking out of the inefficiencies that characterized the past?

Comparing increases in direct subsidies to increases in GDP, it appears that the new strategy is as inefficient as ever. For instance, there was only 0.48 yuan of GDP increase for every yuan of direct budgetary subsidy increase in 2001. Similarly, there was less than one yuan of GDP increase for every one yuan increase in (mostly subsidized) investment in 2002, when investment started to boom due to the railway construction. Considering direct subsidies and investment together, in 2001 there was only 0.34 yuan of GDP increase for every one yuan of increase in subsidies and investment combined. This effectively represents what might be called a "negative multiplier effect" of subsidies to GDP, which has been a consistent characteristic of successive subsidy and investment booms in the TAR. Some northwestern provinces also experienced a few years of a slightly negative multiplier of combined subsidies and investment, although only for short periods during the most intensive phases of industrial restructuring, after which the multiplier became positive. No province experienced a negative multiplier to the degree or consistency as the TAR, where the extreme intensity of subsidization throughout the 1990s and early 2000s does not appear to have improved these multiplier effects right up until the most recent data.

Such inefficiency of direct and indirect subsidization is not new to the TAR. The nominal value of government expenditure almost doubled in 1984 (to 75 percent of GDP and 100 percent of expenditure subsidized), yet the GDP only briefly came out of recession. Government expenditure declined sharply in 1986, and the GDP fell back into recession in the same year. Government expenditure rose gradually thereafter, albeit slower than inflation, and in real terms (indexed to provincial price inflation), it only exceeded its 1984 value in 1998. Correspondingly, real per capita GDP was recessionary from the mid 1980s to the mid 1990s.

These patterns have been noted further in the past by several Chinese scholars and commentators. The earliest and most damning critique was made by Wang and Bai (1990: 72–73), who show that, similar to the above multiplier analysis, for every one yuan increase in the value of output between 1957 and 1983 in the TAR, subsidies increased by 1.24 yuan, that is, a negative multiplier effect of 0.81. They therefore argue that "subsidies have in effect been a powerful disincentive." As noted above, most of this negative multiplier was concentrated after the late 1960s; the level of subsidy started to increase sharply in the TAR from 1968 on, such that the proportion of central government subsidies to output value (equivalent to the subsidy/GDP measure above) increased from 31 percent in the 1950s, to 45 percent in the 1960s, 80 percent in the 1970s, and 97 percent from 1980 to 1983 (Wang and Bai 1990: 73).

In other words, recent strategies have not in any significant way changed the trend of very intense and very inefficient subsidization observed since the late 1960s. Instead, recent rapid growth has entirely been the consequence of another inefficient bout of subsidies. The level of subsidies per se appears inconsequential, to the extent that real per capita GDP was recessionary throughout the 1980s and the first half of the 1990s even while the levels of subsidy and investment were among the highest in the country. Rather, recession appears to have followed more or less in tandem with stagnation in the real value of government expenditure. In other words, GDP growth has acted as a mere reflection of the ebbs and flows in the real value of such subsidies.

The government would argue that there is a lag between increased subsidies and investment now and growth in the future, which is actualized once construction projects have been completed. Yet the argument of a lag factor holds mainly in the realm of productive investment. For instance, investment in a factory now becomes productive in the future once construction of the factory is finished and thus there is a lag between investment and production or employment. Yet, as mentioned above, productive sectors in the TAR, particularly industry, have been completely disconnected from increases in investment. In contrast, the sector that is increasing most rapidly—government administration—is not productive, given that expansion in administration must be sustained by further government revenues. To a limited extent, investment in transport infrastructure might enhance revenues from tourism or trade, but not nearly enough to justify the enormous costs of these projects. Furthermore, the boom in trade in the TAR is also largely fueled by the subsidies themselves and is mostly based on importing goods from elsewhere in China. Despite the market economy ethos, trade itself also cannot sustain growth in absence of wealth created by productive sectors, particularly in locations such as the TAR. In other words, the structure of current growth in the TAR suggests a continuing if not increasing dependence on subsidies and its related inefficiencies.

How has this situation arisen? What are the institutional factors that contribute to the inefficiency of subsidies and investment? These questions are analyzed below.

2. STATE INTERVENTION IN THE CONTEXT OF CHINESE REGIONAL DEVELOPMENT SINCE THE 1950S

As described in the brief historical analysis, the early phase of Communist control over the Tibetan areas laid the foundation for their subsidized and dependent integration into China. By the beginning of the 1960s, the PRC had eliminated the material and social basis on which Tibet could have modernized through locally driven processes. From this point on, there was no other option in the Tibetan areas but to rely on capital accumulation via centralized state planning. This initial expropriation of local assets became the foundation for exile arguments that China profited from its occupation of the Tibetan areas and that subsidies were merely returning to Tibet what had been taken from it in the first place.

This argument would certainly hold true for the money that is now being spent on restoring the various monasteries of Tibet, given that they were destroyed in this initial period. The exile argument also holds in a variety of other areas of the economy which were damaged during this period, such as environmental regeneration projects on lands that were degraded due to misguided agrarian policies and so forth.

More generally, though, subsidization of the western and interior provinces of China has been an explicit policy of regional development throughout China since the 1950s. A system of regional economic planning was set up under Maoism involving two principle strategies: regional redistribution via interior industrialization and the circular payments system. These two strategies still had an impact up to the 1990s and partly explain the lagging of the Tibetan areas throughout the reform period, along with their continued dependence on subsidies. Both strategies were underpinned by the militarization of the western regions, which still holds much weight in the TAR today, as discussed above, whereas it started to have less relevance in the other Tibetan areas from the 1980s on.

Throughout the 1960s and up until the early 1970s, Maoist development strategy pushed industrialization into the interior of China, particularly that of heavy industry, in what later became known as the "Third Front Strategy." The privileged core provinces of the strategy were Sichuan, Gansu, and Qinghai. The orientation was predominantly militaristic, aimed at building up a military-industrial base in the interior of China that would be difficult for potential foes on three fronts—the Soviet Union, India, and the United States, via the coast—to penetrate. The beginning of the end of this strategy was the détente with the United States in 1972 rather than reform in 1978, which removed the coastal military threat and allowed for a reversal of the national industrial strategy back toward the more efficient coastal provinces (Wei 2000: 28; Cannon and Jenkins 1990: 36–38; Yang 1997: 25–26).

The TAR remained far away on the sidelines of such industrialization. It experienced only a slight increase in industrialization, which peaked in 1974 and was likely attributable to the military stationed there (Yang 1997: 22). In general, much of the industrialization of the Third Front Strategy was concentrated in strategic centers that were isolated from military fronts and sensitive border areas, which by definition precluded most of the TAR.

On the other hand, the Tibetan areas outside the TAR were more influenced by this strategy, in particular, Qinghai, which served as a center for prison labor camps as well as several nuclear facilities. The Third Front requirements for regional self-sufficiency also generated considerable demand for forestry and mining resources in the Tibetan areas located close to Chengdu, Lanzhou, or Xining, and also marked the intensification of mineral exploitation in the Tibetan areas of western and northern Qinghai. Nonetheless, most Tibetans were marginal to these developments, remaining mostly agrarian.

The strategy of interior industrialization was supported by the "circular payments system" or the "circular resource allocation system" (Yang 1997: 62). On one hand, state-fixed prices for energy and raw materials (including agricultural products) were kept low in order to subsidize processing industries, which were concentrated in the coastal areas notwithstanding industrialization of the interior. On the other hand, these industries were in turn heavily taxed, and their surpluses were returned in the form of transfer payments to the raw material producing regions, predominantly located in the interior and western regions. Thus, by 1978–80, Shanghai turned over to the central government a surplus equivalent to more than 50 percent of its GDP, while provinces like Inner Mongolia, Ningxia, Xinjiang, and Qinghai received subsidies from the central government equivalent to over 20 percent of their GDP, and the TAR over 60 percent (UNDP 1999: 65).

These subsidies were to a great extent oriented toward the interior industrialization strategy or the parallel and autonomous military structure in the western provinces, mostly bypassing the rural areas. In this regard, the regional development strategy was further complemented by what has been called the "price-scissor" strategy of rural-urban development within regions, whereby agricultural prices were undervalued in order to subsidize urban output and wages. However, unlike the regional transfer system, this rural-urban transfer did not necessarily include a backflow of subsidies from urban to rural areas, given that rural areas were expected to be self-sufficient within this system, despite the fact that much of their output was undervalued (see Knight and Song 1999).

In general, it has been pointed out that the strategies were quite inefficient, particularly in the western economies, where scarce resources were squandered in inefficiently planned and located heavy industries and "projects were built under the direction of a small group of central leaders and with little regard to local interests" (Yang 1997: 24). Because of "the dominance of the unit mentality, which was strengthened owing to the military nature of most of the projects, most of these plants had few linkages with the local economy and contributed little to the development of these localities, including most areas inhabited by ethnic minorities" (Yang 1997: 23). These considerations would have played an especially significant role in the Tibetan areas given their political and security sensitivity.

As a result, by the beginning of the reform period, the TAR was an incoherent mixture of heavily subsidized state and military infrastructures, together with largely self-sufficient rural areas that accounted for most of the Tibetan population. The latter were heavily taxed, mainly through forced quotas for produce such as underpriced wool and grain. In return, the rural areas did gain basic rural health care, education, and limited infrastructure, which were modern novelties in the Tibetan areas.

Nonetheless, the poverty of the Tibetan rural areas astonished Hu Yaobang during his visit to the TAR in 1980, which led him to immediately declare a moratorium on various policies that were accentuating their economic burden (see Teufel Dreyer 2003). This coincided with the general trend of pro-rural reform policies throughout China in the early 1980s, such as decollectivization, which was implemented in most Tibetan areas in 1983 and 1984, as well as improvements in the terms of trade for agricultural goods, that is, better prices for agricultural goods relative to industrial goods. All of these policy changes made a definite improvement in the general standard of living of the Tibetan rural areas, although they were underlain by a collapse in rural public health care (also occurring throughout China), as well as a sudden reduction in the supply of primary education in the early 1980s (on education in the TAR, see Iredale et al. 2001: 144–46).

However, these one-off improvements for rural Tibetans at the beginning of the reform period were undermined by the continuing course of regional development throughout the 1980s and 1990s. Regional development policy embraced the ethos of "comparative advantage," although in effect policies privileged the coastal regions and neglected the interior and western regions. This was done by continuing to underprice the main commodities of the western provinces—a practice that was still largely operative until the early 1990s—while reducing regional transfer payments that were meant to offset this disadvantageous pricing and distribution system. Reductions in transfer payments were enacted through fiscal decentralization, which allowed the richer provinces and localities to retain more of their own resources and reduced the resources available for regional redistribution, thereby having a punitive effect on the poorer provinces and localities. As a result, richer provinces were able to invest more while still profiting from underpriced raw material inputs, which subsidized their dramatic takeoff in the 1980s. The interior and western provinces were inversely disadvantaged.

Essentially, the comparative advantage strategy was concerned about efficiency and the rationalization of the national industrial structure in order to maximize national growth by catalyzing certain coastal growth poles. Regions were divided up into each of their own areas of specialization where they were perceived to have advantage. The coastal region was identified as the industrial engine of the nation, as the logical location for the processing and exporting of the inland raw materials and for absorbing imported technology and finance. The interior was to focus on producing and supplying raw materials. The western region was identified as distinct from the central region of China for the first time in the Seventh Five-Year Plan (1986–90), which also stipulated that the western region would start to receive emphasis at the time of the Ninth Five-Year Plan (Yang 1997: 28).

While this reform of the economic system produced spectacular economic growth in the coastal areas, the gradual and incomplete implementation of the reforms ended by exacerbating regional inequalities throughout the 1980s. This was not apparent in the first years of reform, in part because the end of agricultural collectivization and related reforms catalyzed an initial and sudden increase in rural output and income, which lasted until about 1985 (Brandt et al.: 67–68). However, by the late 1980s, the strains of the strategy were becoming more apparent, given that the interior and western provinces were increasingly strapped for cash, while still facing a disadvantaged price and distribution system. The undervaluation of their products also created a profit disincentive in these provinces, which in turn reinforced the coastal prejudice that interior folk were idle (Yang 1997: 66). Local and provincial governments and people in the interior started to complain, not of the reform per se, but of the unequal manner with which it was being instituted.

Given the heavy dependence of the TAR's economy on central government funding and its complete subordination to central control and policy making, this reorientation of development strategy had a particularly stunting effect on its economic performance. As mentioned previously, the economy of the TAR was experiencing recession in nominal terms from 1981 to 1983 and from 1985 to 1991, even before taking inflation into account (*TSY*, 2005: 2–9). From 1991 to 1995, the TAR was recessionary in real per capita terms, that is, after taking inflation and population growth into account (Fischer 2005: 22–27). Relative to most other Chinese provinces, the economies of the TAR, Qinghai, and Gansu started to fall sharply from the 1980s on. The TAR and Qinghai, which taken together constitute about three-quarters of Tibetans and Tibetan areas in the PRC, were both among the worst-performing provinces up until the mid 1990s (Naughton 2002).

In terms of the experience of the average Tibetan, these dynamics are best represented by wool, which was the main commodity that connected rural Tibetans to the national economy of the PRC. Wool was ironically to become one of the first commodities to be completely liberalized in the 1990s, in terms of both market pricing and international trade (Yang 1997: 72). Thus, the role of administrative controls to keep the prices of wool low was thereby replaced by the impact of cheap imports.

The impact of this, and similar price trends for wheat, barley, and rapeseed that came later, are dramatically represented by the price of sheep's wool. In the late 1980s, wool was selling for about 20 yuan per kilogram, whereas in 2004 it was selling from 6 to 10 yuan per kilogram on average, depending on quality (prices are from field research by the author in 2004). Over the same period of time, the general cost of living in the TAR and Qinghai more than doubled. Therefore, the actual purchasing power of one kilogram of wool had effectively fallen by more than three-quarters since the late 1980s. This explains Tibetan herders' recent lack of incentive to commercialize wool production.

The changing regional economic policies of the 1990s were therefore disadvantageous to the rural economies of the Tibetan areas. The sheer lack of economic diversification in these rural areas meant that the average rural Tibetan had few alternatives to the production of commodities such as wool, barley, wheat, or rapeseed. Meanwhile, due to the success of the competitive advantage strategy, the coastal provinces monopolized most foreign investment, and due to continuing deregulation and decentralization up to the mid 1990s, central subsidies to the western provinces continued to fall as a proportion of their GDP. The TAR was in recession and other western provinces were quickly falling behind the rest of China.

It was in this context that the central government started to prioritize western development in the mid 1990s, as pre-planned in the mid 1980s. This was implemented through several decisive policy initiatives that were taken to curb rising inequalities, such as the 8-7 poverty alleviation plan in 1994, the focus on western development in the Ninth Five-Year Plan (1996–2000), and the WDS in 2000, which complemented the Tenth Five-Year Plan. Certain reforms at the national level also allowed for such initiatives, such as the tax reform of 1994 and related fiscal reforms in the two following years. These crucially re-shifted a large proportion of tax revenues from the provinces back into the hands of the central government, allowing it to finance these various initiatives (Liu and Lin 2001: 96–98).

Thus from the mid 1990s on, spending and investment increased in the western region, and economic growth picked up and sometimes even surpassed national growth rates. The lagging western region was buoyed, and in the case of the TAR and to a lesser extent Qinghai, the backward trend was reversed. This was also partly aided by bumper crops in 1996, coinciding with a sharp rise in the terms of trade of agricultural goods lasting from 1994 to 1997, which together would have had a disproportionately positive impact on the more agricultural western provinces, inverse to the situation from 1985 to 1994 (see Fischer 2005: chap. 2).

The 2001 version of *100 Questions* mostly refers to this recent period of subsidized growth in the TAR, when indeed growth has been spectacular, even if it has also been very inefficient. However, it has been part and parcel of what might be called the "contract" of Chinese regional development policy as it has evolved over the past fifty years, particularly in relation to the occupation and subsequent integration of the Tibetan areas into the Chinese national economy. Through such integration, Tibetan areas have been used by the Chinese state, whether for strategic or economic concerns (more strategic for the TAR, more economic for Qinghai), and have thereby lived through the consequences of the various phases of regional economic planning with very little if any say in the matter. In exchange, the government has provided subsidies, as instituted within such planning.

The problem is that the exchange is asymmetrical at the receiving end. Those who have access to state funds are not necessarily the same as those who suffer from the impacts of regional policy, and thus the burden of adjustment is effectively placed on the losers within growth. In the Tibetan areas, this asymmetry is exacerbated by the fact that there is very little dispersion of subsidies and investment within the local economy due to their concentration in government administration and large-scale construction projects. This makes it increasingly difficult for the have-nots to integrate into the dynamic and growing sectors.

Therefore, the relevant concern is not whether growth can be stimulated through massive injections of external funding, which is self-evident. Rather, the pressing concern is the exclusionary consequence of such artificially stimulated growth, heavily controlled by the state sector and by outside priorities. Those with access to the state sector and who are loyal to its priorities win in this system, but they are few. For instance, 94 percent of staff and workers in the TAR were employed in state-owned units in 2004, and all staff and workers accounted for 11 percent of the provincial workforce and about half of the urban workforce (calculated from *CSY*, 2005: tables 5-4, 5-8, 5-11, 5-20, and 5-21). The losers in this scenario are generally the 85 percent of the population with little or no education and hence little access to state-sector employment. The challenge of subsidies should be to provide opportunities for these disadvantaged citizens, rather than simply enhancing the wealth of a few.

3. WHO CONTROLS AND WHO BENEFITS FROM SUBSIDIES?

All budgetary subsidies are channeled through the government and most investment in the TAR takes place through state-owned units, as discussed previously. Furthermore, the two are interconnected, given that 41 percent of government revenue in the TAR was spent on capital construction in 2003 (i.e., investment), whereas in China as a whole, only 11 percent of government revenue was spent that way. Of the remaining government revenue, the TAR government spent the next largest portion on itself, that is, government administration, at 14 percent of total revenue in 2003 (although higher in other years), compared to 10 percent in China. In contrast, a smaller proportion of total expenditure was spent on education, health, and agricultural production in the TAR than in China (*CSY*, 2005: table 8-22).

In other words, considering the combination of subsidies and investment together, most outside government funding is being spent on the state itself, either directly through government administration or indirectly through state-owned units. Given that growth generated through the expansion of government administration is not self-sustaining and requires further revenues in order to be maintained, the hope that growth might be sustained by current strategies rests on investment, which in the TAR mostly pertains to various construction projects—for example, 87 percent of investment was destined for infrastructure as of 2002.

In these cases, tenders for perhaps all of the large construction projects are contracted to out-of-province companies, as well as many of the small projects. This fact can be clearly observed on the ground, and it is also advertised by the government itself. For instance, the Golmud-Lhasa railway involved a consortium of state-owned construction and engineering companies from around the country, many from the coastal areas. Indeed, it appears that a single construction company from Chengdu constructed almost all of the numerous bridges along the railway (the following qualitative observations are from field visits by the author in 2003 and 2004).

Similarly, the provincial aid projects typically involve construction companies from each of the provinces in question. For instance, the outsized Shandong Hotel in Shigatse was built by a Shandong construction company as part of a Shandong Province aid project. In this very typical case, provincial aid was in effect spent on Shandong itself via one of its companies, which are in most cases state-owned (by Shandong). Aid thereby becomes a form of industrial support for these companies, particularly since the contracts are often very lucrative. This is essentially the same as international tied aid (i.e., aid that requires recipient countries to purchase goods from donor countries, as is the case with much U.S. and EU aid), except that it functions at the national level.

Upon completion of the construction, ownership of the project sometimes remains with the investor (i.e., the Shandong Hotel might still be owned by Shandong) or it might be donated to local governments (as in the case of smaller projects such as schools or clinics). Ownership of the railroad, for instance, will most certainly be retained by the national Ministry of Railways, the main investor. In the case of hydroelectric projects constructed along the Yellow River in the Tibetan areas of Qinghai, ownership is retained by the main investors, who, whether private or public, are mostly non-Tibetans from Xining or elsewhere.

In many cases, even small-scale construction projects, or projects that would be ideally suited for using and improving local Tibetan expertise, are also contracted to out-of-province companies and mostly use Han migrant workers. For instance, as part of village relocations related to poverty alleviation in Nagchu Prefecture in the TAR, houses in the relocated villages were reportedly constructed by teams of Han construction workers from Sichuan. Similarly, the renovation of the façades of new buildings facing the Potala in Lhasa, which was started in 2004 to give these key tourist streets a Tibetan look, and which involves placing Tibetan-style façades on the new buildings (see Question 71), appears to involve only migrant Han workers employed by out-of-province construction companies. Most of the construction work that can be observed in Lhasa, Shigatse, or other centers appears to follow the same pattern. Tibetan participation is usually restricted to the lowest skill levels, such as shoveling in road construction, and is rarely encountered at the level of ownership or management.

In this sense, much of the external funding to the Tibetan areas can be seen as a strategy to nurture and promote regional or national construction companies, subsidizing the development of their expertise and capacity in large, complex engineering projects. The railroad is an excellent example of this, given that it represents a considerable feat of engineering to overcome the challenges of constructing across the high-altitude permafrost. Companies participating in this project acquire a technical and managerial expertise that then prepares them to compete on an international scale. In this sense, the railroad and other large complex projects whose economic rationales remain highly questionable effectively act as lucrative training grounds. This use of public development funds by Beijing or the provinces is comparable to the U.S. strategy of using lucrative defense contracts to subsidize many U.S. businesses, such as in information technology and aeronautics.

While this strategy has been beneficial for building strong, competitive national firms, a large share of western development funding is used for precisely this purpose rather than for local economic needs. The development of locally owned businesses and local expertise tends to be sidelined in the process. Many officials in West China privately admit that in the end, eastern enterprises may benefit more from western development than the western provinces themselves (Goodman 2004: 395). Again, parallels with Western overseas development assistance used to promote Western business interests can be drawn.

On top of the distended administrative apparatus, which is completely out of proportion to the local economy, these institutional characteristics of investment and construction are also key contributors to the high inefficiency of subsidies. To start with, many of the projects are inherently very inefficient and ill conceived for local needs. This is likely due to the status nature of many of the projects, in which the emphasis becomes big and glossy versus functional and appropriate, given that the former promote the fact that aid was given, while the latter do not. For instance, the emphasis in building a clinic might be in the construction of a large, elaborate building, rather than equipping or staffing it sufficiently to realize its purpose. Or, projects in schools might provide satellite TV reception even though the school does not have running water. The houses of the relocated villages in Nagchu, mentioned above, were reportedly constructed in the summer and with little knowledge of the wintertime conditions in these areas. Because they were constructed in eastern Sichuan style, many of them were in a dilapidated state by the end of their first winter. Similarly, many buildings in Lhasa have been poorly constructed, often with corners cut in the quality of materials, with the result that the lifespan of many new buildings is quite short.

These projects often end up being white elephants, draining more from local economies than they contribute once the construction phases have ended. Projects like the Shandong Hotel fall into this category; it apparently had an occupancy rate of only 10 percent on average in 2004 and consumes large amounts of scarce electricity and water. The cities of the TAR are replete with such examples of underutilized or poorly equipped buildings left over from various aid projects. Local governments thereby inherit numerous large, unsustainable buildings that are out of scale with the local capacities, demand, or revenue that would be required to maintain and use the overburdened infrastructure efficiently. In particular, such projects are completely disconnected from local production. They offer little hope that the boom in construction will be self-sustaining. While they do show up as considerable economic activity, this says little about their potential to produce continuing economic activity in the future.

Even aside from the more dramatic cases of wasteful spending, subsidized investment tends to contribute little to the local economy, because out-of-province companies tend to retain and "repatriate" their profits. Companies and their staff and workers usually return home or to other national job sites upon completion of a project, taking acquired skills and earnings with them, rather than investing or spending them locally. The tourism industry functions in a similar manner (see Question 82). In other words, money goes in and out without much turnover to benefit local production or demand.

Corruption further reinforces this process. There is some debate as to whether corruption stunts growth. It appears that corruption can produce either productive results, where it gathers resources in local economies and directs them into productive investment, as in Korea, coastal China, or the United States, or else it can hamper productive outcomes, where corruption diverts resources away from productive uses. Unlike other areas of China, the latter case would apply to the TAR, given that corruption usually diverts project funding outside the TAR. When government departments divert national or foreign aid money into the purchase of land cruisers or condominiums in Chengdu, such funding leaves the region almost before it enters. Its contribution to GDP may simply be an accounting mirage.

In the final analysis, it appears that the government is digging itself deeper and deeper into a form of subsidy dependence. In the absence of significant linkages with local productive sectors, neither government administration nor the construction boom are able autonomously to sustain current economic expansion. Therefore, future growth will depend more or less entirely on increases in government expenditure. In the TAR, this implies quid pro quo increases in subsidies, again because of the limited potential for current activities to produce future revenue. Thus the TAR growth model remains, as it was in the past, effectively dependent on increasing levels of outside funding in order to generate growth.

This places the TAR in a dilemma. The currently high levels of subsidy and investment are in large part determined by the railway and, to a lesser extent, by a handful of supporting projects. Now that the railway has come to fruition, the operation and maintenance expenses will only be a fraction of the current investment demanded by the project. Short of finding some other massive investment project in the region that can be justified to the national leadership, such as the recently discussed Yarlung Tsangpo dam or the planned extension of the railway to Shigatse, it is difficult to see how subsidies could be maintained at their current levels, let alone at increasing levels. Yet if expenditure or investment decrease, the current bubble might burst. Indeed, boom-bust cycles are typical in economies that are dominated by a few large construction projects. Without any serious effort to expand productive linkages within the local economy, particularly in a manner that integrates local (i.e., Tibetan) labor and promotes local (i.e., Tibetan) ownership, the end of subsidy dependence and the polarized growth that it engenders are distant prospects.

Who actually benefits from current strategies is further clarified by the employment dynamics associated with polarized growth. Given the characteristics of growth, related employment gains tend to be disproportionately concentrated in high-wage and high-skill areas. Although low-skill activities have undoubtedly increased with the boom, these have been more limited relative to comparable growth elsewhere in China, and they have been focused in the lower end of construction work or in commercial and service activities, most of which are concentrated in the urban areas. Locally integrated secondary productive activities have been falling as a share of GDP and provide little potential to absorb local low-skilled labor (see also Question 87). In contrast, growth in most other regions in China, including Qinghai, has been rooted in the expansion of secondary productive activities, thereby generating a stronger demand for low-skilled and/or rural migrant labor.

Given that the Tibetan population has by far the lowest level of education in China, there is an important misfit in the TAR between the employment demands of growth and the actual skill levels among local Tibetans. Han migrant workers fill the shortfall in local semi-skilled and skilled labor and even squeeze the low-skill space where Tibetans might be able to integrate into the urban economy. The much higher education levels of migrants in general allow them easily to out-compete local Tibetans in job markets. Several additional factors also give migrants a competitive edge. For instance, low-skilled employment in the areas that are performing well in the TAR—such as in tourism, commerce, or in construction run by out-of-province companies—provides a natural advantage to those who are literate and fluent in Mandarin and who are connected to networks outside the province. Conversely, the sectors of the economy that could provide an advantage for Tibetans or that do not require fluency in Mandarin contribute very little to growth, namely, agriculture or locally integrated secondary activities based on the processing of local inputs for local demand.

Tibetan labor thus confronts a striking disadvantage vis-à-vis net inflows of migrants from other parts of China who come to take advantage of the heavily state-subsidized economic boom. The 85 percent of Tibetans with little or no education are the main cause for concern. These undereducated and lower-skilled Tibetans, in particular, women, are left to compete with out-of-province migrants in the Tibetan urban areas on grossly uneven terms. In the case of the extremely poor education performance among Tibetan women, their restricted options in the urban areas would obviously encourage them to become involved in prostitution, for example. Current education strategies appear ill suited to address this dilemma, given that they largely focus on increasing primary enrollments, which will take at least ten years to have an impact in the labor market, if successful.

The government counters that as the Tibetan workforce becomes more educated or skilled, it will naturally come to fill the roles currently occupied by the migrants. Nonetheless, in light of labor market segmentation and exclusion, this hypothesis cannot simply be taken for granted, particularly in the absence of sufficient secondary, vocational, and adult education, affirmative employment and training policies, or preferential economic strategies. Unless the ethnicity of exclusion is clearly acknowledged and addressed by affirmative and pro-active policies to support Tibetan workers and businesses, less skilled Tibetans may easily lose out in current economic development.

While it might be argued that local workers or businesses are not as efficient or productive as Han workers or businesses, this boils down to an issue of economy-level efficiency versus firm-level efficiency. For instance, locally owned businesses are more likely to invest locally and employ local labor. Therefore, even if they are less efficient than national firms in any given project, funding directed to them will have a much greater chance to circulate within the local economy. This would increase the multiplier effect of subsidies and investment and lessen the dependence on subsidies to sustain growth in the long term.

It is on this basis that many nationalist Tibetans in the Tibetan areas, such as officials and scholars, privately assert that whatever the rest of China pays to the Tibetan areas returns to it. In the final analysis, when all past and present factors are considered, once this boomerang form of funding is deducted from the subsidy equation, the small amount that actually reaches Tibetans, in the form of salaries, poverty assistance, agricultural development, limited health care, education, and so forth, might indeed derive from Tibet. These "Chinese" Tibetan nationalists therefore argue that if the Tibetan areas inside and outside the TAR could be unified under an arrangement of autonomy that allowed them the right to earn royalties on the mineral and oil wealth of the Tsaidam Basin in Qinghai, to give one example, they would be able to generate sufficient revenue to achieve a similar if not more effective form of public intervention in their modern economy than that achieved by the inefficient and self-serving policies of the central government.

Constraints and Favorable Conditions for Development

78
WHAT ADVANTAGES DOES TIBET HAVE FOR ITS ECONOMIC DEVELOPMENT?

Although underdeveloped, Tibet has favorable conditions for economic development: it possesses many natural and mineral resources; its forests can be exploited for the timber industry, and its fauna and medicinal plants are renowned. It is second in China in hydroelectric resources and first in geothermal resources.

Moreover, its splendid landscapes, original folklore, and numerous religious and historical monuments are a very good basis for developing tourism.

Under the Autonomy law and with the central government's authorization, Tibet can take special measures to speed up its economic development. Finally, it benefits from large amounts of aid from the central government and "sister" provinces.

83
WHAT ARE THE MAIN PROBLEMS TIBET FACES
IN DEVELOPING ITS ECONOMY?

The main difficulties Tibet faces at present are "low productivity, difficulties in energy and communications, underdeveloped education, a shortage of trained personnel, poor management of enterprises, low economic efficiency, and poor natural conditions in comparison with other provinces and autonomous regions. Therefore, the per-capita income is fairly low."

[Question 22 in the 2001 version (main factors that restrict economic development in Tibet) is equivalent, and Question 24 (How can Tibet improve its highway transportation?), Question 25 (Why build the railroad?), and Question 26 (modern postal and telecommunications facilities) are also related.]

ANDREW M. FISCHER

In this series of questions, and in particular, in the equivalent question of the 2001 version, the cause of economic backwardness in the TAR is essentially linked to its geographical setting, topographic features, and so forth. However, while many of the points mentioned are in part true, they ignore the impacts of Chinese rule that may have either caused or exacerbated many of the aspects mentioned. For instance, since the 1950s, the military stationed in the TAR has placed enormous pressures on local resources and capacities. To a certain extent many prioritized policies have been aimed at correcting these imbalances. The 2001 version cites a "monopolistic agricultural structure" as an obstacle, probably referring to monopolies of marketing companies in the distribution of agricultural inputs and outputs, which is a legacy of Communist collectivization, not of traditional agricultural production systems.

Finally, there is also a typically China-centric view that identifies the difficulties of integrating the TAR into the national economy as one of the key bottlenecks restricting development. It is true that modern highways and communication systems started with Chinese occupation and that they are still poorly developed relative to the rest of China. However, long-distance networks have been prioritized over local networks such as secondary roads, even though the latter are much more important for stimulating rural economies but continue to be poorly developed in the TAR. The railway is the most extreme (and expensive) expression of this bias to date.

There is an obvious security dimension influencing this bias. Many of the planned infrastructures have dual civilian and military purposes. For instance, priority has been given to the transportation and communications networks that connect Lhasa with Ngari in the west, near one disputed territory with India, or with Nyingtri in the southeast, which is near the other disputed territory with India. It is likely that much of the motivation behind the railroad is similarly based on security concerns, as discussed previously.

The bias nonetheless results in a lopsided developmental dynamic whereby outside integration precedes and in some ways preempts local integration. In the rest of China, the opposite sequencing has usually taken place; local integration within regions has normally been protected and nurtured before opening to outside involvement and competition. The inverse sequencing in the TAR ultimately exacerbates the exclusionary dynamics within growth, given that it becomes easier to establish linkages with the rest of China than with any other Tibetan area.

Ultimately, infrastructural improvements will not, in and of themselves, produce inclusive developmental results. Even if nomads from the Changtang will be able to travel more comfortably to Lhasa, the main factor influencing their employment in Lhasa is education, not the ease of transport. Therefore, education and other social services should be receiving as much if not more priority than physical infrastructure in the sequencing of development policy, although they are not.

In this perspective, by far the greatest bottleneck facing Tibetans is the severe lag in education with every other province of China. Yet this particular bottleneck does not receive any special mention in these questions and answers, besides brief token acknowledgements. While improvements in education have been taking place, it will still take years if not decades to close the gap with the rest of China at current rates, particularly in secondary education.

Also, the current focus on improving education in the TAR is through increasing primary enrollments, thereby lowering illiteracy rates among the young. While this should obviously continue, the problem remains that exclusion in labor markets occurs now, among the adult working-age population, whereas current improvements in primary education will only affect the labor market in about ten years time at best. Education should therefore be brought to the top of the development agenda for the TAR by instituting a massive expansion at all levels of education, in particular adult and vocational education. Otherwise, labor market segmentation will already be heavily entrenched by the time current primary education improvements reach the labor market.

The following are some further comments on two issues related to agriculture.

1. THE 2001 VERSION OF 100 *QUESTIONS* STRESSES THAT VERY LITTLE OF THE TAR IS ARABLE AND THAT EVEN THERE THE ALTITUDE AND CLIMATE LIMIT FARMING

This is true, and it is precisely why pastoralism, whether pure or mixed with farming, has developed as one of the main economic activities over most of the plateau. Thus, while only 0.28 percent of the TAR's land area is arable, more than 40 percent is used as pasture. In fact, almost all of the topography of the Tibetan areas that is suitable for herding has been used intensively for centuries through forms of nomadic or semi-nomadic rangeland use, which can be seen as very efficient adaptations to the ecological conditions of the plateau.

The focus on arable land is therefore misleading and hints at the bias in government policy against pastoralism. This bias underlies policies of settling nomads, fencing rangelands, and attempting to introduce commercial ranching, despite the questionable ecological or economic rationale of such policies. For instance, many scholars specializing on pastoral land use in the Tibetan areas emphasize that policies of settlement or fencing have in many cases accelerated land degradation beyond the primary cause of population growth, principally by increasing the intensity of rangeland use on fixed plots rather than allowing for regular rotation. The economic benefit of such policies is similarly ambiguous. Kenneth Bauer (2006) argues that settlement policies are mostly motivated by state mistrust of mobile peoples and the desire to control such populations.

The pendulum swung further in 1998 when major flooding in central China led to the belief that land degradation on the Tibetan plateau was one of the principal causes of this disaster. The government has since been trying to reduce rangeland use to a minimum, particularly outside the TAR, such as in the "Three Rivers Source Area" in Yushu and Golok in Qinghai. Nomads again bear the brunt of this policy shift, given that the imposed restrictions on rangeland use make it more difficult to sustain the herd sizes necessary for subsistence. Given that most nomadic areas are remote, alternative forms of livelihood are few and far between for them. The government has responded to this dilemma mainly by encouraging or forcing resettlement in urban areas.

Again, the policies appear to be misconceived on two levels. First, several scientific studies have pointed out that medium intensity of pasture use, rather than low- or high-intensity use, may indeed be the best for plant species diversity and density. Nomadic land use systems result precisely in such medium intensity use (Bauer 2006). The second misconception is the failure to recognize that urban growth itself may be a dominant factor causing flooding. Particularly in the more populated areas of central China, urban density reduces the absorption of rainfall, while poorly planned sluice canals passing through successive towns and cities accelerate the passage of water, resulting in often explosive downstream erosion. It is quite possible that much of the flooding in central China has been caused by conditions in central China itself.

A related concern refers to current policies of urban resettlement, which derive from the synthesis of environmental protection and poverty alleviation policies. In some extreme cases of counties outside the TAR, local governments are proposing to move all nomads off the land and into county towns for a period of five years in order to allow for grassland regeneration. Such urbanization is also seen as a solution to rural poverty.

There are two problems with these strategies. First, even though rural Tibetans are poor (in terms of income) and vulnerable, they are also quite effective at providing for themselves. Compared to the rest of rural China, Tibetan areas are relatively rich in terms of subsistence wealth, which allows rural Tibetan households to smooth consumption over time and generally to look after themselves quite independently of the state. If this link to land- and asset-based subsistence is cut, Tibetan rural households might well find themselves worse off, even if their cash incomes rise due to a deepened integration into a market-based economy.

Moreover, the assumption that the incomes of rural people will increase if they move to a town or city is based on the condition that, upon moving, they find employment. However, the strategies for urbanization appear to sideline this employment corollary and instead focus on the supply of physical infrastructure, such as houses, roads, and so forth. In addition, as mentioned previously, infrastructure construction is largely contracted to outside companies, leaving little opportunity for urban growth to catalyze the creation of local employment or local businesses. Instead, there seems to be a sort of mystical belief that urbanization will somehow self-generate jobs or incomes as people become more integrated into the "market" or "commodity" economy. There is a great risk that local governments are simply in the process of creating small town ghettoes, similar to aboriginal reserves in North America, with high unemployment, social breakdown, and welfare dependence.

In any case, rural Tibetans are increasingly moving to towns and cities on their own accord and by their own means as part of calculated household livelihood strategies. These strategies use the subsistence base as a security net and then send one or several family members to the urban areas, either for employment or for education. The main constraints limiting this process are the supply of employment and the supply of affordable and accessible education. In other words, if local governments can solve these two constraints, they will accelerate urbanization and reduce rangeland use in a natural way, following the initiatives of Tibetan households to take care of themselves. Conversely, if governments break the subsistence link, they will make it much more difficult for households to follow such strategies in a sustainable manner. All things considered, current strategies might simply exacerbate poverty by liquidating subsistence wealth and transforming a poor but productive and self-sustaining rural population into a poor but unproductive and welfare-dependent urban population.

2. QUESTION 22, 2001, STIPULATES THAT ONE OF THE MAIN RESTRICTIONS TO ECONOMIC DEVELOPMENT IN TIBET IS A LOW-PRODUCTIVITY AGRICULTURAL SYSTEM CHARACTERIZED BY A SLOW CYCLE OF "LOW OUTPUT–LOW INVESTMENT, LOW ACCUMULATION–LOW OUTPUT"

This assertion is contradicted by official data on agricultural production and rural capital accumulation in the TAR. The theory underlying this answer appears to have been picked from a textbook with little relation to Tibet.

In fact, productivity per hectare in the TAR has consistently been among the highest in western China. By 2004, cereal yields in the TAR were higher than the national average, at 5,300 kg per hectare, versus 5,187 kg per hectare for the PRC as a whole. The only western provinces to surpass the TAR cereal yields were Xinjiang (5,863 kg), and Sichuan (5,420 kg). Per hectare yields were 3,559 kg in Qinghai, 3,409 kg in Gansu, 4,133 kg in Yunnan, and 4,673 kg in Guizhou, the poorest province in China. The TAR yield of rapeseed has also been consistently higher than the national average and the highest of the western region (*CSY*, 2005: table 13-18). The data on output per capita or per agricultural worker show similar patterns with respect to other western provinces (*CSY*, 2005: tables 13-24 and 13-25).

Even greater disparities can be observed in typical livestock output. For instance, the TAR output of milk per agricultural laborer was 239 kg in 2004, versus 73 kg for China overall, although per household sales of milk in the TAR were a small fraction of those in China, reflecting the subsistence or bartered use of such output (*CSY*, 2005: tables 13-25 and 13-26). Output per rural household in the TAR of sheep's wool was 115 kg in 1998, versus 1.2 kg nationally (*CSY*, 1999: 405). Per capita or per laborer productivity data were not available for these livestock outputs.

These provincial differentials in both farming and herding productivity have been more or less consistent over time, increasing in tandem with national productivity increases. In other words, farmers and nomads in the TAR have been at least as successful as the other, predominantly Han Chinese provinces in bringing about increases in agricultural productivity.

Considering that these yields are achieved within a short, harsh growing season (relevant for both farming and herding), they represent impressive productivities, which are supported by field observations. Several agronomists working in the TAR and interviewed by the author in 2004 noted that farmland in the TAR is very productive if irrigated. Given that farmland tends to be concentrated in river valleys, this potential can be realized much more easily than farming in the semi-arid conditions of the loess plateau that covers large parts of northern China, where water is very scarce.

Furthermore, the production systems in the TAR (mostly pastoralism or mixed farming and pastoralism) are in fact characterized by high rather than low savings and investment, reflecting the fact that livestock-intensive economies are very capital-intensive and that pastoralists tend to be quite thrifty (i.e., an increasing herd size is a form of savings). For instance, the original value of productive fixed assets per rural household in the TAR by the end of 2004 was 20,061 yuan, over three times the value of the average Chinese rural household, which was only 5,956 yuan. After the TAR, the next highest value was found in Inner Mongolia at 12,910 yuan per household (*CSY*, 2005: table 13-12).

Predictably, about half of these productive fixed assets were in draft and commodity animals. However, the other half were in the form of non-livestock productive fixed assets such as industrial machinery, transport machinery, buildings for productive purposes, and machinery for farming and animal husbandry, and the values of all of these categories were significantly higher than in the average Chinese rural household. There were 3.8 times the number of motorized vehicles per 100 households in the TAR than on average in China in 2004, 1.6 times the number of large and medium tractors, and twice the number of mini or walking tractors. In other words, the average Tibetan rural household in 2004 was far more capital-intensive than the average Chinese rural household. Therefore, the low incomes of Tibetan rural households are also not related to their relative levels of capitalization or investment.

In contrast to the interpretation of *100 Questions,* rural Tibetans are quite skilled and productive in what they have always done best—farming and herding—even if these traditional activities remain largely subsistence-based and conducted with minimal assistance from the state. It should of course be noted that certain government agencies, such as the Tibetan Academy of Agriculture and Animal Husbandry Sciences in Lhasa, have recently increased assistance to farmers and nomads through a variety of agricultural extension programs. Infrastructure improvements (such as secondary roads) would have also supported productivity increases in the late 1990s and early 2000s. However, these statistics reveal that a fair amount of wealth and accumulation has been consistently generated in these subsistence economies.

The stagnation of rural incomes in the TAR up to the early 2000s, and the continuing stagnation of incomes derived from household agricultural production, has not necessarily been related to deficiencies in productivity or accumulation. Rather, stagnation has been more likely related to the collapse in the prices of the main commodities produced by Tibetans (wool and grains) throughout the 1990s, alongside a shortage of employment opportunities outside farming and herding. Faster rates of population increase among rural Tibetans, as discussed in Part IV above, also add a downward pressure on per capita income measures relative to other Chinese provinces. Collapsing prices of agricultural staples have been compensated for in most other regions of China by rising off-farm rural employment, which has been one of the strongest factors driving growth (and inequality) in rural incomes despite agricultural stagnation. In the TAR, relative to the rest of China, the fate of rural dwellers has been disproportionately determined by the fate of farming and herding. Therefore, although they may be relatively productive and wealthy in subsistence terms (i.e., having more output and animals than the average Chinese farmer), this relative subsistence wealth converts poorly into cash income.

These processes also explain why the preferential (and productive) integration of rural Tibetans into the urban economy is so important and should be prioritized by the government. Cash incomes, as opposed to subsistence wealth, are important for a variety of reasons, particularly with respect to paying tuition and related costs for education, or health costs in the event of illness, both of which are considerable for an average rural Tibetan household. The marginalization of rural Tibetans in urban labor markets also has an important feedback effect on their ability to diversify incomes. In turn, this also has an impact on their capacity to pay for post-primary education or health costs, which reinforces their downward spiral of exclusion.

Foreign Investment and Trade

79
ARE THERE ANY SINO-FOREIGN JOINT VENTURES OR SOLELY FOREIGN-FUNDED PROJECTS IN TIBET?

Since the implementation of the policies of reform and opening, Tibetan investors living abroad, citizens from Hong Kong and Macao, and foreigners have shown interest in investing in Tibet. By the end of 1987, fifteen letters of intent had been signed "with territorial countries and units" [i.e., in China], and three international projects have officially been decided. Tax cuts or exemptions are offered to investors; still, among them, Tibetans living abroad will be favored.

80
HOW DOES TIBET ATTEMPT TO COOPERATE WITH FOREIGN FACTORIES?

More than twenty sectors are waiting for foreign investors, such as energy, communications, building, light industry, textiles, and food processing. Business visits are welcome in Tibet. Agreements could include enterprises with mixed capital or with foreign capital, with joint management or compensatory trade. Agreements will benefit both Tibet and the foreign investors.

81
How do foreign people invest in Tibet?

In 1986, a "Tibetan economic investigation group" went to Hong Kong and signed some letters of intent for cooperation on a number of projects. "The general principles are: expanding possibilities for investment, giving favorable treatment to foreign investors, and welcoming the establishment of working agencies. Any foreign company wishing to invest in Tibet should contact the government of the TAR through Chinese organs residing in foreign countries or by any other way possible."

[The equivalent questions in the 2001 version are: Question 45 (sectors of foreign investment); Question 46 (the workings of investment invitation); Question 47 (international aid projects); Question 48 (preferential policies for foreign investment); Question 49 (services for foreigners from the local government); Question 50 (where to consult); Question 51 (how to apply); and Questions 52 and 53 (both about documentation required). The 2001 version also has a series of questions on foreign trade: Question 42 (changes to policies of opening); Question 43 (exports and imports); and Question 44 (trade system and international norms).]

Andrew M. Fischer

These questions and answers, particularly those of the 2001 version, read as a promotional brochure. They must be understood in the context of the mania for foreign investment and special economic zones that has swept China since the 1990s. Following Deng Xiaoping's "Spring Tour" in June 1992, after which special economic zones were allowed to proliferate across the country in a variety of shapes and forms, there was intense competition among the provinces to attract foreign investment. It was hoped that this would be a way to access the pie of the coastal areas. Even the government of the TAR jumped in, proposing to offer low taxes and tax exemptions wherever it could (Yang 1997: 56).

In the end, regional shares of foreign investment underwent little change as a result of the liberalization of special economic zones. Most foreign investment continued to concentrate in the coastal areas, dispersing along the coast rather than heading into the interior. With the exception of a few western industrial centers, such as Chongqing, Chengdu, Xi'an, and Lanzhou, the west in general still only manages to capture a minute proportion of foreign investment.

The share of the TAR is almost imperceptible at the national level, although some foreign involvement has been recently forthcoming. Much of it has been in the form of bilateral aid projects with foreign countries such as Canada, Australia, the EU, and Japan. Multilateral aid projects have involved UNICEF, the UNDP, and UNESCO, and a handful of NGOs have also made their way in, such as Save the Children (U.K.), Médecins sans frontières/Doctors Without Borders, the Swiss Red Cross, and several smaller Tibet-specific NGOs. A few private sector investments have been notable, such as the purchase of half of the Lhasa Beer Factory by Carlsberg of Denmark in 2003, although in this case the investment represents a transfer of ownership, with a promise to improve facilities, rather than investment in new productive capacity. In many of these cases, involvement in the TAR appears to function as a flagship project, negotiated with the government as a condition for greater and more profitable access to other regions of China. Recent developments with regard to gold or copper mining in the TAR represent the first moves away from this general trend.

However, almost all investment in the TAR is by the state, as analyzed previously. For instance, the combination of foreign-funded economic units and economic units with funds from Hong Kong, Taiwan, or Macao accounted for less than 0.1 percent of total investment in 2004. In other words, even if some headway is made in these shares of foreign involvement, state-owned sources of investment will continue to be the overwhelming determinant of economic activity in the TAR for the foreseeable future. For better or for worse, the fate of the TAR's economy is completely in the hands of Beijing.

82

HOW ABOUT TIBET'S TOURIST RESOURCES? HOW DO FOREIGN PEOPLE TRAVEL IN TIBET? [QUESTIONS 78–82, 2001]

Tibet, the "roof of the world" has abundant tourist resources, in spite of harsh natural conditions. Its natural scenery is colorful, with snow-capped mountains, lakes, forests, and hundreds of geysers and hot springs. It has the world's highest peak, Mount Qomolangma [Everest], and many wild animal species live there.

There are also many historical sites: temples and monasteries, ancient buildings, magnificent palaces and royal tombs. "The region's rich cultural history is reflected in its murals, sculptures, operas, dances, music, poetry and prose, folk tales, and the splendid traditional culture of its people. Tibetans are fond of singing and dancing. Hospitable and warm, they gladly welcome tourists."

The TAR has established several travel organizations, such as the Tibet Branch of the China Travel Service, and so on. There are hotels and restaurants for foreign tourists, whose "quality of service has shown great improvement in recent years."

"People who plan to travel in Tibet should contact the China Travel Service or any of the organizations mentioned."

KATIA BUFFETRILLE

We shall not speak at length about the potential of Tibet for tourism; it has already been mentioned in several questions and has often been discussed in the media. It is more interesting to shed some light on the evolution of tourism in the Land of Snows.

Tourism in China only began in 1978, and the TAR was opened for tourism at the beginning of the 1980s in order to improve its economy. From 1985 on, foreign tourism developed in two different directions: one, favored by the authorities, is group tourism. This involves official guides working for accredited agencies and not only brings financial benefit to the country but also represents little or no political danger. The second type of tourism, that of individual or independent travelers, is also a source of income, but the authorities regard it as potentially risky, in the sense that it cannot easily be controlled. Individual tourists can establish direct contact with Tibetans and often enter areas where the authorities do not wish them to go. In the 1980s and the early 1990s, backpackers commonly wormed their way in almost everywhere.

For several years, the number of foreign tourists was not very high, because of the high cost of traveling to Tibet, the need for special permits, the bureaucratic hurdles placed on getting them (they have to be applied for through official travel agencies), the lack of transport and the bad state of roads, and the rustic style of available accommodation. From the early 1980s through 1991, 17,000 overseas tourists came to the TAR; in 1992, 20,000 tourists were expected.[1] In the same year, the propaganda review *China's Tibet* began to feature a column on tourism.

---

1. *China's Tibet* 1994, no. 1: 6; *China's Tibet* 1993, no. 1: 36.

The emergence of a new, urban middle-class in China and its growing interest in travel led to a boom in domestic tourism. With its rapid expansion, this has become more important than foreign tourism today. For many years, the Chinese saw Tibet as a cold, inhospitable, frightening country inhabited by uneducated people, where even breathing is difficult because of the altitude. In the mid 1990s, however, a more romantic view appeared and "ethnic Tibet" (including the previous Kham and Amdo) began to be an exotic holiday destination for many Chinese. As a result, the TAR hosted over 720,000 visitors from China proper in 2002. During the week-long break of May 2007 alone, 340,000 tourists visited the region, up 31 percent from 2006 (WTN, May 9, 2007).

By the end of October 2000, the TAR had been visited by over 500,000 tourists (domestic and foreign) that year—a 41 percent increase over the same period in 1999. The year 2003 saw 930,000 tourists, among whom only 110,000 were foreigners. At that time, the authorities hoped for 3 million tourists in the following five years, but in 2004, 1.8 million tourists visited the TAR (far exceeding the targets set in 2000), and the Chinese authorities have recently announced that they want to attract more than 5 million visitors a year by the end of the decade, which seems a "reasonable" expectation based on the number given for 2007.[2]

The first consequence of this increase in tourism was the creation and rapid expansion of private travel agencies; 1,400 were listed in 1992, an increase of 80 percent compared to 1991. By the end of 1994, the turnover within this sector was 180 million yuan and the income in foreign currency was U.S.$10 million. These figures rose to 1.87 billion yuan (U.S.$230m) in tourist revenue in the TAR from January to October 2005 according to the regional bureau of tourism in Lhasa (China Tibet Information Center 2005). This sum is now far higher, since the statistics for Tibet's development and reform commission indicate that Tibet is expected to receive 3 million tourists in 2007, for a tourism revenue of 3.4 billion yuan (or U.S.$445 million).

This expectation is in accordance with the middle-term policy that has declared tourism to be one of the three pillars of the economic development of the TAR (the two others being mining and traditional medicine), which was reiterated at the fourth Tibet Work Forum held in Beijing in June 2001. But despite all of the talk of tourism as a new pillar of the economy, it is still small compared to the traditional sources of the state-propelled economy as discussed in Part VIII.

---

2. WTN, July 12, 2006.

The opening of the Qinghai-Tibet Railway (which occurred under very strict security) will help the authorities to reach their goal. Prices are quite attractive—in mid 2006, a hard-seat ticket from Beijing to Lhasa cost 389 yuan (U.S.$48), while a hard sleeper cost 813 yuan (U.S.$101.60), and a soft sleeper cost 1,262 yuan (U.S.$158)—and 2,569 passengers entered the TAR during the first three days of the railroad's operation (www.china broadcast.cn, July 1 and 4, 2006). In July 2006, 391,000 visitors arrived in Tibet, of whom 57 percent flew in (despite the air ticket price of 2,430 yuan, or U.S.$304, one way from Beijing), 29 percent came by rail, and the re-mainder came by road (www.chinabroadcast.cn, July 31, 2006). This "tourist invasion" will perhaps diminish as a result of the "instability of the rail-way line in places where the foundations are sinking into the softening per-mafrost soil," according to a Chinese Railway Ministry spokesman (*Bei jing News*, July 29, 2006).

The number of tourists (mainly Chinese) is already so high that the num-ber of visitors to the Potala Palace has had to be limited. Until 2003, 1,600 visitors a day were allowed. Then the limit was raised to 1,800. On 1st July 2006, when the new railway opened, the daily limit was raised again to 2,300—an almost 50 percent increase since 2003 (WTN, July 12, 2006). In the hope of attracting more Taiwanese and foreigners to the TAR, the Chi-nese authorities proclaimed the lifting of the restrictions on travel to Tibet. This was announced by Wu Jilie, vice-chairman of the TAR government (WTN, September 9, 2006). In spite of this announcement made at local level, nothing concrete happened during the following year. On the contrary, the Chinese authorities, this time at national level, decided to tighten re-strictions on travel by foreigners in Tibet. This followed the unfurling of a banner on which was written in Tibetan and Chinese "One World, One Dream, Free Tibet 2008" by five American activists (among them a young Tibetan born in exile) at the foot of Mount Everest to protest against the occupation of Tibet and the staging of the 2008 Olympics in Beijing (WTN, May 15, 2007). The tightened restrictions seem to concern only the back-packers, however, since the China International Travel Service (CITS, the official travel agency) in Chengdu did not know about these regulations on May 23, 2007.

Such a sudden influx of tourists is likely to accelerate the process, already observed throughout "ethnic Tibet" for more than a decade, whereby local traditions are reduced to a kitsch facsimile of what they once were and is a real threat to Tibetan culture and religion (see Question 68).

One may think that this explosion of tourism benefits Tibetans since, given that most tourists travel in groups, local tour guides are a key element. For many years, there may have been some truth in this, because many of these guides were Tibetans who had been in India and were more or less fluent in English. Now, however, there is a determination to replace these Tibetan tour guides. On April 15, 2003, a group of 100 Chinese tour guides were sent to Tibet not only to "publicize the beautiful mountains and rivers of the Motherland" but also to "enable domestic and foreign tourists to gain a more comprehensive and objective understanding of Tibet's yesterday, today and tomorrow, and resolutely struggle against all words and deeds that distort facts with an attempt to split the Motherland" (Xinhua, April 8, 2003). Moreover, the majority of travel agencies, hotels, and shops belong to Chinese, thus denying the Tibetans much of the benefit brought by tourism.

Huang Fukai, a member of the Chinese Association for the Protection and Development of Tibetan Culture sees the railway as bringing a lot of changes to the Tibetans, among others "they may have coffee and bread in addition to the traditional buttered tea and zanba [tsampa]," not to mention that "jeans and suits might also be welcomed by Tibetans" (items already found in markets in the TAR for some time). He is supported in his defense of the train by An Caidan, a research fellow at the China Tibetology Research Center, for whom "the influx of tourists will not only bring revenue into the region but will also lead to more cultural exchanges between Tibet and other parts of China." And he adds: "Some people may criticize that Tibetan culture will be killed, but this is rather biased, as Tibetan people have the right to share modern civilization" (Xinhua, July 2, 2006).

With such claims coming even from the authorities, one can understand "the doubt and the hostility towards China" expressed in coverage of the railway's opening by foreign journalists, who have asserted "that the railway would threaten the survival of Tibet's culture, and benefit Chinese rather than Tibetans" (*People's Daily*, July 12, 2006), a view strongly criticized by the official Chinese media.

84

It is reported that China has deployed nuclear weapons and dumped nuclear waste in Tibet, damaging the environment there. Is that true?

No. "On the contrary, in comparison with other areas of China, pollution from industrial production and other sources is the slightest."

Thierry Dodin

Playing on words in usual manner, the authors deny that there have ever been nuclear weapons or disposal of nuclear wastes "in the TAR" (Question 32, 2001). However, whereas there are indeed no such reports in the case of the TAR, a quarter of Dashi (Chin. Haiyan) County in Qinghai next to Koko Nor, hence the region traditionally known to Tibetans as Amdo and where Tibetan nomads live in particular, was appropriated, depopulated, and turned into the "221 Bomb Factory," China's nuclear weapons research and development site from 1958 to 1987. There are also serious indications that nuclear wastes have been disposed of in Qinghai. It is just that this region is not recognized as "Tibet" by the Chinese authorities. It is true that no nuclear tests seem to have ever been carried out in any Tibetan region. Tests are well known to have happened at Lop Nor in Xinjiang, however, which is very close to the Qinghai border, raising the question of possible fallout in Tibetan regions. However, for obvious reasons, no independent investigation could ever be conducted to confirm or refute this.

In contrast to the first edition, the 2001 version of *100 Questions* contains several questions (21, 28–30, 32–38) relating to environmental issues in Tibet. Although these offer an abundance of figures and declarations of intention, they do not seem adequate to allay the concerns of environmental experts about the future of Tibet's fragile ecosystem.

The basic problem with the PRC's environmental policy in Tibet (as well as elsewhere in China) is that the understanding of environment implicit in its formulation tends to be functionalistic, and thus often does not match internationally accepted notions. Nature is rarely considered as having any intrinsic value; rather, it is primarily regarded either as a resource or, where it appears uncontrollable, as a threat. When it comes to Tibet, the "wild territory" par excellence in Chinese imagination, Chinese perceptions are generally based on two particular elements: its rich potential in terms of natural resources, and the adversity of its harsh environment. Rivers are valued for their hydroelectric potential, but also feared for their destructive force when in flood. The logic inherent in these perceptions is that the wilderness must be tamed; resources must be tapped, while imminent dangers must be held at bay. From this perspective, nature is ideally a well-ordered park for the enjoyment of man, not a freely growing jungle.

This is not to say that the international debate about ecology has left no trace in contemporary China. In fact, recent years have seen a progressive realization of the link between the thoughtless exploitation of nature and natural catastrophes, a view that has spread rapidly, particularly following the devastating Yangtse floods in the 1990s. But whereas in lowland China this has facilitated the spread of a more modern understanding of ecology, as well as the emergence of NGOs dedicated to the protection of nature, in Tibet, where conservative governance still prevails, environmental policies persist with the paradigm of the old dichotomy of exploitation versus protection. The Chinese authors of *100 Questions* obviously allude to this outdated understanding of nature and environmental protection with their frequent mention of the need "to construct an ecological environment" (e.g., Questions 35–37, 2001), a revealing oxymoron typical of Chinese technocratic jargon. Nevertheless, *100 Questions* does reflect the progress made by China between the first edition in 1989 and the second in 2001, in that the latter dedicates almost a dozen questions directly or indirectly to environmental issues, whereas the original edition effectively ignored the subject altogether, except for this Question 84 dealing with nuclear waste.

This often translates into an almost obsessive use of the buzzword "sustainability," although generally the meaning of the word is distorted, and it tends to amount to a compromise between predatory exploitation and damage limitation, rather than a genuine search for a skillful and meaningful integration of human activity into the processes of nature. "Sustainability" has, as its close relative, the concept of "rational exploitation," which is in no way any less fuzzy. Effectively, development models deployed in Tibet that are labeled "sustainable" tend to impose PRC models while attempting to limit their immediately visible negative impacts. These strategies are pursued instead of offering income opportunities from natural resources, including herding and farming. A sound and truly sustainable environmental policy for Tibet has yet to be formulated.

The assertion made in Question 29, 2001, that the TAR administration has always paid attention to the protection of nature is sheer absurdity. All independent specialists (and, in fact, a number of their Chinese colleagues) agree that wildlife has been seriously diminished since the Chinese takeover in the early 1950s. From the 1960s and 1970s, in particular, contemporary witnesses, supported by ample photographic evidence, give accounts of the mass killings, using machine guns, of complete herds of Tibetan antelopes and *kyang* (wild asses), mostly by or with the support of PLA troops, for the simple "pleasure of hunting." Although the heyday of such destruction is over, and despite official prohibition under Chinese law, PLA detachments still occasionally hunt *kyang* in the border regions of western Tibet, pushing the herds across the border into India. Moreover, until the late 1980s, in eastern Tibet (most of which is today part of the Sichuan province), entire mountain slopes of forest were clear cut, and the timber floated and trucked to lowland China. Small-scale mining, in particular, alluvial gold mining by wildcat prospectors, has left Tibet's grasslands and riverbanks ir-reversibly polluted by harmful chemicals in many areas. Mismanagement and the disruption of traditional economic activities threaten the ecological balance of the Tibetan grasslands and, in parts, have led to desertification. Although industrial developments have yet to be established in many parts of Tibet, until very recently, existing installations have operated without any respect for nature and waste products have simply been dumped in the en-vironment. Gradual urbanization has also created waste disposal problems and water pollution, which is apparent to any visitor. Many county towns still just dump their garbage in the rivers. Traditional Tibetan land man-agement strategies have undoubtedly also left their mark on the landscape. Nevertheless, although the vastness of the land, its sparse population, and its slow economic development render environmental destruction less ob-vious in Tibet than, for example, in the overpopulated and industrialized Chinese lowlands, the second half of the twentieth century nonetheless saw a rapid and unprecedented assault on Tibet's environment.

More recently, however, the first serious and generally laudable mea-sures have been under way to stop environmental degradation. Strict anti-poaching regulations are in place that will, according to some specialists, lead to a regeneration of the Tibetan antelope. Wildcat mining has been widely outlawed (and is currently being replaced by industrial mining, offering greater profits for the state, but with an as yet unknown ecological impact). Extremely polluting plants, like the notorious cement factory in Lhasa, have been closed down or converted to cleaner production processes. Many un-solved environmental problems remain to be addressed though, and, more important, while the new regulations for environmental protection in the TAR and other Tibetan regions appear positive and constructive on paper, the reality on the ground does not always reflect implementation of these rules.

Like PRC propaganda in general, *100 Questions* (e.g., Questions 30 and 34, 2001) vaunts the establishment of natural reserves and protected areas, and produces awesome figures about their size and the level of funding al-legedly invested in them. While there are indeed serious efforts under way, the reality is that many of these reserves only exist on paper. Often there is a marker where a main road enters such an area, but there are rarely sufficiently trained and/or equipped guards, and these are normally a few locals, who have rarely benefited from any appropriate training and are paid 100–300 yuan (U.S.$12.00–37.00) a month. In addition, very little effort is made to involve the locals in these conservation efforts beyond rounding them up for village meetings and describing the harsh penalties for poaching. Local people are mainly engaged in sustainable development in protected areas where foreign organizations are also active, like in the Chomolungma National Park or in the Changtang.

100 Questions (Question 32, 2001) claims that between the 1960s and the end of the century, 70 million trees were planted in the TAR. Experts, however, counter that barely 10 million of these will ever reach maturity. It is common practice in Tibet to count seedlings when planting, but there are no controls or monitoring in later years to see how successful this has been. Apart from that, the arithmetic used by the Chinese authors appears questionable. Calculations based on similar projects in eastern Tibet (Sichuan) suggest that 70 million conifer seedlings (at 250 per mu = 3,000 seedlings per ha) would cover an area of 18,662 ha, which equals 0.25 percent of the land classified as forest area in the TAR, and a total of 2,687 ha is said to have been reforested so far (Chu and Liu 1992). The claim in *100 Questions* that 140,000 hectares are naturally reforested each year therefore seems highly implausible. Perhaps the authors have confused 140,000 ha with 140,000 mu (15 mu = 1 ha), which would appear more realistic. In any case, annual reforestation of 140,000 ha, equaling 1.9 percent of the overall forest area, or 3.5 percent of the actual forests in the TAR, is hard to credit. This seems to be just another example of PRC propagandists using figures whose meaning they don't fully grasp to enliven handouts like *100 Questions*. Apart from suggesting an embarrassing level of incompetence, this points to the fact that official literature like this is produced primarily for its presumed public relation effect, rather than being based on any of the kind of accuracy in reporting, which, political motivations aside, might be expected from a modern state apparatus.

The Chinese authors also remain silent on the fact that reforestation is necessary primarily because the first forty years of Chinese presence in Tibet saw reckless exploitation of forest resources without any compensatory replanting. It was common practice to leave clear-cut areas on slopes unplanted and to allow livestock to enjoy new grazing grounds, thus preventing natural forest regeneration. Only in recent years has reforestation been carried out systematically, but often without any real local involvement. Local Tibetans might be hired for planting in remote areas where there are no Chinese logging units, but they reap no economic benefits aside from the wages of poorly paid manual labor. All the logging proceeds go to county administrations, leaving no incentive to protect forests, since their value is not accessible to local people. Only the collection of mushrooms and medicinal plants generates any local income from forest resources. As a result, many locals regard turning forest areas into grazing as a positive development and consequently grazing takes place even after reforestation. And while forestry bureaus may claim to plant an area with a required amount of seedlings, they fail to work out an arrangement with the local Tibetans that would allow forests to grow by reducing or preventing grazing pressure.

Degraded and completely deforested slopes are common in Tibet, but these are not always the focus of reforestation campaigns. Instead, cadres often plant willows and poplars along rivers and around villages in line with the "Four Arounds/Alongs" (around fields and farms, along roads, rivers, and canals) imported from the lowlands of China. While this is no doubt laudable, it is a disproportionate response to the widespread logging of old growth conifers in Tibet's forest regions that occurred until recently. Also, planting of poplars and willows in river valleys has focused on areas around Chinese settlements or newly built infrastructure projects like Gongkar Airport (serving Lhasa and central Tibet). Winter sandstorms often force flight cancellations, making tree planting in the Tsangpo valley of great interest to cadres who depend on the airport to reach their winter quarters in Chengdu.

A much-publicized environmental measure has been the 1998 logging ban in the upper Yangtse and Yellow River region. However, the nature of the ban might be better understood when it is noted that it only applies in the three counties in the TAR (Gonjo, Jomda, and Markham; Chin. Gonjue, Jiangda, Mangkang) that are adjacent to these two major rivers. In the vicinity of the other major TAR rivers (the Tsangpo/Brahmaputra, Mekong, and Salween), none of which run through traditionally Chinese territory, and all of which exit China soon after leaving the highlands, logging was not actually halted, although it may have slowed down. Significantly, the TAR Forest Bureau was invited to join the logging ban and apply for central government funding but failed for years to apply for grants, leading to the suspicion that revenue generated through logging was more attractive.

A further problem linked to the draconian measures to protect the upper reaches of the great Chinese rivers is that local Tibetans are being forcibly evicted from their traditional homes and relocated in towns, thus implementing the regime's favorite strategy of urbanization of the rural population (see Questions 78 and 83).

A similar problem arises from the Chinese disdain for traditional pastoralism—one of the backbones of the Tibetan economy—which is perceived as "backward." The Chinese authorities acknowledge only two categories, "backward" and "progressive" (often used as a synonym of "scientific"). Most things Tibetan are categorized as "backward" from the outset. This renders a great disservice to the environment and sustainable development, since many of the practices used for centuries, if not millennia, have actually been proven to be sustainable, something that cannot be claimed for most "progressive" technologies recently introduced. Too often, the absorption of traditional techniques into new scientific understanding is not taking place, although even Chinese experts have recommended it. Instead, "scientific development" is used as an argument for implementing policies that terminate well-adapted traditional land use techniques because of old prejudices against mobile livestock rearing and community-managed grazing grounds in favor of sedentary living. The settling of nomadic households—nomadic people were historically perceived as the greatest threat to China—is of such importance to the authorities that these policies are implemented at a high cost not only in financial but in social and ecological terms, with very little to show in return.

With their prioritization of political issues and propaganda over durable and effective measures, China's ecological policies in Tibet hardly seem the model *100 Questions* suggests.

PART NINE

Livelihood of the People

The Chinese questions and answers of this section do not give a real picture of the present conditions of existence of the Tibetans, whether they are city dwellers, farmers, or herders. The Chinese present a very bleak picture of the former "feudal" society in order to show, by contrast, the improvement in Tibetans' standard of living and social status.

The last two questions deal with the customs, habits, and traditional festivals. Katia Buffetrille and Janet Gyatso evoke the authentic Tibetan traditional society and give some insights into the present life of the Tibetans, which appear also in other answers in this volume.

85

How are the living conditions in Tibet today
compared with the past?

"Tibet was a feudal serfdom. . . . Most land and other means of production were owned by the 'three feudal estate-holders' (officials, monasteries and nobles), and the laboring people lived an extremely poor and miserable life."

The "three feudal estate-holders" only accounted for 5 percent of the population, but they monopolized more than half of the production. "All serfs were appendages to feudal lords and had little freedom. . . . In general, serfs worked under the supervision and whips of the serf-owners' stewards." They often were "used as property to be mortgaged or given with their manors as gifts." Their children were enslaved too. Rebels were jailed in private prisons built by the nobles in their manors. People were also overburdened with corvée called *wula [ulag]* and "had to live with debts that could not be cleared up for generations."

In Lhasa, for instance, "there were only 20,000 people living in the city proper, while in the suburbs poor people and beggars were pressed closely together in more than a thousand ragged burlap tents. 'Prisoners' with handcuffs, fetters and wooden yokes were seen begging along the streets."

Since 1959, serfdom has been abolished "and the people have become their own masters." Economy, culture, and other aspects "have developed rapidly and the living standard of the Tibetan people has improved. . . . Farmers and herdsmen have built new houses. Most of the people have adequate clothing and food. . . . Urban and rural markets are thriving."

Katia Buffetrille

Robert Barnett has already discussed the question of "serfdom" in Tibet prior to the "peaceful liberation" (Question 19). It nonetheless seems useful to examine the old social system in somewhat greater detail, since the subject has led to the publication of volumes, articles, films, and propaganda photos that have been used by the Chinese state to propagate a politically convenient view of pre-1950 Tibet.

In the traditional Tibetan economic system, monetary exchange was limited, with most commercial activities taking the form of a direct exchange of goods, lands, or services. The primary area of production was the land, and the land system reflected the social structure, with rights to land linked to social status. Services rendered to the state were often repaid in the form of estates, and rights to land implied social duties and in many cases political offices. Only three groups could be landlords: the state, the clergy, and the aristocracy (the "Three Great Lords" of Chinese propaganda), but ultimately, the land was regarded as belonging to the ruler, and thus to the Dalai Lama in the region under the control of Lhasa. There was no clear separation between economic and political power; those who owned the land exerted political power, even if only locally. However, notable differences existed within the different regions of Tibet. For reasons of space, we shall mainly speak here about central Tibet, the same area *100 Questions* discusses.

Tibet was a very hierarchical society with strata *(rig)* in which there was a separation between clergy and laypeople; the latter were divided into three strata: the aristocracy, the common people, and the lower class (butchers, fishermen, corpse carriers, blacksmiths).

Nobility was hereditary and linked to a fief. There were four grades within the nobility (Petech 1973). Fiefs were inherited, and, in return, the noble families were expected to provide one, or sometimes two sons to serve as officials to the state (army and administration). Also, domains of various sizes were linked to specific offices, such as that of provincial governor, and were returned when the post was left. The highest families generally resided in Lhasa with their lands, often scattered across Tibet, left under the control of a steward.

However, the nobility was not entirely invulnerable. Under certain circumstances, a family could be deprived of its properties. This was often the case with the change of Dalai Lama (also at the time of the accession to power of a regent). The family into which the new Dalai Lama was born, which did not necessarily belonged to the nobility, was ennobled and given considerable lands. With each new Dalai Lama, the demand was substantial. Since the new domains could not come from the transformation of virgin lands into agricultural lands, the only solution was to expropriate land already owned by another family (Goldstein 1973).

The nature of the tie between the people and the landlords is much debated, and we refer the reader to Question 19 in this regard. Nevertheless, it is important to note that the Chinese authorities, in justifying their intervention in Tibet, first emphasized the alleged necessity to liberate the country from "imperialist influences" and only in passing claimed their intention to liberate the Tibetans from "serfdom" and "feudalism" in order to avoid predictably strong reactions from Tibetan society. Indeed, in the early 1950s, they asserted their respect for the traditional system in such documents as the 17-Point Agreement (see Question 14), specifically articles 3, 4, 7, and 11. For some time, they continued to honor their commitments in central Tibet in order to follow the gradualist policy recommended by Mao (Goldstein 1997, 2003), even after the Lhasa uprising and the escape of the Dalai Lama in 1959.

Among the common people, status was variable; there were craftsmen, traders, servants, nomads, and semi-nomads called *samadrog* who practiced both agriculture and herding, but farmers formed the majority.

Whether one uses the term "serfs," defended by Goldstein (1986), "commoners," or "subjects" when discussing farmers, it is important to understand what it denotes. "All serfs were appendages to feudal lords," the Chinese authors claim. Since the term "serf" generally implies a person dependent on a lord, this was not exactly the case. In fact, farmers were hereditarily bound to the land and only indirectly to their landlords. They provided a sort of corvée labor (actually labeled as "tax," *trel*) for the state, a particular estate, or a monastery in exchange for using parts of its land or of the crops produced on it.

However, contrary to the assertions in *100 Questions*, farmers had a legal identity, with rights as well as duties. Landlords, whether lay or religious, did not have the right to increase the amount of tax owed by a serf or to modify the size of his plot. Where this occurred, the serf could have recourse to the courts. Conflicts were generally resolved at a lower level by corporate family units, heads of villages, local authorities of the land (nobility or monastery), or the state (for the lands directly under its authority). The lord had the responsibility to arbitrate disputes between his farmers and to defend them in disputes with farmers from other estates. When property changed hands, the farmer was still bound to the land; if he escaped, his master had the right to summon him and to punish him. The conditions governing these reciprocal obligations were recorded in written documents.

However, farmers did not form an undifferentiated mass, as the Chinese statement suggests. There were in reality several subgroups, and if social mobility hardly existed between nobility and farmers (one of the few exceptions being the families of the Dalai Lamas), it did exist among farmers (as in the clergy or within the aristocracy). The two largest groups were the "taxpayers" *(trelpa)* and the "small householders" (*düchung;* lit. "small smoke"). The first, higher in the hierarchy, could not be deprived of their lands as long as they fulfilled their duties (obligatory labor and taxes) to their master; they could even lease the land allotted to them. The "small householders" were either tied to a property that did not necessarily "belong" to them or they were "human lease" (mibog). The members of this group, while bound to a lord, were still free to go where they wished and to work for the person they chose. Their obligation was to pay a set sum to their lord annually when they were authorized to leave (Goldstein 1986).

Taxes, numerous and various, were owed to the state, the monastery, or the lord. Some were paid in cash, others in kind (grain, materials, and so on), but most took the form of labor, essentially, agricultural work. At the local level, farmers had to build or repair bridges, dikes, and roads. Villagers could be asked to repaint the monastery, to gather wood, or to carry water for their master. Households sometimes had to provide one of their sons to the monastery or to the army, leaving the family minus a worker. Boys from rural countries as young as eight to ten years old could be recruited for the Dalai Lama's dance troupe; in exchange, their families were exempted from taxes (Goldstein et al. 1997). There was also forced labor (ulag); the central government allowed officials and certain other persons to receive, at each stage of their travels, free food, free lodging, and even pack animals to carry their belongings. This was a very heavy burden for those liable to this duty, since it was necessary for them not only to have animals on hand for this purpose but also to feed them. Moreover, people were sometimes compelled to take out a high-interest loan from a monastery, which had to be repaid either by the borrower or by his descendants.

Taxes and forced labor did not bind individuals as much as they did a family, which explains how so many Tibetans could go on pilgrimages or on trading trips for extended periods of time. If two in a household of four people could fulfill its duties, the other two were free to do what they wanted. Sometimes, in well-to-do families, servants did the work, while the members of the family followed occupations of their choice.

Nomads and semi-nomads were subject to a system similar to that of farmers. They were generally the dependents of a noble, a monastery, or of a high religious dignitary. For example, the Phala nomads of western Tibet studied by Melvyn Goldstein and C. M. Beall (1989) were dependent subjects of the Panchen Lama and were bound by hereditary ties to their lord and his lands; they owed him taxes and labor and could not take their cattle and leave the domain they were bound to. However, they were free as soon as they had fulfilled their duties. Some were rich and had large herds.

Let us turn to "the prisoners with handcuffs, fetters and wooden yokes" that were "seen begging along the streets." It is correct that some criminals were sentenced to wear a wooden neck cangue *(go)* for a given time and to beg in the streets, but this did not happen as a rule. The 13th Dalai Lama abolished the death penalty (whereas the PRC not only still practices capital punishment but is the country that makes by far the most extensive use of it), and no document—apart from those provided by the Chinese authorities—corroborates the assertion that "serfs worked under the supervision and whips of the serf-owners' stewards" and that "nobles built private jails in their manors." In any case, considering the appalling record of Chinese prisons up to the present, in particular when it comes to the conditions of Tibetan prisoners, the PRC does not appear in a strong position to criticize the old Tibetan society in this regard; testimonies about the fate of Tibetan prisoners are sufficiently abundant (e.g., Palden Gyatso 1997; Adhe 1997; Goldstein et al. 1997; Marshall 1999, 2000, 2002; Ani Pachen 2000; Goldstein et al. 2004).

It would be unfair not to acknowledge the modernization efforts that have been under way in Tibet under Chinese occupation. However, it is just as unfair and inaccurate to consider this modernization without its manifold negative effects (e.g., on the environment, see Question 84) and the toll it has taken and continues to take in all domains in terms of human suffering, ecological devastation, and architectural and artistic destruction. Traditional Tibetan society had certainly reached a point at which change was necessary, as was recognized by the 13th and 14th Dalai Lamas, who both made serious attempts to introduce necessary reforms (although the former, in particular, was strongly hampered in this endeavor by the conservative establishment, especially the great monasteries). The unquestionable economic development undertaken by the Chinese did not result in wealth for the majority, and China admits that Tibet is one of its poorest regions (see Part VIII above). At the present time, a great number of beggars can be seen in the TAR, mainly in Lhasa. The goods on sale in prosperous markets, sometimes located in ruined old buildings, like the Tromsikhang, on the Barkor, often come from China (and primarily reflect Chinese needs); they also remain beyond the financial means of the majority of the Tibetan population.

Moreover, a sentence such as "the people have become their own masters" appears rather cynical when looking back at Tibet's experience following the Chinese occupation.

The Tibetans from the outset encountered both the carrot and the stick. In the 1950s, after Tibet's "peaceful liberation," Mao wanted the Dalai Lama to accept Chinese sovereignty. His initial policy therefore was, as already said, one of gradualism; the Chinese authorities sought the favor of the aristocracy, painting the "socialist paradise" in glowing colors (Goldstein 1997, 2003). Then, at the beginning of the 1960s, they tried to win the masses' favor by projecting a Marxist-compatible grid over traditional Tibetan society, with subdivisions in various social classes based on political and economic criteria. All monks above the rank of head disciplinarian *(gekö)*, soldiers of the Tibetan army above the *zhelngo* (chief of a section of twenty-five men), and Tibetan officials above the category of "agents" of the landowners—whatever their wealth really was—were assigned to the group of "serf owners." On the economic level, all families who retained more than 50 percent of their income after the deduction of their annual expenses were classified as "serf owners"; those with between 45 and 50 percent as "agents of serf owners"; from 35 to 45 percent as "rich farmers"; from 25 to 35 percent as "middle-class farmers"; and the remainder as "poor people" (Choedon 1978: 33). The Chinese authorities divided Tibetan society into two groups: the "oppressors" and the "oppressed." The latter (that is to say, the underdogs), said to possess the correct political and class backgrounds, were allowed to be "elected" as representatives at district and village levels in 1964. This "election," said by the Chinese to consolidate the "democratic dictatorship," created a new local elite but only a few months later, very few references were made to this "election," and a new system was introduced: the Socialist Education Campaign (Shakya 1999: 259). In this sense, the statement that Tibetans "have become their own masters" distorts rather than accurately depicts the reality of Tibetan society under Chinese occupation.

Certainly, for some Tibetans, life under the current regime is acceptable, and some even express a certain contentment with it (any alternative being unavailable, and, for most, unthinkable). Nevertheless, people who do not enjoy full rights to practice their customs, use their language, and follow their religion without restriction can hardly be labeled "their own masters."

86

WHY ARE THE LIVING STANDARDS OF TIBETANS LOWER THAN [THOSE OF] THE HAN PEOPLE IN OTHER PLACES?

This is because the natural conditions in Tibet are very harsh, with a cold climate and lack of oxygen. "Also, stepping out from a feudal serf society, Tibet had a poor foundation to start with and productivity was very low. After liberation, construction began, but it is still far behind the level of economic development in the interior. Shortages of energy, transportation facilities and qualified personnel have greatly limited the economic development in Tibet."

[The corresponding Question 19, 2001 puts much emphasis on improvements in rural and urban incomes from 1978 to 2001.]

ANDREW M. FISCHER

Most of the government answers that refer to various household income statistics cite nominal yuan values that are not adjusted for inflation, which it is necessary to do in order to get an idea of real purchasing power. Price inflation in the TAR was the highest in the PRC between 1990 and 2000, almost 150 percent (i.e., average prices increasing by 2.5 times). These price indices for the TAR are only publicly available from 1990 on, but based on the experience of Qinghai, inflation between 1985 (the first year available for Qinghai) and 2000 would have been close to 300 percent in the TAR, and using national indices as a reference, inflation between 1978 and 2000 in the TAR would have been over 400 percent (i.e., the general cost of living more than quintupled; for all data given here, see Fischer 2005: chap. 4).

Therefore, to give an example drawn from Question 19, 2001, the actual purchasing power of 200 yuan in 1978—the average net income of farmers and herders in the TAR—would be equivalent to over 1,000 yuan in 2000, according to a conservative estimate of price inflation extrapolated from official data. Therefore, in terms of purchasing power, average net incomes of farmers and herders actually only officially increased at best from about 1,000 yuan to 1,320 yuan over these twenty-two years, or slightly more than 1 percent a year on average, by no means an impressive gain. Hu Yaobang himself was astonished by the poverty of the rural TAR during his visit in 1980.

Furthermore, according to official data, all of this gain in purchasing power was made in the 1980s, and none of it in the 1990s. In fact, average rural incomes in the TAR were stagnant or even falling in the 1990s, taking into account inflation, which was rising faster than average rural incomes throughout the 1990s. As a result, the purchasing power of the average rural income in the TAR in 2000 was lower than in 1990. In other words, according to official data, the 1990s were a particularly punitive decade for rural Tibetans, to a degree not seen in any of the other western provinces of the PRC.

The 2001 answer also states that "at present, most Tibetan residents have no problems making ends meet." As noted in Part VIII above, according to official data and national poverty lines, the rate of absolute rural poverty in the TAR was as high as 25 percent in 1999. Officially, one out of every four rural Tibetans in the TAR, or about 500,000 Tibetans, did in fact have great difficulty making ends meet, to the extent of potential malnourishment. Obviously, these official rural income statistics have been criticized as inaccurate by many, including officials and scholars in China. However, in a five-year survey of thirteen farming villages, Melvyn Goldstein et al. (2003) estimated that 14 percent of the surveyed households were poor in the late 1990s, defined in terms of not having enough production or income to meet basic food needs, although this estimate was around one-third in the two poorest townships. Using this estimate as a benchmark, around 300,000 rural Tibetans in the TAR—one in every seven—would not have been able to make ends meet in 2000. However, Goldstein and his colleagues used only a small survey sample, and their study did not include any pastoral areas.

Average urban household incomes in the TAR similarly mask one of the highest levels of urban poverty in China. According to a study published by the International Labor Organization, also using official data from China, the poverty rate among permanent urban residents in the TAR was 11 percent in 1998. This was the third highest urban poverty rate in China in that year (Hussain 2003: 16). In contrast, average incomes among these same permanent urban residents were the seventh highest in China in 2001, neck and neck with coastal provinces such as Fujian and Jiangsu. Compared with the high urban poverty rate, this suggests a high level of inequality in Tibetan towns and cities.

The sources of the urban wealth explain this contradiction between high urban poverty and high urban income. For instance, 88 percent of average urban income in 2001 was derived from salaries and wages in state-owned units. As discussed before, state-sector salaries in the TAR were the second highest in China in 2001, higher than those of Beijing, although they only represented the earnings of about 12 percent of the total provincial workforce and about 60 percent of the urban workforce (not including migrants). More than two-thirds of these state-sector employees were Tibetans, although since 2001, the Tibetan share of public employment has fallen sharply. Most state-sector employees are also concentrated in cities or towns. Therefore, their salaries weigh heavily in the calculation of average urban income. In comparison, state-sector salaries accounted for only 54 percent of the average urban household income in China, 62 percent for Qinghai and 52 percent for Sichuan (*CSY,* 2002: tables 5-4 and 10-5).

On the flip side, only 12 percent of the average urban household income in the TAR derived from non-state-owned units, which nonetheless accounted for 40 percent of the urban labor force in the TAR (again, none of this includes migrants). This suggests that little urban wealth in the TAR disperses outside the state sector, leaving those without access to employment in it to struggle in the wake of those who do. Essentially, there is a dual economy within the urban areas themselves, which has important implications for exclusion within growth.

Of course, the more fundamental duality concerns the urban-rural divide. Urban-rural inequality in the TAR has been increasing rapidly, far beyond the experience of any other province in China. By 2001, the average urban income was 5.6 times greater than the average rural income. The next highest provincial ratio was seen in Yunnan at 4.4, and all of the other western provinces were below 4. The national average was 2.9, considered to be very high and a source of concern by scholars and policy makers throughout China. The record breaking urban-rural inequality in the TAR has been new since the mid 1990s, before which the TAR was more or less similar to most other western provinces. After 1995, this form of inequality shot up in the TAR, while it briefly fell for about two or three years in almost every other province.

In combination with the dilemmas of rural and urban poverty, the fundamental quandary of current development policy in the TAR is this highly uneven distribution of wealth that excludes those not privileged by the state.

87
DO THE TIBETAN AND HAN PEOPLE ENJOY EQUAL PAYMENT FOR SAME WORK?

"Yes, whether in government offices, enterprises or institutions, they receive equal pay for equal work." [Full quotation of the answer]

KATIA BUFFETRILLE

It is in principle correct to say that Tibetans and Han enjoy equal payment for the same work, but the real question is: do Tibetans and Han perform the same kind of jobs? To that, the answer is negative.

The income gap between rural and urban Tibet is the highest in China, as already noted. The Tibetan workforce in urban areas is generally confined to jobs requiring no qualifications. Fluency in Mandarin is essential for most employment, leaving many Tibetans without any chance to compete in the job market or even to improve their standard of living. In addition, the level of education is lower in Tibet, and the cost of education is steadily increasing. In August 2000, the official Chinese newspaper *Guangming Daily* reported that 54.94 percent of the population of Lhasa was illiterate. Lhasa being the most developed city on the economic and educational levels, this says much about the illiteracy rate in the countryside. According to one study, "the proportion of the local population that cannot read or write increased by more than 10%, to 54,9% in 2003 from 43,8% in 2002" (TibetInfoNet, September 27, 2005). This clarifies why Tibetans cannot compete with Chinese in the market economy. The Chinese have, on average, much better qualifications than Tibetans and are also much better connected; consequently, they have better jobs and better salaries.

Another form of discrimination is that against the women, who receive lower salaries than men (even Tibetan men) for the same job. "[A] Tibetan woman in urban areas spends on average 800 yuan or more each year on cosmetics, approximately half the monthly salary for a government worker in Lhasa," according to *People's Daily Online* (October 3, 2003), and it is true that new cosmetics stores, beauty parlors, and fashionable dress shops are blossoming in Lhasa. In emphasizing such "futile" expenditure, this report obviously intends to demonstrate that Tibetan women are nowadays well-to-do. However, it fails to mention that most of the customers of these cosmetics stores are Chinese (fieldwork, April 2006).

In fact, apart from a very thin layer of privileged Tibetans, the beneficiaries of Tibet's unbalanced economic development are almost entirely Chinese.

88

What customs and habits are there in Tibet?
[Question 77, 2001]

"Tibetans have many customs and habits of their own." Some are listed below.

- Names. "Tibetans do not have surnames. Their personal names are adopted from the names in Buddhist sutras associated with good fortune."

- Terms of address. It is impolite to address someone by his name alone, except in case of an elder to a younger. "To show respect, a title is usually added. In Lhasa, for example, 'la' is said after the name, and in Xigaze region, 'aji' or 'ajue' before male names."

- Dress. Men and women wear "a long gown made of *pula* (a woollen material) and lambskin. The women like to adorn themselves with headdresses decorated with strings inlaid with agate, coral or jade. Felt or fine leather hats are popular with both men and women."

- Food. "In agricultural areas, the staple food is *zanba [tsampa]*, made of roasted highland *qingke* barley [Tib. *nas*] or peas ground into flour and then mixed with buttered tea. In pastoral areas, the Tibetans eat beef and mutton. The favorite drinks of the region are buttered tea, milky tea and *qingke* beer. Lamas are allowed to eat meat."

- Marriage. "Monogamy is the standard practice. Young people are quite free to choose their own partners. The head of a family is always male, and only men can inherit property. All monks are permitted to marry, except those belonging to the Gelug (Yellow) Sect."

- Funerals. The corpse of an ordinary person is carried to a mountain, dismembered, and offered to vultures. "Ordinary living Buddhas are cremated. When an incarnated grand living Buddha dies, after a solemn ceremony, his body is covered with spices and medicine and dried. Sitting cross-legged, it is covered with incense paste, in some cases, preserved in a pagoda."

- Taboos. The Tibetans do not eat the meat of horses, rabbits, or dogs, and in many places, birds, eggs, and fish are not eaten either. "For religious reasons, the killing of wild animals is generally prohibited. People are not allowed to stride across Buddhist vessels and basins for holding fires, and prayer wheels may not be turned counterclockwise. To touch one's head is resented."

- Greetings. "At formal introductions, people exchange *hatas [katas]*, ceremonial silk scarves." They pay great attention to presenting gifts. They offer tea or beer to a relative going on a long journey. "The construction of a new house is celebrated with gifts from relatives and friends."

KATIA BUFFETRILLE AND JANET GYATSO

Tibetan culture is the expression of a civilization so complex that its description would require several books. Numerous regional communities have developed traditions in the domains of social organization, arts, language, and so on, such that it is impossible to attribute the specific customs of one region to the whole of Tibet. The following answer deals only with topics mentioned in *100 Questions*.

Names

Tibetans indeed do not use surnames. They are often known by their first name (generally composed of two), which, in most cases, reflects religious values such as Sönam ("Merit") or Yeshe ("Wisdom"). They can also bear the name of the day of their birth: Nyima ("Sunday") or Dawa ("Monday"). In the case of sickness, a pejorative name like "Small Dog" is chosen in order to divert evil spirits. In the same way, a temporary appellation can be given to a baby to distract evil forces, or, in the case of the death of a previous baby, the newborn child may receive a name like "Free from demons." Nicknames are often given to reflect a physical characteristic ("The Dumb," "The Deaf"). The name of the household, estate, or clan is sometimes added before the first name, or that of the village, the region, or even the professional occupation. With nomads, the tribe's name is added before the personal name.

It is "impolite to address someone directly by his name alone." Generally, one uses a term corresponding to his or her generation, like *Ama la* for a mother and all women of the same generation (*la* is an honorific particle used mainly in central Tibet). On the other hand, a child might be called by its first name or simply *bu* ("son") or *bu mo* ("daughter").

Incarnate lamas (*trülkus*) are often known by their personal names or that of their monastery, the seat of their line of reincarnations. Religious titles and epithets like Rinpoche ("Precious One"), Khenpo ("Abbot"), or Lama ("Guru") are also added to their name. "Secret names" and other appellations are given during rituals, initiations, or other occasions, which lead to difficulties in the identification of a person: an author may sign a work with any of his names.

Clothes

Nowadays, many city dwellers wear "Western clothes," not only for convenience and fashion, but also because it is strongly advisable not to look "too Tibetan" while working for the government.

Traditionally, and this is still the case in the agricultural areas and among the herders, laymen and women wear—above pants and shirt—a long-sleeved gown called a *chuba*, which they pull up and tie at the waist with a belt. The pocket so formed is used as a bag to carry everything from a bowl to a child. A new, perhaps temporary, fashion of wearing *chubas* adorned with very large borders of fur, often tiger fur, appeared in the 1990s, mainly among nomads, which the Chinese authorities promoted for propaganda and commercial purposes, despite its official prohibition (TibetInfoNet, January

31, 2006). But the Dalai Lama made strong statements during the *Kâlacakra* initiation in India in January 2006 about the importance of wildlife conservation (an idea actually foreign to Buddhist doctrine) and asked the Tibetans not to wear fur anymore. Tibetans reacted very quickly, and reports soon came of Tibetans in Qinghai, Sichuan, and also in Lhasa collecting and burning fur and animal skins in a spontaneous response to the Dalai Lama's appeal. The Chinese authorities tried to stop these actions showing the Tibetan support for the Dalai Lama (WTN, February 24, 2006) and even ordered Tibetan television broadcasters to continue wearing fur-trimmed *chubas*. In addition, traditionally, the Tibetans wore embroidered boots, replaced nowadays by Chinese sneakers, and they are fond of hats; but despite the cold, they rarely use gloves.

Monks and nuns must dress in conformity with the rules of the monastic discipline *(vinaya)*. The monastic dress, yellow and maroon, is composed of a vest without sleeves and of a long skirt made of three materials sewed according to strict rules. Monks drape themselves in a stole but leave the right arm bare, a sign of respect to the Buddha. Religious robes may be cut in sumptuous brocades, and one finds a large selection of hats, corresponding to different schools, ceremonies, and rituals. During sacred dances *(cham)*, monks wear various costumes, masks, hats, and aprons to help the performer, the other participants, and the spectators to imagine the character as a deity or religious or historical personage.

Men and women wear jewelry, especially turquoise, amber, coral, silver, and gold, as well as a special black or brown agate called *zi*. This stone is regarded as of supernatural origin with the power to protect its wearer from catastrophe. Traditionally, jewelry could indicate the rank of the person in society. The *gao*, a silver or golden box containing relics or an image of a master or a deity, is worn across the chest.

Food

Dietary customs have changed with the coming of Chinese products, but *tsampa*, roasted barley flour, mixed with butter and salted tea, is still the staple food for many Tibetans. Another very common dish is *tugpa*, a soup made with noodles, flour balls, and small pieces of meat. Tibetans also enjoy dry cheese *(chura)* and other dairy products. Yak meat, mutton, and pork are widely consumed, but not fish, dogs, or rabbits. The traditional alcohol, *chang* (Chin. *qingke* beer), is a kind of beer made from the fermentation of barley or other grains. Since the occupation, Chinese alcohols often replace *chang*, causing serious health problems.

Marriage

Several forms of marriage coexist in Tibet. The most frequent is monogamy, but fraternal polyandry (a woman married to several brothers) and sororal polygyny (a man married to several sisters) were and still are practiced in some areas despite their legal prohibition. The woman generally goes to live in her husband's house. When a family has only daughters, a man is invited in as son-in-law *(magpa)*. He lives in the house of his wife and takes the name of her household. Traditionally, weddings were a secular event, in the sense that the presence of the clergy was not necessary; divorce was not uncommon. Usually, the estate is inherited patrilineally, but personal belongings are often passed on matrilineally.

Contrary to what the Chinese authors assert, no monk, whatever his school, can marry (see Question 54).

Funerals

A variety of funerary practices exist according to the region and the climate. In central Tibet, an almost treeless region with frozen ground for part of the year, bodies are usually cut up in a special place and given to the vultures. In other regions, the dead are buried, cremated, or sometimes thrown in the river. The bodies of newborn children are often abandoned in the mountains. Important religious persons are cremated, while the most exalted masters are mummified and their corpse placed in a stupa reliquary.

In accordance with the belief in reincarnation, the "soul" of the dead person must be guided toward liberation or to a fortunate rebirth. To this end, clerics recite texts for the dead, among them *The Great Liberation through Hearing, in the Intermediate State between Death and Rebirth (Bardo)*, well known as *The Tibetan Book of the Dead*, in order to help the wandering "soul" find its way during the forty-nine days of the *bardo*.

Social Life and Behavior

It is not possible to describe Tibetan social life in a few lines. Tibetans enjoy festivals, dance, songs, games, and picnics. Upon arrival and departure, guests receive a ceremonial scarf *(kata)* and other presents. Tea is always offered. A respectful way of greeting is to touch the other person's head with one's own. To step over the hearth, considered the residence of a god, is prohibited, as stepping over or sitting on a book, symbol of the word of the Buddha.

89
WHAT FESTIVALS ARE THERE IN TIBET? [QUESTION 76, 2001]

Apart from national [i.e., Chinese] holidays (New Year, May 1, and the National Day, October 1, etc.), "the Tibetans also celebrate some of their own traditional festivals, which include":

- Tibetan New Year *[Losar]* "is the most important event of the Tibetan calendar. . . . It falls around the beginning of February." People wish each other a happy new year "and every household makes offerings for good fortune."

- The *Monlam*, known as "the Grand Summons Ceremony," "takes place in Lhasa during the first month of the Tibetan calendar. . . . Monks and lay people from Tibet and other provinces meet to recite and analyze sutras and offer praises to Buddha. Alms are given to the lamas, offerings are made to the statue of Buddha Champa, dike-reinforcement ceremonies are held on the banks of Lhasa River, and butter lantern festivals take place across the city."

- The "World Public Memorial Festival (also known as the Lingka Festival)," on the 15th day of the fifth month of the Tibetan calendar, is "reputedly the day on which Sakyamuni defeated the pagans." On this day, people dressed at their best go for picnics "in the *lingka* parks."

- The "Sour Milk Drinking Festival" *[zhotön]* falls around the first day of the seventh month of the Tibetan calendar and lasts about one week. It "was originally purely a religious festival. It has now developed into a celebration of Tibetan operas, and therefore is also called the 'Tibetan Opera Festival.'"

- The Ongkor Festival, or "Bumper Harvest Festival," in the eighth month of the Tibetan calendar. "Farmers dressed in new clothes carry Buddhist statues and walk around their crops, reciting sutras and bowing. Afterwards they gather in their villages to dance and drink. In some places, horse races, ox races and wrestling also take place."

- The Lamp Festival, on the 25th day of the twelfth month of the Tibetan calendar, is said to be "the day when Tsong-kha-pa, founder of the Gelug (Yellow) Sect, completed his enlightenment to Buddhahood. To celebrate, many people light rows of butter lamps on the roofs and windowsills of their homes."

KATIA BUFFETRILLE AND JANET GYATSO

The state festivals, religious festivals, and local festivals that punctuated Tibetans' lives were initially banned by the Chinese and then slowly reintroduced beginning in 1985, but often severed from their ritual context. These festivals take place at precise dates of the Tibetan calendar.

The Tibetan year is composed of twelve lunar months named "first month, second month, and so on," requiring the insertion of an additional month every thirty-two months to be in accordance with the solar calendar. In 1027, following the *Kâlacakra tantra*, the Tibetans adopted a sexagesimal cycle, combining the Chinese system of a cycle of twelve years, each designated by an animal (rat, ox, tiger, rabbit, dragon, snake, horse, sheep, monkey, cock, dog, pig) with one of the five elements (fire, water, earth, iron, wood). The animal years are designated as male or female in each sixty-year cycle. For example, 2006 was the year Fire-Male-Dog.

Auspicious days within the lunar calendar fall on the fifteenth and thirtieth days of each month and are associated with Shâkyamuni, the tenth with Padmasambhava (who brought tantric Buddhism to Tibet in the eighth century), and the twenty-fifth with the *dâkinî*, female tantric figures who are the embodiment of Wisdom.

The Chinese authors describe only the main festivals held in Lhasa, which for all Tibetans is not only the capital but also the holy city. Some further explanations and corrections seem necessary.

Most Tibetan festivals have two parts: the religious part includes a visit to a monastery to offer butter lamps, ceremonial scarves, or money; to show veneration through prostrations; and to burn juniper, whose fragrant smoke is an offering to the gods. (This ritual is also performed at home every day. Early in the morning, the head of the household burns juniper in a hearth generally located on the roof terrace, makes an offering of *tsampa*, and recites invocations.) The secular aspect is always present, and food, drinks, and songs are parts of the celebration.

The Tibetan New Year is truly "the most important event of the Tibetan calendar." In former times, the New Year festival in Lhasa lasted the whole first month (February–March). On the last day of the old year, the evil forces were expelled through various rituals. State ceremonies took place in the Potala and in Nechung, the monastery of the state Oracle. Thousands of Tibetans gathered in the city for religious purposes (mainly to visit the Jokhang temple) but also to watch horse races, archery competitions, foot races, and dances. Gifts of food and good wishes were exchanged.

The Great Prayer *(Mönlam chenmo)*, introduced in 1409 by Tsongkhapa (1357–1419), took place from the third to the twenty-fifth day of the first month. During these three weeks, monks prayed for the well-being and the prosperity of the state, of the Buddhist religion, of the people, and of all sentient beings. Rituals to hasten the coming of the future Buddha, Jampa (Sanskrit, Maitreya), were celebrated and huge butter sculptures erected outside the Jokhang. The dikes in Lhasa were also repaired. During the festival, civil authority was transferred to the monks of Drepung monastery, and thousands of monks from all over the country gathered in the Jokhang and filled the streets. The *Mönlam chenmo* festival was banned by the Chinese until 1986, when an abbreviated version was permitted, before being banned again and then again permitted. It is obvious that such a concentration of monks, although much smaller than in the past, must be perceived as a threat by the PRC authorities.

What the Chinese authors strangely call "The World Public Festival (also known as the Lingka festival) . . . the day on which Sakyamuni defeated the pagans" does not fall on the fifteenth day of the fifth month. The authors have confused two festivals. "The Festival of the Great Miracle and the Offering of the Fifteenth" *(Chotrül düchen dang conga chöpa)*, on the fifteenth day of the first month, celebrates the defeat of the heretics by the Buddha at Shrâvasti. "The Universal Incense-Offering" *(Dzamling chisang)*, on the fifteenth day of the fifth month (June–July), commemorates the foundation of Samye monastery and the subjugation of the demons by Padmasambhava. On this day, people go picnicking in the parks.

Regarding the "Yogurt Feast" *(zhotön)*, see Question 68. It occurred annually on the 29th and 30th of the sixth month (July–August) in Sera and Drepung, and from the 1st to the 5th of the seventh month (August–September) in Lhasa.

The *Ongkor* festival is a harvest festival held on the first fortnight of the seventh month (August–September). On this occasion, the farmers go around their fields in procession, led by a tantrist priest. They carry statues, symbols of the body of the Buddha; books, symbols of his word; and stupas, symbols of his mind.

What the Chinese call "The Lamp Festival" is in fact the offering on the twenty-fifth day in Ganden *(Ganden ngachö)* that commemorates the death of Tsongkhapa on the twenty-fifth day of the tenth month and not of the twelfth. During the night of the twenty-fourth, small butter lamps are lighted everywhere in the city.

There are many more festivals. In particular, the cults of territorial gods and their associated festivals are being revived all over Tibet. The beliefs underlying these cults, classed as superstitions by the PRC authorities, are often denigrated, and their manifestations are sometimes repressed. Horse races and archery are associated with these rituals, and the PRC authorities encourage the "folklorization" of these festivals.

PART TEN

About the Riots in Lhasa

What the Chinese call "riots" started out as peaceful demonstrations. As explained by Robert Barnett, violence by the Tibetans, when it occurred, was in response to aggression by the Chinese security forces.

The 2001 edition of *100 Questions* only once refers to demonstrations and unrest in Tibet, and then only to accuse the Dalai Lama of plotting them. It does not mention issues of restrictions on assembly or on opinion, political imprisonment, or the maltreatment of detainees, although there were more than 150 demonstrations in Tibet against Chinese rule after 1987, and several thousand political arrests. The earlier edition, however, had devoted ten questions to the street protests and related arrests that took place in Lhasa in the late 1980s, including a unique acknowledgment that some Tibetans imprisoned in the 1980s were wrongly detained. Those questions and discussions are included here, together with comments on them.

90

SOME PEOPLE HAVE SAID THAT THE DEMONSTRATIONS WHICH
OCCURRED IN LHASA IN 1987 AND 1988, DESPITE BEING PEACEFUL,
WERE FORCIBLY SUPPRESSED. IS THIS TRUE?

The demonstrations were riots that were not at all peaceful. They were "deliberately instigated by a handful of separatists," who illegally aimed to dismember the state. On September 27, 1987, 24 policemen were wounded and two vehicles destroyed. On October 1, 1987, 43 vehicles were destroyed or burned, the Barkor police station was burned down, and 325 cadres and policemen were wounded. On March 5, 1988, a member of the People's Armed Police was beaten to death, and 328 policemen were wounded. Article 4 of the constitution and article 92 of the criminal code forbid all separatist activity and counterrevolutionary acts. The group of separatists who misled the innocent masses therefore infringed the constitution and the criminal code.

ROBERT BARNETT

The official account here argues that the use of force to suppress these three demonstrations was legitimate because the demonstrations were in fact violent riots, and secondly because the demonstrators "were deliberately instigated by a handful of separatists," and "splittism"—the Chinese term for calls for Tibetan independence—is illegal in the PRC. From this account, it is clear that the demonstrations would therefore have been forcibly suppressed whether or not they included any violence.

The Chinese constitution and criminal code forbid "counterrevolutionary" acts; this in effect authorizes the use of lethal force against them. A new version of the PRC's criminal code in 1997 replaced the term "counterrevolutionary" with "acts that endanger state security," "undermine national unity," or "subvert the political power of the state" (articles 102–13 of the revised criminal code [see Xinhua 1997]), but this made little difference in practice.

Lethal force has been used against at least one demonstration where there was no violence at all, because the participants were deemed to be "splittists." This was on December 10, 1988, when paramilitary police approached two unarmed Tibetans leading a demonstration in Lhasa and shot them dead without warning and at close range. The police then, again without warning, opened fire at random on bystanders in the main square who were watching the demonstration, injuring several dozen people, including a foreigner. The Chinese authorities have never claimed there was any suggestion of violence in that incident or explained why these killings took place.

This was one of some 150 peaceful demonstrations in Lhasa suppressed by force between 1987 and 1996 (see TIN 1992a, 1993a). Fortunately, after 1990, the police rarely opened fire on protesters, and there were few such killings reported after that date. However, the police often severely beat participants in such events. Even the PRC authorities have suggested that violence was involved or intended in only four of these incidents. Security forces did use firearms to suppress demonstrations after 1990 in rural areas, such as in the military interventions at Kyimshi in Chideshol and at Nyemo in 1993 (see TIN 1993b).

There were, in fact, three incidents in Lhasa that involved violence by protesters—those of October 1, 1987, March 5, 1988, and March 5, 1989 (the claim in *100 Questions* that there was violence during the demonstration of September 27, 1987, is not supported by any eyewitnesses). These three incidents, however, began peacefully and became violent only in response to members of the security forces beating participants or opening fire on them.

The demonstration of October 1, 1987, for example, began when some sixty or so monks staged a peaceful demonstration around the Barkor. When police stopped the march to arrest the monks, however, they beat the monks with such force that many of them were covered with blood, according to Western eyewitnesses who saw the incident. An American tourist who was briefly detained for taking photographs of the beatings reported that inside the police station, he saw a policeman hitting some monks over the head with a shovel. As a result of the police violence, several hundred laypeople gathered outside the police station and called on the police to release the monks being held inside the building. Their first act of violence occurred about two hours later in response to a specific act by the security forces, which was perceived as aggressive—the decision of officials to bring in a cameraman to film the crowd. The first stone was thrown to smash the camera, because Tibetans were not wearing masks and knew that if the filming continued, they would later be identified from the video footage and severely punished. In addition, police snatch squads were trying to drag random people from the crowd. After the stone throwing began, Chinese police opened fire, and a number of Tibetans were shot dead; hundreds of others were wounded or later arrested, many of them identified by photographs or film taken at the time.

The demonstration on March 5, 1988, began when monks shouted at PRC political leaders sitting on a stage in front of the Jokhang, calling on them to release a leading lama, Yulu Dawa Tsering (a lecturer at Tibet University and a former abbot at Ganden monastery), who had been detained and imprisoned for political reasons some weeks earlier. Some unconfirmed reports say that a single stone was thrown toward the officials, and that a security official on the stage opened fire into the crowd at this point, killing one Tibetan in the crowd. This led to a rapid increase in tension: the monks reportedly paraded the body around the streets, probably throwing stones at the police, until the security forces intervened in large numbers, using tear gas. Thousands of laypeople joined in by throwing stones at the police, apparently in protest at the police attempts to stop the monks' protests. The Chinese police killed at least three Tibetans that day, according to official Chinese reports. At some point during the protests, a Chinese plainclothes security man called Yuan Shisheng was beaten and pushed to his death from a third-floor window. This is the only known case of a Chinese person being killed in Tibet in any recent protests. Several other policemen were beaten or wounded by stones.

Video footage of this protest taken by Chinese officials and later leaked to TIN—distributed under the title *Chinese Police Film of Demonstration, March 1988*—has had all police shooting edited out, but it does show paramilitary police severely beating monks who had taken shelter inside the Jokhang temple. The monks are then thrown into trucks for transportation to prison. The demonstration had finished by the time these paramilitary police arrived, and there was no evidence that these monks had been involved in the unrest. The details of this event are unclear, but it appears that initial police overreaction and later brutality was a major factor in the escalation of the incident from shouting to stone throwing.

The demonstration of March 5, 1989, led to three days of violent unrest in Lhasa, which culminated in the declaration of martial law. Western tourists who saw the start of that unrest described a peaceful demonstration by a dozen people chanting slogans in the main square of Lhasa. A policeman standing on a rooftop threw a bottle at the group, which led one Tibetan youth to throw a stone toward the police. Although the stone fell well short of the policeman, another officer opened fire immediately into the crowd, wounding the youth and two other Tibetans who tried to assist him after he fell. The incident led, for the third time in three years, to a mass response by laypeople, who gathered together to throw stones at police, and later to ransack some shops.

Later that day and on the following two days, the paramilitary police responded by making a number of mass sorties into the Old City of Lhasa, during which they shot at random down streets and into people's houses, killing many people. There were no incidents or crowds in the streets at the time of these sorties, and the shootings were punitive or intimidatory, not efforts to disperse a crowd. At least seventy-five bystanders and local residents, perhaps many more, were shot dead. The tactics used by the security forces during these three days provoked further stone throwing and burning of vehicles. There was no attempt by the authorities to restore calm to the area during this period. On the fourth day, the army moved in, and set up checkpoints throughout the area without meeting any resistance. This suggests that violence by protesters would have been minimal if police had not opened fire and repeatedly shot innocent bystanders.

There have been various attempts by the Chinese authorities to suggest that in one or other of these incidents, the Tibetans had firearms, but these claims have all since been dropped. It is generally agreed by most observers that in the three demonstrations where there was violence, the only weapons used were stones.

The Chinese authors of *100 Questions* claim that over 300 police were wounded in the October 1987 incident, but this seems unlikely, since few police or their agents went near the demonstrators after the initial attempts at arrest, and most remained well out of range of stones throughout the rest of the day.

Between 1995 and 1997, there were nine small incidents involving explosions, usually near official buildings or monuments (see TIN 1996a, 1996b), as well as a small one in Lhasa in 2000 (see TIN 2000a). Exiles are accused by China of organizing these incidents, but no evidence has been produced to support this, and no convictions have been reported. A series of six small explosions in Sichuan in 2000–2002 reportedly led to one death, for which a Tibetan farmer was controversially executed in 2003 and a Tibetan lama, Tenzin Delek, given a life sentence in 2005 (see Spiegel 2004).

91
WHAT CAUSED THE RIOTS, AND DID IT HAVE ANYTHING TO DO WITH THE DALAI CLIQUE?

The TAR government has plenty of evidence that the Lhasa riots were caused by a handful of splittists at the instigation of the Dalai clique, which has been advocating "independence" since its armed rebellion failed in 1959. It provoked the riots by sending people to Tibet disguised as tourists to distribute secessionist leaflets, while the Dalai

Lama tried to get support through his "Five-Point Peace Plan" for Tibetan independence during his visit to the United States in September 1987. News of this was broadcast to Tibet by radio and in other ways. The separatists took advantage of people's religious sentiments and used as a pretext the mistakes made by the TAR authorities during the "special historical conditions of the 'cultural revolution,'" which are already being corrected [from the 1989 edition]. In September 1987, the Dalai Lama . . . continued to advocate "Tibetan independence" through radio broadcasts and other channels and instigated and plotted a number of riots in Lhasa [from the 2001 edition].

ROBERT BARNETT

The elements listed here as causes of unrest in Tibet—the desire for independence, the failure of the 1959 uprising, the Americanization of the Tibetan issue, the Dalai Lama's activities abroad, return visits to Tibet by individual exiles during the early 1980s, and legacy of the Cultural Revolution—were indeed among the factors that shaped Tibetan politics and protests from the mid 1980s on. However, there is little evidence that these factors became significant because of manipulation by leaders in exile. There were existing reasons for Tibetans to have become discontented with Communist rule, even without any news or information reaching Tibet from the exiles.

Even Chinese historians admit that the notion of Tibetan independence had been around since the late nineteenth century (they say it was deliberately introduced by the British). Except for a few aspects of elite function—the presence of an *amban* and a small garrison in Lhasa and the use of some seals or titles for appointments, for example—there was little between 1792 and 1910 to indicate to any ordinary Tibetan that Tibet was not a separate political entity, and from 1913 to 1950 Tibet was in practice independent and declared itself to be so. So the existence of the Dalai Lama in exile is likely to have represented to many Tibetans the continuing possibility of reclaiming their national identity in one form or another, and it is unlikely that a conspiracy was required to provoke this after twenty years of largely catastrophic rule by Beijing. The only evidence so far produced of an outside effort to provoke such support is the fact that two American tourists were caught in Lhasa the week before the October 1987 demonstration carrying leaflets from India describing the Dalai Lama's recent visit to Washington—but their materials were confiscated by the Chinese authorities before they could be handed out. In any case, these materials were informational and did not call for a protest.

In fact, extensive interviews with the monks who started the protests in September 1987 have not revealed any signs that their actions were organized from outside. They described having learnt about Tibetan history from their families in secret, and they had read a few books or leaflets smuggled to Tibet after 1980 (some exiles had brought publications to Tibet after the Chinese relaxed travel restrictions in 1979, but the only Tibetan-language broadcasts were via All India Radio and were generally not political). They had been troubled by increasing restrictions on entry to monasteries, on pilgrimages, on visits to India, on monastery elections, on religious teachings, on study time, and by other such issues, as well as by issues such as freedom, political rights, religious beliefs, and independence.

In addition, many Tibetans seem to have been angered by official media attacks on the Dalai Lama that month, after some years of relative restraint, triggered by his speech on the Five-Point Peace Plan in Washington on September 21. Some Lhasans appear to have been provoked by the mass sentencing rally at the Lhasa Sports Stadium on September 24 (see Question 23). There was also dissatisfaction about a propaganda campaign associated with a marathon race staged by the Lhasa authorities, which was intended to symbolize the integration of Tibet into China. These were, however, minor factors that affected the timing of the first event that September. There seems little reason to doubt the participants' own statements that they wanted independence, or freedom from Chinese rule, and the return of the Dalai Lama. (The claim of an American sinologist that Tibetans did not express support for independence to him [Grunfeld 1988] can be discounted, because any Tibetan admitting a political motivation to him would have been liable to arrest [Sperling 1994].) It could not have been predicted that the police beatings would lead to major popular unrest in Lhasa, or that the events would have worldwide impact because of news reports carried out of Tibet by tourists who saw them.

92
SOME PEOPLE HAVE SAID THAT IN PUTTING DOWN THE RIOTS IN LHASA, THE POLICE ARRESTED AND BEAT PEOPLE INDISCRIMINATELY, KILLING QUITE A FEW. WHAT IS THE TRUTH?

It is true that there were some wrongful arrests in the heat of the moment, but these people were freed as soon as they were found not guilty. Others were freed once they had confessed after interrogation or because their crimes were not serious. Principal troublemakers who took the lead in smashing, sabotaging, looting, and burning were arrested. As for those killed, police were ordered not to open fire but a few had to fire in self-defense when they were in danger. Six Tibetans were killed on October 1, 1987, and four on March 5, 1988, of whom four were killed by stones thrown by Tibetans, five by police bullets, and one by an accidental fall from a high building.

Robert Barnett

This acknowledgment that there were wrongful arrests during the 1980s is unique (it has not, apparently, been made to the detainees involved). The claim that protest-related arrests in Tibet focused on identifying demonstrators involved in violence or damage has some basis but is not fully supported by the evidence. Of the 3,000 or so Tibetans detained for involvement in protests and dissent from 1987 to 1989, several hundred fled to India after being released, where they were interviewed. Few if any reported that they or other prisoners were accused of violence or damage to property or even asked about it: all the interrogations and accusations related to their support of Tibetan independence or the Dalai Lama. The security forces in Tibet were interested almost exclusively in identifying the political leaders of the protests and intimidating their followers, in most cases through beatings and torture.

This is borne out by the court documents of the relevant trials. Of the 179 Tibetans known to have received court sentences as a result of involvement in the demonstrations during the period 1987–91 (as opposed to the 2,000 or so who were held in detention without any trial), only 16 are known to have been held for offenses relating to any form of criminal activity or violence (see TIN 1992b, 1992c). Six of those accused of violence were involved in the murder of Yuan Shisheng, the policeman killed during the March 1988 demonstration. The other ten cases involved damaging property, burning vehicles, or throwing stones during demonstrations. In all except one of these ten cases (that of Penpa Tsering, who set a police car on fire), court documents show that sentences were imposed primarily for political offenses and only secondarily for acts of violence. Tsering Ngodrup, for example, was sentenced to twelve years' imprisonment because he had incited young people to sing "reactionary" Tibetan independence songs and also "delivered speeches stirring up separatist emotion, wantonly robbed, destroyed and set on fire public and private properties, and beat up public security officers" (Radio Lhasa broadcast, September 13, 1989). The documents show that the courts in Tibet treated political offenses as more serious than crimes of violence.

The remaining 92 percent of those who were tried were sentenced for nonviolent political activities because they called for Tibetan independence. Almost all were convicted of "through counterrevolutionary slogans, leaflets, or other means, propagandizing for and inciting the overthrow of the political power of the dictatorship of the proletariat and the socialist system" (article 102, subsection 2 of the 1980 PRC criminal code). Some of the court cases involved Tibetans who were sentenced, usually much more severely than those involved in demonstrations, for having sent or received literature or letters from exiles in India. The overwhelming evidence suggests that most detentions and arrests in Tibet during protests have been intended to suppress certain political views and were rarely connected to acts of violence or damage to property.

The second argument, that police used lethal force only in self-defense, is also difficult to sustain. For the first six months after the October 1987 protest, the Chinese authorities maintained that police had not opened fire at all—they insisted that Tibetans had seized guns from the police and then fired into the crowd. Even the Panchen Lama, then a senior official in China, refuted this claim, saying publicly in February 1988 that the police had fired "warning shots" and killed one person during the incident (Radio Lhasa, February 8 and 9, 1988). The Chinese claim was dropped when Western tourists who had seen the incident presented testimonies and photographs to the United Nations in March 1988, along with photographs showing Chinese police firing into the crowd. The following day the Chinese government, without acknowledging its shift in position, informed the United Nations that on October 1, 1987, "policemen were forced to . . . fire into the air [and] three people died of bullet wounds." The allegation that Tibetans had had firearms was dropped and never repeated. It was replaced by the claim that police had fired in self-defense, a claim weakened by the fact that it took five months for it to be produced.

In fact, the police in Lhasa on October 1, 1987, faced little direct danger, since they were out of range of stone throwers except when they chose to walk toward the crowd, which was stationary. The few police in the police station were able to exit from the back of the building, since only the front was on fire. The crowd of demonstrators had a clear objective: to enable prisoners held inside the police station to escape, and apart from this, the protesters made no attempt to move elsewhere or to attack police. They dispersed once firing began in earnest, but police units patrolled the streets for some three or four hours afterwards, firing in sustained bursts on stragglers. None of these shootings involved self-defense, and it is not possible that they were carried out without orders.

The first shootings on March 5, 1988, and March 5, 1989, were in each case a response to a single stone being thrown, representing little or no danger to the police, and thus were a disproportionate use of force. In the 1988 demonstration, there is also a report that a Tibetan was shot dead when he tried to enter a room inside the Jokhang temple in which a number of Chinese leaders were taking shelter, and there may have been an understandable perception of serious danger in that case. As explained in Question 90, subsequent shootings during the three days after the March 5, 1989, demonstration consisted of the People's Armed Police firing at random in the streets of Lhasa Old City without provocation, as far as we know. There was likewise no apparent reason or purpose for the shooting dead by paramilitary police, at point blank range, of two monks carrying the forbidden Tibetan flag in Lhasa on December 10, 1988 (for eyewitness accounts, see TIN 1991). The claims of self-defense and of shooting without orders are not tenable in any of these cases.

As noted above, the official Chinese video footage of the March 1988 protest shows Chinese paramilitary police dragging Tibetan monks from their rooms in the Jokhang temple and kicking and beating them, with no sign of provocation by the monks and long after the protests had finished. The evidence that Chinese security forces are prone to use excessive force is therefore quite strong.

93
OF ALL THOSE ARRESTED IN THE RIOTS, HOW MANY HAVE BEEN SET FREE AND HOW MANY ARE STILL IN PRISON? HOW WELL ARE THEY TREATED IN PRISON? WHAT WILL HAPPEN TO THEM? HOW MANY RIOTERS, IF ANY, WERE EXECUTED?

According to the governor of the TAR, Doji Cairen [Dorje Tsering], out of 220 detained after the March 1988 demonstration, about 20 were still in custody by August that year. Of those detained after the October 1987 demonstrations, most were released within three months. Everyone remaining in custody has been well treated and judged according to the severity of his or her crimes. No one has been executed for his or her participation in the riots.

ROBERT BARNETT

No Tibetans are known to have been judicially executed for a political offense between 1987 and 2004. This restraint was probably intended to avoid
inflaming local unrest or attracting international attention. About seventy-
five to one hundred Tibetans were, however, shot by police, without the sanc-
tion of a court, during demonstrations in this period. Since, as we have seen,
few if any of these killings can be claimed to have been in self-defense, these
were, in legal terms, nonjudicial or summary executions. Most of these
deaths occurred during March 5–7, 1989. It appears that since then police
have been ordered not to shoot demonstrators on sight.

There is one exception to the claim that there have been no judicial executions: the case of Migmar Tashi and Dawa (see Question 23).

It is correct that in the period 1987–90, the vast majority of those detained in connection with the three or four major demonstrations of that
period were released, usually within three to six months. However, a very
large percentage of these prisoners were drastically tortured before they
were released, and extensive documentation of such cases has been provided in reports by Amnesty International and other organizations. Most
cases of severe torture took place in the first three months after detention;
those who were held longer risked other kinds of abuse, such as lack of
medical treatment in prison, excessive labor requirements, and severe beatings during protests. Exiles have documented at least eighty-seven suspicious deaths in custody among Tibetan political prisoners since 1987 (see
TCHRD 2005).

The prisoners who received the worst treatment and the longest sentences
were not those detained during any of the major protests in this period. The
Chinese legal system identifies as the most serious criminals those who
influence others to commit crimes or who in any way initiate or encourage
crime or dissent. Those involved in the major demonstrations were regarded
as having been "misled" and received relatively light sentences or were released without charge after a few months. But in the 150 or so small demonstrations that are not discussed in *100 Questions*, all the participants received
extremely long sentences—an average of 6.5 years—for protests seen as liable to influence and mislead others. These protests were entirely peaceful
events, which typically lasted less than five minutes and involved fewer than
half a dozen people.

A large percentage of long-term prisoners, and usually those with the
longest sentences, are Tibetans never accused of any involvement in a
demonstration but convicted of producing dissident literature, sending in-

formation to the exiles in India, or spreading ideas in some way. A recent example is Dolma Kyab, who was sentenced to ten years' imprisonment on September 16, 2005, for having written a private, unpublished text about the situation in Tibet (see TCHRD 2006). Long-term political imprisonment in Tibet therefore targets those involved in dissident leadership, ideas, distribution of information, or initiatives, rather than those involved in mass protests.

94
WERE ANY FOREIGN TOURISTS OR REPORTERS AT THE SCENE OF THE RIOTS? IF THERE WERE, WERE THEY DETAINED, WARNED, OR DEPORTED?

There were foreigners present at the riots of October 1, 1987, and March 5, 1988. Some of them participated in the riots, and they were given a warning or fined by the police. Fifteen foreign journalists based in Beijing who traveled to Tibet in October 1987 were ordered to leave Tibet for breaking official regulations covering news gathering in China.

ROBERT BARNETT

Four foreigners participated in the demonstration of October 1, 1987, and were criticized for doing so in a statement issued at the time by other tourists in Lhasa who witnessed the events. There is no evidence that these four foreigners had any prior knowledge that demonstrations were going to happen or that they had instigated them (one had carried in leaflets from India, but these had been confiscated earlier by police). One foreigner briefly joined a demonstration on December 10, 1988.

In some cases, police used considerable violence to deport or threaten the foreigners, shooting a Dutch woman who was watching a demonstration on December 10, 1988, in the shoulder, and expelling a Swiss tourist and an English journalist at gunpoint in March 1989. Subsequently, police focused attention on foreigners who were fluent in Tibetan, sometimes searching them at Lhasa airport for letters they might be carrying from Tibetan friends.

But in the 1987 events, police punished, not tourists who witnessed or took part in demonstrations, but the six or seven Westerners who were at the time working in Tibet as English teachers. They were deported at short notice, and in one case fined a large amount, for no apparent reason, even though most had legal work permits and had not even seen any protests. These deportations were perhaps meant as a warning to other tourists, or perhaps as a warning to Tibetans who were learning English from them. Since that time almost no Westerners have been allowed into Tibet as resident teachers, apart from members of fundamentalist Christian organizations, whose presence appears to be welcomed by the authorities, presumably because they disdain Buddhism and any involvement in Tibetan politics.

95
How do religious leaders and the residents of Lhasa view these riots since September 1987?

Local people and religious leaders in Tibet have been incensed by the riots and condemned the "handful of separatists" who instigated the riots in coordination with the Dalai clique in an effort to split Tibet from China. Several religious figures publicly condemned these actions and the part played in them by monks—the Banchen Erdeni [the Panchen Lama], Cemolin Danzengchilie [Tenzin Trinley], and others. The majority of the population of Lhasa are firmly opposed to the riots. These separatists are few in number, they are criminals who are controlled by the exiles, and they do not represent the will of the Tibetan people and are unpopular.

Robert Barnett

It is illegal in Tibet or China to express views that criticize the authorities or their actions, if these views question the supremacy of the Communist Party or the socialist system, territorial claims, or other political principles. This was made clear to Tibetans in December 1987 by the highly publicized arrest of the Tibet University lecturer Yulu Dawa Tsering (see Question 90), who was given a ten-year sentence for a conversation he had had six months earlier at a private dinner in his cousin's house, in which he had mildly criticized Chinese policy. It would therefore not be surprising if few people in Tibet were to praise demonstrators, even in private.

There are many Tibetans who have doubts about the methods and aims pursued by demonstrators, especially when those have led to violence or to state crackdowns and to the withdrawal of earlier concessions. There may also be a number who are suspicious of the exile leadership. But even these same Tibetans are likely to sympathize broadly with the protesters' objective of removing or at least drastically reducing Chinese presence and influence in the region. This almost certainly applies to a number of Tibetan leaders too, though no one will say this in public. Indications of these views are discernible from a widely circulated tape-recording of an internal discussion between the Panchen Lama and two other senior Tibetan leaders, in which all three appear to agree that public statements made by them or their colleagues are lies (transcript of tape recording of Panchen Lama's talk at the China Tibetology Institute).

96

WHY WERE FOREIGNERS NOT ALLOWED TO TRAVEL NOR FOREIGN REPORTERS PERMITTED TO COVER NEWS IN TIBET DURING RIOTS?

Tibet is an area of China that is open to the outside world and foreigners, tourists and journalists are welcome there. During the riots there was only a short period when tourists were not allowed in, for safety reasons. Foreign journalists who wish to go to Tibet should submit a request to the Foreign Affairs Bureau of the TAR, and a number of foreign journalists have already visited.

ROBERT BARNETT

Almost all of Tibet in fact remains closed to foreigners. Although most areas of the former Tibetan province of Kham, now parts of Sichuan and Yunnan, were opened to tourists in spring 1999, as of 2007 no foreigner could enter the TAR without a special invitation or as a member of a tour group that had obtained special permission (see Question 82). Such restrictions do not exist anywhere in China proper. Once they have entered the TAR, foreigners can leave their group and travel as individuals—but only to Lhasa and Shigatse, and along the main roads to Qinghai and Nepal. An additional permit is required for any other place in the TAR. Foreigners found in closed areas are regularly fined, detained, or even deported. Foreign journalists still require a permit in order to visit the TAR, and these permits are rarely given.

97
After the riots in Lhasa, were any leaders of the Tibet Autonomous Region dismissed or promoted? Are more soldiers or policemen to be sent to Tibet?

The riots were instigated by a handful of splittists and so were quickly subdued. No leaders were dismissed or promoted because of the riots, and the state did not need to send any more soldiers and policemen.

Robert Barnett

History has been unkind to the writers of *100 Questions*: in March 1989, a few months after the book was first produced, 10,000 or more Tibetans took part in a pro-independence demonstration, which continued for three days, and the Chinese responded by sending at least 14,000 extra troops into Tibet. The whole region was placed under martial law and handed over to the PLA for thirteen months, the first time in the history of the PRC that martial law had been formally declared in a part of its territory.

Even before *100 Questions* was published, it was clear that moderate leaders in Tibet were going to lose their positions because of the earlier demonstrations. In mid 1988, the then Party secretary of the TAR, Wu Jinghua, a member of the Yi nationality who was popular among Tibetans, was dismissed for "right deviationism," meaning he was too moderate in policy (Wang Xiaoqiang 1994). He was replaced in December 1988 by Hu Jintao, later to become China's president, and regarded as hard-line on Tibet issues, who imposed martial law in 1989. He was succeeded in 1992 by Chen Kuiyuan, a Chinese cadre specializing in dealing with "frontier minorities," who is associated with ultraconservative policies toward Tibetan culture and any expression of dissent (Barnett 2003). Other sackings followed: in January 1993, the popular mayor of Lhasa, Loga, was dismissed, reportedly because of his failure to criticize those involved in the protests with sufficient rigor; a move to dismiss him in June 1990 had been delayed because of popular support for him at the time.

98
WHAT COUNTERMEASURES HAVE THE TIBETAN AUTHORITIES TAKEN SINCE THE RIOTS? ARE THE MASSES ALLOWED TO HOLD PARADES AND DEMONSTRATIONS?

Measures have been taken to intensify education on patriotism and national unity, and to denounce and expose separatist plots. In line with the Party's nationalities and religion policy, Tibet's economic and cultural development is being accelerated. All demonstrations are permitted in Lhasa, provided they obey regulations issued on October 9, 1987. According to the regulations, any assemblies that do not have prior police approval, which take place in the Barkor area [the Old City], or which encourage splittism or undermine national unity are forbidden. Those who contravene these regulations, who are involved in violence during a demonstration, or who interfere with the functioning of state institutions or infringe the law in any manner are liable to criminal proceedings.

ROBERT BARNETT

A number of demonstrations have been allowed since these rules were issued—in one, university students held a march about language rights in December 1988, which avoided the Barkor area. Some brief street protests against price increases in the city were also allowed. In May 1993, Tibetans led a march through the new areas of the city protesting against educational and medical fees without problem until the marchers approached the Barkor area and began to call for independence, at which point the protest was violently broken up by police.

This relative tolerance changed in May 1994 when a tax protest by shopkeepers was also violently broken up by police. The new hard-line leadership in the TAR had ruled that demonstrations about what they called "hot topics in society"—inflation, unemployment, immigration, prices, and so on—were in fact disguised methods by supporters of the Dalai Lama to disrupt society in order to promote Tibetan independence (see TIN 1994c). Even though the rest of the PRC has become more open in terms of economics and access to the outside world, restrictions on political thought and expression have increased in Tibet, and few political demonstrations have been attempted in Lhasa since 1996.

99
WHAT IS THE SITUATION IN TIBET NOW?

In general, the post-riot situation in Tibet is stable and good, because the majority of Tibetans treasure a hard-earned, happy life, stability, and unity. The riots were limited to a small area around Lhasa and involved only 0.5 percent of the Tibetan population. All evidence shows that they did not enjoy popular support.

100
SOME FOREIGN NEWSPAPERS SAID RECENTLY THAT THE TIBET AUTHORITIES HAVE DISPATCHED PEOPLE TO TEMPLES AND MONASTERIES TO THROW OUT THOSE LAMAS AND NUNS WHO PARTICIPATED IN THE RIOTS. IS THIS TRUE?

Some "work teams composed mainly of Tibetans" were sent to some temples and monasteries involved in riots, but their mission was not to pursue lamas. They were sent to help the administration committees of these temples and monasteries to put things back in order, to educate those monks and nuns who were led astray by deceiving propaganda and participated in the riots, and to ferret out major criminals.

ROBERT BARNETT

These two questions are best taken together, since both can be judged by subsequent events. At least 130 pro-independence demonstrations took place in Tibet in the six years after *100 Questions* was first published, including the three-day protest in March 1989 that led to the imposition of martial law. This suggests that the demonstrations did enjoy some popular support. Many of these incidents were reported from rural areas well removed from Lhasa, including parts of Kham and Amdo, many hundreds of miles to the east. After 1989, the "revolving door" policy of arresting thousands of Tibetans for relatively short periods was replaced by a policy of more selective, longer-term arrests. The number of political prisoners in Tibet was estimated in 2000 at around 500 and is believed to have decreased since. Although the security forces have assumed a lower profile since 1990, the numbers of police and soldiers in Tibet have not been reduced, and there has been no change in restrictions on tourists and foreign journalists visiting the area, despite frequent promises by tourism officials (see Question 82). The number of Tibetans fleeing to India via Nepal has remained at around 2,500 a year since 1990, a large proportion of them from rural areas of eastern Tibet. These figures strongly suggest that many Tibetans are unhappy with the Chinese regime and support the Dalai Lama. In March 2006, thousands of Tibetans publicly burnt animal furs after the Dalai Lama called for an end to the killing of endangered species (see Question 88), and in July, some 8,000 Tibetans gathered near his birthplace in Qinghai after a rumor spread that he might be allowed to visit.

The restrictions on religion since the Third Tibet Work Forum (1994) described in Part V above remain in place. The "patriotic education" drive that required each monk and nun in the TAR to sign a written document denouncing the Dalai Lama, led to some major demonstrations in monasteries, a number of reported deaths of monks in custody, and hundreds of expulsions of monks and nuns from their institutions.

Chinese leaders in Tibet continue to say that the struggle against "the splittists" is still "intense" and "grim." Since there have been few demonstrations as of 1996, this suggests that opposition to the Chinese and support for the Dalai Lama are widespread and cover all areas of Tibetan society—including rural communities and even some relatively senior figures within the administration—and remain a permanent concern for the Chinese leaders.

Since 1995, Beijing seems to have decided that the problem of political opposition in Tibet is not limited to a "handful of splittists," supposedly instigated by the exiles in Dharamsala, but is rooted in Tibetan culture. Officials then began to put pressure on (though not, as some have claimed, to destroy) Tibetan culture and religion, such as diminishing the status of translation projects, ending secondary school teaching in Tibetan in the TAR, rewriting textbooks used at the University of Tibet, the early retirement of some Tibetan scholars, and a two-year ban on admission of students to the Tibetan Department of the university.

These pressures on cultural life have been combined with the rapid acceleration of a market economy in the region (see Part VIII above), which has led, often beneficially, to dramatic shifts in urban culture. Mobile phones, private houses and vehicles, fax machines, luxury commodities, and computers have all become available. For the new Tibetan middle class, whose salaries and bonuses have surged, these developments have brought enhanced opportunities for wealth, travel, and leisure. As already noted, they have also exposed Tibetans to direct and unequal competition with Chinese entrepreneurs and have marginalized some sectors. At the same time, re-strictions on travel and access have not diminished for much of the popu-lation, and there has been a major effort to diminish the role and standing of religion in Tibetan society. In addition, the role of Tibetan language and culture has been reduced. Rigid demands by propaganda teams requiring obedience to the Communist Party still dominate the media and the legal and political systems, probably more than they did fifteen years ago. The policy of economic relaxation remains in contradiction with the ongoing political rigidity in the region.

A COMPARATIVE CHRONOLOGY

OF TIBET AND CHINA

Tibet	China
	Tang Dynasty, 618–907

617–649/650 Songtsen Gampo defeats and brings under his rule several independent kingdoms, including Zhangzhung in west. Invention of Tibetan alphabet on basis of Indian script; construction of several Buddhist temples, among them the Jokhang. Beginning of "first diffusion of Buddhism" *(ngadar)*.	618 Tang dynasty established in Chang'an. Period of great territorial expansion.
	629–645 Buddhist monk Xuanzang translates Indian Buddhist texts. Influence of Central Asian cultures on China.
680 Numerous Tibetan incursions into northwestern and central Asia.	
	Eighth century Development of Esoteric *(mizong)* and Chan Buddhism.
742–797 (?) Trisong Detsen, second "Dharma king," makes Buddhism state religion; invites Indian masters Shantarakshita and Padmasambhava; builds Samye, first Buddhist monastery. Main texts of Indian Buddhism translated from Sanskrit into Tibetan. Bön religion repressed. Doctrinal controversy at Samye between Indian	755–763 An Lushan Rebellion.

331

Tibet China

Tang Dynasty, 618–907

---

and Chinese Buddhist factions.
Period of great territorial expansion.

763 Tibetans take the Chinese capital,
Chang'an.

787 Peace treaty between Tang and
Tibetans.

821/822 Sino-Tibetan treaty concluded
in Chang'an. Tibet and China
regarded as two sovereign states.

ca. 842 Death of Langdarma, last Tibetan   842–846 Persecution of Buddhists.
monarch, famous in later sources for
his persecution of Buddhism. End of
"first diffusion of Buddhism."
Establishment of principalities, among
them the kingdom of Ngari in western
Tibet, by Langdarma's descendants.
Dislocation of Tibetan empire following
internal quarrels and military reverses,
such as loss of Dunhuang in 851 (in
the PRC's present-day Gansu province).

Period of the Five Dynasties, 907–960
Song Dynasty, 960–1279

Northern Song, 960–1127

958–1055 Buddhist scholar Rinchen   Economic development; expansion
Zangpo travels from western Tibet to   of literati.
bring back Indian masters, artists, and
texts. Beginning of the "second
diffusion of Buddhism" *(chidar)*.

1042 Arrival of Atisha (whose teachings
form the base of the Kadampa School)
in Tibet, where he dies in 1054.
Tibetans travel to India to study
Buddhism. Founding of Buddhist
monasteries and schools in Tibet,
including Reting monastery (1057)
in central Tibet, by Dromtön, chief
disciple of Atisha; Sakya monastery

Tibet	*China*
	Northern Song, 960–1127

(1073) in Tsang, by Könchog Gyeltsen; and Densathil monastery (1158) in central Tibet, which will become Phagmodrupas' seat.	
	Occupation of northern China by Jin (Jürchen). Chinese court takes refuge in south.

	Southern Song, 1127–1279

	Influence of Buddhism on some literati and appearance of neo-Confucianism.
	1206 Gengis Khan takes power in Mongolia.
1235–1280 Phagpa, nephew of Sakya Pandita (1182–1251), of Khön lineage and Sakyapa order, becomes one of the architects of the "priest-patron" relationship *(chöyön)*. Kublai Khan, future emperor of China and founder of the Yuan dynasty, delegates authority over Tibet to him.	1260 Phagpa is placed in charge of religious communities of northern China.
	1269 Script invented by Phagpa is adopted to transcribe the Mongol language. Translation into Chinese of several works written by Phagpa.

	Yuan Dynasty, 1279–1368

1302–1364 Changchub Gyeltsen, of the Phagmodrupas, based in Neudong (central Tibet), defeats Sakyapas and comes to power in 1358.	China integrated into Mongol empire. Coming of first Western travelers.

	Ming Dynasty, 1368–1644

1357–1419 Tsongkhapa, founder of Gelugpa school, builds Ganden monastery in 1409; later, his disciples construct two other important	Mongols pushed back; beginning of commercial relations with West (coming of Portuguese in sixteenth century). Construction and

Tibet	*China*

monasteries, Drepung in 1416 and Sera in 1419.

1434 Decline of Phagmodrupas, replaced by lords of Ringpung, patrons of Karma kagyüs. They are expelled in 1565 by the kings of Tsang, supporting the "Red Hats" Karmapas.

1578 Sönam Gyatso receives title of Dalai Lama from Altan Khan, chief of Tumed Mongols. His two previous incarnations are retroactively recognized as 1st and 2nd Dalai Lamas.

1588 Death of Sönam Gyatso. His reincarnation, the 4th Dalai Lama, is discovered in Altan Khan's family.

1617–1682 Ngawang Lobsang Gyatso, 5th Dalai Lama.

1642 Gushri Khan, chief of Qoshot Mongols, confers temporal authority over Tibet on 5th Dalai Lama. Construction of Potala Palace begins.

restoration of numerous Buddhist temples.

Construction and restoration of numerous Buddhist temples. Manchus recognize Lamaism as their official religion.

1644–1662 Reign of Shunzhi.

1662–1723 Reign of Kangxi. Construction of Jehol.

1674–1681 Wu Sangui's rebellion against Qing.

1682 Death of 5th Dalai Lama; regent Sangye Gyatso keeps it secret until 1696 to complete Potala.

1683–1705 6th Dalai Lama is uninterested in monastic life and governing. Lhazang Khan, grandson of Gushri Khan, with Chinese support, attacks Lhasa, kills regent, and kidnaps Dalai

Tibet	*China*

Tibet	*China*
Lama, who dies in captivity. Lhazang tries to impose a Dalai Lama of his own choice, whom Tibetans—allied with Dzungars—oppose.	
1717 Tibetans kill Lhazang Khan.	
1720–1757 Manchus install 7th Dalai Lama in 1720 but give him no temporal power.	1723–1735 Reign of Yongzheng.
1728 Pholane, a nobleman (1689–1747), aided by Manchus, becomes ruler of Tibet until his death. *Amban*s in Lhasa. Jesuits and Capuchins arrive in Lhasa.	
1758–1804 8th Dalai Lama, who never wielded power.	1736–1795 Reign of Qianlong. Period of great territorial expansion.
	1750 Qianlong sends an army to Lhasa following anti-Chinese riots.
1788,1791 Gurkhas invade Tsang province and defeat Tibetans.	
	1792 Qianlong sends an army against Gurkhas.
	1796–1814 Uprisings in China.
1805–1875 9th (1805–1815) to 12th (1856–1875) Dalai Lamas die at an early age. Gelugpa regents, supported by Chinese, rule Tibet.	1839 Beginning of Opium Wars.
	1842 Nanking treatise.
	1850–1864 Taiping Rebellion. Decline of Qing.
1876–1933 13th Dalai Lama assumes power in 1895.	1876 Chefoo Convention.
1904 Younghusband expedition to Lhasa and flight of Dalai Lama to Mongolia.	
	1908 Zhao Erh-feng invades eastern Tibet to "restore order."
1909 Dalai Lama returns to Tibet but then escapes to India, fleeing Chinese army.	
	1911 Qing dynasty ends.

Tibet	*China*

Tibet	*China*
1913 13th Dalai Lama proclaims Tibetan independence.	1912 Yuan Shikai becomes first president of Chinese Republic.
1914 Simla Convention. Dalai Lama undertakes reforms.	
1918 Truce of Rongbatse (eastern Tibet) demarcates eastern borders between Tibet and China.	
1923 Escape of 9th Panchen Lama to Mongolia, then to China.	
	1928 Chiang Kai-shek unifies China under his own leadership.
	1934 Beginning of Communist "Long March."
1935 Birth of 14th Dalai Lama in northeastern Tibet.	
1940 Enthronement ceremony of 14th Dalai Lama in Potala.	
1947 Failure of a coup d'état by ex-regent Reting Rinpoche.	

Tibet	*China*
	1949 PRC proclaimed by Mao Zedong on October 1. Nationalist government takes refuge in Taiwan.
1950 PLA invades Tibet.	
1951 17-Point Agreement.	
1955 Uprising in eastern Tibet following forced collectivization.	
	1958 "Great Leap Forward"; enforcement of communes followed by severe famine.
1959 Repression of uprising in Lhasa; escape of Dalai Lama to India.	
	1962 Border conflict between China and India.
1965 Creation of Tibet Autonomous Region.	
1966–1976 Cultural Revolution: destruction of most religious buildings,	1966–1976 Cultural Revolution.

Tibet	*China*
	People's Republic of China, 1949–

books, and sacred images; prohibition of monastic life; imprisonment of many Tibetans.

1976 Death of Mao Zedong.

1978 Deng Xiaoping comes to power. Beginning of a period of relative liberalization. Launching of "Four modernizations" policy.

1970s Reconstruction of some monasteries.

1980 Visit of Hu Yaobang to Tibet; economic and political reforms; relative religious liberalization.

1982 Economic development becomes main Chinese objective.

1987–1989 Demonstrations in Lhasa following a period of repression.

1989 Hu Jintao, Tibet Party secretary, imposes martial law. Nobel Peace Prize awarded to Dalai Lama. Death of 10th Panchen Lama.

1989 Demonstrations in Tiananmen Square. Policy of repression throughout China.

1993 Jiang Zemin becomes president of PRC.

1995 Dalai Lama recognizes 11th Panchen Lama. Panchen Lama is abducted by PRC authorities and replaced by another boy of their choice.

1996 Demonstrations in Lhasa.

1997 Deng Xiaoping dies.

1999 Chinese government represses Falun Gong movement.

2000 17th Karmapa escapes to India.

2001 Construction of Golmud-Lhasa railroad begins. Dalai Lama meets U.S. president. Hu Jintao visits Tibet for commemoration of "Peaceful Liberation of Tibet."

2001 International Olympic Committee selects Beijing to host 2008 Olympic Games. PRC enters World Trade Organization.

2002 PRC and Dharamsala resume contact for first time since 1993.

2003 2nd round of PRC-Dharamsala contacts.

2003 Hu Jintao becomes president of PRC.

Tibet	China
	People's Republic of China, 1949–

2004 3rd round of PRC-Dharamsala contacts.

2005 40th anniversary of TAR; rebuilding and "renovation" of Lhasa begins; 4th round of PRC-Dharamsala contacts.

2006 Golmud-Lhasa railway opened July 1; Tibet-India trade route through Nathu la reopened July 6.

2007 5th round of PRC-Dharamsala contacts.

Altan Khan	Tumed Mongol khan who conferred the title Dalai Lama on Sönam Gyatso in 1578
Amdo [A mdo]	the northeastern part of "ethnic Tibet," incorporated into the present-day Chinese provinces of Qinghai, Sichuan, and Gansu
Amitâbha	[Sanskrit] Tib. *Öpame ['Od dpag med]*, "Buddha of the Infinite Light"
ani [a ne]	lit. "paternal aunt," a common term for a Tibetan nun
Atisha, 958–1054	[Sanskrit] a Bengali monk who came to Tibet in 1042, whose teachings are the basis of the Kadampa school
Avalokiteshvara	[Sanskrit] Tib. Chenrezi [sPyan ras gzigs], the bodhisattva of compassion, protector of Tibet, manifested as Songtsen Gampo and the Dalai Lamas, among others
bardo [bar do]	the intermediate state between death and rebirth
Barkor [Bar skor]	"Middle circumambulation path" surrounding the Jokhang, the great temple of Lhasa
Batang ['Ba' thang]	a city in traditional Kham
Beri [Be ri]	a region of Kham, on the southern bank of the Yalung River [Tib. Nyag chu]; a Bönpo principality until the seventeenth century, then a "semi-independent" state run by hereditary chiefs
Bö [Bod]	the local name of the country called Tibet by Westerners
bodhisattva	[Sanskrit] a person who has vowed to achieve buddhahood but who renounces it in order to work for the welfare of all living beings

339

Bön [Bon]   For Tibetans, the surviving pre-Buddhist religion,
                         codified only in the tenth and eleventh centuries
                         and heavily influenced by Buddhism

Bönpo [bon po]   a follower of the Bön religion

Cagpori [lCags po ri]   "Iron Mountain:" a hill in Lhasa, near the Potala
                         where the College of Medicine founded at the end
                         of the seventeenth century stood

Chadrel Rinpoche [Bya bral rin po che] the abbot of Tashilhünpo monastery,
                         head of the mission commissioned by the Chinese
                         government for the search of the reincarnation of
                         the 10th Panchen Lama

Chamdo [Chab mdo]   "Confluence," a city in Kham, so called because
                         of its location at the confluence of the Ngomchu
                         [Ngom chu] and the Dzachu [rDza chu] Rivers

chang   a kind of beer produced from the fermentation of
                         barley or other cereals

Changchub Gyeltsen [Byang chub rgyal mtshan], 1302–1364 the founder
                         of the Phagmodrupa dynasty, established in central
                         Tibet, at Neudong [sNe'u gdong], who defeated the
                         Sakyapas and took power in 1358

Changtang [Byang thang] "Northern Plateau," with an average altitude of
                         4,500 meters; inhabited only by nomads

Chateng [Cha/Phyag phreng] located in Kham, a Gelugpa monastery since
                         the seventeenth century

chidar [phyi dar]   the second diffusion of Buddhism beginning in the
                         tenth century

Chingwa ['Phying ba]   in the Yarlung Valley, where the royal tombs were
                         located; the old castle of Chingwa Tagtse ['Phying
                         ba stag rtse] is famous as the birthplace of the 5th
                         Dalai Lama

chö [chos] (Sanskrit dharma) the standard term for Buddhism or religion

Chögyel [chos rgyal]   "King ruling according to the Buddhist Law"

chöjung [chos 'byung]   "Origins of the Doctrine," a historiographical genre
                         presenting the history of Buddhism

chölkha-sum [chol kha gsum] "The Three Districts," a territorial division
                         introduced by the Yuan (1276–1368) covering all
                         of "ethnic Tibet"

Chotrül düchen dang conga chöpa [Cho 'phrul dus chen dang bco lnga
                         mchodpa] "Festival of the Great Miracle and the
                         Offerings of the Fifteenth," commemorating the

	Great Miracle performed by the Buddha in Shrâvasti when he defeated the heretics and preached the Law
chöyön [mchod yon]	"Priest and Patron," a politico-religious relation (see Questions 2, 5, and 6)
chuba [phyu pa]	a long coat of wool or sheepskin with very long sleeves, worn by men and women
chura [phyu ra]	dried cheese made from the milk of the female yak *(dri)*
dâkinî	[Sanskrit] female figures personifying Wisdom who appear to tantric practitioners in peaceful or fierce aspects
Derge [sDe dge]	an old independent kingdom of Kham famous for its printing press, particularly for its edition of the Buddhist canon; today's Derge County (TAP of Kandze, Sichuan) is on the eastern border of the TAR

Desi Sangye Gyatso [sDe srid Sangs rgyas rgya mtsho], 1679–1703 the last regent of the 5th Dalai Lama, whose death he concealed for fourteen years while the construction of the Potala was completed

Dingri [Ding ri]	a county *(dzong)* and a small city in Shigatse Prefecture

Döndrup Gyel [Don grub rgyal] a famous writer from Amdo who committed suicide in 1985

Dorje Tseten [rDo rje tshe brtan] a contemporary scholar and politician, former Director of the China Tibetan Studies Center (Beijing)

Dratang [Gra thang]	a monastery founded in the eleventh century, not far from Tsetang
Drepung ['Bras spungs]	one of the three seats of the Gelugpas, founded in 1416, and located to the northwest of Lhasa
dri ['bri]	female yak

Drigungpa ['Bri gung pa] one of the subsects of the Kagyüpa School, named after the monastery founded in 1179 by Jigten Gönpo ['Jig rten mgon po], 1143–1217

drongkyer [grong khyer]	(Chin. *shi*) municipality
düchung [dud chung]	lit. "small smoke," meaning "small household" (see Question 85)

Düsong ['Dus srong] or *Tridu Songtsen [Khri 'du srong btsan], 676–704* a Tibetan emperor

Dzayül [rDza yul]   an area located in southeast Tibet, and south of Chamdo, at the Burmese border

dzong [rdzong]   lit. "fortress": during Changchub Gyeltsen's time, the term came to mean a territorial division; today, it means "county" (Chin. *xian*)

Gaden ngachö [dGa' ldan lnga mchod] a festival commemorating the death of Tsongkhapa (1419)

Galdan Khan [dGa' ldan Khan], 1676–1697   khan of the Dzungar Mongols

Ganden [dGa' ldan]   one of the three seats of the Gelugpas, located about forty kilometers east of Lhasa; founded in 1409 by Tsongkhapa

Gar [mGar]   a powerful clan in the seventh century, whose members held hereditarily the office of Great Councilor

Gartok [sGar tog?]   in western Tibet, one of the two places opened to British trade by the 1904 Lhasa Treaty

Gedün Chökyi Nyima [dGe 'dun chos kyi nyi ma] the 11th Panchen Lama recognized by the Dalai Lama

Gedün Chöphel [dGe 'dun chos 'phel], 1903–1951 a nonconformist Gelugpa monk, scholar, poet, and artist

Gedün Drup [dGe 'dun grub], 1391–1475 a disciple of Tsongkhapa and founder of Tashilhünpo monastery (Tsang), which later became the seat of the Panchen Lamas; regarded as the first Dalai Lama

gekö [dge skos]   a chief monastic disciplinarian

Gelugpa [dGe lugs pa]   lit. "The Virtuous," a Buddhist School founded by Tsongkhapa in the fifteenth century whose leading figures are the Dalai Lama and the Panchen Lama

genyen [dge bsnyen] (Sanskrit *upâsaka*) a lay disciple who has taken five vows

Gesar [Ge sar]   Tibetan epic hero

geshe [dge bshes]   the highest scholastic rank in the Gelugpa curriculum

Geta [dGe stag]   one of the reincarnations of the Gelugpa monastery of Beri, in Kham, who sided with the Communists during the Chinese invasion and died of poisoning in 1950

Godan   grandson of Genghis Khan, son of Ogodai (see Sakya Pandita)

Golok [mGo log]   name of a tribe living in the Amye Machen area and of one of the TAPs of Qinghai

Gongkar [dGongs dkar] a county south of Lhasa where Gongkar Airport was built; also the name of a fifteenth-century Sakya monastery, Gongkar chöde [dGongs dkar chos sde]

Gönpo Tseten [mGon po tshe brtan] one of the candidates for the position of the 9th Panchen Lama

Gushri Khan the head of the Qoshot Mongols, patron of the 5th Dalai Lama, to whom he entrusted power over Tibet in 1642

Gyantse [rGyal rtse] a town in Tsang province dominated by the ruins of the fortress destroyed during the Younghusband expedition in 1904 and famous for the Pelkor Chöde monastery and the monumental Kumbum stupa

Gyaza Belza [rGya bza' Bal bza'] the term for the Chinese and Nepalese wives of Songtsen Gampo

gyelrab [rgyal rabs] "royal chronicles," a historiographical genre that focuses on the succession of the lay and religious leaders of Tibet

Gyeltsen Norbu [rGyal mtshan nor bu] (Chin. *Gyaincain Norbu*) the 11th Panchen Lama recognized by the PRC

Gyurme Namgyel ['Gyur med rnam rgyal] the son of Pholane, who took power at the death of his father (1747) but was soon murdered

Gyüzhi [rGyud bzhi] "The Four Tantras," a fundamental work of Tibetan medicine in four parts

Jampa [Byams pa] (Sanskrit *Maitreya*) the future Buddha

Jang ['Jang] (Chin. *Nanzhao*) an ancient kingdom located in what is now Yunnan province, defeated by the Tibetans in the eighth century

Jokhang [Jo khang] "House of the Lord," the great temple of Lhasa, said to have been founded by Songtsen Gampo's Nepalese wife in the seventh century, and named for an image of the Buddha brought by the Chinese wife of Songtsen Gampo that is the most venerated image in Tibet

Jyekundo [sKye rgu mdo] a town in northwest Kham (in present-day Sichuan)

Kadampa [bKa' gdams pa] the sect of "those who follow the oral instructions," stemming from Atisha's teachings (eleventh century)

Kagyüpa [bKa' brgyud pa] the sect of "those of the oral transmission", its

most famous representatives are Marpa (1012–1097)
and Milarepa (1040–1123)

Kandze [dKar mdzes] (Chin. *Ganzi*) the capital of the TAP of the same
name; located in Kham (in present-day Sichuan)

Kangding (Tib. *Dartsedo [Dar rtse mdo]*), a county in the
Kandze TAP (in present-day Sichuan)

kangso [bskang gso] "to satisfy and restore [the ties with a deity]," a
ritual for propitiating wrathful protective deities

Karmapa [Karma pa] a school of Tibetan Buddhism; one of the subdivisions of the Kagyüpas, founded in the twelfth
century by Düsum Khyenpa [Dus gsum mkhyen
pa], 1110–1193

Kashag [bKa' shag] the cabinet of ministers, the highest government
office in the former Tibet, composed of three lay
officials and a monk

Kashöba [Ka shod pa], 1903–? a lay minister under the 14th Dalai Lama who
was banished to southern Tibet in 1949, accused of
having spread rumors about an imminent war with
the Chinese

kata [kha btags] a ceremonial scarf offered by the Tibetans as a sign
of respect

Kham [Khams] the traditional eastern province of "ethnic Tibet,"
now divided among the Chinese provinces of
Qinghai, Sichuan, and Yunnan

Khampa [Khams pa] a Tibetan from Kham

Khangchene [Khang chen nas] the governor of western Tibet under Pholane
(see "The Qing Dynasty," Question 5)

Khenpo [mkhan po] "abbot"

Khenpo Jigphün mKhan po 'Jigs [med] phun [tshogs] (1933–2004) A high
Nyingmapa lama from Khams, founder of Larung
Gar Buddhist Institute, near the town of Serthar
(Chin. Seda, in present day Sichuan), a vast
monastic encampment

Khyentse Rinpoche [mKhyen brtse rin po che], 1910–1991 a famous
Nyingmapa master from Kham who left Tibet
in 1959 and died in Bhutan

Kumbum [sKu 'bum] (Chin. *Taer si*) an important Gelugpa monastery
of Amdo founded in 1560 at the birthplace of
Tsongkhapa; enlarged by the 3rd Dalai Lama
Sönam Gyatso (1543–1588)

kyang [rkyang] a wild ass

Labrang [Bla brang] (Chin. *Labulang si*) the largest Gelugpa monastery of Amdo, founded in 1709 by Jamyang Zhepa ['Jam dbyangs bzhad pa]

Lama [bla ma] (Sanskrit *guru*) a spiritual master; also a common term for a *trülku*

Langdarma [Glang dar ma], whose real name was Ü Dumtsen [U'i dum btsan], r. 838–841?-842? the last Tibetan emperor, described in later Tibetan sources as the persecutor of Buddhism

Lazang Khan [lHa bzang Khan], ?–1717 eighteenth-century Qoshot Mongol chieftain allied with China who killed the Desi Sangye Gyatso when he learned that the latter had hidden the death of the 5th Dalai Lama, but was himself murdered soon after

Lhagpa Phuntso [lHag pa phun tshogs] the present (2007) director of the China Tibetan Studies Center (Beijing)

Lhalu Tsewang Dorje [lHa klu Tshe dbang rdo rje] a scion of the family of the 12th Dalai Lama who was governor of Kham from 1947 to 1950

Lhasa [lHa sa] — "Place of the Gods," the capital of Tibet since the seventeenth century, and now of the TAR; the Lhasa municipality covers a territory as large as a prefecture's

Lhopa [LHo pa] — people from southeastern Tibet, north and south of the McMahon line

Lhoyül [LHo yul] — "Country of Lho[pa]"; the region where the Lhopas live

Litang [Li thang] — the capital of the county of the same name located in Kham, now part of Sichuan

Loga [Blo dga'] — mayor of Lhasa who had to resign in 1993 following his moderate reactions to demonstrations

Lozang Chöki Gyeltsen [Blo bzang chos kyi rgyal mtshan], 1570–1662 the teacher of the 5th Dalai Lama; the 1st Panchen Lama (according to the Tibetan government) or the 4th (according to the tradition of Tashilhünpo followed by the Chinese)

Lozang/Losang Yeshe [Blo bzang ye shes], 1663–1737 the 2nd Panchen Lama

magpa [mag pa] — "son in law," a term used for the man who marries the daughter(s) of a household without a male heir

Malho [rMa lho] — "South of [the river] Ma[chu]," a TAP in Qinghai

Manglong Mangtsen [Mang slong mang btsan], 649–676 the grandson and successor of Songtsen Gampo

Mañjushrî [Sanskrit] Tib. Jampelyang ['Jam dpal dbyangs], one of the most important bodhisattvas of the Mahâyâna

Markam [sMar kham] the capital of the county of the same name located in Kham, now part of Sichuan

Marpa [Mar pa], 1012–1096 a famous mystic and translator, the master of Milarepa and the first Tibetan in the Kagyüpa lineage, who traveled to India where he received the teachings of Nâropa

Meldro Gungkar [Mal gro gung dkar] the capital of the county of the same name, located about sixty kilometers east of Lhasa

Mentsikhang [sMan rtsis khang] the "Center of medicine and astrology" (see Question 74)

mibog [mi 'bogs] "human lease" (see Question 85)

Milarepa [Mi la ras pa], 1040–1123 the main disciple of Marpa, of the Kagyüpa tradition, famous for his mystical songs

Mönlam chenmo [smon lam chen mo] "The Great Prayer" (see Question 89)

Mönpa [Mon pa] a term used by Tibetans to designate the Tibeto-Burmese populations living in the southern regions of the Himalayas, implying a non-Buddhist person, a barbarian

Mönyul [Mon yul] the region where the Mönpas live

Nagchu [Nag chu] a prefecture located to the north of Lhasa (TAR)

Nagchuka [Nag chu kha] a city located in Nagchu Prefecture

Namri Longtsen [gNam ri slong btsan], 7th century the father of Songtsen Gampo and the 32nd king according to the Tibetan tradition

Nangang [Nang sgang] the name given to the entourage of the Panchen Lamas

Nechung [gNas chung] a monastery founded in the seventeenth century, the residence of the state Oracle until 1959; located below Drepung, west of Lhasa

Ngapo Ngawang Jigme [Nga phod Ngag dbang 'jigs med], 1910– governor of Chamdo (Kham) at the time of the Chinese invasion in 1950 and signatory in 1951 of the 17-Point Agreement

Ngari [mNga' ris] one of the three districts of Ngarikorsum (western Tibet), the others being Purang and Guge; now western TAR

Ngawa [rNga ba] a TAP in present-day Sichuan

Nyarong [Nyag rong] originally, a semi-independent state of Kham, under the Lhasa government from 1865 until its

annexation by Chao Erh-feng at the beginning
of the twentieth century

Nyemo [sNye mo]   a county and a town located northeast of Shigatse

Nyingmapa [rNying ma pa] "The Ancients," a school of Tibetan Buddhism

Nyingtri [Nying khri]   a county in the Nyingtri Prefecture (Kongpo),
southeast of Lhasa

ongkor ['ong skor]   the harvest festival occurring during the first
fortnight of the seventh month (August-September)

Padmasambhava   [Sanskrit] an Indian tantric master, said to have
introduced tantric Buddhism in Tibet in the eighth
century

Panchen Lama Chökyi Gyeltsen [Pan chen bla ma Chos kyi rgyal mtshan]
see Lozang Chöki Gyeltsen

Pelkor Chöde [dPal 'khor chos sde] a monastery in Gyantse (Tsang) founded
by Rabten Künzang [Rab brtan kun bzang] in 1418

Pelyön [dPal yon]   monk and Great Counselor who negotiated the
821–22 treaty with China and was later murdered

Phagmodrupa [Phag mo gru pa] a subsect of the Kagyüpas that became an
important political power in the fourteenth century

Phagpa ['Phags pa], 1235–1280 nephew of Sakya Pandita who was one of the
architects of the "priest-patron" *(chöyön)* relation;
made regent of Tibet by Kublai Khan

Pholane [Pho la nas], 1689–1747 rebelled against the Dzungars and became
the master of Tibet with the aid of the Manchus

Potala [Po ta la]   the Dalai Lamas' winter palace on a hill west of
Lhasa, built by the 5th Dalai Lama

Raidi/Ragdi/Radi [Tib.?] chairman of the standing committee of the
People's Congress of the TAR (1993–2003) and
subsequently (August 2006) vice-chairman of the
National People's Congress in Beijing

Ramoche [Ra mo che]   temple in Lhasa built in the seventh century to
shelter the statue of the Buddha that the Chinese
wife of Songtsen Gampo brought

Reting Rinpoche [Rwa sgreng rin po che] regent from 1934 to 1941; died
in prison in 1947 after a failed coup d'état

rig [rigs]   "social strata"

Rinpoche [rin po che]   "Precious One": title given to reincarnate lamas
and great religious figures

Sagadawa [sa ga zla ba] the festival commemorating the birth, enlightenment, and death of the Buddha

sakhül [sa khul] (Chin. *di qu*) "prefecture"

Sakya Pandita ('Sa pan'), 1182–1251 Sakyapa hierarch appointed to rule Ü and Tsang provinces by the Mongol prince Godan in 1249

Sakyapa [Sa skya pa]   a major sect of Tibetan Buddhism

Samye [bSam yas]   the first Buddhist monastery in Tibet, built by Trisong Detsen in the eighth century

sane zhung [sa gnas gzhung] the government of an area

Sangye Gyatso [Sangs rgyas rgya mtsho] see Desi Sangye Gyatso

Sangye ki chö [sangs rgyas kyi chos] "Doctrine of the Buddha," Buddhism

Sengdong [Seng gdong] one of the candidates for 9th Panchen Lama

Sera [Se ra]   one of the three seats of the Gelugpas

Shâkyamuni [Sanskrit] the name of the historical Buddha

shang (Chin. *shang*)   "township" (sometimes "subdistrict")

Shelkar [Shel dkar]   a town in Tsang whose monastery, Shelkar chöde [Shel dkar chos sde], was founded in 1266 by a Kagyüpa lama, but became Gelugpa in the seventeenth century

Sherpa   a community of Tibetan culture and language (see Question 47)

Shigatse [gZhis ka rtse] the capital of the prefecture of the same name in Tsang and the site of Tashilhünpo monastery

Sönam Gyatso [bSod nams rgya mtsho], 1543–1588 abbot of Drepung monastery who received the title of Dalai Lama from Altan Khan; counted as the 3rd Dalai Lama

Songtsen Gampo [Srong btsan sgam po], 620?-649? the first historical emperor of Tibet

stûpa   originally, funeral monuments erected to house the Buddha's relics, *stûpa*s are among the main monuments of Tibetan Buddhism and contain not only relics of great masters but also texts and other objects

Sumpa [Sum pa]   a population from northeast Tibet subjugated by the Tibetans in the sixth and seventh centuries C.E.

sûtra   [Sanskrit] lit. "aphorism," a text traditionally regarded as having been spoken by Shâkyamuni, although numerous *sûtra*s were composed several centuries after the death of the Buddha

Taktra [sTag brag]   regent from 1941 to 1950

tantra [Sanskrit]   canonical text that appeared in India around the fifth–sixth centuries C.E., traditionally regarded as the esoteric teaching of the Buddha and providing techniques using rituals, meditation, and yoga

Tara Lugong [sTag sgra Klu gong] minister of Trisong Detsen

Tashilhünpo [bKra shis lhun po] the largest monastery in Tsang, seat of the Panchen Lamas

thangka [thang ka] a representation of a sacred image on a cotton or silk scroll (see Question 70)

Tölung Dechen [sTod lung bDe chen] a county in central Tibet, west of Lhasa

torma [gtor ma] a sacrificial cake used during rituals

trelpa [khral pa] "tax-payers" (see Question 85)

Tride Songtsen [Khri lde srong btsan], 800?-871 also called Senaleg [Sad na legs], the son of Trisong Detsen

Tride Tsugtsen [Khri lde gtsug btsan], 704–755 a Tibetan emperor, married to a Chinese princess originally intended for his father Tridu Songtsen (Khri 'du srong btsan, 676–704)

Tripitaka [Sanskrit] "The Three Baskets," the three collections of the early Buddhist canon: *sûtra*, *vinaya*, and *abhidharma* (metaphysics)

Trisong Detsen [Khri srong lde btsan], 742–797? the Tibetan emperor who proclaimed Buddhism as the state religion

Trisong Tsen [Khri srong btsan] or Songtsen Gampo see Songtsen Gampo

Tritsug Detsen [Khri gtsug lde btsan], r. 817–838 or 817–841? a Tibetan emperor better known under the name of Relpacen [Ral pa can]

Tromsikhang [Khrom gzigs khang] "House from which one sees the market," a palace located in the north of the Barkor, built during the time of the 6th Dalai Lama; only the façade survives, the interior having been transformed into a market

trülku [sprul sku] a religious figure regarded as an emanation of a buddha or a bodhisattva

tsampa [rtsam pa] flour of roasted barley, which, mixed with Tibetan tea, was the staple food of the Tibetans

Tsang [gTsang] one of the two provinces of central Tibet, with Shigatse as the main town

Tsangpo [gTsang po] river that crosses Tibet from west to east and becomes the Brahmaputra in India

tsenpo [btsan po] "the mighty one": title given to Tibetan monarchs of the imperial period

Tsetang [rTse thang] the capital of Lhokha prefecture, regarded as the cradle of the Tibetan people

Tsochang [mTsho byang] "North of the lake [Koko Nor]": TAP in Qinghai

Tsolho [mTsho lho] "South of the lake [Koko Nor]": TAP in Qinghai

Tsongkhapa [Tsong kha pa], *1357–1419* the founder of the Gelugpa School, who emphasized monastic discipline and the importance of the gradual path to enlightenment

Tsonub [mTsho nub] "West of the lake [Koko Nor]": TAP in Qinghai

Tsurphu [mTshur phu] the seat of the Karmapas, founded in 1189, located in Tölung Dechen

tukpa [thug pa] soup made with noodles, flour balls, and small pieces of meat

Ü [dBus] "Center": one of the two provinces of central Tibet, with Lhasa, the capital, as the most important city

ulag ['u lag] corvée owed by Tibetans to a local lord, monastery, or the state

Xining [Tib. Zi ling] the capital of Qinghai

Yarlung [Yar lung] a valley in the southeast of Lhasa, the cradle of the Tibetan royal dynasty

Yushu [Tib. sKye rgu mdo] TAP in Qinghai

Zhalu [Zha lu] monastery built in 1040 near Shigatse, famous for its mural paintings and its Chinese-style roof; the seat of the Zhalupas, a school founded by Butön Rinchendrup (1290–1364)

Zhamar [Zhwa dmar] Karmapa "Red Hat," the name of a Karmapa lineage founded in the thirteenth century, whose main seat since the fifteenth century has been the monastery of Yangpachen [Yang pa can], north of Tsurphu

Zhanag [Zhwa nag] Karmapa "Black Hat," the oldest lineage of the Karma kagyü School, founded in the twelfth century, and established at Tsurphu Monastery

Zhangzhung [Zhang zhung] independent kingdom to the west of Tibet that was defeated and incorporated into Tibet in the seventh century

zhelngo [zhal ngo] an officer in charge of twenty-five soldiers in the traditional Tibetan army; a term for *gekö* in some monasteries

zhotön [zho ston] the "Yogurt Feast" (see Questions 68 and 89)

zhung [gzhung] "government"

Adhe, Tapongtsang. 1997. *Ama Adhe: The Voice That Remembers: The Heroic Story of a Woman's Fight to Free Tibet*. Boston.

Alexander, André. 2005. *The Temples of Lhasa: Tibetan Buddhist Architecture from the 7th to the 21st Centuries*. Tibet Heritage Fund's Conservation Inventory, vol. 1. Chicago.

Alexander, André, and Pimpim de Azevedo. 1998. *The Old City of Lhasa: Report from a Conservation Project*. Tibet Heritage Fund, VI. Berlin.

Alme, Oystein, and Morten Vågen. 2006. *Silenced—China's Great Wall of Censorship*. Stockholm.

Anand, R. P. 1969. "The Status of Tibet in International Law." *International Studies* 10, 4: 401–45.

Ani, Pachen, and Adelaide Donnelley. 2000. *Sorrow Mountain: The Remarkable Story of a Tibetan Warrior Nun*. New York.

Arpi, Claude. 1999. *The Fate of Tibet: When Big Insects Eat Small Insects*. New Delhi.

Avedon, John F. 1984. *In Exile from the Land of Snows*. New York. Reissued as *In Exile from the Land of Snows: The Definitive Account of the Dalai Lama and Tibet since the Chinese Conquest* (New York, 1997).

Barnett, Robert, ed. 1998a. *A Poisoned Arrow—The Secret Report of the 10th Panchen Lama*. London.

———. 1998b. "Lhasa, la ville illisible." In *Tibétains, 1959–1999: 40 ans de colonisation*, ed. Katia Buffetrille and Charles Ramble, 129–62. Paris.

———. 2003. "Chen Kuiyuan and the Marketisation of Policy." In *Tibet and Her Neighbours*, ed. Alex McKay, 229–39. London.

———. 2005. "Women and Politics in Contemporary Tibet." In *Women in Tibet*, ed. Janet Gyatso and Hanna Havnevik, 285–366. New York.

———. 2006. *Lhasa: Streets with Memories*. New York.

Barnett, Robert, and Shirin Akiner, eds. 1994. *Resistance and Reform in Tibet*. London.

Bass, Catriona. 1998. *Education in Tibet: Policy and Practice since 1950*. London.

Bauer, Kenneth. 2006. "State and Range: Pastoral Development Policies in the TAR since 1951." Paper presented at the 10th International Conference of the IATS. Oxford, September 2003.

Becker, Jasper. 1996. *Hungry Ghosts: Mao's Secret Famine.* New York.

Beijing Review. 1992. *White Paper on Tibet.* Beijing.

Brandt, H. Loren, Huang Jikun, Li Guo, and Scott Rozelle. 2002. "Land Right in Rural China: Facts, Fictions and Issues." *China Journal* 47: 67–97.

Buffetrille, Katia. 1989. "La restauration du monastère de bSam yas: Un exemple de la continuité de la relation chapelain-donateur au Tibet?" *Journal Asiatique* 277, 3–4: 363–411.

Buffetrille, Katia, and Charles Ramble, eds. 1998. *Tibétains, 1959–1999: 40 ans de colonisation.* Paris.

Burjgin, Jirgal, and Naran Bilik. 2003. "Contemporary Mongolian Population Distribution, Migration, Cultural Change and Identity." In *China's Minorities on the Move: Selected Case Studies,* ed. A. Iredale et al., 53–68. New York.

Cannon, Terry, and Alan Jenkins, eds. 1990. *The Geography of Contemporary China: The Impact of Deng Xiaoping's Decade.* London.

Chayet, Anne. 1994. *Art et archéologie du Tibet.* Paris.

———. 1997. "Pays réel et pays sacré, réflexions sur les toponymes tibétains." In *Les habitants du toit du monde: Études recueillies en hommage à Alexander W. Macdonald,* ed. Samten Karmay and Philippe Sagant, 35–51. Nanterre.

Childs, Geoffrey. 2003. "Namas *(mna'-ma)* and Nyelus *(nyal-bu):* Marriage, Fertility, and Illegitimacy in Tibetan Societies." Paper read at the 10th Conference of the IATS, Oxford, September 2003.

Childs, Geoffrey, M. C. Goldstein, Ben Jiao, and C. M. Beall. 2005. "Tibetan Fertility Transitions in China and South Asia." *Population and Development Review* 31, 2 (June): 337–49.

China Daily. 1998. Interview with the Panchen Lama. September 29.

———. 2005. "Changes Transform Childbirth in Tibet." January 19.

China Directory [Zhongguo zu zhi bie ren ming bu]. Annual. Tokyo. In Mandarin with pinyin transliteration.

China Tibet Information Center. 2005. "Tibet Becomes Attractive Tourist Destination." http://info.tibet.cn/en/news/tin/t20051124_73634.htm (accessed March 25, 2007).

Choedon, Dhondub. 1978. *Life in the Red Flag People's Commune.* Dharamsala.

Chu Yushan and Liu Jiyuan. 1992. *Land Use of Tibet Autonomous Region.* Compiled by Tibet Land Use and Management Bureau. Beijing.

Coleman, William M. 1998. *Writing Tibetan History: The Discourses of Feudalism and Serfdom in Chinese and Western Historiography.* Ann Arbor, Mich.

Conner, Victoria, and Robert Barnett. 1997. *Leaders in Tibet: A Directory.* London.

Dalai Lama, 14th [Tenzin Gyatso]. 1962. *My Land and My People: The Memoirs of H.H. the Dalai Lama of Tibet.* London.

David-Neel, Alexandra. 1930. *La vie surhumaine de Guésar de Ling, le héros thibétain.* Paris. Translated as *The Superhuman Life of Gesar of Ling the Legendary Tibetan Hero* (London, 1933; reprint, New York, 1978).

Deshayes, Laurent. 1997. *Histoire du Tibet*. Paris.

Diemberger, Hildegard. 2005. "Female Oracles in Modern Tibet." In *Women in Tibet*, ed. Janet Gyatso and Hanna Havnevik, 113–68. New York.

Domenach, Jean-Luc, and Philippe Richer. 1987. *La Chine, 1949–1985*. 2 vols. Paris.

Dorje, Gyurme. 1996. *Tibet Handbook with Bhutan*. Chicago.

Dreyfus, Georges B. J. 2001. *The Sound of Two Hands Clapping: The Education of a Tibetan Buddhist Monk*. Berkeley, Calif.

Feng Jianhua. 2005. "Reducing Infant Mortality." *Beijing Review* 48, 26 (June 30).

Fischer, Andrew M. 2002. *Poverty by Design: The Economics of Discrimination in Tibet*. Montréal.

———. 2004. *Urban Fault Lines in Shangri-La: Population and Economic Foundations of Inter-ethnic Conflict in the Tibetan Areas of Western China*. London School of Economics and Political Science, Crisis States Programme, Working Paper No. 42. London.

———. 2005. *State Growth and Social Exclusion in Tibet: Challenges of Recent Economic Growth*. Copenhagen.

Ford, Robert. 1957. *Captured in Tibet*. London.

Gernet, Jacques. 1972. *Le monde chinois*. Paris.

Gittings, John. 2002. "Cultural Clash in Land on the Roof of the World." *Guardian* (London), February 8.

Goldstein, Melvyn C. 1973. "The Circulation of Estates in Tibet: Reincarnation, Land and Politics." *Journal of Asian Studies* 32, 3: 445–54.

———. 1986. "Re-examining Choice, Dependency and Command in the Tibetan Social System—'Tax Appendages' and Other Landless Serfs." *Tibet Journal* 11, 4: 79–112.

———. 1988. "On the Nature of Tibetan Peasantry." *Tibet Journal* 13, 1: 61–65.

———. 1989. *A History of Modern Tibet: The Demise of the Lamaist State, 1913–1951*. Berkeley, Calif.

———. 1997. *The Snow Lion and the Dragon: China, Tibet, and the Dalai Lama*. Berkeley, Calif.

———. 1998. "The Revival of Monastic Life in Drepung Monastery." In *Buddhism in Contemporary Tibet. Religious Revival and Cultural Identity*, ed. id. and Matthew T. Kapstein, 15–52. Berkeley, Calif.

Goldstein, Melvyn C., and Cynthia M. Beall. 1989. *Nomads of Western Tibet. The Survival of a Way of Life*. London.

Goldstein, Melvyn C., B. Jiao, Cynthia M. Beall, and Phuntsog Tsering. 2002. "Fertility and Family Planning in Rural Tibet." *China Journal* 47 (January): 19–40.

———. 2003. "Development and Change in Rural Tibet: Problems and Adaptations." *Asian Survey* 43, 5: 758–79.

Goldstein, Melvyn C., William Siebenschuh, and Tashi Tsering. 1997. *The Struggle for Modern Tibet. The Autobiography of Tashi Tsering*. Armonk, N.Y.

Goldstein, Melvyn C., Dawei Sherap, and William R. Siebenschuh. 2004. *A Tibetan Revolutionary: The Political Life and Times of Bapa Phüntso Wangye*. Berkeley, Calif.

Goodman, D. 2004. "Qinghai and the Emergence of the West: Nationalities, Communal Interaction and National Integration." *China Quarterly* 178 (June): 379–99.

Grousset, René. 1941. *L'empire des steppes.* Paris.

Grunfeld, A. Tom. 1988. "Independence Is Second to Dalai Lama's Return." *Far Eastern Economic Review,* October 13.

Gyatso, Janet, and Hanna Havnevik, eds. 2005. *Women in Tibet.* New York.

Harrell, Stevan, ed. 2001. *Perspectives on the Yi of Southwest China.* Berkeley, Calif.

Harris, Nancy S., et al. 2001. "Nutritional and Health Status of Tibetan Children Living at High Altitudes." *New England Journal of Medicine* 344: 341–47.

Heath, John. 2005. *Tibet and China in the Twenty-first Century.* London.

Heller, Amy. 1993. "La sauvegarde des monuments historiques." In *Tibet, l'envers du décor,* ed. O. Moulin, 177–82. Geneva.

Hulme, Bill, Tom Ingram, and David Lonsdale-Eccles. 2000. "Seven Weeks in Tibet." *Student BMJ* [British Medical Journal], 08 (May): 131–74. www.studentbmj.com/issues/00/05/life/160.php (accessed February 17, 2007).

Human Rights Watch. 1996. *Cutting off the Serpent's Head: Tightening Control in Tibet, 1994–1995.* New York.

Hussain, Athar. 2003. *Urban Poverty in China: Measurement, Patterns and Policies.* InFocus Programme on Socio-Economic Security. Geneva. www.ilo.org/public/english/protection/ses/download/docs/china.pdf (accessed February 17, 2007).

Intercontinental Pan-Chinese Network Information Co. 2001. *100 Questions and Answers about Tibet.* Beijing. www.tibet.cn/tibetzt/question_e/index.htm (accessed February 17, 2007).

International Campaign for Tibet [cited as ICT]. 1990. *Forbidden Freedoms. Beijing's Control of Religion in Tibet.* Washington, D.C.

International Commission of Jurists [cited as ICJ]. 1960. *Tibet and the Chinese People's Republic: A Report to the International Commission of Jurists.* Geneva.

Iredale, Robyn, Naran Bilik, Wang Su, et al. 2001. *Contemporary Minority Migration, Education, and Ethnicity in China.* Cheltenham, U.K.

Jagou, Fabienne. 2000. "Le contrôle des marches sino-tibétaines à l'époque de la Chine républicaine." *Géographie et cultures* 34: 5–23.

Jamyang Norbu. 1994. "The Tibetan Resistance Movement and the Role of the C.I.A." In Barnett and Akiner 1994: 186–96.

Ji Youquan. 1993. *Xizang pingpan jishi* [An Account of the Suppression of Tibet]. Beijing.

Jing Wei, ed. 1988. *Le Tibet: Cent questions et réponses.* Beijing.

———. 1989. *100 Questions about Tibet.* Beijing.

———. *100 Questions and Answers about Tibet.* 2001. Beijing.

Karmay, Samtem G. 1994. "Mountain Cults and National Identity in Tibet." In Barnett and Akiner 1994: 112–20.

Karmay, Samtem G., and Philippe Sagant. 1998. *Les neuf forces de l'homme: Récits des confins du Tibet.* Nanterre.

Knaus, John K. 1999. *Orphans of the Cold War: America and the Tibetan Struggle for Survival.* New York.

Knight, John, and Lina Song. 1999. *The Rural-Urban Divide: Economic Disparities and Interactions in China.* Oxford.

Kunsang Paljor. 1977. *Tibet: The Undying Flame.* Dharamsala.

Kvaerne, Per. 1994. "The Ideological Impact on Tibetan Art." In Barnett and Akiner 1994: 166–85.

———. 1998. "Le Bön, l'autre religion." In Buffetrille and Ramble 1998: 58–73.

Li Xiao. 2002. "Tibet to Popularize Compulsory Education by 2010." October 26. www.china.org.cn/english/2002/Oct/46880.htm (accessed May 24, 2007).

Liu, Yi, and Lin Chusheng. 2001. "The Tax Division Scheme: Central-Local Financial Relations in the 1990s." In *China's Regional Disparities: Issues and Policies,* ed. V. F. S. Sit and D. Lu, 85–104. Huntington, N.Y.

Lo Bue, Erberto. 2004. "Problems of Conservation of Murals in Tibetan Temples." At the 2nd International Conference on Tibetan Archeology and Arts (Beijing, September 5, 2004) and at the International Conference on Traditional Architecture and Murals Conservation (Lhasa, September 24, 2004).

Lobsang. 1989. "The Memory of the Panchen Lama." *China in Focus* 37. Beijing.

Lopez, Donald S., Jr. 1998. *Prisoners of Shangri-La: Tibetan Buddhism and the West.* Chicago.

———. 2006. *The Madman's Middle Way: Reflections on Reality of the Tibetan Monk Gendun Chopel.* Chicago.

Ma Yin, ed. 1989. *China's Minority Nationalities.* Beijing.

MacInnis, D. E. 1989. *Religion in China Today: Policy and Practice.* Maryknoll, N.Y. Includes translation of the CCP's "Document 19."

MacLean, M. G. H., ed. 1993. *Cultural Heritage in Asia and the Pacific: Conservation and Policy.* Proceedings of a Symposium Held in Honolulu, Hawaii, September 8–13, 1991, Organized by the U.S. Committee of the International Council on Monuments and Sites for the U.S. Information Agency with the Cooperation of the Getty Conservation Institute. Marina Del Rey, Calif.

Marshall, Steven D. 1999. *Hostile Elements: A Study of Political Imprisonment in Tibet, 1987–1998.* London.

———. 2000. *Rukhag 3: The Nuns of Drapchi Prison.* London.

———. 2001. *Suppressing Dissent. Hostile Elements II—Political Imprisonment in Tibet, 1987–2000.* London.

———. 2002. *In the Interests of the State. Hostile Elements III—Political Imprisonment in Tibet, 1987–2001.* London.

Marshall, Steven, and Suzette Cooke. 1997. *Tibet outside the TAR.* Alliance for Research in Tibet. Distributed as a CD-ROM by the International Campaign for Tibet. Washington, D.C.

Meyer, Fernand. 1981. *Gso-ba rig-pa: Le système médical tibétain.* Paris.

Michael, Franz. 1986. "Tibetan Traditional Polity and Its Potential for Modernisation." *Tibet Journal* 11, 4: 70–78.

———. 1987. "Letter to the Editor: Tibetan Social System." *Tibet Journal* 13, 3: 78.

Miller, Beatrice D. 1987. "A Response to Goldstein's 'Re-examining Choice, Dependency and Command in the Tibetan Social System.'" *Tibet Journal* 12, 2: 65–67.

———. 1988. "Last Rejoinder to Goldstein Social System." *Tibet Journal* 13, 3: 64–66.

Naughton, Barry. 2002. "Provincial Economic Growth in China: Causes and Consequences of Regional Differentiation." In *China and Its Regions: Economic Growth and Reform in Chinese Provinces*, ed. M.-F. Renard, 57–86. Cheltenham, U.K.

Palden Gyatso. 1997. *The Autobiography of a Tibetan Monk*. Translated from the Tibetan by Tsering Shakya. New York.

Parfianovic, Yuri, and Gyurme Dorje, eds. 1992. *Tibetan Medical Paintings: Illustrations to the "Blue Beryl" Treatise of Sangye Gyamtso (1653–1705)*. London.

Pelliot, Paul. 1961. *Histoire ancienne du Tibet*. Paris.

People's Daily [Renmin Ribao]. 2001. "Fewer Prisoners in Tibet on Charges of Threatening State Security." May 20.

People's Daily Online. 2005. http://english.people.com.cn. March 31.

People's Republic of China [cited as PRC]. 1993. *Zhongguo gongchandang Xizang zizhiqu zuzhishi ziliao 1950–1987* [Materials on the History of the CCP in the TAR from 1950 to 1987]. Lhasa.

———. Information Office of the State Council. 1999. *La politique chinoise à l'égard des ethnies minoritaires et son application*. Beijing.

———. 2001. "Statistical Communiqué of PRC on 2000 National Economic and Social Development." January 1.

———. National Bureau of Statistics. Department of Population, Social, Science and Technology Statistics. 2002. *Tabulation on the 2000 Population Census of the People's Republic of China*. Beijing.

———. National Bureau of Statistics. Department of Population, Social, Science and Technology Statistics. Various years. *China Statistical Yearbook* [cited as *CSY*]. Beijing.

———. National Bureau of Statistics. Various years. *China Population Statistical Yearbook* [cited as *CPSY*]. Beijing.

———. Qinghai Bureau of Statistics. Various years. *Qinghai Statistical Yearbook* [cited as *QSY*]. Beijing.

———. Tibet Bureau of Statistics. Various years. *Tibet Statistical Yearbook* [cited as *TSY*]. Beijing.

Petech, Luciano. 1972. *China and Tibet in the Early XVIIIth Century*. Leiden.

———. 1973. *Aristocracy and Government in Tibet: 1728–1959*. Rome.

———. 1990. *Central Tibet and the Mongols: The Yüan–Sa-skya Period of Tibetan History*. Rome.

Powers, John. 2004. *History as Propaganda: Tibetan Exiles versus the People's Republic of China*. Oxford.

Ricca, Franco. 1999. *Il tempio oracolare di gNas chung: Gli dei del Tibet più magico e segreto.* Turin.

Richardson, Hugh E. 1993. *Ceremonies of the Lhasa Year.* London.

Saklani, Girija. 1978. "The Hierarchical Pattern of Tibetan Society." *Tibet Journal* 3, 4: 27–33.

Samuel, Geoffrey. 1995. *Civilized Shamans: Buddhism in Tibetan Societies.* Washington, D.C.

Sautman, Barry, and June Teufel Dreyer, eds. 2006. *Contemporary Tibet: Politics, Development and Society in a Disputed Region.* Armonk, N.Y.

Schuh, Dieter. 1988. *Das Archiv des Klosters bKra-shis-bsam-gtan-gling von sKyid-grong.* Bonn.

Schwartz, Ronald D. 1994. *Circle of Protest: Political Ritual in the Tibetan Uprising.* New York.

Shakabpa, Tsepon W. D. 1967. *Tibet. A Political History.* New Haven, Conn. Reprint, New York, 1984.

Shakya, Tsering. 1994. "The Genesis of the Sino-Tibetan Agreement of 1951." In *Tibetan Studies: Proceedings of the 6th Seminar of the International Association for Tibetan Studies, Fagernes, 1992,* ed. Per Kvaerne 2: 739–54. Oslo.

———. 1999. *The Dragon in the Land of Snows: A History of Modern Tibet since 1947.* London.

———. 2000. "'The Waterfall and Fragrant Flowers': Literature or Propaganda? The Development of Tibetan Literature since 1950." *Mânoa: A Pacific Journal of International Writing* 12, 2: 28–40. See also www.tibet.net/en/tibbul/2001/0107/shakya.html (accessed June 21, 2007).

Smith, Warren W., Jr. 1996. *Tibetan Nation: A History of Tibetan Nationalism and Sino-Tibetan Relations.* Boulder, Colo.

Sperling, Elliot. 1994. "The Rhetoric of Dissent: The Intellectual Milieu of Tibetan Pamphleteers." In Barnett and Akiner 1994: 267–84.

[Spiegel, Mickey]. 2004. *Trials of a Tibetan Monk: The Case of Tenzin Delek.* New York.

Stoddard, Heather. 1985. *Le mendiant de l'Amdo.* Nanterre.

———. 1988. "The Long Life of rDo-sbyis dGe-bshes Shes-rab rGya-mtsho (1884–1968)." In *Studia Tibetica,* ed. Helga Uebach and Panglung Rinpoche, 2: 465–72. Munich.

———. 1994a. "Don grub rgyal (1953–1985): Suicide of a Modern Tibetan Writer and Scholar." In *Tibetan Studies: Proceedings of the 6th Seminar of the International Association for Tibetan Studies, Fagernes, 1992,* ed. Per Kvaerne, 2: 825–36. Oslo.

———. 1994b. "Tibetan Publications and National Identity." In Barnett and Akiner 1994: 121–56.

———. 2000. "La peinture contemporaine à la fin du XXe siècle." *Action poétique* 157: 61–67.

Tan Hongkai. 2000. "Experts on Tibet Have More Work to Do." *People's Daily* [*Renmin Ribao*], June 13. Translated June 13, 2000, www.tibet.ca/en/wtnarchive/2000/6/13–2_3.html (accessed February 17, 2007).

Teufel Dreyer, June. 2003. "Economic Development in Tibet under the People's Republic of China," *Journal of Contemporary China* 12, 36: 411–30.

Thöndrupgyäl. 2007. *L'artiste tibétain (Sha dang rus pa'i brtse dungs).* Translated by Françoise Robin. Paris.

Tibetan Centre for Human Rights and Democracy [TCHRD; www.tchrd.org]. 2001. "Drapchi Prison: Tibet's Most Dreaded Prison." August. Dharamsala.

———. 2005. "Tibetan Prisoner Serving Life Sentence Dies in Prison." February 4. Dharamsala. www.studentsforafreetibet.org/article.php?id=529 (accessed February 28, 2007).

———. 2006. "Commentary Manuscript Lands Tibetan Youth Ten Years in Prison." Press Release. July 25. Dharamsala.

Tibet Daily (Xizang Ribao). 1990. May 8. See BBC Summary of World Broadcasts, May 22, 1990, for the Lhasa TV version.

———. 1998. "Tibet Leader Raidi's Work Report." July 29. In Mandarin. See BBC Summary of World Broadcasts, October 26, 1998, for a translation.

Tibet Government-in-exile [cited as Dharamsala]. Central Tibetan Administration. Department of Information and International Affairs. 1991. *The Panchen Lama Speaks.* Dharamsala. Reprint of the Panchen Lama's Speech to the TAR Standing Committee Meeting of the National People's Congress, Beijing, 28th March 1987.

———. 1993. "Official Document Reveals Coercive Birth Control Policy in Tibet." August 17. Dharamsala.

———. 1995. "Document 17. TAR Lhasa People's Intermediate Court, 1982." October 24. Dharamsala.

———. 2000. *China's Current Policy on Tibet: Life-and-Death Struggle to Crush an Ancient Civilization.* Dharamsala.

———. 2001. *Tibet under Communist China: 50 Years.* Dharamsala.

Tibet Heritage Fund [cited as THF]. 1999. *Annual Report, 1998.* Hong Kong.

TibetInfoNet. www.tibetinfonet.net. An independent information service on contemporary Tibet. Germany.

Tibet Information Network [cited as TIN]. 1989. "Lhasa Interview No. 22." Document T5(H). April.

———. 1991. *Defying the Dragon: China and Human Rights in Tibet.* London.

———. 1992a. *Background Papers on Tibet.* September. Includes "Reported Demonstrations in Tibet, 1987–92."

———. 1992b. *Political Prisoners in Tibet.* New York.

———. 1992c. "Political Prisoners 2: Sentences and Offences—Further Analysis of a New List of Political Prisoners in Tibet." *TIN News Update,* February 18.

———. 1992d. "Tibet Birth Control Regulations." *TIN News Update,* October 5.

———. N.d. [1992]. [TIN ref:] Yishu doc. Unpublished Document. In Mandarin.

———. 1993a. "Reported Demonstrations in Tibet, 1992–93." *TIN News Compilation,* October.

———. 1993b. "Troops Take Over Tibet Village: Villagers Appeal to UN." *TIN News Update,* August 11.

———. 1994a. *Documents on Birth Control.*

———. 1994b. *Survey of Birth Control Policies in Tibet.* Background Briefing Paper, March 30.

———. 1994c. "Tax Protest Deemed 'Political': Arrests Follow." *TIN News Update,* June 2.

———. 1994d. *TIN Background Briefing Paper,* March 30.

———. 1995a. "Ban on Education in India First Planned in 1993." *TIN News Update,* March 15.

———. 1995b. "Chinese Extend Ban on Tibetan Children Going to Exile Schools." *TIN News Update,* March 20.

———. 1996a. "Bombing in Sog County: 'Strike Hard' to Continue." *TIN News Update,* December 26.

———. 1996b. "Major Bomb Blast in Lhasa." *TIN News Update,* December 28.

———. 1997. "Tibetans Sacked after Visiting India." *TIN News Update,* March 27.

———. 1998. "Political Prisoners Held in New Lhasa Detention Centre." *TIN News Update,* November 17.

———. 1999a. "Definitive New Book on Education in Tibet." *TIN News Update,* January 8.

———. 1999b. *Social Evils: Prostitution and Pornography in Lhasa.* London.

———. 2000a. "Bomb Blast in Lhasa: No Injuries, Minor Disruption." *TIN News Update,* November 8.

———. 2000b. *China's Great Leap West.* London.

———. 2000c. "Increased Restrictions on Birth of Children in Tibet." *TIN News Update,* February 9.

———. 2000d. "Personal View: Tibetan Perspectives on Lhasa Today." *TIN News Update,* December 29.

———. 2000e. "Shol Dawa: Obituary of a Political Activist." *TIN News Update,* December 14.

———. 2000f. *TIN News Update,* July 26.

———. 2001. *News Review: Reports from Tibet 2000.* No. 29. London.

———. 2002. "Initial Reports on Fourth Tibet Work Forum." *TIN News Update,* July 27.

Tibet Poverty Alleviation Fund. N.d. "Strengthening of Rural Reproductive Health Services in Eight Tibetan Townships of Lhoka and Nagchu Prefectures, Tibet Autonomous Region, PRC." Cited in Sera Bonds and Adam Rosenbloom, "Women's Health Needs Assessment, Nagchu Prefecture, Tibet, China, June–August 2004" (Baltimore: Circle of Health International, 2004), 20, 50n21.

Tofani, Loretta. 1996. "Bodies Scarred, Spirits Broken." *Philadelphia Inquirer,* December 6.

Tournadre, Nicolas. 1999. Interview by Bruno Philip. *Le Monde,* January 26, 17.

Trebinjac, Sabine. 1990. "Que cent chants rivalisent, qu'une musique éclose: Étude sur le traditionalisme d'État en Chine." *Archives européennes de sociologie* 31: 60–79.

Union Research Institute [Hong Kong]. 1968. *Tibet, 1950–1967.* Official Chinese documents concerning Tibet's incorporation into China.

United Nations. 2000. *China Human Development Report 1999: Transition and the State.* Edited by Carl Riskin. New York.

———. Population Division of the UN Secretariat [cited as UN Population Division]. 2002. *World Population Prospects: The 2002 Revision, Volume I: Comprehensive Tables.* Geneva.

———. UN News Centre. 2004. "UNICEF Head Wraps Up Tibet Visit Aimed at Slashing Disparities with Rest of China." Geneva.

United Nations Children's Fund [cited as UNICEF]. 2004. "[UNICEF Executive Director Carol] Bellamy Urges Tibet to Reach for New Heights for Children." August 31. www.tibet.ca/en/wtnarchive/2004/3/9–2_4.html (accessed February 17, 2007).

Unrepresented Nations and Peoples Organization [cited as UNPO]. 1997. "'China's Tibet': The World's Largest Remaining Colony." Report of a Fact-Finding Mission and Analyses of Colonialism and Chinese Rule in Tibet. www .tibet.com/Humanrights/Unpo/index.html (accessed February 17, 2007).

———. 2006. "Tibet: Dalai Lama's India-Based Representatives Report Progress after Visit to China." February 27, www.unpo.org/article.php?id=3848 (accessed March 30, 2007).

U.S. Embassy, Beijing. 2000. "Health Policy Challenges in the Tibet Autonomous Region." December. www.usembassy-china.org.cn/sandt/tib-health.htm (accessed February 17, 2007).

Van Walt van Praag, Michael C. 1987. *The Status of Tibet: History, Rights, and Prospects in International Law.* Boulder, Colo.

Vandermeersch, Léon. 1989. *Bouddhisme et politique en Asie orientale.* Problèmes politiques et sociaux, no. 603. Paris.

Virtanen, Riika J., comp. and ed. 2000. *A Blighted Flower and Other Stories.* Dharamsala.

Wang Xiaoqiang. 1994. "The Dispute between the Tibetans and the Han: When Will It Be Solved?" In Barnett and Akiner 1994: 290–95.

Wang Xiaoqiang and Bai Nanfeng. [1986] 1990. *The Poverty of Plenty.* Translated by Angela Knox. Basingstoke, U.K.

Wang-Toutain, Françoise. 1997. "*La voix du Dharma* se fait-elle de nouveau entendre en Chine?" In *Renouveaux religieux en Asie,* ed. Catherine Clémentin-Ojha, 61–81. Paris.

Wei, Yehua D. 2000. *Regional Development in China: States, Globalization, and Inequality.* London.

World Tibet Network News [cited as WTN]. 1994. "Dalai Lama Wants Referendum on Tibet." June 8, 1994. www.tibet.cn (accessed March 30, 2007).

Xinhua [News Agency]. 1997. "The PRC Criminal Law . . . Amended March 14, 1997." In Mandarin. Translated FBIS-CHI-97–056. March 17, 1997, as "China: Text of Criminal Law."

———. 1998. "Danish Delegation Visits Tibetan Prison." August 7. In Mandarin.

Yan Hao. 2000. "Tibetan Population in China: Myths and Facts Re-examined." *Asian Ethnicity* 1, 1: 11–36.

Yang, Dali L. 1996. *Calamity and Reform in China: State, Rural Society, and Institutional Change since the Great Leap Famine.* Stanford, Calif.

———. 1997. *Beyond Beijing: Liberalization and the Regions in China.* London.

Yang Enhong. 1999. "The Study of Singing Tradition of the Tibetan Epic 'King Gesar.'" *IIAS Newsletter* 18: 16.

Yedor. 2006. "'Enlarged Tibet Autonomous Region' Pursued by Dalai Not Exists." *People's Daily,* July 28. Translated July 30, 2006, www.tibet.ca/en/wtnarchive/2006/7/30_1.html (accessed February 17, 2007).

Zhang Qingli. 2006. "Dalai Lama 'Deceived His Motherland.'" Interview. *Der Spiegel Magazine,* August 16, www.spiegel.de/international/spiegel/0,1518,431922,00.html (accessed March 26, 2007).

ROBERT BARNETT is an adjunct professor of Modern Tibetan Studies at Columbia University, New York, and director of the Modern Tibetan Studies Program. He was the founder and the first director of the former Tibet Information Network (TIN), an independent news agency.

ANNE-MARIE BLONDEAU is *directeur d'études* emeritus at the École pratique des Hautes Études (Sciences religieuses), Paris.

KATIA BUFFETRILLE is an anthropologist working at the École pratique des Hautes Études (Sciences religieuses), Paris.

ANNE CHAYET is *directeur de recherche* at the Centre national de la recherche scientifique in Paris.

THIERRY DODIN is a Tibetologist at the University of Bonn. He is a former director of the Tibet Information Network and the founding director of TibetInfoNet.

ANDREW M. FISCHER is a development economist based at the Development Studies Institute, London School of Economics.

JANET GYATSO is Hershey Professor of Buddhist Studies at the Divinity School, Harvard University. She was president of the International Association of Tibetan Studies from 2000 to 2006.

AMY HELLER is a Tibetologist and art historian. She is a collaborator of the Centre de recherche sur les civilisations chinoise, japonaise et tibétaine (UMR 8155, EPHE/CNRS) in Paris and a consultant on conservation and restoration projects for the Swiss government.

SAMTEN G. KARMAY is a former *directeur de recherche* at the Centre national de la recherche scientifique in Paris. He was president of the International Association of Tibetan Studies from 1995 to 2000.

PER KVAERNE is professor at the University of Oslo and director of the Institute of Comparative Research in Human Culture.

FERNAND MEYER is *directeur d'études* at the École pratique des Hautes Études (Sciences historiques et philologiques), Paris.

JAMPA L. PANGLUNG (Ph.D., Ludwig-Maximilians-Universität, Munich) obtained the title of *geshe* at the Sera Monastery in Tibet in 1959. Subsequently, he worked until 2004 at the Central Asiatic Studies Committee of the Bavarian Academy of Sciences and Humanities.

TSERING SHAKYA is professor at the Institute of Asian Research of the University of British Columbia, where he holds the Canadian Research Chair of Contemporary Society in Asia.

ELLIOT SPERLING is associate professor and holds the Chair of Central Eurasian Studies at Indiana University.

HELGA UEBACH (Ph.D., Ludwig-Maximilians-Universität, Munich) is a former researcher at the Central Asiatic Studies Committee of the Bavarian Academy of Sciences and Humanities.

Text:	10/13 Aldus
Display:	Aldus
Cartographer:	Bill Nelson
Compositor:	Integrated Composition Systems
Printer and binder:	Sheridan Books, Inc.